Revised and Expanded Edition

A Research Guide to CENTRAL PARTY and GOVERNMENT MEETINGS in CHINA 1949·1986

Kenneth G. Lieberthal
Bruce J. Dickson

D0208541

An East Gate Book

M. E. Sharpe, Inc.
Armonk, New York
London, England

An East Gate Book

Available in the United Kingdom and Europe from M. E. Sharpe,
Publishers, 3 Henrietta Street, London WC2E 8LU.

Library of Congress Cataloging-in-Publication Data

Lieberthal, Kenneth.
    Research guide to central party and government meetings in China,
1949–1987 / by Kenneth Lieberthal and Bruce Dickson.
        p.   cm.
    Bibliography: p.
    Includes index.
    ISBN 0-87332-492-7
    1. Chung-kuo kung ch'an tang—Congresses—History—Sources.
2. China—Politics and government—1949-   —Sources. I. Dickson,
Bruce J. II. Title.
JQ1519.A5L474   1989
324.251'075—dc19   88-18527
                                                                  CIP

Printed in the United States of America

A Research Guide to
CENTRAL PARTY
and GOVERNMENT
MEETINGS in CHINA
1949·1986

To Michel Oksenberg
In appreciation

Contents

Abbreviations

CAC	Central Advisory Committee
CB	*Current Background*
CC	Central Committee
CCGPR	Central Commission for Party Rectification
CCP	Chinese Communist Party
CDIC	Central Discipline Inspection Commission
CPPCC	Chinese People's Political Consultative Conference
CPSU	Communist Party of the Soviet Union
GPCR	Great Proletarian Cultural Revolution
JPRS	Joint Publications Research Service
NPC	National People's Congress
PLA	People's Liberation Army
PRC	People's Republic of China
RMRB	*Renmin ribao*
SCMM	*Selections from China Mainland Magazines*
SCMM-S	*Selections from China Mainland Magazines* (Supplement)
SCMP	*Survey of China Mainland Press*
SCMP-S	*Survey of China Mainland Press* (Supplement)
SEZ	Special economic zone
SSC	Supreme State Conference

Introduction

This volume, like its predecessor in 1976, provides information on all top-level meetings convened by Chinese officials since 1949 for which there is concrete documentary evidence. In so doing, it seeks to provide a vehicle for capturing a part of China's elite decision making, for tracking the appearance of various issues on the agenda of the leaders, for documenting major decisions taken, and for gaining increased bibliographic control over a scattered and unsystematic literature. The original edition of this volume appeared in 1976 and contained summaries of 298 meetings. These formally covered the period 1949–1975, but in fact the distribution was highly skewed: only 41 meetings were summarized for 1949–1955, and a mere 11 meetings were identified for the period 1968–1975. The introduction to that volume (reprinted below) commented somewhat wistfully, "It is to be hoped that the Chinese will fill some of the major gaps in documentation in the future." The Chinese subsequently obliged.

Since Mao Zedong's death and Beijing's turn toward openness and reform under Deng Xiaoping, numerous new sources have appeared that cast additional light on the 1949–1975 period as well as providing documentation on the events during 1976–1986. At the beginning of the 1980s, the Chinese began publishing many histories of the Chinese Communist Party.[1] Compendia of documents for particular periods[2] and of speeches by given leaders[3] have also contributed to the record. Many older leaders and important officials retired and published their memoirs,[4] and these were supplemented by other volumes published in memorium.[5] Compendia and chronologies of decisions were put out in fields as diverse as education,[6] economics,[7] economic management,[8] and so forth. Other helpful volumes analyzed the development and operation of particular sectors, such as state planning.[9] Indeed, the Chinese even published a reference volume on central meetings![10] While there is considerable overlap among these various sources—especially among the party histories, many of which were drawn from the same central guidance volume—each nevertheless has made some contribution to providing a more complete understanding of the consultations that have taken place among the highest level leaders since the founding of the PRC.

This outpouring of information has greatly enhanced our ability to analyze both political history and policy process during the period under consideration. The major difficulty, though, has remained that of achieving bibliographic control over a mushrooming body of scattered data. This revised and updated version of the 1976 *Research Guide* seeks to make a contribution to this effort. The definition of the types of meetings that qualify for inclusion in this volume is the same as that for 1976. The current edition, however, both adds eleven important years to the story and significantly enhances the information base for the period covered in the 1976 edition.

The *Research Guide* cannot pretend to exhaustive coverage of all of the many millions of words that have been published in China that might contain pertinent data. Undoubtedly, one or another user of this book will wonder why we have missed some important fact that has been published in a Chinese paper, journal, or book. Recognizing that 100 percent coverage is simply beyond our capabilities, we have, nevertheless, tried to cast our net widely in the data-gathering effort that undergirds this volume.

This volume includes information that was published by the U.S. government translation services as well as much that appeared in the Chinese print media. It also brings to bear numerous articles from publications in Hong Kong and elsewhere. We culled relevant information from a large percentage of the biographical materials published in China (including official biographies, memoirs, memorial collections of essays, and collections of speeches and writings), as well as from the Chinese official histories and reference books on developments in various fields. We have included some formally "internal" (*neibu*) materials in this *Research Guide*, where those materials are available in the major libraries on China in the United States.

This new information has increased from 298 to 513 the number of meetings summarized in this volume. It has also produced considerably more even coverage, with 14 new meetings recorded for the period 1949–1955 and 178 additional meetings after 1968. In addition, we have been able to add new substantive information to the summaries of 103 (that is, 34.5 percent) of the meetings that were included in the 1976 version of the *Research Guide*. Table 1 details these changes in coverage.

The table provides a first impression of the areas in which the Chinese have significantly added to the historical record over the past twelve years. While the first two columns present a quick index to the number of meetings on which there is information for each year, the last two columns highlight the changes from the 1976 to the 1988 editions. The third column shows the number of meetings on which there is documentation in 1988 for which there was no concrete evidence in 1976. This table shows a relatively even spread of new information, with the exceptionally large numbers for 1974 and 1975 explained by the fact that the original *Research Guide* was written immediately after this period and during a

Table 1

Changes in Meeting Coverage

Year	No. of meetings, 1976 ed.	No. of meetings, 1988 ed.	No. of new meetings in 1988 ed.	No. of 1976 ed. meetings revised in 1988 ed.
1949	3	4	1	2
1950	3	3	—	1
1951	4	7	3	3
1952	1	2	1	—
1953	11	13	2	5
1954	6	9	3	2
1955	13	17	4	4
1956	19	21	2	8
1957	15	16	3	7
1958	26	28	2	18
1959	24	27	3	12
1960	19	21	2	4
1961	20	22	2	8
1962	19	20	1	9
1963	18	18	—	3
1964	23	24	1	4
1965	23	22	–1	4
1966	28	33	5	8
1967	12	16	4	2
1968	2	2	—	1
1969	2	4	2	1
1970	2	8	6	2
1971	1	6	5	1
1972	—	2	—	—
1973	2	9	7	1
1974	—	5	5	1
1975	1	15	14	1
1976	—	22	22	—
1977	—	12	12	—
1978	—	13	13	—
1979	—	9	9	—
1980	—	16	16	—
1981	—	13	13	—
1982	—	15	15	—
1983	—	6	6	—
1984	—	10	10	—
1985	—	12	12	—
1986	—	9	9	—
Totals	297	511	214	112

time of continuing political tension. Column 4 gives an important additional indication of the distribution of new information. It shows, for example, that the Chinese have significantly increased the documentation of the events of 1958–1959 and 1961–1962, but relatively little has been added to the available record for 1960 and 1963–1965.

The period 1968–1969 in particular and 1968–1974 in general continues to yield almost no information about the types of meetings covered in this *Research Guide*. Given the period of time that has elapsed and the extensive exposés on the Cultural Revolution period that have been published, it now seems safe to conclude that this lack of documentation reflects a significant change in the policy process at the top of the Chinese system during these years. The previous practice of holding fairly regular meetings of top bodies, along with central work conferences, fell victim to the extraordinary political infighting of the time. Regular consultation gave way to personal intrigue, and the bodies whose activities are detailed in this volume virtually ceased to function. This volume also documents, however, the reemergence since the mid–1970s of a system of elite consultation that in many ways harks back to that of the pre-Cultural Revolution years.

We therefore feel that the overview of the role of Central meetings in the Chinese policy-making process provided in the introduction to the 1976 edition remains generally accurate (or, more precisely, that the post–1976 system in China has in this respect largely retained the basic procedural features identified as having characterized the pre–1966 system). We have therefore chosen to reprint this introduction in the current volume, not only for reasons of continuity but also because we feel it still offers a useful set of generalizations about the system portrayed in detail in the various meeting summaries. For a similar reason, we are also retaining Michel Oksenberg's very useful review of bibliographic sources, which he wrote especially for the 1976 edition, even though this obviously does not introduce the important sources that have become available more recently.[11]

As noted above, the scope of coverage in this revised edition remains the same as that in the 1976 version. Our information given for each meeting has, however, changed somewhat. The original version of this *Research Guide* contained the results of an appearance file that tracked the public appearances of roughly thirty top leaders. The present version of the *Research Guide* discontinues the appearance file data. The original edition also had a category that indicated particularly useful secondary sources that enhance our knowledge of individual meetings. Space considerations have required that we exclude this category from our current edition.

With the above minor exceptions, this *Research Guide* seeks to accomplish the same task as its predecessor: to provide accurate information on the primary sources available for certain categories of central meetings. The information on each meeting (where available) includes the type, date, place convened, participants, agenda, speeches and reports, documents passed, and, occasionally, a final section of helpful additional comments. The contents of all reports and speeches are summarized and the volume is indexed by proper name, meeting type, and subject matter to facilitate use of this book for various types of research. The introduction to the 1976 edition contains detailed information on our criteria for selection, guidelines for including information, and other matters. We encourage users of this volume to take the time to read the pertinent sections of that essay.

Given the welcome fact that new materials continue to pour out of China at a prodigious rate, we decided to produce this volume even though we recognize that it is chasing a very rapidly moving target. We believe that it captures the major materials that became available up to the summer of 1987. We also want to note that this has been truly a joint effort. For any errors of omission or commission contained herein, therefore, we have nobody to blame but each other.

Notes

1. See, e.g., *Zhongguo gongchandang liushi nian* (Beijing: Jiefangjun chubanshe, 1984).

2. E.g., *Sanzhong quanhui yilai zhongyao wenxian xuanbian* (Changchun: Renmin chubanshe, 1983).

3. The selected works of Deng Xiaoping, Chen Yun, Liu Shaoqi, Mao Zedong, Zhang Wentian, and Zhou Enlai, among others, have been used in the present volume.

4. For a variant of this, see *Peng Dehuai zishu* (Beijing: Renmin chubanshe, 1981).

5. E.g., *Huiyi Zhang Wentian* (Hunan: Hunan chubanshe, 1985).

6. See *Zhongguo jiaoyu nianjian, 1949–1981* (Shanghai: Zhongguo dabaike quanshu chubanshe, 1984).

7. See the very informative *Zhonghua Renmin Gongheguo jingji dashiji (1949–1980)* (Beijing: Zhongguo shehui kexue chubanshe, 1984).

8. *Zhonghua Renmin Gongheguo jingji guanli dashiji* (Beijing: Zhongguo jingji chubanshe, 1987).

9. See, e.g., He Jianzhang et al., *Zhongguo jihua guanli wenti* (Beijing: Zhongguo shehui kexue chubanshe, 1984).

10. *Zhongguo gongchandang lizi zhongyao huiyi ji (xia)* (Shanghai: Shanghai renmin chubanshe, 1984). This volume contained no information not already in our files.

11. Professor Oksenberg has published a more up-to-date bibliographical overview that provides a significant part of this missing data: "Politics Takes Command: An Essay on the Study of Post-1949 China," *Cambridge History of China*, vol. 14 (People's Republic of China, Part I) (New York: Cambridge University Press, 1987), pp. 543–90. We are grateful to him for his permission to reprint his original essay here despite his misgivings concerning the omission of new sources.

Foreword to the 1976 Edition

Michel Oksenberg

Establishing Bibliographic Control Over Sources
On Post–1949 Chinese Politics

One indication of the maturity of a field is the bibliographic aids and study guides that facilitate research in the field. By that standard, contemporary Chinese studies are coming of age.[1]

G. William Skinner's mammoth effort to obtain bibliographic control over major secondary analyses of Chinese society,[2] coupled with several more select bibliographies,[3] provide entree into the secondary sources. Indeed, according to one academic wag, the dynamism and creativity of a field probably are inversely correlated with its bibliographic control over previous monographic work. In the extreme instance of total bibliographic control, scholars would feel compelled to pore over so many previous, mediocre analyses that they would devote too little time to primary sources and fresh interpretation. If there is any truth to this saw, the contemporary Chinese field may be approaching saturation in its control over secondary Western-language sources.[4]

Such is not the case, however, for invaluable secondary Chinese-language analyses appearing in Taiwan and Hong Kong. Researchers face a formidable task in identifying the valuable analyses in the Union Research Institute's *Zuguo*, the Hong Kong monthly *Mingbao*, or the various metamorphoses of Taiwan's *Zhonggong yanjiu*. In fact, one wishes Taiwan authorities would turn their bibliographic skills to this task.

This situation is also less than ideal for primary sources, where efforts to obtain bibliographic control are still in an emergent stage. Professor Lieberthal's *Guide* to central party and government meetings is a major step forward, a pioneering effort to establish bibliographic control over higher-level party and government meetings in China. Henceforth, any researcher interested in studying virtually any aspect of policy formulation and implementation in China, be it at the highest or lowest levels, will wish to consult this *Guide*. Particularly for the 1955–1966 era, it provides an excellent sense of the evolving agenda of issues and problems confronting Peking's top decision-makers. Those wishing to understand local affairs will wish to know whether the initiatives for change came from the local level or from the top. Those interested in specific time spans will certainly wish to know what major meetings occurred then. And students of particular leaders, bureaucracies (the military, finance and trade organizations, and so on), or issue areas (public health, literature and art, and so on) will wish to know when their interest was crucially involved at the highest levels. The *Research Guide* gathers the known evidence on these matters.

Perhaps it would be useful to place the Lieberthal *Guide* in context, in terms both of what aspect of the policy process it illuminates and where it fits in the emerging group of research aids. To do this requires some sense of the communication processes of the Chinese political system. In overly schematic terms we can identify the following methods of communication: (1) formal and informal meetings of higher- and lower-level officials convened by higher-level organs; (2) formal written communications—directives, petitions, circulars, notices, reports, etc.—within the bureaucracy; (3) in-house journals, bulletins, and newspapers; (4) the mass media, including radio broadcasts; (5) informal written communications such as personal notes, letters, and poems which officials send to one another; (6) telephone calls, either informal or formal, and bureaucratic telephone conferences; (7) visits by higher-level officials to lower levels for inspection, investigation, or integration purposes. The relative importance of each channel varies over time, region, level, organization, issue area, and stage in the policy process. To acquire a total grasp of the Chinese policy process would require a keen sense of how each is used and, more importantly, how the channels are interrelated. And to acquire total bibliographic control over the various dimensions of the policy process would involve knowing about the available sources on each channel.

In this context, we can appreciate the contribution Lieberthal has made, for it is the most extensive effort to date to order the available information on meetings convened at the national level. His appendices refer to regular meetings of the Government Administrative Council, the State Council, the Standing Committee of the National People's Congress, and occasional, specialized meetings convened by various ministerial and Chinese Communist Party bodies. The *Guide* itself focuses on a range of central party, government, and military gatherings which Lieberthal adequately describes in his introduction. Given the importance of the meeting channels, Lieberthal's effort is particularly welcome and important—even if, as he recognizes, for certain kinds of meetings that he catalogues (meetings of the Politburo or Secretariat), his *Guide* contains but a small percentage of the total—for, with this *Guide*, it will be possible for the first time to begin to explore precisely how central meetings have been related to other communication channels, when and how the results of the meetings are reported in the mass media, what the sequence is between activities at the lower levels and the central meetings, what links exist between high-level officials and their subordinates or various public sectors, and so on.

Indeed, the Lieberthal *Guide*, when combined with other sources, will enable us to begin to acquire a more refined sense of how the policy process actually has *varied* over time, region, organization, issue area, and level of the hierarchy. For example, do the mass media more readily reflect central meetings dealing with agriculture than those dealing with literature and art? A careful tracing of the evolution of different policies may enable more rigorous insights into the determinants and trends of the Chinese policy process. But the key, as Lieberthal himself would note, would be to weave the data he draws to our attention in this *Guide* with data derived from the other communication channels. If we are to monitor the Chinese policy process successfully, in short, we must plug into as many of the diverse channels as possible.

It seems wise at this juncture, therefore, to assess briefly the state of the art and remind ourselves of the available research aids that facilitate entry into the other communication channels. At the same time, we should note those channels that elude the current penetrative capacities of academicians: informal meetings and informal written communications,[5] in-house journals,[6] telephone calls, and visits of higher-level officials to lower levels. The available official information comes overwhelmingly from the mass media and to a lesser extent from formal bureaucratic communications. Non-system-produced data come from interviews and direct observation.

Formal, Written Bureaucratic Communications

Only a small portion of the bureaucratic flow has come to light. The major openly available series are legal compendia of the central government[7] and particular ministries.[8] The Union Research Institute also has assembled many major Central Committee directives as well as Central Committee Plenum communiqués,[9] major military directives,[10] and documents on Tibet.[11] As to classified, illicitly obtained inner-party and inner-government directives, the now famous "Lian-jiang documents"—inner-party documents secured through a Taiwan raid on party headquarters within a local county—yielded a remarkable but limited cache.[12] During the Cultural Revolution a number of central directives came to light for the era both preceding and during the Cultural Revolution.[13] And since 1969 a number of significant inner-party documents somehow have come to light,[14] so much so that the U.S. intelligence community probably understands the contents of a high portion of the sequentially numbered Central Committee documents (*zhongfa*) of 1973–75. In addition, of course, a large number of reports by leading officials are available, particularly for the 1950s and early 1960s; many appeared in the mass media.

Unfortunately, there is no easy route to achieving bibliographic control over these diverse written bureaucratic communications. For example, no published union list exists of the Chinese legal compendia available in Western and Japanese libraries. Perhaps the best guide has been compiled in Japan. [15] A complete index to central government legal compendia is available: T. T. Hsia's *Guide to Selected Legal Sources of Mainland China*. [16]

Control over reports by leading central government officials is best obtained through the biographical files compiled by the U.S. Consulate General in Hong Kong, a record of the known daily activities of China's elite. [17] This series is available on microfilm through 1967 and on index cards thereafter, filed at leading China centers. [18] If one wants, for example, available reports by leading Ministry of Commerce officials, the researcher should compile a list of these officials through consulting the invaluable appendices to Klein and Clark's *Biographic Dictionary of Chinese Communism, 1921–1965*, [19] and then trace the known activities of each official through the biographical files, where most of his reports will be indexed. During the 1950s, many of these reports were reprinted in the major, invaluable publication of official record, *Xinhua yue bao* (New China Monthly), which from 1955 to 1959 was *Xinhua ban yue kan* (New China Semimonthly). For the fifties these journals contained major statements, directives, and news items from all major sectors of the bureaucracy, but since then the publication has concentrated more on foreign affairs. The annual *Renmin shouce* (People's Handbook, 1948–1965, except for 1954) is also an invaluable publication of record. Again for the 1950s, the reports that ministries submitted to the National People's Congress and the 1956 and 1958 CCP National Congress are available in the compendia detailing the proceedings of these meetings. [20]

In the foreign policy realm, the Chinese to the eve of the Cultural Revolution published two important series, *Zhonghua Renmin Gongheguo tiaoyue ji* (Collected Treaties of the People's Republic of China) and *Zhonghua Renmin Gongheguo dui wai guanxi wenjian ji* (Documents on Foreign Affairs of the People's Republic of China). [21] The annual *Shijie zhishi nianjian* (World Knowledge Yearbook) authoritatively surveyed the world scene. [22] Since the termination of these publications, the U.S. Consulate General in Hong Kong has attempted to monitor the situation through various occasional foreign policy research aids in its *Current Background* series. [23]

Bibliographical control over existing provincial-level directives, reports, plans, and statistics is significantly enhanced with John P. Emerson's important *The Provinces of the People's Republic of China: An Economic and Political Bibliography*. [24] This invaluable research aid lists such items as known provincial budgets, First Party Secretary reports, and government work reports. Provincial-level economic statistics have also been conveniently gathered in a number of recent publications, with some of the statistical estimates pieced together after much painstaking scholarship.[25] Lists of provincial-level officials are in the now annual U.S. government publication *Directory of Chinese Communist Officials*.[26] These provincial sources enable interesting, rigorous interprovincial comparisons.

Unfortunately, researchers confront a near-total lack of access to subprovincial internal bureaucratic messages.[27]

Finally, we should note the several significant documentary collections that have been assembled in translation that bring together official documents and mass media commentary on specialized aspects of the Chinese system.[28]

Mass Media

Since the routes to obtaining bibliographic control differ, let us, for convenience sake, distinguish among: (1) newspapers and journals with broad appeal (e.g., *Red Flag*); (2) Chinese-language specialist journals, frequently published by specific ministries or mass organizations; (3) radio broadcasts; (4) Chinese-language pamphlets and books; (5) Cultural Revolution publications; (6) foreign-language publications (e.g., *Peking Review* or pamphlets from Foreign Languages Press).

As to newspapers and general journals, the first step for the researcher obviously is to identify the useful serial publications and, when possible, the specific articles of interest. Several research guides list Chinese periodical publications.[29] The major national newspapers—*Renmin ribao*, *Guangming ribao*, and until 1966, *Da gong bao*—are widely available. These newspapers publish(ed) their own indexes, but only for *Renmin ribao* does a complete set exist in Western libraries.[30] Most national journals—*Hongqi* (Red Flag),[31] *Zhongguo qingnian* (Chinese Youth, suspended in 1966), *Jingji yanjiu* (Economic Research, suspended in 1966),[32] and *Xuexi* (Study, 1949–1958) are also widely available. The Chinese publish(ed) two very useful indexes to the periodical press, the *Quanguo zhuyao baokan ziliao suoyin* (National Index to Important Periodical Materials) and the *Guonei baokan ziliao youguan dili ziliao suoyin* (Index to Domestic Publications Concerning Geographic Materials). Unfortunately, these two are available only for the 1950s. The Japanese have published two useful indexes to national media articles on local units. These sources are arranged by locality, so that a complete listing of articles on particular factories and communes can be obtained.[33]

After compiling a list of publications and articles, the next research task is to identify which actually are available and which library contains them. The existing union lists of Western and Japanese holdings of Chinese newspapers and periodicals are now somewhat dated,[34] for in recent years the U.S. government has released extensive holdings, and several exchanges were arranged with Eastern European libraries. The most extensive holdings of original editions are now at the Hoover Institution of Stanford University, with significant holdings also at California (Berkeley), Michigan, Columbia, and Harvard. However, a substantial portion of the available provincial newspapers are now on microfilm in most major libraries. And most China Center librarians have on their shelves a collection of untitled, looseleaf, mimeographed sheets indicating the precise dates available for each provincial newspaper. With these lists of available newspapers and periodicals and with the Chinese indexes, library research based on the mass media for the 1955–1960 era is a pleasure. The researcher makes a list of the articles relevant to his subject, derived from the Chinese indexes, and then finds out which of those articles are available. But for earlier or later periods, the only recourse is to go through the relevant publications, searching for items of interest.

This raises the obvious question: what about the translations of the Chinese media, whether done by the Chinese in their daily New China News Agency (NCNA) release and their English-language journals or by the U.S. government in its Hong Kong Consulate General translation series or its Joint Publications Research Service (JPRS) series? Bibliographical control over NCNA and JPRS is lacking.[35] The Chinese provide annual indexes to their journals (e.g., *Beijing Review, China Pictorial*) which usually appear in the last issue of the year. (For some years, *Beijing Review* was indexed semi-annually, that is, in numbers 26 and 52.) The Hong Kong Consulate General indexes its various publication series, although the quality of the index is not perfect: not much cross-indexing; perhaps overly refined categories; underdeveloped, underutilized place index.

A greater problem in relying extensively upon translations of the Chinese mass media, however, is the built-in biases in the selection process. Scholars should not forget that government officials, whether American or Chinese, are doing the selection. For obvious reasons, the needs of government may differ from the needs of scholars. What is included or excluded reflects governmental interests and concerns. In addition, the criteria of selection reflect the existing limits of comprehension about what is and is not important. Items that retrospectively may seem crucial easily could have been overlooked at the time. For example, the Consulate General did not reproduce Yao Wenyuan's now famous opening shot of the Cultural Revolution, "On the New Historical Play *Dismissal of Hai Rui*," until March 21, 1966, although it appeared in *People's Daily* on November 30, 1965. And in no year through 1970 did the Consulate General see fit to translate all *People's Daily* editorials (see table 1).[36] The point of all this is not to denigrate the contribution of the government translation services. To the contrary, particularly the Hong Kong press monitoring unit's contribution to a scholarly understanding of Chinese politics has been monumental. Nonetheless, we must recognize that while the translations of the Chinese mass media facilitate research somewhat, the field has developed to such an extent that serious work now requires extensive consultation of Chinese-language sources.

Percentage of Different Types of *People's Daily* Articles Carried in Hong Kong Consulate General Translation Series, 1951–1970[36]

	Editorials (*Shelun*)		Observations (*Guancha*)		Commentaries (*Pinglun*)	
	Total number	Percentage translated	Total number	Percentage translated	Total number	Percentage translated
1951	193	88%	—	—	—	—
1952	140	90%	—	—	—	—
1953	232	83%	—	—	—	—
1954	284	80%	—	—	—	—
1955	370	86%	74	82%	1	100%
1956	372	80%	136	78%	19	0%
1957	296	80%	47	87%	174	42%
1958	446	65%	23	70%	210	46%
1959	343	56%	17	60%	195	25%
1960	456	44%	9	67%	167	17%
1961	245	70%	15	100%	92	63%
1962	149	89%	12	91%	63	72%
1963	206	93%	15	100%	67	76%
1964	221	94%	12	100%	81	88%
1965	274	88%	19	84%	184	60%
1966	191	85%	15	94%	100	90%
1967	125	96%	9	89%	140	68%
1968	42	90%	—	—	97	68%
1969	15	93%	—	—	17	94%
1970	41	90%	—	—	43	93%

It is also next to impossible to obtain bibliographic control over books and pamphlets published in China—be they in Chinese or English. The Chinese publish a widely available list of all new books,[37] but to identify potentially useful titles from this list is not helpful, since only a small portion of the titles is available outside of China. My own approach is to consult library card catalogs and ideally to wander through the stacks of the major libraries, exploring the relevant call numbers.

The monitored and translated radio broadcasts—Foreign Broadcast Information Service (FBIS), British Broadcasting Company Summary of World Broadcasts/Far East, and News from Chinese Radios (to 1968)—have no index. The Central Intelligence Agency's daily appearance list for Chinese officials keys the appearance to the broadcast that noted the appearance, but other than through this limited lead, the only way to use the radio materials is to plow through the voluminous materials, issue by issue. In the absence of provincial newspapers after 1966, however, the broadcasts are the best way to acquire provincial-level information about China: officeholders, production trends, and implementation of policy.

The situation is somewhat better with respect to the available Cultural Revolution materials in the United States: Red Guard newspapers, wall posters, pamphlets.[38] These have been gathered by the Center for Chinese Research Materials (CCRM) into the twenty-volume *Red Guard Publications*. The first volume lists all titles and dates of available issues. In addition, under the same Department of State Office of External Research contract that helped sponsor the present volume, Dr. Hong Yung Lee of the University of Michigan is preparing a research guide to the CCRM volumes. The extensive Ting Wang clipping file on the Cultural Revolution, arranged by various subjects, is well indexed; it is available at the University of Michigan. Extensive Red Guard holdings are also thought to exist in Japan and Taiwan, but access to these collections appears to be restricted. The Cultural Revolution sources, although demanding careful use, yield enormous insight into not only the mass media but the other modes of communication as well, for they describe many instances of more private informal communications.

Trip Notes and Interview Protocols

Thus far, we have described ''official'' sources: products of the Chinese political system. But two other sources of information greatly illuminate Chinese politics: interviews of former Chinese residents and notes of travelers of varying duration to China. Many visitors or interviewers are willing to share their notes. But here, too, the problems of bibliographic control are forbidding.[39] I would suggest the following procedure to researchers. Lists of known visitors to China, mentioning dates of visit and purpose (if known), are contained in the *China Exchange Newsletter*, published by the Committee on Scholarly Communication with the People's Republic of China. Lists of scholars who have done research in Hong Kong, the time of their sojourn, and their topic of research are on file at the Universities Service Center in Hong Kong. The Chinese themselves report the occasions on which high-level officials have granted off-the-record interviews with foreigners. And one could add the observations of China-based diplomats, journalists, and businessmen to this list. Informally held wisdom exists at the major China centers as to whose trip or interview notes and recollections are accessible and worthwhile. Researchers can plug into this network to identify people they should contact for direct assistance. Three examples suffice: Ezra Vogel and John Pelzel of Harvard headed an excellent interview project in 1963–65 that gathered rich information on various aspects of local organization in China; they have provided generous access to their files through the years. Several scientific delegations to China have prepared excellent summary reports of their observations.[40] And Zhou Enlai's interviews in the summer of 1971 make fascinating retrospective reading in the light of the struggle against Lin Biao then going on—unbeknownst to the interviewer. Such sources cast light upon the informal dimensions of Chinese politics which the official, written communications seek to cloak. Research on any time period in China, then, is greatly enhanced by the inclusion of ephemeral materials such as refugee interviewing and trip notes that recapture the era.[41] But again, no research aids exist to guide one to the sources, and ingenuity is required to surmount the obstacles.

Chronologies

To round out the picture, particularly for the Lieberthal *Guide*, we should mention several good chronologies. The Lieberthal *Guide* can be used profitably in conjunction with several chronologies that indicate what else was occurring during the higher-level meetings.[42] In foreign relations, David Floyd and John Gittings rehearse the evolution of the Sino-Soviet dispute.[43] And the Center for Chinese Studies at the University of Michigan is preparing a chronological list of all *People's Daily* editorials.

Conclusion

The above sources have supported the recent, expanding literature on the Chinese policy process. This is not the place to analyze the strengths and weaknesses of these sources, or to explore methodologies for utilizing the information well.[44] Rather let us conclude with a general observation which the Lieberthal *Guide* reinforces. Empirical research on Chinese politics is not easy, and any findings are likely to be quite tentative. Nonetheless a significant number of topics remain unexplored. The topics require a good reading knowledge of Chinese and a determination patiently to search out and sift through many diverse sources. And one value of Professor Lieberthal's work is that he both identifies a number of specific, researchable topics and provides leads to begin the research.

Notes

1. See in particular Peter Berton and Eugene Wu, *Contemporary China, A Research Guide* (Stanford: The Hoover Institution of War, Revolution, and Peace, 1967); Andrew J. Nathan, *Modern China, 1840-1972: An Introduction to Sources and Research Aids* (Ann Arbor: Center for Chinese Studies, 1973).

2. G. William Skinner, Winston Hsieh, and Shigeaki Tomita, eds., *Modern Chinese Society*, 3 vols. (Stanford University Press, 1973).

3. See, for example, Wing-tsit Chan, ed. *Chinese Philosophy 1949-1963* (Honolulu: University Press of Hawaii, 1967); Nairuenn Chenn, *The Economy of Mainland China, 1949-1963: A Bibliography of Materials in English* (Berkeley: Committee on the Economy of China, SSRC, 1963); Roger Dial, *Studies on Chinese External Affairs: An Instructional Bibliography of Commonwealth and American Literature* (Halifax: Center for Foreign Policy Studies, 1973); Stewart E. Fraser and Kuang-liang Hsu, *Chinese Education and Society, A Bibliographic Guide: The Cultural Revolution and Its*

Aftermath (White Plains, N.Y.: International Arts and Sciences Press, 1972); W. P. J. Hall, *A Bibliographic Guide to Japanese Research on the Chinese Economy, 1958–1970* (Cambridge: Harvard University Press, 1972); U.S. Bureau of the Census, *The Population and Manpower of China: An Annotated Bibliography*, International Population Statistics Reports, Series P-90, no. 8 (Washington, D.C.: U.S. Government Printing Office, 1958); U.S. Department of Health, Education, and Welfare Public Health Service, National Institutes of Health, *A Bibliography of Chinese Sources on Medicine and Public Health in the People's Republic of China: 1960–1970*, DHEW Publication no. (NIH) 73–439 (Washington, D.C.: U.S. Department of Health, Education, and Welfare, 1973); Michel C. Oksenberg, *A Bibliography of Secondary English Language Literature on Contemporary Chinese Politics* (New York: Columbia University, 1970); Edward J. M. Rhoads, ed., *The Chinese Red Army, 1927–1963: An Annotated Bibliography* (Cambridge: Harvard University Press, 1964); Leonard H. D. Gordon and Frank J. Shulman, eds., *Doctoral Dissertations on China, a Bibliography of Studies in Western Languages, 1945–1970* (Seattle: University of Washington Press, 1972); Chi Wang, *Nuclear Science in Mainland China, A Selected Bibliography* (Washington, D.C.: Library of Congress, 1968).

4. The exception is for post–1971 secondary publications, with the annual Bibliography of the Journal of Asian Studies suffering from production difficulties and the Skinner bibliography project not being maintained.

5. The Red Guard publications do provide some information about these channels, but nothing very systematic. And some of Mao's personal letters and poems have come to light.

6. The major exception is the People's Liberation Army's in-house *Work Bulletin*. See J. Chester Cheng, *The Politics of the Chinese Red Army: A Translation of the Bulletin of Activities of the People's Liberation Army* (Stanford: The Hoover Institution, 1966).

7. China Commission of Legislative Affairs, *Zhongyang renmin zhengfu faling huibian* (Compendium of Laws and Decrees of the Central People's Government), 5 vols. (Beijing: Renmin chubanshe, 1952–1954, Fal chubanshe, 1955); China State Council, Bureau of Legislative Affairs, *Zhonghua Renmin Gongheguo fagui huibian* (Compendium of Laws and Regulations of the People's Republic of China) (Beijing: Falü chubanshe, 1956–).

8. See, for example, the *Jinrong fagui huibian* (Compendium of Fiscal Laws and Regulations) published by the People's Bank of China and the *Zhongyang caizheng fagui huibian* (Compendium of Central Financial Laws and Regulations). Both series are available for the 1950s.

9. Union Research Institute, *Documents of Chinese Communist Party Central Committee, September 1956–April 1969*, vol. 1. (Hong Kong: Union Research Institute, 1971).

10. Jiang Yishan, ed., *Zhonggong junshi wenjian huibian* (Compendia of Documents on Chinese Communist Military Affairs) (Hong Kong: Union Research Institute, 1965).

11. Union Research Institute, *Tibet: 1950–1967* (Hong Kong: Union Research Institute, 1968).

12. See S. C. Chen and Charles Ridley, *The Rural People's Communes in Lien-Chiang* (Stanford: The Hoover Institution, 1969).

13. Some are collected in Richard Baum and Fredrick C. Teiwes, *Ssu-Ch'ing: The Socialist Education Movement of 1962–1966* (Berkeley: University of California Press, 1968); and Union Research Institute, ed., *CCP Documents of the Great Proleterian Cultural Revolution 1966–1967* (Hong Kong: Union Research Institute, 1968).

14. Several of these are collected in Michael Y. M. Kau, *The Lin Piao Affair, Power Politics and Military Coup* (White Plains, N.Y.: International Arts and Sciences Press, 1975).

15. Ajia Sekai Gakkai, *Chūgoku seiji keizai sōran* (Chinese Political and Economic Almanac) (Tokyo: 1954–).

16. T. T. Hsia, *Guide to Selected Legal Sources of Mainland China* (Washington, D.C.: Library of Congress, 1967).

17. Exceptions in English involve Mao Zedong, Liu Shaoqi, and Lin Biao, where efforts have been made to compile and translate the known post–1949 writings of each. For Mao *inter alia*, see Stuart Schram, *The Political Thought of Mao Tse-tung* (New York: Praeger, 1963); and Stuart Schram, *Chairman Mao Talks to the People, Talks and Letters: 1956–1971* (New York: Pantheon Books, a division of Random House, 1974). John Starr at the University of California (Berkeley) and Michael Y. M. Kau at Brown University are involved in separate projects to establish total control over available post–1949 writings of Mao.

18. In more recent years, the Central Intelligence Agency has also provided university libraries with a periodical publication alphabetically listing the publicly known activities of higher-level officials.

19. Donald W. Klein and Anne B. Clark, *Biographic Dictionary of Chinese Communism 1921–1965*, 2 vols. (Cambridge: Harvard University Press, 1971).

20. These are indexed in the Lieberthal *Guide*.

21. China Ministry of Foreign Affairs, *Zhonghua Renmin Gongheguo tiaoyue ji* (Collected Treaties of the People's Republic of China) (Beijing: Falü chubanshe, 1957); World Knowledge Publishing Company, *Zhonghua Renmin Gongheguo duiwai guanxi wenjian ji* (Documents on Foreign Affairs of the People's Republic of China) (Beijing: Shijie jishi chubanshe, 1957). See also Douglas Johnston and Hungdah Chiu, *Agreements of the People's Republic of China: A Calendar* (Cambridge: Harvard University Press, 1968).

22. Also important through 1965 was the authoritative foreign affairs journal *Shijie jishi* (World Knowledge).

23. See especially *Current Background* (*CB*), nos. 545, 651, 928, 934, and 1014 for indexing of treaties. Other *CB*s group Chinese statements at the United Nations and their major pronouncements on various bilateral concerns.

24. John Emerson, *The Provinces of the People's Republic of China: An Economic and Political Biography* (U.S. Department of Commerce, forthcoming).

25. Kang Chao, *Provincial Agricultural Statistics for Communist China* (Ithaca, N.Y.: Committee on the Economy of China, SSRC, 1969); Chen Nai-ruenn, *Chinese Economic Statistics: A Handbook for Mainland China* (Chicago: Aldine Publishing Co., 1967); and Robert Field, Nicholas R. Lardy, and John Philip Emerson, "Industrial Output by Province in China 1949–1973," *The China Quarterly* 63 (September 1975): 409–434.

26. For more extensive treatment of provincial (and national) elite analysis, see Donald Klein, "Sources for Elite Studies and Biographical Materials on China" in Robert Scalapino, *Elites in the People's Republic of China* (Seattle: University of Washington Press, 1972).

27. An exception would be the few cities in the early 1950s where directives can be culled from the available mass media. These directives help sustain several recently completed theses, particularly Kenneth Guy Lieberthal, "Reconstruction and Revolution in a Chinese City: The Case of Tientsin, 1949–1953" (Ph.D. dissertation, Columbia University, 1972); and Lynn T. White III, "Careers in Communist Shanghai" (Ph.D. dissertation, University of California [Berkeley], 1973).

28. See *inter alia*, Robert Bowie and John Fairbank, eds., *Communist China, 1955–1959: Policy Documents with Analysis* (Cambridge: Harvard University Press, 1962); Albert P. Blaustein, ed., *Fundamental Legal Documents of Communist China* (South Hackensack, N.J.: Fred B. Rothman, 1962); Kuo-chün Chao, *Economic Planning and Organization in Mainland China: A Documentary Study (1949–1957)*, vol. 1. (Cambridge: Harvard University Press, 1959); Kuo-chün Chao, *Agrarian Policies of Mainland*

China: A Documentary Study (1949–1956) (Cambridge: Harvard University Press, 1963); Stewart Fraser, *Chinese Communist Education: Records of the First Decade* (Nashville: Vanderbilt University Press, 1965); Ying-mao Kau, *The Political Work System of the Chinese Communist Military: Analysis and Documents* (Providence, R.I.: East Asia Language and Area Center, Brown University, 1971); Ying-mao Kau, *The People's Liberation Army and China's Nation-building* (White Plains, N.Y.: International Arts and Sciences Press, 1973); John Wilson Lewis, *Major Doctrines of Communist China* (New York: Norton, 1964); Peter J. Seybolt, *Revolutionary Education in China: Documents and Commentary* (White Plains, N.Y.: International Arts and Sciences Press, 1973).

29. See especially Berton and Wu, *Contemporary China.*

30. These are titled *Renmin ribao suoyin, Guangming ribao suoyin,* and *Da gong bao suoyin.* Another valuable index is the *Renmin ribao shelun suoyin, 1949–1958* (Index to *People's Daily* Editorials), which lists and indexes by subject all editorials from 1949 to 1958.

31. See James Chu-yul Soong, *Red Flag, 1958–1968: A Research Guide* (Washington: Center for Chinese Research Materials, Bibliographic series no. 3, 1969). *Hongqi* produces its own annual index, and since February 1961 the contents of each have been translated in their entirety in separate issues of *Survey of People's Republic of China Magazines (SPRCM).* (Before 1973, this series was *Survey of China Mainland Magazines* [*SCMM*]).

32. See James Nickum, *A Research Guide to Jingji Yanjiu (Economic Studies)* (Berkeley: University of California Press for Center of Chinese Studies, 1972). This guide contains a subject and author index, as well as the table of contents for each issue for the duration of the publication.

33. Asia Research Office, ed., *Jimmin koshı sōran* (Concordance to People's Communes) (n.p., 1965); Asia Research Office, ed., *Chugoku kogyō kojo sōran* (Concordance to Chinese Industrial Factories) (n.p., 1965). See also Richard Baum, *Bibliographic Guide to Kwang-tung Communes 1959–1967* (Hong Kong: Union Research Institute, 1968).

34. Union lists are in Raymond G. Nunn, comp., *Chinese Periodicals International Holdings, 1949–1960,* 3 vols. (Ann Arbor: Association for Asian Studies, 1961); Bernadette P. N. Shih and Richard L. Snyder, *International Union List of Communist Chinese Serials: Scientific, Technical and Medical with Selected Social Science Titles* (Cambridge: Massachusetts Institute of Technology, 1963). The important holdings of the Union Research Institute are in *Catalogue of Mainland Chinese Magazines and Newspapers Held by Union Research Institute* (Hong Kong: Union Research Institute, 1968); *Index to Classified Files on Communist China Held by the Union Research Institute* (Hong Kong: Union Research Institute, 1962); and *Hongweibing ziliao mulu* (Catalogue of Red Guard Publications) (Hong Kong: Union Research Institute, 1970).

35. For 1957–1960, see Richard Sorich, *Contemporary China: A Bibliography of Reports on China Published by the United States Joint Publications Research Service* (New York: Joint Committee on Contemporary China, 1961). For 1960–63, see Berton and Wu, *Contemporary China.*

36. I am indebted to Dr. James Reardon-Anderson for preparing this table, which is derived from a larger analysis of *People's Daily* editorials in which I am now engaged.

37. This is the *Zhongguo zongshu mulu* (Catalogue of All Chinese Books).

38. See Hong Yung Lee, "Utility and Limitation of the Red Guard Publications as Source Materials: A Bibliographical Survey," *Journal of Asian Studies* 34, 3 (May 1975): 779–794.

39. Exceptions are the interviews conducted by the Union Research Institute and by the U.S. Department of Agriculture attaché in Hong Kong (prior to 1966). The records of both interview series are available on microfilm in most China centers.

40. See, for example, National Academy of Sciences, *Plant Studies in the People's*

Republic of China: A Trip Report of the American Plant Studies Delegation (Washington, D.C.: National Academy of Sciences, 1975); and William Kessen, ed., *Childhood in China* (New Haven: Yale University Press, 1975).

41. An instance of excellent use of such sources is in Roderick MacFarquhar, *Origins of the Cultural Revolution* (New York: Columbia University Press, 1974).

42. See *inter alia*, Peter Cheng, *A Chronology of the People's Republic of China from October 1, 1949* (Totowa, N.J.: Littlefield, Adams, 1972); E. Stuart Kirby, *Contemporary China*, vols. 1–4 (Hong Kong: Oxford University Press, 1956–1966); *Current Background*, scattered issues; *Xinhua banyue kan shiqi* (Chronology from New China Monthly), 3 vols. (Washington: Center for Chinese Research Materials, 1972).

43. David Floyd, *Mao Against Khrushchev: A Short History of the Sino-Soviet Conflict* (New York: Praeger, 1964); John Gittings, *Survey of the Sino-Soviet Dispute: A Commentary and Extracts from the Recent Polemics, 1963–67* (London: Oxford University Press, 1968).

44. For such discussion, see my "Sources and Methodological Problems in the Study of Contemporary China," in *Chinese Communist Politics in Action*, ed. A. Doak Barnett (Seattle: University of Washington Press, 1969).

Introduction to the 1976 Edition

1. The Policy-making System

In 1960 Mao Zedong commented that eight hundred people—the remaining survivors of the Long March—rule China.[1] A growing body of literature in the West is gradually illuminating how these people interact with each other and with their subordinates. A. Doak Barnett wrote the pioneering work in this field,[2] and others have followed. Michel Oksenberg has written on the policy process in water conservancy,[3] Mao Zedong's own roles in the system,[4] the various "arenas" in which policy is made,[5] and the methods of communication within the post–1949 Chinese bureaucracy.[6] Roderick MacFarquhar has masterfully analyzed the interactions among the very highest-level leaders during the 1956–57 period,[7] with volumes bringing the analysis forward to 1966 in the offing. Parris Chang has focused on certain elements of continuity and change in the forums in which party leaders gather to discuss policy, highlighting especially the importance of Central Work Conferences starting in 1960,[8] and in a more recent work the same author examines the Chinese policy process in broader perspective based on his intensive investigation of several cases.[9] Byung-joon Ahn's excellent dissertation,[10] a part of which has been distilled in published form,[11] continues in this same analytical vein. David Lampton has examined policy making through the operations of the Ministry of Public Health,[12] considerably enhancing our knowledge of policy making in a field in which both highly technical and broadly motivational factors are of great import. Numerous other works have contributed more or less directly to our understanding of the Chinese policy process.[13] A major goal of the present *Research Guide* is to facilitate further work in this field.

The picture that emerges from the currently available literature is that of a highly complex process of decision making, one that cannot be comprehended solely through an appreciation of the tenets of democratic centralism.[14] It is a system, moreover, that has changed over time in response to both technological[15] and political[16] considerations. One senses a constant tension in the system between formal organizations and procedures, recognized as indispensable for governing a country as vast as China, and informal means of communicating and deliberating, required to circumvent bureaucratic rigidities and, in some instances, to allow for wide consultation while maintaining strict secrecy. Thus, for instance, while there are elaborate codified rules for circulating documents[17] and convening meetings of people's congresses[18] and other bodies, the leadership has at times gathered together as many as seven *thousand* of the highest-ranking cadres in the country for almost a month of discussion[19] without any mention of this event in the public media and without recourse to any known provision in statutes for bringing together such a group.

In their attempt to reap the benefits of bureaucracy without suffering its consequences,[20] the Chinese leaders have developed a highly flexible system of interagency meetings—symposia, work conferences, telephone conferences, etc.[21]—in addition to formal meetings of bodies that themselves are designed to play a generalist policy role in the system, such as the Politburo and its Standing Committee. This *Research Guide* provides the basis for a more detailed understanding especially of the consultative process at the highest levels of the Chinese system through providing all currently available information both on meetings of these generalist bodies and on interagency gatherings from 1949 through January 1975.[22] Through the information it provides on these meetings, moreover, the *Research Guide* highlights related aspects of the policy process, such as conducting investigations and circulating reports and comments.[23]

The policy process itself has evolved over time. During 1949–1954, China was divided into six large military-administrative regions.[24] These areas differed immensely in their economic structure and recent political history. A poor transportation system and lack of experience in governing a complex society added to the difficulties in establishing a strongly centralized political system at the time. During these years, therefore, the leadership convened relatively few gatherings in Beijing. Those that did meet tended to be specialized in nature, although these frequently in fact discussed a broader range of topics than the meeting rubrics would suggest.[25]

In 1954 the Chinese established a permanent Central People's Government and abolished the six large regions.[26] The Central Committee also established a range of specialized departments to oversee work in various functional areas.[27] Thenceforth, the more specialized meetings in Beijing were usually convoked by these departments or by government ministries. At the same time, the party began convening a large number of more general meetings under a range of rubrics. Essentially this system of both specialized and general policy meetings continued until the advent of the Great Proletarian Cultural Revolution in 1966.

In 1967 the Cultural Revolution wrecked the meeting system that had characterized the policy process of the previous decade. Ad hoc meetings between central leaders and representatives of various local groups became the order of the day, and within Peking itself the Military Affairs Committee and the Cultural Revolution Group—which had been organized specifically for this campaign—

became the key decision-making bodies.[28] With the conclusion of the Cultural Revolution in 1969 and the subsequent reconstruction of the party and government apparatus, the policy process has clearly reverted to some approximation of its pre–1966 incarnation.[29] Just how close an approximation and with what innovations remains unclear, however, as the Chinese have again become extremely secretive about their own policy-making process.

The materials in the body of this *Research Guide* speak to a range of questions about this evolving policy process in China. When have the top leaders gathered together and what issues have they discussed? How important have formal organizations been in the policy process? How much consultation occurs between leaders in Peking and those in the provinces? To what degree are decisions made by a small group that meets secretly and then communicates *faits accomplis* to the larger leadership stratum? How detailed and rigid are instructions from the party center and how much allowance is made for local adaptation and subsequent review and modification of policy? Can individual leaders convene meetings of their colleagues and aids to discuss policy problems, or does the ban on factions preclude this? Indeed, to what degree are China's leaders fully in control of events in the country versus having to respond to problems that the situation forces onto their agenda? The answers to these questions, not surprisingly, vary somewhat by time and issue. Nevertheless, as can be richly documented by the information in this *Guide*, the following observations in general hold true concerning the Chinese policy process.

Formal tables of organization reveal little about the way top leaders interact. Many important decisions are made in gatherings such as Central Work Conferences that cannot be found on any organizational chart. For instance, the decision to purge Peng Dehuai and launch an anti-rightist campaign was taken at the July 2–August 1, 1959, Lushan Conference (meeting 138), and that to issue the Twenty-three Points ("Some Problems Currently Arising in the Course of the Rural Socialist Education Movement") was made by the December 15, 1964–January 14, 1965, Central Work Conference (meeting 247). Many other decisions, moreover, are made at "enlarged" meetings of designated organizational units, where the group that is gathered together includes a significant number of individuals who do not belong to the unit concerned. Thus, the August 17–30, 1958, Enlarged Meeting of the Politburo at Beidaihe (meeting 113), which was attended by the first secretaries of the CCP committees of all provinces, autonomous regions, and municipalities directly under the central government and responsible members of the party organs in various relevant government departments, in addition to members of the Politburo, made the decision to promote communes throughout the country. Even formal meetings of clearly designated organizational structures, therefore, frequently provide relatively imperfect information concerning the composition of the group that has gathered to consult together.

In view of the extreme secrecy surrounding the Chinese policy process, not surprisingly only about 10 percent of the nearly three hundred meetings summarized in this *Research Guide* received substantial notice in the contemporary media. If one excludes Central Committee plenums and party congresses, this figure drops to 1–2 percent![30]

Indeed, the secrecy that has remained a pervasive characteristic of the Chinese policy-making system can produce serious misunderstanding of the way that system functions.[31] For example, the evidence at first glance indicates that Central Committee plenums have served two major functions: "housekeeping" in preparation for or directly following a party congress; and policy making with respect to major political issues. Thus, the Seventh Plenum of the Seventh CC and the Fourth Plenum of the Eighth CC prepared for the first and second sessions of the Eighth Party Congress, while the first plenums of the Eighth, Ninth, and Tenth Central Committees have "elected" the leadership organs of the new Central Committees directly following the respective party congresses. On the policy-making side, the Eighth Plenum of the Eighth CC issued revised production figures for 1958 and launched an antirightist campaign, the Ninth Plenum of the same CC announced the policy of "agriculture as the foundation and industry as the leading factor," and the Tenth Plenum of the Eighth CC issued the call for renewed emphasis on class struggle. A closer look, however, reveals that in fact in each of these cases the plenum actually merely announced (and legitimized?) a policy that had already been decided at a secret conclave—the July 2–August 1, 1959, Lushan Conference (meeting 138), the July 5–August 10, 1960, Central Committee Conference (meeting 160), and the August 6–September 23, 1962, Central Work Conference (meeting 203), respectively. Indeed, it is now possible to document that of the sixteen ostensibly policy-making CC plenums, at least seven convened directly following secret Central Work Conferences.[32]

Although secrecy and informality characterize much of the policy process at the highest levels, the few highest-ranking leaders have not taken advantage of this to seal themselves off from the rest of the elite. Many important decisions are in fact taken at meetings that bring together a substantial range of important central and provincial leaders and thus reflect the deliberations of more than only a small coterie of people. This is not to suggest that a group as small as the Standing Committee of the Politburo[33] has not exercised tremendous policy-making power over the years, or that all participants at a large meeting decide the major issues through some sort of democratic voting procedure. The centralization of ultimate decision-making power on major issues in China has remained impressive. Rather, it is to recognize that the leadership fairly frequently convenes conferences of a large number of high-ranking individuals in Beijing and the provinces to review problems and policy options and consult on the requirements for future actions. Clear evidence exists that these meetings are not "staged" affairs where the consultation and discussion are pro forma and without real influence on policy.[34] Indeed, the duration, substance, and conclusions of some of these meetings seem to have come as a surprise to a number of the principal

participants. By way of example, the October 9–28, 1966, Central Work Conference (meeting 304) was originally convened for three days but lasted nineteen as
the nature and extent of the problems under review became clear. The July 2–
August 1, 1959, Lushan Conference (meeting 138) and the August 6–September
23, 1962, Central Work Conference (meeting 203) also give every indication of
having taken turns unforeseen by many of the major participants.

The Chinese have varied somewhat the rubrics under which they have convened these consultative meetings, but the underlying uniformities are striking.
For instance, Parris Chang has analyzed the appearance of a seemingly new form
of meeting as of 1960—the Central Work Conference—that generally brought
together a range of central and provincial leaders for policy discussions.[35] As
suggested in the above discussion, however, the Chinese system prior to 1960
made provision for convening similar types of meetings, albeit under different
names. These earlier gatherings frequently assumed the identity of the place
where they met—Nanning,[36] Chengdu,[37] Zhengzhou,[38] Lushan,[39] and so forth.
Like the known Central Work Conferences of the 1960s, they brought together
key leaders from Beijing and the provinces for a wide-ranging review of one or
more major issues, which usually produced some policy decisions (frequently in
the form of tentative proposals for discussion at lower levels, experimental
implementation, and subsequent review within the next three to four months).[40]
These meetings of the 1950s also paralleled those of the following decade in their
seemingly variable roster of participants.[41] At all times during at least the period
1955–1966, therefore, the Chinese leadership included as a regular part of the
policy process meetings under various rubrics that brought together a considerable number of central and provincial leaders for prolonged consultation and
discussion.

The "summer gathering" provides another notable regularity in this consultative process in China. This is a Central Work Conference type meeting that
convenes for several weeks to two months at one of China's summer resorts,
provides the forum for a major review of the current state of the country, and sets
a tentative agenda for the coming year's activities. The two most famous of these
summer gatherings occurred at Beidaihe in 1958 and at Lushan in 1959. In fact,
however, documentary evidence is available concerning such meetings in May–
June 1951,[42] June–August 1953,[43] summer 1955,[44] June 1956,[45] July 1957,[46]
August 1958,[47] June–August 1959,[48] July–August 1960,[49] May–June and August–
September 1961,[50] July–September 1962,[51] June 1964,[52] and September 1965[53]
(the politics of the Cultural Revolution prevented such gatherings in 1966–69).[54]
These summertime gatherings usually took place after the spring harvest had
been completed and the leadership had received the first estimates of the fall
harvest, and thus they provided an opportunity for the leadership to discuss plans
with a relatively clear sense of the resources available for the following year. It
seems likely that similar types of gatherings are still convened in China, although
direct evidence to that effect in recent years is lacking.[55]

The "summer gathering" may convey the incorrect impression that the Chinese leaders enjoy excellent information about the state of the country and can pretty much select the issue on which they want to concentrate at any given time. There is ample evidence in this *Research Guide* to indicate that such is frequently not the case. Indeed, their stress on consultation reflects the Chinese leaders' keen sensitivity to the fact that they operate in an environment of poor information and therefore need to "touch base" often with people in key positions in the central and provincial bureaucracies.[56] Relatedly, for that period when our information on such things is best (late 1950s to mid-1960s), it is striking to observe the degree to which the leadership viewed major policy decisions as temporary, subject to almost immediate review and modification as additional information became available. Not surprisingly, these decisions were frequently cast in general terms allowing for considerable local flexibility in implementation. In this sense, the decisions emanating from the Chinese policy process have tended to be incremental rather than the decisive ukazes one might expect from a more totalitarian model of the system, and they have allowed for considerable local initiative during the process of implementation. A perusal of the meetings from late 1958 through the spring of 1959 demonstrates that even during a political campaign as momentous as the Great Leap Forward this constant review and modification remained an integral part of top-level decision making.[57]

Within this consultative system, how constrained are individual leaders in their ability to bring together colleagues, supporters, and relevant specialists to discuss policy problems and prepare for their own participation in other policy-making forums? Does the strict ban on factionalism preclude this type of individual fact-finding and consultation so necessary to the development of knowledgeable input into complex policy decisions? The meeting summaries in this *Research Guide* suggest that the system makes ample provision for this type of gathering; they demonstrate also that at times leaders have abused this privilege by using it to advance personal political interests. A brief glance at the spring of 1966 vividly illustrates this latter point.

The early spring of 1966 found Peng Zhen trying to defend Wu Han (and himself) against attacks on the play *Hai Rui Dismissed from Office*, with Mao firmly in Jiang Qing and Lin Biao's camp. Deng Xiaoping and Liu Shaoqi initially inclined toward Peng Zhen but then increasingly tried to put some distance between themselves and the first secretary of Beijing. In this tense situation, Peng Zhen on February 3 convened an enlarged meeting of the Five-man Cultural Revolution Group (meeting 279), which decided to draft a report that favored Peng's position in the debate over Wu Han. Two days later, Liu Shaoqi convened a meeting of the Standing Committee of the Politburo (meeting 280) (Mao was absent from Beijing at the time), which approved Peng's report for dissemination. Peng and Liu may have been acting to preempt a challenge from the Left on this issue, for under Lin Biao's aegis and the direct guidance of Jiang Qing, the PLA on February 2–20 convened a Forum on Work in Literature and Art for the Armed Forces (meeting 278), which produced a "forum summary" that sharply contradicted the key points of Peng's report. Lin then convened a meeting of the Military Affairs Committee on March 30 (meeting 284) that approved Jiang Qing's "forum summary" and then transmitted it to the Central Committee.

During March 3-April 8, Lin Biao pressed forward his campaign to oust his rival, Luo Ruiqing, from his position as chief of staff by convening a meeting (meeting 281) of an ad hoc group that he headed, the Central Committee Work Group to Investigate Luo (which had been established the previous winter). This meeting condemned Luo and called for his removal.

Mao Zedong convened an Enlarged Standing Committee Meeting of the Politburo on March 17-20 (meeting 282) and a Central Committee Work Conference on March 28-30 (meeting 283) to intensify his attack on Peng Zhen and to bolster the positions of Lin Biao and Jiang Qing. Peng Zhen, now realizing the full gravity of his situation, tried to mobilize support through convening a meeting of the Standing Committee of the Beijing Municipal Party Committee on April 3 and a joint meeting of the Beijing Municipal Party Committee and the Five-man Cultural Revolution Group on April 6 (meeting 285). Deng Xiaoping then convened an enlarged meeting of the Secretariat on April 9-12 (meeting 287), at which he, Kang Sheng, Chen Boda, and ("finally") Zhou Enlai criticized Peng Zhen. Mao Zedong followed up Deng's initiative with a strong attack on Peng Zhen at a Politburo Standing Committee meeting that he convened on April 16 (meeting 287), and Peng was formally purged and the Five-man Cultural Revolution Group disbanded at an Enlarged Politburo meeting that Mao convened for May 4-26 (meeting 289). The same gathering sealed Luo Ruiqing's fate and formally accepted Jiang Qing's "forum summary."

This synopsis only skims the surface of the events during this very complicated period. Still, it shows that during this time of intense political activity, each of the principals turned to a range of meeting formats that would allow him to air his views and defend his position. For Peng Zhen, these included meetings of the Five-man Cultural Revolution Group, the Beijing Municipal Party Committee, and the Standing Committee of the Beijing Party Committee, all of which he headed. Liu Shaoqi convened the Standing Committee of the Politburo in Mao's absence, and the party chairman in turn called meetings of the Politburo Standing Committee, the full Politburo, and a Central Committee Conference. Lin Biao arranged a special military forum and convened meetings of the Military Affairs Committee, while Deng Xiaoping called together the Secretariat of the Central Committee. Significantly, many of these meetings were "enlarged," indicating that the convener could manipulate the roster of participants to meet his political requirements. The above list, moreover, by no means exhausts the possibilities for meetings that each of the leaders could convene.[58] The Chinese in fact seem quite flexible in assigning names to meetings, and this flexibility undoubtedly facilitates having a leader call together his colleagues in a "legitimate" forum to discuss current issues and problems. Thus, while factions are formally banned in the CCP, there is ample provision for each central leader to meet with aides and supporters to discuss that leader's current concerns.

The image that emerges from the above is one of a secretive system, not closely constrained by organizational boundaries and formal rules, but nevertheless one that places high value on consultation and that retains for the most part a profound awareness of its own limitations on information and resources. It is a system whose major characteristic is flexibility in format of meetings as much as in the substantive debates about policy. Three techniques have ensured this continuing flexibility in the meeting system: convening "enlarged" meetings, where the roster of participants need not be confined to members of the convening unit; utilizing a wide range of rubrics (Central Work Conference, Central Committee Conference, etc.) that permit the leaders to bring together almost any particular body of people at any time to discuss any issue; and consenting to have the role of a given type of meeting change substantially over time. The above analysis of the spring of 1966 illustrates the point concerning "enlarged meetings," and the earlier discussion of Central Work Conferences demonstrates the use of a new meeting rubric to convene essentially the same types of meetings that had met before.

The changing functions of Supreme State Conferences points up the degree to which even a single type of meeting can undergo substantive mutation over time. The Chairman of the People's Republic of China is empowered by Article 43 of the 1954 Constitution (in effect until January 1975)[59] to convene Supreme State Conferences. Mao Zedong exercised this prerogative fifteen times during his tenure as State Chairman from September 1954 to April 1959, and Liu Shaoqi did likewise on six known occasions during his effective term in this office from April 1959 to 1966. The Constitution prescribes no particular composition for Supreme State Conferences, although official reference in two instances to "enlarged" SSCs[60] suggests that there was some understanding as to the types and number of people who might attend. Mao Zedong frequently used the Supreme State Conference format to announce and mobilize support for his major policies, as the Chairman's promotion of the Twelve-Year National Program for Agricultural Development and his speech "On the Correct Handling of Contradictions among the People" at two of these conferences indicate.[61] Liu Shaoqi, by contrast, almost always utilized this forum after 1959 to take care of organizational issues involved in the convening of various sessions of the National People's Congress.[62] Thus, in a real sense, the nature of the Supreme State Conference and its function in the system changed substantially, with 1959 demarcating this shift.

The above discussion highlights some major characteristics of the Chinese policy process at the highest levels. The following brief review of the sequence of meetings held during the spring of 1958 through the summer of 1959 conveys a sense of how the system has worked in practice. Four major issues dominated the agenda of the Chinese leaders during this period: (1) the Great Leap Forward as a general strategy of economic and political development; (2) more specific questions about the administration of communes, concrete investment priorities in industry, the 1959 economic plan figures, and so forth; (3) party rectification and relations with nonparty people ("united front work"); and (4) relations with other countries in the Communist bloc. The following review focuses on the various types of meetings and their roles in the policy process, bringing in these substantive policy issues only as necessary to highlight the interplay of various types of meetings.

The May 1958 eighteen-day session of the Eighth Party Congress (meeting 103) dealt with all the issues noted above and generally endorsed the Great Leap Forward strategy. A "housekeeping" Central Committee plenum (meeting 104) convened two days after this Congress to elect additional people to the Politburo, the Standing Committee of the Politburo, the Secretariat, and the Central Committee.[63] Thereupon followed a period of frantic activity throughout the country, where hundreds of thousands of local units went "all out" in searching for the best ways to implement the Great Leap Forward strategy of development.

In late summer the Chinese leadership convened a major "summer gathering"—the August 17–30 Enlarged Conference of the Politburo at Beidaihe (meeting 113)—to sum up the experiences of the previous few months and lay down policy guidelines to direct the surging mass campaign. Preparations for this meeting included the following: inspection tours by the Chinese leaders, where they gathered information on the types of innovations being made in different areas;[64] regional meetings of agricultural leaders in North and South China to sum up their experiences;[65] two national telephone conferences of provincial party secretaries during July and August (meeting 112) to discuss priorities in the movement to reform farm implements; a national united front work conference in mid-July (meeting 111) to discuss and more systematically articulate policy in that delicate arena; a national conference of the political and legal system in early August; and a national forum on party school work just prior to the Beidaihe gathering.

The August Beidaihe meeting made communization the nationwide policy, decided that agriculture was already progressing very rapidly, and stressed that the emphasis should fall on increasing industrial output, especially that of iron and steel. During the final week of this conference, the Central Committee convened a separate meeting on industrial production attended by party secretaries in charge of industry for the party committees of the various provinces, autonomous regions, and directly administered cities. This industrial conference undoubtedly served both to provide the Politburo meeting with necessary information and to inform the "industrial secretaries" of the new policy in detail. In addition, the September 5–9 Fifteenth Supreme State Conference (meeting 115) transmitted the results of the Beidaihe meeting in detail to over 100 high-ranking party and nonparty people.[66]

With policy set at Beidaihe, the country embarked on a massive program of communization and tremendous efforts at increasing production.[67] For the leadership in Beijing, accurate information rapidly became a scarce commodity as administrative boundaries changed, new small-scale production units sprang up overnight in large numbers, and the experts who staffed the country's statistical system were shoved aside in the political enthusiasm of the moment. By late fall Mao and others sensed astounding progress combined with costly excesses that required remedial action. Again the leaders made inspection trips to the provinces. As a result, in early November Mao convened a meeting for eight days in the city of Zhengzhou (meeting 116), at which he discussed the situation with some of his colleagues from Beijing and a number of leading provincial officials. This conference formulated measures to correct "deviations" in the commune movement.

After further inspection tours by some central leaders, Mao convened a second meeting of central and provincial officials, this time in the Hubei city of Wuchang on November 21–27 (meeting 117). The Wuchang gathering decided on further measures to consolidate the communes and also resolved to reduce the 1959 steel production target by a third. The leadership then convened the Sixth (Enlarged) Plenum of the Eighth Central Committee in Wuchang from November 28 to December 10 (meeting 118) to formalize the consolidation policies decided upon at this November 21–27 meeting. This plenum, which brought together over 160 full and alternate members of the Central Committee and all provincial, municipal, and autonomous region party first secretaries, also dealt with the politically sensitive problem of Mao's stated desire to retire from his post as chairman of the government.

Other meetings convened in tandem with the Sixth Plenum. The Politburo met on December 1 (meeting 120) and most likely at other times as well. It in all probability served essentially as a steering committee for the plenum. A conference of directors of various cooperative areas met through the Sixth Plenum, and Mao remained in contact with them, briefing them on the plenum results directly after it adjourned. Other known efforts to transmit and discuss the results of the Sixth Plenum include a telephone conference with the provinces to convey Mao's reasons for resigning as State Chairman and a National Conference of Directors of the Party's Rural Work Departments (convened by the Rural Work Department of the Central Committee on January 12–26, 1959 [meeting 123]).

After the New Year the party leadership began to acquire complete figures for state procurement of agricultural goods during 1958. These showed that the harvest had not been as good as had been thought and that in many areas the peasants were resisting procurement measures. The attention of national leaders, therefore, turned increasingly toward correcting errors in commune organization and practice, and another round of consultative conferences met to work out appropriate measures.

The first of these, attended by provincial and municipal party secretaries, met in late January and early February to discuss continuing adjustments required by communization. Mao Zedong addressed this meeting. Then in late February and early March Mao called an enlarged meeting of the Politburo at Zhengzhou (meeting 126—the "Second Zhengzhou" conference), at which he demanded urgent measures to correct leftist deviations in commune policy lest these errors wreck the Great Leap Forward as a whole. Mao's own preferences as articulated at this meeting read very much like the policies actually adopted by the party at the Ninth Plenum of the Eighth CC in January 1961 (meeting 172). The party chairman, for instance, favored making the production team the basic level of accounting in the communes.

Leading cadres from the provinces attended the Second Zhengzhou meeting, and upon the conclusion of this conference they went back to their provinces and, in accordance with Mao's instructions, convened a series of multilevel cadre conferences to gather information on the problems raised at Second Zhengzhou and prepare position papers for the next enlarged Politburo meeting, scheduled for March 25 in Shanghai.[68] The brief interlude between these enlarged Politburo conferences also witnessed a meeting of the CC Secretariat (meeting 128) devoted to problems of consolidation in the communes. This meeting directed Wu Lengxi, the director of the New China News Agency, to collect pertinent materials on the communes and publish these in *Cankao ziliao* (Reference Materials), an internal publication for ranking party cadres.

The March 25–April 1 enlarged Politburo meeting in Shanghai (meeting 129), attended by the first secretaries of provincial, municipal, and special district party committees and the central leaders, continued discussing policies to rectify the communes and also revised the 1959 plan targets, effecting another substantial reduction in the steel output target. The Seventh (enlarged) Plenum of the Eighth Central Committee then convened in Shanghai on April 2–5 (meeting 130) to codify and make official the decisions that had been taken at the preceding conferences. That one of these decisions specified the commune's brigade as the basic accounting unit indicates that Mao's own opinions as expressed at Second Zhengzhou did not always carry the day.[69]

Clearly as a follow-up to the March 25–April 1 enlarged Politburo meeting (meeting 129), Xue Muqiao and Sun Yefang convened a conference in Shanghai for April 3–22 that focused on a discussion of economic theories. The Seventh Plenum itself had prepared for the April 18–28 First Session of the Second NPC (meeting 132) (and simultaneous meeting of the National Committee of the CPPCC [meeting 133]), which spelled out officially the 1959 Economic Plan and formally accepted Mao Zedong's resignation as chairman of the PRC. Mao Zedong convened his last Supreme State Conference (meeting 131) two days before this NPC meeting to discuss his decision to resign as chairman of the PRC, foreign affairs, and united front work, undoubtedly taking advantage of the presence of the delegates in Beijing for the larger NPC and CPPCC meetings about to begin.

The above meetings of February–April set policy in a number of realms for the period lasting at least through the spring harvest. It became clear by June, however, that the country faced an increasingly difficult situation, with agricultural production falling well below expectations. Thus, on June 18–23 the Central Committee convened a conference (meeting 137) on nonstaple food and handicraft production in the cities, which called on each city to solve its own nonstaple food supply problems. Then the central and provincial leaders convened a "summer gathering" at Lushan (meeting 138) for a general review of the situation, commencing in late June. This meeting came to grips with the economic difficulties of the time and also witnessed the now-famous clash between Mao Zedong and Peng Dehuai. It reached conclusions relating to both problems, and toward the end of this conference the leadership decided to convene the Eighth Plenum of the Eighth Central Committee (meeting 139) to embody the results of the Lushan Conference in formal Central Committee resolutions. The fact that the three provinces of Guangdong, Liaoning, and Shanxi (at a minimum) started carrying out an antirightist campaign directly after the conference—almost two weeks before the plenum issued a resolution calling for this campaign—highlights the reality that it was the conference and not the plenum that made the basic decision in this realm.

As frequently occurs, the Lushan Conference and Plenum sparked several other meetings. On August 24 Liu Shaoqi convened an enlarged Supreme State Conference (meeting 140) to transmit the decisions of the plenum to a wide range of party and nonparty personages. And in early September Lin Biao convened an enlarged meeting of the Military Affairs Committee of the CCP (meeting 141) to circulate documents on Peng Dehuai's errors and condemn his crimes. This meeting all but determined that Peng would undertake several years of study.

The above review does not include all gatherings of central leaders during this period of some sixteen months. It slights both specialized conferences and meetings devoted to foreign affairs. In addition, evidence gathered on appearances of central leaders suggests that a Politburo meeting convened approximately every nine days throughout this period, although direct documentation of these regular meetings is not available. Unfortunately, too, many important questions about the functions of different types of meetings and the "rules of the game" for convening them remain unanswered. Nevertheless, this overview of May 1958–September 1959 highlights the basic pattern of decision making at the highest levels in China at the time.

Typically, both specialized meetings convened by Central Committee departments and regional conferences met prior to a major central meeting to sum up experiences and prepare for the larger gathering. Then the major leaders in Beijing and the provinces met for anywhere from a week to over a month to grapple with a series of complex issues. Not infrequently, another meeting of people whose expertise and responsibilities related to the subjects at issue convened in tandem with this central gathering and maintained liaison with it. A range of meetings transmitted the decisions reached by the central conference to relevant people throughout the country. This in turn began a process of implementation that entailed investigations and reports which then led to more local and specialized gatherings that preceded the next major central meeting. The central meetings tended to focus on major issues such as priorities for capital investment, basic principles for remuneration, and the administrative system in communes, issues that had wide-ranging repercussions across a number of policy areas. At the same time, Central Committee departments, the Secretariat, and other organs convened meetings that dealt with narrower problems. During the period under review, moreover, the phasing of this meeting activity remained attuned to the agricultural cycle.

Some central conferences—those at Wuchang, Shanghai, and Lushan in the above review—led directly to Central Committee plenums that promulgated the decisions in the form of official resolutions. It is difficult to determine, however, the precise functions that such plenums played. The plenum certainly did not simply provide a forum for making decisions public, as in fact a number of plenum resolutions were kept secret (such as the Lushan Plenum's resolution on Peng Dehuai), while some central meeting decisions (such as many of those taken at Beidaihe in August 1958) were widely publicized. It also cannot merely signify that the leadership was united and had reached an important decision, for there is no indication of significant dissent at Beidaihe in 1958, and the decisions reached at that gathering were among the most momentous in the twenty-five-year history of the PRC. Indeed, it even remains unclear who decided to convene each Central Committee plenum. In all probability, though, where a CC plenum was convened and passed a resolution, that policy did enjoy a great measure of legitimacy and would be almost impossible to challenge successfully in its fundamentals.

The above review of May 1958–September 1959 also demonstrates a point raised earlier in this essay—the apparent flexibility of the Chinese meeting system. It seems that roughly the same people attended the First Zhengzhou, Wuchang, Second Zhengzhou, and Shanghai meetings, and yet the latter two were called "enlarged meetings of the Politburo" while the former were not. Almost all meetings of formal organizational units were enlarged, including even the August 1959 Supreme State Conference, which has no known statutory membership or size. Thus, there seem to have been few if any constraints on having the leadership gather together whatever group seemed most relevant for discussing a problem as the need arose, and the rubrics assigned to such meetings often appear arbitrary to the outside observer.

This brief case history illustrates additional points made earlier in this essay. Most of the above meetings became known only years after they had met, with the contemporary press giving attention only to the Central Committee plenums and very few others. Indeed, in almost all cases, the critical decisions were taken at gatherings that lacked a statutory basis, although implementation of these decisions tended to take place through more regular channels. Also, this was clearly a system that involved very extensive and frequent consultations between central and provincial officials. The disruption of the normal channels of communication via the state bureaucracy and the magnitude of changes taking place, however, may have made this central-provincial consultation more necessary during 1958–59 than is normally the case. Lastly, the decisions produced by these meetings tended to be short-term, in expectation of continual review and modification as information on conditions throughout the country filtered back to the leaders.

As the above demonstrates, the study of central party and government meetings can reveal much about the policy process at the highest levels. Summaries of these meetings also reflect in rather great detail the ongoing political history of post–1949 China,[70] a history that has largely been shrouded in official secrecy. By focusing on central meetings, moreover, this *Research Guide* has the additional advantage of highlighting the *grouping* of issues in the minds of national leaders at any given time. It can, therefore, provide both researchers concerned with the evolution of policy in a given functional area and scholars directing their attention to the politics of a particular locale with important information on the larger context of the policies they are studying.

The very diffuseness of meetings as a focus of study presents special problems of achieving bibliographic control over the data. The purpose of this *Research Guide* is to establish such control for the important meetings summarized individually herein, with somewhat less complete guidance to numerous additional gatherings. Part 2 of this introduction provides technical details on the scope of coverage and format of presentation.

This *Research Guide* attempts to be comprehensive with respect to the information currently available on meetings that fall within its purview. Still, the available information is itself far less than comprehensive on the subject at issue. There are data, for instance, on probably less than 1 percent of the Politburo meetings over the past twenty-five years, and no one can state with certainty how many Central Work Conferences and other types of nonserial meetings have been convened. Indeed, even where documentation on a gathering is relatively abundant as is that for the Lushan Conference of 1959, stenographic reports and other important items are usually lacking. It is to be hoped that the Chinese will fill some of the major gaps in documentation in the future. Until then, this *Research Guide* seeks to facilitate maximum utilization of the considerable body of information already in hand on central party and government meetings in China.

2. The Research Guide

A. *Scope*

This *Research Guide* specifies the documentary information available on all of the following types of gatherings: meetings of the Politburo, Standing Committee of the Politburo, Secretariat, Military Affairs Committee,[71] Central Cultural Revolution Group (original and revamped);[72] Central Committee Plenums; Central Work Conferences; Supreme State Conferences (and "enlarged" meetings of the above); All-PLA Political Work Conferences;[73] National People's Congresses; and the CPPCC and its National Committee.

A number of other types of meetings, less readily identified by category, are also included so as to encompass all those interagency meetings that have drawn a range of central leaders together to review and make policy. These include conferences between central party leaders and provincial party secretaries (e.g., the July 31, 1955, meeting [meeting 50]), convocations of a portion of the central and provincial leadership identified only by the place in which they gathered (e.g., the November 2-10, 1958, First Zhengzhou Meeting [meeting 116]), meetings of special subgroups of the Central Committee (e.g., the March 4-April 8, 1966, meeting [meeting 281]), and some particularly important "report meetings" (e.g., that of July 22, 1966 [meeting 298]), "forums" (e.g., that of February 13, 1964 [meeting 231]), and "symposia" (e.g., that of October 29, 1955 [meeting 52]). Because the object of this guide is to provide data on meetings critical to the policy-making process in China, some other meetings (e.g., the mid-November 1961 Changguanlou meeting [meeting 188]) that cannot be justified on grounds other than their involvement of central leaders and importance for understanding the politics of the period have also found their way into this volume. Which gatherings to include and which to exclude has unavoidably involved, in some instances, a degree of personal discretion.

No meeting is included for which direct documentation on the meeting itself is lacking. The Central Committee, for instance, may issue a document without holding a meeting, as certain officials can "chop" documents in the name of the Central Committee. This guide thus does not take note of instances where the Central Committee has "passed" or "approved" a document unless sources specifically state that this action occurred *at a meeting*.[74] The guide similarly ignores instances where *indirect* evidence strongly suggests that a meeting was held but no direct documentation of the meeting is available.

B. Meeting Rubrics

The following are brief synopses of the major types of meetings included in this *Research Guide*.

Standing Committee of the Politburo. Established by the September 1956 First Session of the Eighth Party Congress (meeting 70), the Standing Committee includes the five to ten highest-ranking members of the Politburo. It is the functional equivalent of the pre-1956 Secretariat. It probably meets at least weekly, although available documentation mentions only about ten meetings, of which half were "enlarged" and therefore included more than the Standing Committee's formal membership.

Politburo. Includes approximately twenty of the highest-ranking party members and usually has about five additional "alternate" members. Almost certainly meets every week to ten days, although available documentation provides information on only twenty to twenty-five of these meetings, of which roughly a third are "enlarged."

Secretariat. Before 1956 acted as the Standing Committee of the Politburo, and from then until 1967 served as an executive organ of the Politburo. Presumably, the Secretariat met frequently until its demise during the early stages of the Cultural Revolution. (It was formally abolished at the Ninth Party Congress in April 1969 [meeting 327].) There is available documentary evidence on approximately twenty of these meetings, the last convening in April 1966 (meeting 286).

Military Affairs Committee. Highest-level party body in charge of military affairs. The frequency of its meetings is unknown. Documentation on thirteen of its meetings is available, of which nine were "enlarged."

Central Committee Plenums. Numbered, and there is documentation available on all twenty-two that convened during 1949–January 1975. At least twelve of these plenums included people other than, and in addition to, the full and alternate members of the Central Committee in attendance.

Party Congresses. Promulgate new party constitutions and usually occasion significant reports and policy statements. Two sessions of the Eighth Party Congress[75] and one each of the Ninth and Tenth congresses have convened since 1949, and there is documentation available on each of these meetings.

Central Work Conferences. Usually rather large gatherings of central and provincial party leaders to consider a range of issues. Roughly thirty-five meetings since 1960 have been labeled either "Central Work Conferences" or "Central Committee Work Conferences." This is an imprecise rubric, evidently somewhat loosely applied.

Conferences of Provincial and Municipal Party Secretaries: Usually focused on a specific problem area, and typically at least some major central party leaders attended. Ten to twenty of these conferences can be documented during the 1950s, but none has been mentioned since then.

Supreme State Conferences. According to the 1954 Constitution could be convened by the Chairman of the PRC (Mao until April 1959; Liu from April 1959 to 1968), who was presumably empowered to specify who attended. Some of these meetings are numbered: seventeen met during the 1950s, of which documentary materials are available on nine; another four are known to have met during 1960–64, each of which is covered by available documentary evidence.

All-PLA Political Work Conferences. Convened by the General Political Department, the major party organ within the army. Only three of these have been documented; all convened under Lin Biao's auspices during 1961–63.

Report Meetings. Oral briefings used by subordinates to inform their superiors about meetings attended, inspections made, and so forth; presumably take place constantly at various levels of the hierarchy. While typically devoted to a particular subject (as the name implies), they can provide the forum for rather wide-ranging discussion, and five of the most important of these for which there is documentation are included in this volume. All five met during 1963–66.

NPC, CPPCC, and CPPCC National Committee. Governmental bodies whose meetings usually occasioned important reports by high-level leaders. There is available documentation on all these meetings, which total twenty-one over the period 1949–1975. The CPPCC ceased meeting in 1954, at which time it was replaced by the NPC and the CPPCC National Committee (which in turn met jointly with the NPC from 1959 through its final convocation in 1965).

NPC, CPPCC, and CPPCC National Committee meetings have played important roles in communicating, but not in *making*, policy in China. They are included in this *Research Guide* because the many detailed and useful reports delivered to them comprise a vital resource for the study of post–1949 national politics. At the same time, their lesser importance in the policy-making process is reflected in the somewhat abbreviated treatment the guide accords to these meetings. Specifically, summaries of these meetings, unlike those for all other types of gatherings, exclude synopses of speeches and reports, mention of who attended, and analysis of actions or decisions taken that were not embodied in documents formally passed by the meetings. In addition, only the most important speeches, reports, and resolutions from these meetings are enumerated separately in the text, and in most cases the sources cited are in either English or Chinese (usually the latter) but not both.

[Deleted here is a brief discussion of the three appendices that accompanied the first edition of this book.]

C. Explanation of Categories in Meeting Summaries

There are potentially eleven categories of data in each meeting summary. For any single meeting, only those categories appear for which documentary information is available. The following explanations define the boundaries and criteria for each of these categories.

Category I: Date(s) of meetings. Where precise dates for a meeting are available, these are given. Uncertainty about whether a meeting began before a specific date or ended after it is indicated by appropriate question marks. For instance, the only available documentation of the CCP's May 1954 Second National Propaganda Work Conference consists of excerpts of speeches to the conference on May 22 and May 25. The meeting clearly could have begun before the twenty-second and concluded after the twenty-fifth, and therefore the date for this meeting is given as May ?–22–25–?, 1954. Where dates for a meeting have been derived from the appearance file, this is noted. Otherwise, the dates come from the documentary sources cited for the meeting.

Meetings are arranged chronologically, according to the earliest date on which they could have started. For instance, the February 2–20, 1966, Forum on the Work in Literature and Art for the Armed Forces comes before the February 3, 1966, Enlarged Meeting of the Five-man Cultural Revolution Group, and the "1961" Central Work Conference summary precedes that of the Expanded Central Work Conference convened between January 1 and 14, 1961.

Category II: Type of meeting. The meeting rubric (Central Work Conference, Politburo Meeting, and so forth) is presented as given in the documentary sources. Where different sources provide dissimilar titles for the same meeting, this is noted. In some instances, a meeting is referred to in the Chinese press both by its organizational rubric and (more commonly) by the place in which it convened. Again, in such cases both are noted. For example, category II for the meeting of February 27–March 10, 1959, reads: "Enlarged Meeting of the Politburo ('Second Zhengzhou Meeting')." The most common types of meetings, with their Chinese equivalents, are given in the above discussion.

Category III: Place of meeting. The place the meeting convened is given only in instances where available documents specify it. No attempt has been made to infer the meeting location if this information is not verified by documents.

Category IV: Attendance. All information in this category comes from the available documents, either through direct quotes or by noting the audience mentioned in speeches to the meeting. This category is excluded for all NPC and CPPCC National Committee meetings.

Category V: Major agenda items. Presents a brief listing of the most important topics under consideration at the particular meeting. It is very important to note that the information in this category is derived exclusively from the available documentary evidence. Thus this category provides guidance to the major items *in the available documents*, which *may or may not* accurately reflect the full agenda of the meeting concerned. In some cases, for instance, category V is based solely on the one available short excerpt from a speech given to the meeting or from the mere mention of a topic discussed there.[76] This category is thus designed simply to provide quick reference to the major topics covered by the available documentation on a given meeting. It is excluded for all NPC and CPPCC National Committee meetings.

Category VI: Speeches and reports. Includes all speeches and remarks made at a meeting, reports submitted to it, and, in most cases, other documents that were circulated at it.[77] Summaries are provided of all materials cited in this category (except for NPC and CPPCC National Committee meetings), as is notation of whether the original(s) contain a full text, partial text, excerpt, or simply mention of the contents of the speech or report. Major textual differences are also noted. Where dates are known, these are used as the basis for arranging the order of items presented in the category. No attempt is made to judge the degree to which available excerpts from a speech accurately reflect the substance of the entire speech.

Category VII: Documents passed. Presents all documents formally passed at a meeting, including notation of whether the available sources simply mention the document or present a partial or complete text. Summaries of these documents are not provided, except in the case of "Communiqués," where decisions noted in the communiqués are given if not revealed elsewhere.

Category VIII: Other decisions and/or actions. Meetings frequently reached decisions and took actions that were not embodied in known documents passed by the gathering. All such decisions and actions are noted under category IX.

Category IX: Remarks. As the name implies, a catchall category designed to allow inclusion of important data that do not neatly fit under the other rubrics. This category is frequently used to make observations about how a meeting was conducted,[78] to bring in relevant information about recent or contemporaneous events,[79] to cross-reference the current proceedings with those of other relevant meetings in the guide,[80] and to take note of more specialized preparatory or follow-up meetings that do not themselves qualify for separate treatment in the guide.[81] Many other types of information are also included in this category, as appropriate.

D. Reference Bibliography

The *Research Guide* employs a flexible format for citation of sources. All numbers in brackets refer to sources listed in the bibliography. Additional bibliographical information, as appropriate, is presented in the text in the following order: volume: number: date: page, with a colon separating each item of information. Only that information is included in the meeting summary which could not conveniently be placed in the bibliography itself. Where the bibliography provides both the Chinese source and its translation, the page number(s) in the meeting summary refer to the translation. "Ibid." refers to the entire bibliographic unit immediately preceding, i.e., all citations within one set of parentheses.

Every effort has been made to cite both English and Chinese texts, where both are available. In a few instances, documents translated in U.S. government translation series were not available in Chinese, and therefore only the English source is given. Occasionally, a given datum appeared in a wide range of sources, and in these cases the *Research Guide* includes references only to those primary materials to which any serious scholar of China is likely to have access. This volume does not, therefore, present an exhaustive listing of available documentation for each item. It does, however, seek to provide bibliographic guidance to primary source documentation for all available data on the central party and government meetings included herein.

E. Note on Sources

Most references in this volume relate to Chinese publications and translation series that are familiar to all researchers on contemporary China. Materials published during the Cultural Revolution are also included, such as internal party documents, official statements, and publications by various Red Guard and other mass organizations. These latter have until recently been difficult to locate, even where title and date were known. The Center for Chinese Research Materials in Washington has now published a multivolume collection of the copious unofficial Cultural Revolution publications made available by the U.S. government and has arranged these materials alphabetically according to title (Wade Giles romanization) and, within a given series, by date. Over 90 percent of such materials cited herein come from this collection and thus are readily traceable. Some additional publications are also included—drawing from the Ting Wang collection and various documents acquired by the University of Michigan library. All of these can be located in the Asia section of the University of Michigan library, and a number are available elsewhere as well.

Indeed, one of the major features of the *Research Guide* is its bibliographic guidance to the large body of official and unofficial Cultural Revolution materials as these relate to central party and government meetings. The origins and polemical nature of these documents, however, demand serious evaluation of their accuracy as sources for research on Chinese politics. Are these materials more likely to enlighten or distort inquiries into pre–1966 political history?

The Cultural Revolution materials clearly are biased. The Red Guards and other Cultural Revolution polemicists gained access to many government and party archives and acquired the stenographic records of a number of important political meetings. They often attempted to utilize these records to blacken the names of political opponents through selective quotation, ex post facto imputation of sinister motives, and skewed interpretation of the available record. The resulting materials are least reliable, therefore, precisely when they ascribe motives to the participants. Relatedly, brief excerpts from speeches and reports frequently are—as with any selective quotation—highly misleading. Words that appeared politically suspect during the Cultural Revolution, moreover, may have been completely orthodox within the context in which they were uttered years earlier.[82] For all these reasons, analysts must carefully separate the quotations cited in the Cultural Revolution materials from the analytical statements appended to these citations.

What, then, remains that is of research value? First, the research for this volume, which often provides cross-checks, strongly suggests that the Cultural Revolution documents are generally reliable when they assert that a person made a speech or remark at a particular meeting. Thus, these materials help to specify when meetings occurred, the type of meeting concerned, and who participated actively. In addition, direct quotations are usually accurate, albeit prior selection may render them unrepresentative. Where the quotations consist of entire speeches or reports, they provide an important source of documentation for the study of the politics of the period.[83]

Certain tests can also be applied to winnow out the wheat from the chaff in the Cultural Revolution materials. Few of these documents refer to periods or issues completely undocumented in the contemporary media, and it is therefore usually possible to determine, at a minimum, whether these materials make sense in terms of the previously available data and the degree to which they are in subtle harmony with contemporary documentation. Also, the Red Guards were by no means unanimous in their interpretations of pre-1966 Chinese political history. Indeed, different central leaders utilized different Red Guard organizations to "leak" materials favorable to their own interests. The subsequent use of these materials in internecine polemics in turn mitigates the one-sidedness that characterizes these documents.

In sum, the Cultural Revolution materials can provide important information about pre-GPCR political history. They help pinpoint when meetings occurred and, to a degree, who participated. They provide the full texts of some speeches, reports, and discussions and make available brief (and probably frequently misleading) excerpts from the contributions in many more instances. For these reasons, the *Research Guide* seeks to provide bibliographic control over the Cultural Revolution materials relevant to central party and government meetings. At the same time, when a single Red Guard source provides the sole documentary evidence for a gathering, category IX of the meeting summary takes note of that fact. Additionally, as with all other sources, to help distinguish the relatively reliable full texts from less reliable excerpts in Cultural Revolution materials, each entry notes whether the documentary source provides a full text, excerpt, summary, or simply brief mention of the particular report or speech.

As reflected in the body of the guide, the GPCR materials do not provide information about all aspects of 1949–1966 political history equally. The temporal bias in favor of 1955–1966 in general and 1959–1966 in particular is noted above. There is also a functional bias, as these materials reveal little data on the particularly sensitive spheres of foreign affairs, public security concerns, and military affairs, indicating that the central leaders at all times retained some modicum of control over the types of documentation the Red Guards could disseminate.

Finally, information about the proceedings of certain types of meetings— especially those of the Secretariat and the Politburo—is usually impossible to confirm through techniques such as the appearance file because so few people were involved. But the record on other forms of meetings that were attended by larger numbers of people creates confidence in the general accuracy of the Cultural Revolution materials on these smaller and unverifiable gatherings—at least within the boundaries delineated above.

Notes

1. This remark, attributed by Edgar Snow to "a man very high in the Party," almost certainly came directly from Mao Zedong. Edgar Snow, *The Other Side of the River* (New York: Random House, 1961), p. 331.

2. A. Doak Barnett, *Cadres, Bureaucracy and Political Power in Communist China* (New York: Columbia University Press, 1967).

3. Michel Oksenberg, "Policy Formulation in Communist China: The Case of the Mass Irrigation Campaign, 1957–1958" (Ph.D. dissertation, Columbia University, 1969).

4. Michel Oksenberg, "Policy Making Under Mao, 1949–1968: An Overview," in *China, Management of a Revolutionary Society*, ed. John M. H. Lindbeck (Seattle: University of Washington Press, 1971), pp. 79–115.

5. Michel Oksenberg, "The Chinese Policy Process and the Public Health Issue: An Arena Approach," *Studies in Comparative Communism* 7, 4 (Winter 1974), 375–408.

6. Michel Oksenberg, "Methods of Communication Within the Chinese Bureaucracy," *The China Quarterly* (January-March 1974), 1–39.

7. Roderick MacFarquhar, *The Origins of the Cultural Revolution*, vol. 1 (New York: Columbia University Press, 1974).

8. Parris Chang, "Research Notes on the Changing Loci of Decision in the CCP," *The China Quarterly*, no. 44 (October-December 1970), 169-94.

9. Parris Chang, *Power and Policy in China* (University Park: Pennsylvania State University Press, 1975), esp. chap. 7.

10. Byung-joon Ahn, "Ideology, Policy and Power in Chinese Politics and the Evolution of the Cultural Revolution, 1959-1965" (Ph.D. dissertation, Columbia University, 1971).

11. Byung-joon Ahn, "Adjustments in the Great Leap Forward and Their Ideological Legacy, 1959-62," in *Ideology and Politics in Contemporary China*, ed. Chalmers Johnson (Seattle: University of Washington Press, 1973), pp. 257-300.

12. David Lampton, "The Politics of Public Health in China, 1949-1969" (Ph.D. dissertation, Stanford University, 1973); and "Health Policy During the Great Leap Forward," *The China Quarterly*, no. 60 (October-December 1974), 668-98.

13. For example: Richard Baum and Frederick Teiwes, *Ssu-Ch'ing: The Socialist Education Movement of 1962-1966* (Berkeley: University of California Press, 1968); Linda Perkin, "The Chinese Communist Party: The Lushan Meeting and Plenum, July-August 1959" (M.A. essay, Columbia University, 1971); David Charles, "The Dismissal of Marshal P'eng Teh-huai," *The China Quarterly*, no. 8 (October-December 1961), 63-76; J. D. Simmonds, "P'eng Teh-huai: A Chronological Reexamination," *The China Quarterly*, no. 37 (January-March 1969), 120-38; Michael Pillsbury, "Patterns of Chinese Power Struggles: Three Models" (unpublished paper delivered to the University Seminar on Modern China, Columbia University, March 27, 1974). James Townsend provides a summary of some of the pertinent literature in his *Politics in China* (Boston: Little, Brown, 1974), pp. 286-334.

14. "Democratic centralism" provides for relatively wide-ranging discussion until a decision is made, followed by absolute discipline in implementation once a policy has been set. It suggests far less ongoing policy review than in fact occurs in China.

15. Oksenberg, "Methods," pp. 33 and 35.

16. Cf. Ahn, "Adjustments."

17. See the sources cited by Oksenberg in "Methods," p. 16, n. 26.

18. *Collection of Laws and Decrees of the Chinese People's Government, 1949-1950*, vol. 1 (Peking: People's Publishing House, 1952), pp. 109-16.

19. The Enlarged Work Conference of the CC CCP that convened from mid-January to early February 1962 (meeting 192). In all cases, information contained in the meeting summaries in this volume is not separately footnoted in this introduction other than to indicate the appropriate meeting summary to check.

20. Martin K. Whyte analyzes the differences between Maoist and Western concepts of bureaucracy in "Bureaucracy and Modernization in China: The Maoist Critique," *American Sociological Review* 38, 2 (April 1973), 149-65.

21. Oksenberg describes this in "Methods," pp. 3-16.

22. Part 2 of this introduction discusses in detail the scope of the *Research Guide*.

23. The Lushan Conference and Plenum of June-August 1959 (meetings 138 and 139) provide good examples of this.

24. These were the Northeast, East, Northwest, North, Central-South, and Southwest.

25. For instance, the June-August 1953 National Finance and Economics Conference (meeting 22) worked out the General Line for the Transition to Socialism.

26. For the specific dates when each government was abolished, see Donald Klein and Anne B. Clark, *Biographical Dictionary of Chinese Communism* (Cambridge: Harvard University Press, 1971), pp. 1116-19. This was in fact part of a process of centralization that had been in evidence since 1952.

27. For an enumeration of pre-Cultural Revolution Central Committee departments and their dates of establishment, see ibid., pp. 1092-93. About half of these departments date back to pre-1949.

28. The best information on the membership of the Cultural Revolution Group is Kao Ch'ung-yen, *Changes of Personnel in Communist China, 1959-1969* (Kowloon: Union Research Institute, 1970), pp. 58-64. For examples of this type of ad hoc meeting, see, for example, *SCMP-S*, no. 226 (May 20, 1968), 1-12; no. 225 (May 14, 1968), 1-14.

29. Frederick Teiwes, "Before and After the Cultural Revolution," *The China Quarterly*, no. 58 (April-May 1974), 336-37.

30. The editors of *Current Background*, a publication put together by the U.S. Hong Kong Consulate, have collated all Chinese news articles on national meetings of various types. There is only a minuscule overlap between this *Current Background* list and the meetings included in this *Research Guide*.

31. This secrecy was broken only during the flood of revelations that occurred during the Cultural Revolution. Otherwise, while the degree of secrecy regarding administrative difficulties, economic statistics, and so forth has varied considerably over time, that concerning the policy-making process at the highest levels has unfortunately remained high.

32. Information on party conferences preceding "policy-making" CC plenums is as follows (meeting numbers are in parentheses):

Dates of Plenums	Dates of Preceding Conference, where known
3/5-13/49 (1)	
6/6-9/50 (5)	
2/6-10/54 (24)	
4/455 (32)	3/21-31/55 (30)
10/4-11/55 (37)	
11/10-15/56 (57)	
9/20-10/9/57 (73)	
11/28-12/10/58 (99)	11/21-27/58 (98)
4/2-5/59 (111)	3/25-4/1/59 (110)
8/2-16/59 (118)	6/26-8/1/59 (117)
1/14-18/61 (148)	Between 1/1 and 1/14/61 (147)
9/24-27/62 (179)	Late July-9/23/62 (176) (and the 7-8/60 Central Committee Conference [137])
8/1-12/66 (272)	Between 7/24 and 7/31/66 (see the information in Category X of the 7/24/66 Enlarged Meeting of the Cultural Revolution Group [271]).
10/13-31/68 (289)	
8/23-9/6/70 (292)	
1/8-10/75 (297)	

Information on attendance is available for fourteen of the sixteen "nonhousekeeping" CC plenums convened during 1948-1975. Twelve of these were enlarged. The two exceptions were the March 5-13, 1949, Second Plenum of the Seventh CC (meeting 2) and the August 23-September 6, 1970, Second Plenum of the Ninth CC (meeting 334).

33. Typically has five to ten members at any given time.

34. As, for instance, seems to be the case with the Supreme Soviet in the USSR.

35. Chang, "Research Notes."

36. Convened January 11-22, 1958 (meeting 94).

37. Convened for March 8 or 9-26, 1958 (meeting 98), with a hiatus midway for participants to make inspection tours of the countryside.

38. First Zhengzhou meeting convened for November 2-10, 1958 (meeting 116), and the Second Zhengzhou meeting met, under the formal rubric of an "Enlarged Meeting of the Politburo," for February 27-March 5, 1959 (meeting 126).

39. Convened July 2-August 1, 1959 (meeting 138).

40. See, for instance, the February 27-March 5, 1959, Second Zhengzhou meeting (meeting 126) and the March 25-April 1, 1959, Shanghai Conference (meeting 129).

41. Only weak evidence is available to specify the typical size of these meetings, and the pertinent documentation indicates clearly that considerable flexibility characterized the determination of the participants. Chang ("Research Notes," pp. 170-71) suggests that usually somewhat under one hundred people attended. This seems to be a reasonable estimate, although one must stress that it was not necessarily always the same hundred or so people who attended.

42. The National Conference on Propaganda Work (meeting 11), which also discussed cooperativization in agriculture.

43. The June 13-August 12, 1953, National Conference on Financial and Economic Work (meeting 22), which developed the General Line for the Transition to Socialism.

44. Beidaihe Conference (meeting 47), which probably convened in August.

45. Beidaihe Conference (meeting 65), which discussed the pace of economic advance.

46. The Qingdao Conference (meeting 86), which marked the beginning of the radicalization that led to the Great Leap Forward.

47. The August 17-30, 1958, Beidaihe Conference (meeting 113), which made communization the official policy of the PRC.

48. The July 2-August 1, 1959, Lushan Conference (meeting 138), which initiated the Antirightist campaign and issued orders for the further consolidation of the communes.

49. A Central Committee Conference at Beidaihe (meeting 160), which evidently marked the turn to the economic and administrative policies that were formally announced at the January 1961 Ninth Plenum of the CC CCP (meeting 172).

50. The May-June Central Work Conference (meeting 178) convened in Beijing, reviewed the failure of the Great Leap Forward, initiated a movement for investigation and study, and concluded with Mao Zedong's self-criticism. The August-September Central Work Conference (meeting 184) met in Lushan and was concerned with adjusting the communes.

51. This August 6-September 23, 1962, Central Work Conference (meeting 203) convened in Beidaihe and then moved to Beijing. It set the stage for the September 24-27, 1962, Tenth Plenum of the Eighth CC (meeting 206).

52. (Meeting 238); convened May 15-June 17, 1964, in Beijing and discussed a wide range of domestic and foreign issues. In 1963 a meeting that convened for May 2-12 in Hangzhou (meeting 220) discussed a similarly broad spectrum of domestic and foreign issues, although the fact that this meeting concluded in May suggests it should not be regarded as a "summer gathering."

53. This September 1965 meeting (meeting 264) may have been different from the other "summer gatherings" mentioned above in that fewer people may have attended and its agenda may have been narrowly fixed on political issues that would play a major role in the Cultural Revolution. Too little information is available to be more precise.

54. Given the political situation of the time, the series of meetings of July 19-August

12, 1966 (meetings 297–300) should perhaps be considered the functional equivalent of the annual "summer gathering."

55. The fact that the important Second Plenum of the Ninth CC (meeting 334) began on August 23, 1970, and that the Tenth Party Congress (meeting 350) convened on August 24, 1973, suggests that these major summer conferences have again become a regular part of the policy process in post-Cultural Revolution China, as such conferences often precede CC plenums and party congresses. Of course, not all important Central Work Conferences lead directly to CC plenums or party congresses, and thus the possibility of "summer gatherings" in 1971, 1972, and 1974 cannot be excluded.

56. Oksenberg briefly assesses the feedback mechanisms in the Chinese bureaucracy in "Methods," pp. 30–31.

57. See note 40 above and the more detailed review of this period below.

58. At any given time almost every central leader belongs to a considerable range of committees and units that can provide the pretext (and context) for convening a meeting.

59. The September 15–28, 1954, First Session of the First National People's Congress (meeting 36) passed the 1954 Constitution, and the January 13–17, 1975, First Session of the Fourth NPC (meeting 361) passed the 1975 Constitution. The texts of both are given in *The China Quarterly*, no. 62 (June 1975), 386–406.

60. On February 27–March 1, 1957 (meeting 80), attended by over 1,800 people, and on August 24, 1959 (meeting 140). Most other Supreme State Conferences on which such information exists were attended by 150–200 people, although only 61 people attended the SSC convened by Mao Zedong on October 13, 1957 (meeting 90), and over 300 attended the SSC on January 25, 1956 (meeting 58).

61. On January 25, 1956 (meeting 58), and February 27-March 1, 1957 (meeting 80), respectively.

62. As noted below, Liu convened the August 24, 1959, SSC (meeting 140) to transmit the results of the Eighth Plenum of the Eighth CC. The sole additional exception seems to be the December 30, 1964, meeting (meeting 252), and the evidence for regarding even this meeting as an exception is weak.

63. The basic memberships of these organs had been elected at the First Plenum of the Eighth CC in September 1956 (meeting 71), directly following the First Session of the Eighth Party Congress (meeting 70).

64. In some cases, individual leaders publicized their feelings about one or another experiment, essentially making that unit a national "model" even before the higher levels of the party as a whole could discuss it. The most famous example is Mao Zedong's remark that "People's communes are good," made during an inspection trip on August 9, 1958: *Renmin ribao* (People's Daily), August 13, 1958.

65. In North China on July 18 and in South China on July 6–16. A similar conference was held on June 25–July 7 by representatives of the Northwestern provinces. See *CB*, no. 593 (September 22, 1959), 7–8.

66. The Supreme State Conference also considered in detail China's policy in the Taiwan Straits crisis, which peaked during the first week in September. See, e.g., Allen Whiting, "New Light on Mao: Quemoy 1958: Mao's Miscalculations," *The China Quarterly*, no. 62 (June 1975), 263–70.

67. The communization had actually begun in parts of the country before Peitaiho but was carried through on a nationwide scale after this meeting: Parris Chang, "Patterns and Processes of Policy-Making in Communist China, 1955–1962: Three Case Studies" (Ph.D. dissertation, Columbia University, 1969), pp. 175–82.

68. For additional information on these subprovincial meetings, see *Mao Zedong sixiang wan sui* (1967), pp. 104–107, translated in *Miscellany of Mao Tse-tung Thought (1949–1968)*, part 1 (Washington, D.C.: *JPRS*, no. 61269-1, February 20, 1964), pp. 164–67.

69. Mao had indicated that these lower-level meetings should make recommendations for modification in the program he put forth at Second Zhengzhou (meeting 126).

70. Especially for the period 1955–1967.

71. After the Cultural Revolution this became the "Military Commission," but for simplicity the *Research Guide* utilizes the pre-Cultural Revolution rubric throughout.

72. The May 4–26, 1966, Enlarged Politburo Meeting (meeting 289) substantially reconstituted this group.

73. Considered as party meetings because the General Political Department of the PLA convened them.

74. This accounts for the guide's exclusion of some of the "meetings," such as the December 15, 1951, Politburo Conference, listed by Parris Chang in his "Research Notes."

75. The Second Session of the Eighth Party Congress did not produce a new constitution.

76. This is, for instance, the case with the April 1965 Politburo Meeting (meeting 249).

77. In some instances, these latter are included under category IX.

78. For example, the April 1–24, 1969, Ninth Party Congress (meeting 327).

79. For instance, the September 5–9, 1958, Supreme State Conference (meeting 115).

80. For example, the March 6–13, 1957, National Conference on Propaganda Work (meeting 82).

81. For instance, the March 25–April 1, 1959, Enlarged Meeting of the Politburo (meeting 129) and the February 13, 1964, Spring Festival Forum (meeting 231).

82. Cf. Kenneth Lieberthal, "Mao Versus Liu? Policy Toward Industry and Commerce, 1946–1949," *The China Quarterly*, no. 47 (July-September 1971), 494–520.

83. Cf. Hong Yung Lee, "Utility and Limitation of the Red Guard Publications as Source Materials: A Bibliographical Survey," *Journal of Asian Studies* 34, 3 (May 1975), 789.

MEETING SUMMARIES

1949-1986

Key to Categories
in Meeting Summaries*

I	Date(s) of Meeting
II	Type of Meeting
III	Place of Meeting
IV	Attendance
V	Major Agenda Items [based solely on available documents]
VI	Speeches and Reports
VII	Documents Passed
VIII	Other Decisions and/or Actions
IX	Remarks

---

*See Introduction to the 1976 Edition, pp. xlvii–xlix, for a fuller explanation of each of these categories.

Meeting Summaries, 1949–1986

1949

1

I. *January 6–8, 1949*
II. **POLITBURO MEETING**
III. Xibaibo village, Hebei
V. Plans for 1949 and 1950
IX. Decision on "The Current Situation and the Party's Tasks in 1949" (mention: [270]: 215): the CCP will capture nationwide power during 1949 and 1950.

2

I. *March 5–13, 1949*
II. **SECOND PLENUM OF THE SEVENTH CC CCP**
III. Xibaibo village, Hebei
IV. Thirty-four full and nineteen alternate members of the CC CCP.
V. Transition to urban revolution; exercise of state power
VI. Mao Zedong: "Report," March 5, 1949 (text: [204]: 361–75): the PLA must continue to push hard for military victory; must prepare to rule the country; will establish a four-class alliance; need to restore production; the state will control foreign trade; will establish diplomatic relations with all countries that treat China as an equal; conditions are ripe for convening a political consultative conference; must firmly establish a united front policy that includes nonparty democrats; the period of basing the revolution in the rural areas has now ended, and the period of "from the cities to the villages" has begun; we have completed only the first step in a march of ten thousand *li*.

Liu Shaoqi: Speech "Several Questions Regarding Urban Work," March 12, 1949 (text: [146]: *shang*: 419–25): discusses the need to unite urban and rural areas; the problems of taking over control of the cities; guarantee the livelihood of workers, educate them, and organize them into unions.

VIII. Approved the work of the Politburo of the CC CCP since the First Plenum of the Seventh CC in June 1945 (mention: [43]: 410: September 25, 1956: 40; [195]: 1957: 146).

Approved a proposal to establish a new CPPCC and establish a democratic coalition government (mention: ibid.).

Approved Mao Zedong's January 14, 1949, "Statement on the Current Situation" (text: [204]: 315–19) and his eight conditions for talks with the Nationalist government enumerated therein (mention: [43]: 410: September 25, 1956: 40; [195]: 1957: 146).

Decided to increase the percentage of proletarian members of the CCP via worker recruitment and restricting future recruitment from among the peasantry (mention: ibid.).

Affirmed that the center of party work had shifted from the rural to the urban areas (mention: ibid.).

Dismissed Liu Zijiu from full membership in the CC CCP for betraying the revolution in the Henan "white" areas (mention: [53]: 11).

IX. Several regulations adopted but not written into resolution: no birthday celebrations; no gifts, at least within the party; keep toasts and applause to a minimum; ban on naming places after persons and placing Chinese leaders on par with Marx, Engels, Lenin, and Stalin (mention: [163]:111).

On the basis of this meeting, the Common Program was drafted [mention: [282]: 1).

3

I. *September 21–30, 1949*

II. **FIRST CPPCC**

III. Beijing

VI. Liu Shaoqi: Speech, September 21, 1949 (text: [144]: 157–60; [146]: 432–35): the significance and role of the CPPCC; CCP support of the Common Program.

VII. "Organization Law of the Central People's Government" (text: [284]: 146–52).

"Common Program of the CPPCC" (text: [284]: 161–73).

"Organization Law of the Central People's Government" (summary: [284]: 241–45).

VIII. Elected the Central People's Government, headed by Mao Zedong, with six vice-chairmen and fifty-six members (name list: [284]: 280–81).

    Elected the National Committee of the CPPCC (name list: [284]: 276–80).

IX.   This convocation officially founded the Chinese People's Republic. Participants heard 100 speeches from representatives of political parties, districts, armed forces, groups, and from specially invited personages, as well as opening and closing remarks by the major leaders (texts: [278]; many also in [284]: 3–13, 57–227).

4

I.   *October 9, 1949*

II.   **FIRST SESSION OF THE FIRST NATIONAL COMMITTEE OF THE CPPCC**

III.   Beijing

VIII.   Established the following groups (*zu*): Political-legal, finance and economics, culture and education, foreign affairs, overseas Chinese affairs, political parties and groups (mention: [195]: 1951: 35).

    Approved the name lists for the positions of chairman, vice-chairman, standing committee members, and secretary general (*mishu zhang*) (mention: ibid).

    Requested the government to designate October 1 as National Day (mention: ibid.).

1950

5

I.   *1950*

II.   **FIRST NATIONAL CONFERENCE ON PUBLIC SECURITY**

V.   Public security work

VI.   Peng Zhen (excerpt: [267]): complains of a previous "left" deviation in public security work.

IX.   All information on this meeting comes from the single Red Guard source cited above.

6

I.   *June 6–9, 1950*
II.   **THIRD (ENLARGED) PLENUM OF THE SEVENTH CC CCP**
III.   Beijing
IV.   Thirty-five full and twenty-seven alternate members of the CC CCP and forty-three party committee secretaries of the provinces and municipalities and other work personnel.
V.   Land reform, financial and economic policy
VI.   Mao Zedong: written report, "Fight for a Fundamental Turn for the Better in the Financial and Economic Situation in China," June 6, 1950 (texts: [43]: 1: June 1950; [76]; [194]: June 13, 1950; [11]: July 1, 1950: 4–6; [163]: 26–32): wide-ranging review of the international and domestic situations; specifies that the domestic situation will undergo a fundamental turn for the better during the coming three years; advocates rich peasant economy, partial demobilization of PLA, and assertion of unified control and leadership in financial and economic work.

Liu Shaoqi: "Report on the Question of Land Reform" (mention: [194]: June 13, 1950).

Zhou Enlai: "Report on Foreign Affairs Work and on United Front Work" (mention: ibid.).

Chen Yun: "Report on Finance and Economic Work" (excerpt: [27]: 92–98; mention: [194]: June 13, 1950): discusses revising the relationship between state and private ownership and the tax collection system and tax rates.

Nie Rongzhen: "Report on Military Affairs Work" (mention: ibid.).

An Ziwen: "On the Question of the Party's Organizational Condition and Developing and Consolidating the Organization of the Party" (mention: ibid.; [273]: 388).

Bo Yibo: "On the Question of Adjusting Taxes" (mention: [108]: 29).

Hu Qiaomu: "On the Question of Party Style" (mention: ibid.).

Su Yu: "On the Question of Army Affairs" (mention: ibid.)

Lu Dingyi: "On the Question of Education Within the Party" (mention: ibid.).

Mao: Speech, "Don't Hit Out in All Directions," June 6, 1950 (partial text: [163]: 33–36): suggests conciliatory policy toward national and petty bourgeoisie to convert them into supporters.

Mao: Summation speech (mention: [108]: 29) (possibly same as above).
VIII. Approved draft of Land Reform Law ([108]: 47; [273]: 394). Meeting criticized the erroneous tendency to eliminate capitalism at an early stage and realize socialism; called for the overall rectification, consolidation,

and development of the party ([273]: 388, 405–406).

IX.   Liu Shaoqi, Chen Yun, and Nie Rongzhen gave reports on identical topics at the June 14–23, 1950, Second Session of the First CPPCC (meeting 7).

This plenum convened during a radical retrenchment in fiscal policy that had produced a temporary but severe recession in China by late spring 1950.

7

I.   *June 14–23, 1950*

II.   **SECOND SESSION OF THE FIRST NATIONAL COMMITTEE OF THE CPPCC**

III.   Beijing

VI.   Liu Shaoqi: "On the Problem of Land Reform," June 14, 1950 (texts: [43]: 43: December 22, 1950; [195]: 1951: *chen* 32–43; [144]: 215–33; [147]: *xia*: 29–47).

Zhou Enlai: "Political Report" (mention: [195]: 1951: 35).

Bo Yibo: "Finance and Economics Report" (mention: ibid.).

Bo Yibo: "Report on the Question of Adjusting Tax," June 15, 1950 (text: [194]: June 22, 1950).

Guo Moruo: "Work Report on Culture and Education," June 17, 1950 (text: [194]: June 20, 1950).

Nie Rongzhen: "Report on Military Affairs" (mention: [195]: 1951: *yin*-35).

Shen Junru: "Report on the Work of the People's Courts," June 17, 1950 (text: [194]: June 21, 1950).

Chen Yun: "Questions on the Economic Situation and the Readjustment of Industry, Commerce, and Taxation," June 15, 1950 (texts: [43]: June 15, 1950: 2; [194]: June 19, 1950; [27]: 99–110).

Mao Zedong: Closing Speech (texts: [43]: June 23, 1950: 3; [194]: June 24, 1950).

Chen Shutong: "Work Report of the Standing Committee of the National Committee of the CPPCC," June 14, 1950 (text: [194]: June 18, 1950).

Also numerous other minor speeches: (texts of some: [194]: June 24, 1950).

VII.   "Method for Calling on the People of the Whole Country to Unfold a Signature Campaign to Protect World Peace" (mention: [195]: 1951: *yin*-35).

VIII.   Passed in principle the draft of the Land Reform Law of the PRC and asked the government to implement it after proper inquiry and approval (mention: [195]: 1951: 75).

Agreed with the reports listed above (except Chen Yun) (mention: ibid.).

Decided to designate the week of July 1–7 as "Peace Signature Movement Week" (mention: ibid.).

Decided to send a "comfort telegram" to the fighters of the army (mention: ibid.).

1951

8

I.	*Mid-February 1951*
II.	**ENLARGED MEETING OF THE POLITBURO OF THE CC CCP**
V.	Party rectification and other issues
VIII.	Decided upon a three-year rectification by conducting widespread education throughout the party on how to be a party member (mention: [273]: 406). Also dealt with the following issues: economic construction based on three years of preparation and ten years of planned economic construction; Resist America-Aid Korea propaganda work; land reform; suppression of counterrevolution; urban work; united front work; and party building (mention: [270]: 241).

9

I.	*March 28–April 9, 1951*
II.	**FIRST NATIONAL ORGANIZATIONAL WORK CONFERENCE**
V.	Party rectification
VI.	Liu Shaoqi: Gave a report and made the meeting summary (mention and excerpts: [116]: April 16, 1967; [98]; [106]; [152]: 20; [53]: 12; [270]: 242 [147]: *xia*: 62–64, 65–77): the Chinese revolution has been led by the proletariat and the semiproletariat; the *xian* party committee should dispatch people to the villages twice a year—if there is not time to do so, they may go to the cities.
	Chen Yun: Speech, April 4, 1951 (text: [27]: 126–39): discusses exchanges between urban and rural areas; increase agricultural production; economic accounting; implement measures to suit local conditions under the principle of unified management; rectify the ranks of financial and economic workers.
VIII.	Passed a resolution on tidying up the party's basic-level organization

(mention: [255]: 3: 1953: 23); posed eight criteria for party membership (text of criteria: [194]: July 1, 1952; [53]: 12; summary in [270]: 242).

IX.   An Ziwen presided over this meeting (mention: ibid.).

Both resolution and eight criteria were written by Liu Shaoqi (mention: [194]: December 16, 1985, tr. in [82]: December 20, 1985: K14).

This conference played a key role in launching a rectification of basic-level party units, especially in the countryside, during the following three years (mention: [266]: 29–30; [255]: 3: 1953: 23; [187]: July 1, 1953).

Liu said the party at this time consisted of 5.8 million members and 250,000 basic organs (mention: [273]: 406).

10

I.   *May 10–16, 1951*

II.   **THIRD NATIONAL CONFERENCE ON PUBLIC SECURITY WORK**

V.   Suppression of Counterrevolutionaries Campaign

VI.   Liu Shaoqi (excerpt: [267]): it is now better to err to the Right than to the Left in the Suppression of Counterrevolutionaries Campaign.

Peng Zhen (excerpt: [267]): affirms the point made above by Liu Shaoqi.

Mao Zedong, May 15, 1951 (excerpt: [167]: 5–6; [174]: 9–10): articulates the resolutions of the conference as enumerated in VIII below.

Luo Ruiqing, Speech (mention: [108]: 54): summarizes the experience with counterrevolutionaries during the previous seven months.

VIII.   Conference adopted resolution with the following measures ([174]: 9–10; [108]: 54–55):

—Take steps immediately to organize reform through labor;

—Have the public security organs conduct inspection in a more systematic way;

—Execute 10–20 percent of those sentenced to death and place the remainder on probation with forced labor to see whether they reform adequately;

—Err on the side of leniency rather than severity in passing sentences;

—Strictly examine the name lists of the people identified for arrest or execution and carry out propaganda work and education extensively and well.

IX.   Resolution drafted under Mao's personal supervision (mention: [176]: November 28, 1977, tr. in [82]: November 29, 1977: E2; Mao's personal instructions in [163]: 50–52).

This meeting convened toward the end of a very severe campaign to suppress counterrevolutionary elements in the urban areas.

11

I.   *May–June 1951*
II.   **NATIONAL CONFERENCE ON PROPAGANDA WORK**
V.   Initiation of cooperativization in agriculture
VI.   Liu Shaoqi: Speech, May 7, 1951 (excerpts: [24]; [116]: April 16, 1967; [97]: 3: February 28, 1970: 78; [194]: November 23, 1967; [182]: 49: December 1, 1967: 14; [205]: 633: November 4, 1968: 8): asserts that nationalization of land and collectivization of agriculture must be preceded by supplying the peasants with large quantities of machinery, which in turn could be accomplished only after the nationalization of industry.

      Chen Yun: Speech, "Developing Rural Industry Is of Primary Importance," May 16, 1951 (excerpt: [27]: 140–43): the key to increasing agricultural production is completing the land reform in the newly liberated areas, avoiding drought, and building railways in the southwest and northwest.

      Liu Shaoqi: Speech, "The Party's Tasks on the Propaganda Front," May 23, 1951 (partial text: [147]: *xia*: 78–91): assesses past propaganda work and outlines present and future tasks in propaganda.

X.   Liu took charge of convening this conference (mention: [194]: December 16, 1985, tr. in [82]: December 20, 1985: K14).

12

I.   *September 9–?, 1951*
II.   **FIRST CONFERENCE ON MUTUAL AID AND COOPERATION**
VII.   "Draft Resolution on Mutual Aid and Cooperation in Agricultural Production" (mention: [108]: 51; [273]: 396; summary: [270]: 243–44).
IX.   This conference began the rapid development of the mutual aid and cooperation movement. By 1952, 40 percent of rural households belonged to mutual aid and cooperative organizations.

      This conference was convened by the CC CCP.

13

I.   *October 1951*
II.   **ENLARGED MEETING OF THE POLITBURO OF THE CC CCP**
VIII. Decided to implement a program to streamline and improve the administrative staff and increase production and practice economy (mention: [273]: 400; [270]: 244).

14

I.   *October 23–November 1, 1951*
II.   **THIRD SESSION OF THE FIRST NATIONAL COMMITTEE OF THE CPPCC**
III. Beijing
VI.   Mao Zedong: Opening Speech, October 23, 1951 (texts: [43]: 130: October 25, 1951; [195]; 1952: 163).

Zhou Enlai: "Political Report," October 23, 1951 (text: [43]: 134: November 5, 1951).

Reports by representatives of national minorities (texts: [43]: 139: November 22, 1951).

Guo Moruo: "Report on Cultural and Education Work," October 25, 1951 (text: [43]: 140: November 22, 1951).

Reports on the following regions in China: Northeast, North, East, Central-South, South, Northwest, Southwest (texts: [43]: 141: December 28, 1951).

Shen Junru: "Report on Judicial Work," October 31, 1951 (text: [43]: 147: December 28, 1951).

Li Fuchun: "Report on Industry," October 31, 1951 (text: ibid.).

Ye Jizhuang: "Report on Trade," October 31, 1951 (text: ibid.).

Teng Daiyuan: "Report on Railways," October 31, 1951 (text: ibid.).

Li Shucheng: "Report on Agriculture" (text: ibid.).

Liang Xi: "Report on Forestry," October 31, 1951 (text: ibid.).

Fu Zuoyi: "Report on Water Conservancy," October 31, 1951 (text: ibid.).

Li Dechuan: "Report on Public Health" (text: ibid.).

Chen Shutong: "Report on Committee Affairs," October 24, 1951 (mention: [216]: 202: October 26, 1951: 27).

Peng Zhen: "Report on Resist America-Aid Korea and Safeguard the Homelands Campaign" (excerpts: [216]: 202: October 25, 1951: 13–16).

Chen Yun: "Report on Economic and Financial Work," October 25, 1951 (mention: [216]: 203: October 26, 1951: 27).

Mao Zedong: Closing Speech, November 1, 1951 (texts: [195]: 1952: 164; [216]: 208: November 2–3, 1951: 1).

Zhou Enlai: "Report Summing Up the Meeting" (mention: ibid.).

VIII. Passed a resolution supporting the appeal of the World Peace Council for conclusion of a Five-Power Peace Pact (mention: [216]: 208: November 2–3, 1951: 2).

Also passed resolution endorsing the reports on the work of government, National Committee affairs, and the proposal examination committee, November 1, 1951 (mention: [216]: 208: November 2–3, 1951: 3).

Passed resolution on the work to Resist America and Aid Korea, October 24, 1951 (text: [216]: 202: October 25, 1951: 11–12).

1952_____

15

I.   *August 1952*
II.   **NATIONAL PUBLIC SECURITY WORK CONFERENCE**
V.   Public security work
VI.   Luo Ruiqing (excerpts: [128]; [140]): the problem of the Shanghai Public Security Bureau is one of work method, while that of the Canton Bureau is one of class enemies.
IX.   On August 10, 1952, the Central Public Security Department announced the "Temporary Organizational Regulations for the Public Order Preservation Committees" (mention: [195]: 1953: 441). It is unclear whether these were discussed at this conference.

16

I.   *Late December 1952 (between 28th and 31st)*
II.   **ENLARGED MEETING OF THE POLITBURO OF THE CC CCP**
VI.   Mao Zedong: Speech (mention: [282]: 85): general line and tasks for the long transitional period are to realize socialist industrialization and the gradual socialist transformation of industry, agriculture, handicrafts, and capitalist industry and commerce.

1953_____

17

I.   *1953*
II.   **CENTRAL MEETING**
V.   Purge of Gao Gang and Rao Shushi

IX.   The party center headed by Mao Zedong waged a determined struggle against Gao Gang and Rao Shushi at this meeting. Tao Zhu originally supported Gao and Rao but then changed his stance when he saw how things were going at this meeting (mention: [69]).

All information on this meeting comes from the single Red Guard source cited above.

This meeting is very likely identical with the December 24, 1953, Politburo Meeting (meeting 29), in which case the latter was in fact an enlarged meeting of the Politburo.

18

I.   *February 4-7, 1953*
II.   **FOURTH SESSION OF THE FIRST NATIONAL COMMITTEE OF THE CPPCC**
III.   Beijing
VI.   Zhou Enlai: "Political Report," February 4, 1953 (text: [43]: 228: February 8, 1953).

Chen Shutong: "Work Report of the Standing Committee of the National Committee of the CPPCC," February 4, 1953 (text: [216]: 508: February 6, 1953: 1-5).

Guo Moruo: "Report on the Congress of the People for Peace," February 4, 1953 (mention: [216]: 507: February 5, 1953: 1).

Other minor speeches (excerpts: [216]: 509: February 7-8, 1953: 4-7).

Mao Zedong: Closing Speech, February 7, 1953 (Summary: [216]: 509: February 7-8, 1953: 3).

VII.   Passed resolution in support of reports by Zhou, Chen, and Guo (texts: ibid.).

19

I.   *April 3-23, 1953*
II.   **FIRST RURAL WORK CONFERENCE**
VI.   Deng Zihui: Summary Report, April 23, 1959 (mention: [112]: 299-302; [273]: 417; [270]: 252): review of mutual aid and cooperation movement over previous three years; criticizes rash advance and advocates steady advance; dissatisfaction of middle peasants is primary cause of tension. cause of tension.
VIII.   Made preparations for the First Five-Year Plan's mutual aid and cooperation movement (mention: [112]: 299).

IX.   This meeting was convened by the Rural Work Department.

20

I.   *May 17, 1953*
II.   **MEETING OF THE POLITBURO OF THE CC CCP**
V.   Educational work
VI.   Mao Zedong: Speech (mention and excerpts: [165]: 7; [208]): the two most fundamental tasks are the improvement of the leadership core in institutes of higher learning and guiding the compilation of teaching materials; should place special emphasis on cultivating cadres from worker backgrounds; must stop burdening students with too much work and giving them too little to eat; labor education should be emphasized in primary education; the "five-year system" is good; local "popularly run" (*minban*) schools should be permitted; Xi Zhongxun's opposition to many of the above points is wrong.

21

I.   *June ?-15-?, 1953*
II.   **MEETING OF THE POLITBURO OF THE CC CCP**
V.   General Line for the Transition to Socialism
VI.   Mao Zedong (text: [163]: 93–94; excerpt: [259]: 11; summary: [270]: 254): should bring about, in a ten- to fifteen-year period, the transition to socialism in all spheres of the economy; those who believe the transition period is too long commit a leftist mistake; others commit a rightist mistake by persisting in "New Democracy" without engaging in socialist transformation.
IX.   This meeting occurred at the start of the National Conference on Financial and Economic Work (meeting 22) and set the stage for it.

22

I.   *June 13–August 12, 1953*
II.   **NATIONAL CONFERENCE ON FINANCIAL AND ECONOMIC WORK**
V.   Generai Line for the Transition to Socialism
VI.   Mao Zedong: Speech, "Combat Bourgeois Ideas in the Party," August 12, 1953 (text: [163]: 103–11): strong criticism of Bo Yibo's proposed tax

plan; combat "erroneous Right opportunist tendencies" in the party; strengthen collective leadership; fight subjectivism and decentralization.

Zhou Enlai: Concluding remarks (summary: [273]: 422–23): the 1953 revision of the tax system was a mistake because it put a heavier burden on the public sector than on the private and on industry than on commerce; violated party policy of utilizing, regulating, and transforming capitalist commerce.

IX.   This meeting was convened by the CC CCP (mention: [72]: 204–205).

Mao Zedong subsequently commented that this conference set forth the General Line for Transition to Socialism, but that the leaders felt it was not yet time to propagate this throughout the entire party ([167]: 122; [174]: 72). He also later commented that at this conference some comrades did not speak appropriately, some were criticized, and some did not dare to speak at all. He vaguely linked this meeting with the Gao-Rao affair ([167]: 35, 36; [174]: 30, 31).

The dispute with Gao Gang and Rao Shushi seems to date back to this meeting, although little specific information is available on the nature of the dispute at this early stage (mention: [72]: 204–205; [167]: 479; [174]: 345; [273]: 425; [108]: 90; [270]: 255–56). Gao initiated vigorous criticism of Bo Yibo's tax policies at this meeting ([223]: 100).

Bo Yibo came under criticism for Right opportunism but was defended by Peng Zhen, An Ziwen, and Liu Shaoqi (the latter basing this defense in part on Bo's steadfastness when he had been imprisoned by the Kuomintang) (mention: [24]).

Participants representing various locales criticized the "excessive" and "rigid" control that the central government had been exercising through its policy of financial unification and its method of recovering all local balances at the end of the year (mention: [119]).

Mao subsequently noted ([167]: 655; [201]: 267) that after this meeting (and as a result of the discussions at the conference itself?) he had asked the major central and regional leaders to keep one another and the Central Committee, as well as the local administrations, informed. He made this remark in the context of lamenting the decrease in centralism that characterized the party after it gained control over China's major cities in 1949.

The June 1953 Politburo meeting (meeting 21) set the stage for this conference, and the July 18, 1953, National United Front Work Conference (meeting 23) also dealt with problems of integral importance to the questions at issue here.

Deng Xiaoping's speech to the Eighth Party Congress stated that this conference ended on August 11 ([72]: 197), but the date of Mao Zedong's speech cited in VI above implies that the closing date was in fact August 12.

23

I.   *July ?-18-?, 1953*
II.   **NATIONAL UNITED FRONT WORK CONFERENCE**
III.   United front work
VI.   Liu Shaoqi: Speech, July 18, 1953 (text: [147]: *xia*: 117–24; excerpts: [29]; [123]: April 11, 1967; [106]; [130]: 17, 21; [239]: April 18, 1967): if united front work is done well, the capitalists and intellectuals will not oppose the transition to socialism; if united front work is stopped, these people will oppose us, and they can make things very difficult for us; in the minority areas, a united front approach toward the upper strata is, in the long run, the most efficacious method of achieving our goals; thus, united front work is central to the accomplishment of the party's main tasks.
IX.   The June 13–August 12, 1953, National Conference on Financial and Economic Work (meeting 22), which worked out the General Line for Transition to Socialism, met during the period of this United Front Work Conference.

24

I.   *September–October 1953*
II.   **SECOND NATIONAL ORGANIZATION WORK CONFERENCE**
III.   Beijing
V.   Material incentives; qualifications for party membership
VIII.   Drafted a Central Committee document that raised the level of material incentives for technical personnel (mention: [53]: 13).

Stipulated the party's organizational tasks as guaranteeing the general line and implementation of the Five-Year Plan; enlarging and consolidating the party; and raising the party's ideological level. Also discussed cadre policy and inner-party democracy and discipline (mention: [270]: 256–57).
IX.   Liu Shaoqi and Deng Xiaoping approved the opinions (submitted to the conference?) on experimental work in party registration (mention: [94]: 24).

Rao Shushi reportedly attempted to pursue his and Gao Gang's plans to split the party at this conference (mention: [273]: 425; [270]: 257). Rao did so by attacking his deputy An Ziwen, who had close ties with Liu Shaoqi (mention: [223]: 99–100).

25

I.   *October 26–November 5, 1953*
II.   **THIRD MUTUAL AID AND COOPERATION WORK CONFERENCE**
V.   Transition to socialism in agriculture
VI.   Mao Zedong: Speech (excerpt: [195]: 1956: 93; [9]: November 5, 1977, tr. in [82]: November 10, 1977: E1): if socialism does not occupy a leading position in agriculture, then capitalism will; one cannot straddle the middle between socialism and capitalism in agriculture; correct the Right opportunist thinking in guiding the movement for agricultural co-operativization.
IX.   On October 15 and November 4 Mao Zedong discussed these issues with cadres from the party's Rural Work Department (summary: [270]: 257).

26

I.   *October 1953*
II.   **MEETING OF THE POLITBURO OF THE CC CCP**
V.   Public health
VI.   Mao Zedong (mention: [191]: 17: June 26, 1967): attacks the Ministry of Health for failing to exercise leadership over doctors.

27

I.   *October 10–12, 1953*
II.   **NATIONAL CONFERENCE ON PLANNED PURCHASING AND MARKETING OF GRAIN**
V.   Planned purchasing and marketing of grain
VI.   Chen Yun: Speech, "Implement the State Monopoly on Purchasing and Marketing of Grain," October 10, 1953 (text: [27]: 202–16): implement state purchases of grain in the villages and rationed distribution in the cities; strictly regulate merchants; readjust relations among regions and between the center and local areas.
IX.   This conference was convened by the CC CCP (mention: [72]: 197).

28

I. *November–December 1953*
II. **NATIONAL CONFERENCE OF HANDICRAFT COOPERATIVES**
VIII. Determined the policy of "active leadership, steady advance" regarding the socialist transformation of the handicraft industry (mention: [108]: 107).
IX. This conference was convened by the CC CCP.

29

I. *December 24, 1953*
II. **ONE OR MORE MEETINGS OF THE POLITBURO OF THE CC CCP**
III. Beijing
V. Purge of Gao Gang and Rao Shushi
VI. Mao Zedong (mention: [195]: 1955: 343; [216]: 751: February 19, 1954: 3): makes a proposal on party unity.
    Mao Zedong (mention: [163]: 162): there are two party headquarters in Beijing: one stirs an open wind and lights an open fire, the other stirs a sinister wind, lights a sinister fire, and operates underground.
VII. "Resolution on Strengthening Party Unity (Draft)" (mention: [195]: 1955: 343; [216]: 751: February 19, 1954: 3).
IX. The February 6–10, 1954, Enlarged Fourth Plenum of the Seventh CC CCP (meeting 32) formally adopted the "Resolution on Strengthening Party Unity."
    Gao Gang's attempts to become secretary-general or vice-chairman of the party at this meeting led Mao to criticize him and propose strengthening party unity (mention: [91]: June 3, 1977, tr. in [82]: June 9, 1977: E3; [223]: 102).
    See also meeting 17, which may be identical with this meeting.

1954

30

I. *Winter 1954*
II. **MEETING OF THE STANDING COMMITTEE OF THE CC CCP** (so identified in [257]: 9)
V. Traditional Chinese medicine

VI.   Mao Zedong (excerpt: ibid.): should neither look down on nor exaggerate the importance of traditional Chinese medicine—both it and Western medicine have contributions to make.

IX.   This dovetails nicely with Mao Zedong's expressed support for the integration of traditional Chinese medicine and Western medicine in July 1954 (excerpt: [138]: 73–74) and at other times.

31

I.   *February 1954*

II.   **SYMPOSIA ON GAO GANG AND RAO SHUSHI**

IV.   Thirty-seven members and alternate members of the Central Committee, forty important workers ([273]: 428).

V.   Exposure and criticism of Gao Gang and Rao Shushi ([273]: 428; [108]: 90; [91]: June 3, 1977, tr. in [82]: June 9, 1977).

IX.   Zhou Enlai chaired the symposium on Gao Gang; Deng Xiaoping, Chen Yi, and Tan Zhenlin chaired the one on Rao Shushi.

    Under the leadership of the Politburo, the North China Bureau held a similar meeting in April ([273]: 428).

32

I.   *February 6–10, 1954*

II.   **FOURTH (ENLARGED) PLENUM OF THE SEVENTH CC CCP**

III.   Beijing

IV.   Thirty-five full and twenty-six alternate members of the CC CCP; fifty-two main responsible cadres of the party, government, military, and people's groups. Nine full and alternate CC CCP members were absent for reasons of health or were otherwise engaged. Mao Zedong was "on holiday" and did not attend (mention: [195]: 1955: 342; [216]: 751: February 19, 1954: 1).

V.   Purge of Gao Gang and Rao Shushi

VI.   Liu Shaoqi: "Report of the Politburo of the CC CCP to the Fourth Plenary Session of the Seventh CC," February 6, 1954 (partial text: [147]: *xia*: 125–31; summary: [195]: 1955: 343–44; [216]: 751: February 19, 1954: 1–4; [273]: 426): reviews the work of the Politburo since the June 6–9, 1950, Third Plenum of the Seventh CC CCP (meeting 5); requests the plenum approve the convening of a party conference during 1954 to discuss the outlines of the state's first five-year construction plan and other relevant questions; warns that the party must remain vigilant against the creation of intraparty factions.

Zhou Enlai: Speech, "Strengthen Party Unity, Oppose Bourgeois Individualism," February 10, 1954 (excerpt: [286]: 119–28): discusses the need to improve inner-party life and party unity in light of the Gao Gang-Rao Shushi affair.

Chen Yun: Speech, "High-Ranking Leaders Must Raise Revolutionary Consciousness," February 10, 1954 (excerpt: [27]: 229–33): responsibility for maintaining party unity and preventing divisiveness belongs to high-ranking leading personnel.

Zhu De and forty-two others make important speeches (mention: [195]: 1955: 342; [216]: 751: February 19, 1954: 1).

VII.   "Resolution on Strengthening Party Unity" (summary: [195]: 1955: 344–45; [216]: 751: February 19, 1954: 4–5; [273]: 426–27).

"Communique," February 18, 1954 (texts: [195]: 1955: 342–45; [216]: 751: February 19, 1954: 1–8): notes that the plenum adopted resolutions approving the work of the Politburo since the June 6–9, 1950, Third Plenum of the Seventh CC CCP (meeting 5) and calling for convening a party conference during 1954 (mention: [195]: 1955: 342; [216]: 751: February 19, 1954: 1; [282]: 113).

VIII.   Formally approved the Common Program for the Period of Transition, which had been proposed by the Politburo (mention: [89]: 28; [108]: 80).

IX.   This plenum "exposed and criticized the conspiracy of the Gao Gang-Rao Shushi antiparty alliance" and called on them to admit their crimes, but they refused (mention: [91]: June 3, 1977, tr. in [82]: June 9, 1977: E3). Neither one appeared in public after the conclusion of this meeting ([224]: 210: 215–16). "After [this] plenary session, the party proceeded to expose and liquidate the crimes of the Gao Gang-Rao Shushi antiparty alliance" ([43]: 410: September 25, 1956: 41; [195]: 1957: 146). The February 1954 symposia (listed above) were part of this effort.

Peng Zhen had to make a self-examination at this meeting (mention: [250]: June 10, 1967; [206]: 27: July 8, 1968: 56).

Liu Shaoqi presided over this plenum (mention: [195]: 1955: 342; [216]: 751: February 19, 1954: 1).

The party conference called for at this plenum did not in fact convene until March 21–31, 1955 (meeting 41).

33

I.   *April 1954*
II.   **SECOND CONFERENCE ON RURAL WORK**
VIII.   Further clarified the guiding principles of the cooperativization movement; reviewed the situation in the countryside (peasant attitudes, party's

work and policies) (mention: [273]: 418).

IX. Between spring and fall, 130,405 new producer cooperatives were established, bringing the total to 225,405 (mention: ibid.).

This meeting was convened by the Rural Work Department.

34

I.   *May ?–22–25–?, 1954*
II. **SECOND NATIONAL PROPAGANDA WORK CONFERENCE OF THE CCP**
V.   Cultural questions; commercial problems
VI. Zhou Yang: Speech, May 22, 1954 (excerpts: [237]: 12, 15): "letting one hundred flowers bloom" means allowing free competition in the realm of culture; "getting rid of the old to usher in the new" means allowing the masses and history to judge things.

Chen Yun: "Report on Commercial Questions," May 25, 1954 (excerpts: [10]: January 28, 1967): a shortage of goods relative to demand is a long-term phenomenon which is beneficial in that it serves as a spur to industrial and agricultural production.

IX. Chen Yun's report was delivered to a joint meeting of this conference and the May 25, 1954, Sixth National Public Security Work Conference (meeting 35) (mention: ibid.).

35

I.   *May ?–25–?, 1954*
II. **SIXTH NATIONAL PUBLIC SECURITY WORK CONFERENCE**
V.   Commercial questions; role of law
VI. Chen Yun: "Report on Commercial Questions," May 25, 1954 (excerpts: [10]: January 28, 1967): a shortage of goods relative to demand is a long-term phenomenon which is beneficial in that it serves as a spur to industrial and agricultural production.

Peng Zhen: "Report" (excerpts: [265]): the period of major campaigns is over; we are now in the era of large-scale economic construction, and for this the need is for a more complete body of law and a greater role for the law.

IX.   Chen Yun delivered his report to a joint meeting of this conference and the May 22–25, 1954, Second National Propaganda Work Conference of the CCP (meeting 34) (mention: [10]: January 28, 1967).

36

I.   *September 15–28, 1954*
II.   **FIRST SESSION OF THE FIRST NPC**
III.   Beijing
V.   Draw up constitution and several important laws; adopt government work report; elect new government leaders
VI.   Mao Zedong: "Opening Speech," September 15, 1954 (text: [195]: 1955: 41–42; [163]: 148–49).

Liu Shaoqi: "Report on the Draft Constitution of the People's Republic of China" (texts: [195]: 1955: 44–48; [145]; [144]: 275–316; [147]: *xia*: 132–70).

Zhou Enlai: "Government Work Report" (text: [195]: 1955: 129–40).

Chen Yun: "On Planned Procurement and Planned Supply," September 23, 1954 (text: [27]: 254–63).

Speeches by eighty-nine representatives concerning Liu Shaoqi's report (texts: [195]: 1955: 59–113).

Speeches by seventy-five representatives concerning Zhou Enlai's report (texts: [195]: 1955: 141–215).

Other minor reports.

VII.   "Constitution of the People's Republic of China" (text: [195]: 1955: 1–15).

"Organizational Law for the NPC of the People's Republic of China" (text: [195]: 1955: 214–17).

"Organizational Law for the State Council of the People's Republic of China" (text: [195]: 1955: 117–18).

"Organizational Law for the Courts of the People's Republic of China" (text: [195]: 1955: 118–23).

"Organizational Law for the Various Levels of the People's Congresses and People's Councils of the People's Republic of China" (text: [195]: 1955: 124–29).

Other minor resolutions and decisions.

VIII.   Made appointments to leading organs of the state (name lists: [195]: 1955: 216–18).

IX.   Complete documentation for this meeting is in [279]; [195]: 1955: 33–224.

This meeting marked the formal end to the transition period in China.

It officially inaugurated the Central People's Government and abolished the six military-administrative regions into which the country had been divided since 1949. The State Council replaced the Government Administrative Council as China's highest government executive organ.

37

I.   *October 1954*
II.   **FOURTH NATIONAL CONFERENCE ON MUTUAL AID AND COOPERATION**
VI.   Deng Zihui (mention: [108]: 100): cooperatives should include twenty to thirty households, after several years they can be enlarged; in the past cooperatives were run by cadres, next year they must rely on peasants to run them.
VIII.   Decided that the number of coops would expand from 100,000 to 600,000 by the spring of 1955. The party approved the report of this conference (mention: [273]: 418), as reflected in Mao Zedong's July 31, 1955, speech "On the Cooperative Transformation of Agriculture" (mention: [163]: 186; [195]: 1956: 81).
IX.   This meeting was convened by the Central Rural Work Department ([273]).

38

I.   *December 21–25, 1954*
II.   **FIRST SESSION OF THE NATIONAL COMMITTEE OF THE SECOND CPPCC**
III.   Beijing
VI.   Zhou Enlai: "Political Report," December 21, 1954 (summary: [195]: 1956: 259–60).
        Chen Shutong: "Work Report of the First CPPCC," December 21, 1954 (text: [195]: 1956: 260–62).
        Zhang Bojun: "Explanation of the (Draft) Charter of the CPPCC," December 21, 1954 (text: [195]: 1956: 264–65).
VII.   "Charter of the CPPCC," December 25, 1954 (text: [195]: 1956: 262–64).
        "Proclamation of the First Session of the Second CPPCC," December 25, 1954 (text: [195]: 1956: 265–66).
IX.   Texts of these documents also available in [277]: I.

1955

39

I.   *Early January 1955*
II.   **MEETING OF THE POLITBURO OF THE CC CCP**
V.   Nuclear energy
IX.   According to Qian Sanjiang, president of the Chinese Academy of Sciences as of October 1978, he was inspired by Mao Zedong's comments at this meeting that protons, electrons, and neutrons should be divisible, since one divides into two and opposites unite. This wisdom encouraged Qian to pursue atomic energy research, and he later came to be known abroad as the "father of China's atomic bomb" (mention: [9]: October 8, 1978, tr. in [82]: October 17, 1978: E19).

40

I.   *Late February or early March 1955*
II.   **FIRST NATIONAL VILLAGE-LEVEL ORGANIZATIONS WORK CONFERENCE OF THE CCP**
V.   Party-building and party work in China's rural villages, including consideration of the best form for party branches, strengthening educational work of the village party branches, rectification of backward village party branches, strengthening internal leadership of party within villages, and encouraging the use of persuasion instead of coercion by village party branches ([195]: 1956: 268; [206]: 1005: March 1955: 4–6).
VIII.   (All of following from ibid.:)

Must continue basic-level party building in the villages so that by the end of the First Five-Year Plan every village that has gone through land reform will have a basic-level party organization.

Party must link up with the rural cooperative production campaign and the mutual-aid teams to develop new party members.

Villages may henceforth organize village party branches on the basis of either geographical district (*diqu*) or production instead of organizing on the basis of district alone.

Basic-level village party organizations must strengthen collective leadership and engage in criticism and self-criticism.

Should establish party classes and carry out education that stresses unity ("in the spirit of the [February 6–10, 1954] Fourth CC Plenum" [meeting 32]), knowledge of the General Line, knowledge of the party's policies of mutual aid and cooperation, and basic knowledge of the party and communism.

Must strengthen the development and consolidation of the party in the agricultural cooperatives. *Xian* and district party committees must strengthen their leadership of village party branches.

41

I. *March 21–31, 1955*
II. **NATIONAL CONFERENCE OF THE CCP**
III. Beijing
IV. Sixty-two full and alternate members of the CC and 257 representatives elected by party organizations throughout the country ([43]: 324: April 5, 1955: 1).
V. First Five-Year Plan; Gao-Rao Affair; establishment of a Central Control Commission
VI. Mao Zedong, opening speech, March 21, 1955 (text: [163]: 154–58; excerpt: [43]: 891: October 8, 1969: 18): conceit and complacency within the party due to past accomplishments caused the Gao-Rao affair; must observe and help erring comrades who are willing to reform; international situation is favorable but China must be prepared for a surprise attack.

Chen Yun: "Report on the First Five-Year Plan for the Development of the National Economy" (mention: [43]: 324: April 5, 1955: 1; [63]: 7–10; [195]: 1956: 77).

Deng Xiaoping: "Report on the Gao Gang-Rao Shushi Anti-Party Alliance" (mention: ibid.).

Additionally, 100 people spoke at the eight days of plenary meetings, including "important speeches" by Liu Shaoqi, Zhou Enlai, Zhu De, Kang Sheng, Zhang Wentian, Peng Zhen, Dong Biwu, Lin Boqu, Peng Dehuai (mention: ibid.).

Mao: Closing speech, March 31, 1955 (text: [163]: 158–71): period of socialist industrialization, socialist transformation, modernization of national defense, and atomic energy has begun; party secretaries and heads of central departments should become political and economic experts; Gao-Rao affair; policy toward national minorities.

VII. (All passed on March 31, 1955): "Resolution on the First Five-Year Plan for the Development of the National Economy" (texts: [43]: 324: April 5, 1955: 3; [63]: 11–12; [195]: 1956: 11).

"Resolution on the Gao Gang-Rao Shushi Anti-Party Alliance" (texts: [43]: 324: April 5, 1955: 4–6; [63]: 13–20; [195]: 1956: 78–79).

"Resolution on the Establishment of Central and Local Control Committees of the Party'' (texts: [43]: 324: April 5, 1955: 7–9; [63]: 21–25; [195]: 1956: 79).

VIII. Elected a Central Control Committee with Dong Biwu as secretary ([43]: 324: April 5, 1955: 2).

IX. Mao's closing speech suggests that so many self-criticisms were given at this meeting in connection with Gao-Rao there was not time for all of them: Mao told the rest to submit written reports to the Central Committee (mention: [163]: 163,168).

A series of *Renmin ribao* (People's Daily) editorials reflected the decisions of this conference. These were the editorials of April 5, 1955, on the party conference; April 7, 1955, on the First Five-Year Plan; April 10, 1955, on the Gao-Rao purge; and April 14, 1955, again on the purge and its lessons. All of these editorials are reprinted in [63]: 29–64.

42

I. *Spring 1955*

II. **STANDING COMMITTEE OF THE POLITBURO OF THE CC CCP**

V. Traditional Chinese medicine

VI. Mao Zedong (excerpt: [257]: 9): affirms value of traditional Chinese medicine. Recommends that the authorities set up institutions to study traditional Chinese medicine; require future graduates of Chinese medical schools to study traditional Chinese medicine for two years; regard traditional doctors as specialists and pay them accordingly; and make Qizhou in Hubei the place for concentration and dispersal of medicinal herbs.

IX. Although first called for in 1950, research centers for the study of traditional medicine were not established until 1955 ([138]: 64).

43

I. *April 1955*

II. **THIRD NATIONAL CONFERENCE ON RURAL WORK**

V. The ''stop, contract, develop'' policy for agricultural cooperativization

VI. Deng Zihui (mention: [273]: 439–40): the phenomenon of blind advance has appeared in some areas; conveys the proposed ''stop expansion, all-out consolidation'' of coops which the Secretariat had approved (Secretariat meeting had been convened by Liu Shaoqi).

VIII. Based on the spirit of the central decision mentioned above, the meeting proposed four requirements: generally stop expansion of coops; immediately focus on production; go all-out to consolidate (a small number of provinces—Zhejiang, Shandong, Hebei, and Anhui are mentioned in Deng's speech—and counties must reduce the number [or size?] of coops); run and consolidate the mutual aid teams properly; make allowances for individual peasants (ibid.: 440).

IX. Results of this meeting were reported to the Politburo in June 1955 (mention: ibid.: 442).

This meeting was convened by the Rural Work Department.

44

I. *April 4, 1955*

II. **FIFTH PLENUM OF THE SEVENTH CC CCP**

V. Approve and carry out the resolutions of the National Party Conference of March 21–31, 1955 (meeting 41); additional elections to the Politburo.

VII. "Communique" (texts: [43]: 324: April 5, 1955: 1–2; [63]: 7–10; [195]: 1956: 77): notes that the plenum did the following:

—Approved the three resolutions passed by the National Party Conference on March 21–32, 1955 (meeting 41) and the composition of the Central Control Committee elected at that conference.

—Instructed the Politburo of the CC to make appropriate revisions to the draft of the First Five-Year Plan (the relevant resolution of the National Party Conference had instructed the CC to make these revisions) and then to submit the revised plan to the July 5–30, 1955, Second Session of the First NPC (meeting 49) for examination and adoption.

—Added Lin Biao and Deng Xiaoping to the Politburo of the CC CCP.

45

I. *May 1955*

II. **RURAL WORK CONFERENCE OF THE CC CCP**

V. Consolidation of rural cooperatives

VI. Deng Zihui proposes to "retrench and dissolve" 200,000 cooperatives (mention: [3]; [272]: IV: 1: January 10, 1970: 125; [148]).

IX. In his confession of October 23, 1966, at the October 9–28, 1966, CC Work Conference (meeting 303), Liu Shaoqi mentioned that he presided over an earlier "Central Meeting" in 1955 at which Deng Zihui voiced this proposal and Liu did not oppose it ([272]: IV: 1: January 10, 1970: 125).

Bowie and Fairbank ([14]: 92) assert there was criticism of "rightist tendencies" at the May Rural Work Conference but cite no sources for this statement. A contemporary source ([253]: 5: 1956: 89) indicates that at this meeting there was a battle between socialism and capitalism over the question of cooperativization in agriculture but provides no details.

In May 1955, Mao Zedong mentioned that 20,000 cooperatives—not the 200,000 mentioned above—had been dissolved during that spring ([14]: 95).

According to *Dangshi yanjiu ziliao* 3, p. 701, this meeting convened for April 21–May 7, 1955, and Deng Zihui proposed to "retrench and dissolve" 50,000–100,000 cooperatives.

46

I.   *May 17, 1955*
II.   **MEETING OF PARTY SECRETARIES**
IV.   Party secretaries from fifteen provinces and municipalities of North China, Central-South China, Hebei, Tianjin, and Beijing.
V.   Agricultural cooperativization
VI.   Mao Zedong: Speech (mention: [273]: 441; [17]: no. 1, 1982: 111): repeats policy of "stop, contract, develop" but with an emphasis on "develop."

47

I.   *Summer 1955*
II.   **BEIDAIHE CONFERENCE**
III.   Beidaihe, Hebei
V.   The economy
VIII.   According to a subsequent reminiscence by Mao Zedong in January 1958, this conference decided that China would produce fifteen million tons of steel in the Second Five-Year Plan (mention: [167]: 149; [174]: 80).

48

I.   *Mid-June 1955*
II.   **MEETING OF THE POLITBURO OF THE CC CCP**
V.   Agricultural cooperativization
VI.   Liu Shaoqi (mention: [273]: 442): if the policy of cooperativization is handled properly through next spring, peasants will voluntarily join coops.

Rural Work Department (mention: [273]: 442): report on the Third National Rural Work Conference.

VIII.   Politburo approved policy suggested by Rural Work Department, on the basis of the May 17, 1955, conference of fifteen party secretaries, to increase the number of coops from 650,000 to one million within one year.

IX.   After this meeting, debate emerged within the party on agricultural and cooperativization policy (mention: [273]: 442).

49

I.   *July 5–30, 1955*

II.   **SECOND SESSION OF THE FIRST NPC**

III.   Beijing

VI.   Li Fuchun: "Report on the First Five-Year Plan for the Development of the National Economy," July 5–6, 1955 (text: [195]: 1956: 160–68).

Deng Zihui: "Report on the Summary Plan for Controlling Yellow River Floods and Opening Yellow River Irrigation Projects," July 8, 1955 (text: [195]: 1956: 168–74).

Li Xiannian: "Report on the 1954 State Budget and the 1955 Draft Budget" (text: [194]: July 10, 1955).

Peng Zhen: "Work Report of the Standing Committee of the National People's Congress of the PRC," July 16, 1955 (text: [195]: 1956: 175).

Peng Dehuai: "Report on the Draft of the National Military Conscription Law," July 16, 1955 (text: [195]: 1956: 176–77).

Zhou Enlai: "The Current International Situation and Our Foreign Policy," July 30, 1955 (text: [195]: 1956: 186–88).

Chen Yun: "On the Question of Unified Purchase and Unified Supply of Food," July 21, 1955 (text: [195]: 1956: 191–95; [27]: 272–79).

Luo Ruiqing: "The Whole Country Unite—Resolutely, Thoroughly, and Completely Wipe Out All Counterrevolutionary Elements," July 27, 1955 (text: [195]: 1956: 196–200).

Altogether 147 people spoke at this meeting (texts not included above: [285]: 8: 1955: 43–204; [195]: 1956: 178–86, 188–91, 195–96, 200–38).

VIII.   Resolutions and decision approving the substance of the above (texts: [195]: 1956: 12, 239–43).

50

I.   *July 31–August 1, 1955*

II.   **CONFERENCE OF SECRETARIES OF PROVINCIAL, MUNICIPAL, AND DISTRICT PARTY COMMITTEES**

V.   Agricultural cooperativization

VI.   Mao Zedong: "On the Question of Agricultural Cooperativization," July 31, 1955 (texts: [14]: 94–105; [186]; [175]: 389–420; [163]: 184–207): advocates strengthened efforts to consolidate existing cooperatives and the new cooperatives being formed; suggests two months of study to work out a plan for speeding up the cooperative movement, at the end of which the provinces should submit their plans to the CC; affirms that cooperativization can be carried out before and concurrent with industrialization, rather than having to await the basic completion of industrialization, and raises the target number for the formation of agricultural cooperatives over that advocated by Li Fuchun in his report to the July 5-30, 1955, NPC (meeting 49).

IX.   This meeting was convened by the party center ([106]).

The meeting criticized the right deviationist thoughts that had emerged within the party during the cooperativization period, in particular the Third Rural Work Conference and Zhejiang's reduction of cooperatives. The meeting also encouraged what was subsequently called "rash advance" in the socialist transformation of agriculture. Afterwards, provincial, municipal, and autonomous region party secretaries investigated anew the plans for cooperativization and stepped up the pace of organizing elementary cooperatives (mention: [282]: 150–51).

51

I.   *October 4–11, 1955*
II.   **SIXTH (ENLARGED) PLENUM OF THE SEVENTH CC CCP**
IV.   Thirty-eight full and 25 candidate members of the CC; secretaries of the Shanghai Bureau, the Beijing, Tianjin, and Shanghai municipal committees, and the various provincial, autonomous region, and special district committees; and responsible comrades of the committees of the party center's departments and of the party organs in the branches (*bumen*) of the state organs: a total of 388 nonvoting people attended ([195]: 1956: 87).

V.   Agricultural cooperativization; the Eighth Party Congress
VI.   Mao Zedong: Opening address, October 4, 1955 (mention: [195]: 1956: 87).

Chen Boda: "Explanation of the Draft Decision on the Question of Agricultural Cooperativization" (delivered on behalf of the Politburo), October 4, 1955 (text: [195]: 1956: 92–95): must combine industrialization with agricultural cooperativization; specific recommendations about work during the high tide of cooperativization.

Deng Xiaoping: "Explanation of the Draft Decision to Convene the Eighth Party Congress" (delivered on behalf of the Politburo), October 4, 1955 (mention: [195]: 1956: 87).

Liu Shaoqi, Zhou Enlai, Zhu De, Chen Yun, Peng Dehuai, and Peng Zhen gave "important speeches" (mention: [158]: 25; [174]: 26).

Local leaders gave speeches based on their investigations of the local areas over the previous two months and presented plans for agricultural cooperativization in their locales. Others gave speeches on how to relate the following areas to agricultural cooperativization: industry, communications and transport, handicrafts, finance, banking, trade, culture, education, science, hygiene, military, politics, law, Communist Youth League, trade unions, and the Federation of Women. Altogether 80 people spoke at the meeting; another 167 speeches were circulated but could not be given because of time (ibid.). Zhou Enlai's speech concerned current events (mention: ibid.).

Mao Zedong: Summing-up speech, October 11, 1955 (texts: [167]: 12–25; [174]: 14–26; [163]: 211–34): this conference has included a wide-ranging and vigorous debate on the whole General Line, resulting in agreement to speed up cooperativization and socialist transformation.

VII.   "Decision of the Sixth (Enlarged) Plenum of the Seventh CC on the Question of Agricultural Cooperativization," October 11, 1955 (text: [195]: 1956: 87–92).

"Decision on Convening the Eighth Party Congress," October 11, 1955 (text: ibid.: 95).

IX.   Mao presaged this conference when in his July 31, 1955, speech to the Conference of Secretaries of Provincial, Municipal, and District Party Committees (meeting 50) he called for his audience to conduct two months of investigations and then write up reports and plans. These reports and plans were distributed in advance to the people attending the Sixth Plenum ([164]), and they formed the basis of discussion at this conference. They indicated that conditions in the countryside were ripe to accelerate cooperativization.

At this plenum, Liu Shaoqi purportedly criticized himself for going too slow on the formation of agricultural producers' cooperatives ([179]), and Deng Zihui along with the party's Rural Work Department were criticized for "rightist empiricism" ([112]: 325–26; [167]: 25; [174]: 27; [273]: 445 renders this as "right opportunism"). Rightism (lack of enthusiasm regarding cooperatives) in general was criticized at this meeting (mentions: [108]: 103; [282]: 153; [273]: 445).

52

I.   *October 29, 1955*
II.   **SYMPOSIUM**
III.   Beijing

IV.   Over 500 people, including Mao Zedong, Liu Shaoqi, Zhou Enlai, Zhu
        De, Chen Yun, Kang Sheng, Peng Zhen, Zhang Wentian, Peng Dehuai,
        Deng Xiaoping, He Long, Chen Yi, Li Fuchun, Li Xiannian, members of
        the Executive Committee of the All-China Federation of Industry and
        Commerce in Beijing for a meeting of the federation, full and candidate
        CC members in Beijing, vice-chairmen of the Standing Committee of the
        NPC, vice-chairmen of the CPPCC, and responsible people in the various
        people's groups, central government ministries, and enterprise units
        ([195]: 1956: 104).
V.   Socialist transformation of industry and commerce
VI.   Mao Zedong (mention: [233]; summaries: [273]: 452; [108]: 117–18):
        tells audience to recognize the law of socialist development, actively
        participate in the socialist transformation rather than oppose it; calls for
        radical speedup in the socialist transformation of industry and commerce.
            Zhou Enlai, Chen Yun, Chen Shutong, and other prominent members
        of the All-China Federation of Industry and Commerce (mention: [195]:
        1956: 104).
IX.   This meeting provided a significant impetus to the acceleration of the
        socialist transformation of industry and commerce in the fall 1955–winter
        1955–56 period as witnessed, for instance, in Canton ([235]: 164).
            Mao convened a second symposium with representatives of the bour-
        geoisie at the end of 1955, at which he asserted that acceptance of socialist
        transformation is their only option for the future (mention: [18]). There is
        no other information available on this meeting.

53

I.   *November 1955* ([158]: 27, citing: [194]: January 26, 1956)
II.   **MEETING OF MAO ZEDONG AND PROVINCIAL PARTY
        SECRETARIES**
III.   Tianjin, Hebei
IV.   Mao Zedong and the secretaries of fifteen provincial party committees
        (ibid.).
V.   Twelve-Year National Program for the Development of Agriculture
VIII.   Increased from eleven to seventeen the number of articles in the document
        that in January 1956 became the forty-article Twelve-Year National Pro-
        gram for the Development of Agriculture (ibid.; [167]: 150; [174]: 81).
IX.   The initial eleven-point draft which was expanded at this meeting origi-
        nated at a Hangzhou meeting for which no other information is available
        (ibid.).

54

I.   *November 16–24, 1955*

II.   **CC CCP-SPONSORED CONFERENCE ON TRANSFORMATION OF CAPITALIST INDUSTRY AND COMMERCE** (mention: [72]: 197)

V.   Socialist transformation of industry and commerce

VI.   Liu Shaoqi, November 16, 1955 (text: [147]: *xia*: 176–83): stresses the difficulty of the struggle for socialist transformation of industry, handicrafts, and agriculture, but affirms that once it is completed the capitalist will have no choice and the question of who wins over whom will "have already been settled."

Chen Yun: Speech, "New Circumstances and New Tasks in the Transformation of Capitalist Industry and Commerce," November 6, 1955 (text: [27]: 280–92): all industries must be reorganized; conduct joint state-private ownership in all industries; popularize the fixed interest (*dingxi*) method for paying capitalists; organize the specialized professions.

VIII.   Meeting passed a draft resolution on the question of the transformation of capitalist industry and commerce, which was revised by the Politburo on February 24, 1956, and subsequently officially adopted (mention: [108]: 118).

IX.   On November 9–10, 1955, the Shanghai Bureau of the CC CCP had convened an enlarged meeting to discuss plans for the socialist transformation of private industry and commerce ([194]: November 25, 1955).

55

I.   *December ?–6–?, 1955*

II.   (No information available)

V.   Oppose rightist conservatism

VI.   Mao Zedong: "Talk Opposing Right-Deviation and Conservatism," December 6, 1955 (texts: [167]: 25–27; [174]: 27–29): must oppose conservatism, Right deviation, passivity, and arrogance; should review the industrial situation and make industry go through campaigns on schedule; should carry out an inspection of finance, trade, and culture and education; should carry out a review and summing up at the forthcoming Eighth Party Congress; must achieve "more, faster, and better results"; and the "Seventeen Articles" (see the November 1955 meeting in Tianjin [meeting 53]) are good.

1956_____

56

I.   *January 14–20, 1956*
II.   **CC CCP-SPONSORED CONFERENCE ON THE QUESTION OF THE INTELLECTUALS**
III. Beijing
IV.   1,279 people, including full and candidate members of the CC; secretaries or vice-secretaries of the party's Shanghai Bureau, Beijing, Tianjin, and Shanghai municipal committees, provincial committees, autonomous regions, and twenty-six cities directly under control of provincial governments; responsible members of the party in various government departments and committees of the CC; responsible members of the party in various government departments of the central government, in various national mass organizations, and in the important higher institutions of learning, scientific research bodies, factories, mines, designing bodies, hospitals, literary organizations, and military establishments ([43]: 376: February 7, 1956: 2; [216]: 1220: February 1, 1956: 56).
V.   The treatment and tasks of intellectuals; Twelve-Year Program for Agricultural Development
VI.   Zhou Enlai: "Report on the Question of the Intellectuals," January 14, 1956 (texts: [14]: 128–43; [43]: 376: February 7, 1956: 3–23; [286]: 158–91): reviews recent policy toward intellectuals; discusses the current conditions of intellectuals; castigates party sectarianism toward intellectuals; stresses the need to give intellectuals appropriate work assignments, sufficient prestige, and adequate promotions; discusses the need for continuing reform of the intellectuals; stresses the urgency of increasing the number and quality of Chinese intellectuals; warns not to become too dependent on the USSR in the sphere of science; calls for cultural and educational departments to draw up twelve-year plans (1956–1967); announces the pending establishment of a Chinese Experts Bureau under the State Council; and reviews the administrative division of labor that will apply to work in this field in the future.

Liao Luyan: "Explanation of the Draft 1956–1967 National Program for Agricultural Development" (text: [216]: 1219: January 31, 1956): explanation of the provisions of this program, which had been developed over the previous few months.

Mao Zedong: Closing speech on the question of intellectuals, January 20, 1956 (excerpts: [26]: 21; [43]: 891: October 8, 1969: [194]: January 30, 1956; [187]: February 16, 1956; [273]: 455–56; [89]: 243): articulates general support for the policies discussed at this conference.

IX.   On the basis of this meeting, the party issued "Instructions Regarding the Intellectual Question" on February 20, 1956, which included a twelve-year plan for scientific development and called on party committees at all levels to put the intellectual question on the agenda of all departments (mention: [108]: 124–25).

The State Scientific Planning Commission was established as a result of this meeting (mention: [108]: 241).

57

I.   *January 23, 1956*

II.   **MEETING OF THE POLITBURO OF THE CC CCP**

V.   Draft of the Twelve-Year National Program for the Development of Agriculture

VII.   Draft Twelve-Year National Program for the Development of Agriculture (also called the "Forty Points") (text: [40]: 119–26)—submitted this document to the January 25, 1956, Supreme State Conference (meeting 58) ([158]: 28).

IX.   The "Forty Points" represent an expanded version of the Seventeen-Article draft of the Twelve-Year National Program that had been developed at the November 1955 meeting of Mao with provincial party secretaries in Tianjin (meeting 53). This expansion of the draft occurred on the basis of continuing consultations between Mao and provincial officials ([158]: 27).

58

I.   *January 25, 1956*

II.   **SUPREME STATE CONFERENCE**

III.   Beijing

IV.   More than 300, including Communist and non-Communist officials and many prominent democratic personages ([22]: 32). Deng Zihui did not attend ([158]: 19).

V.   Draft Twelve-Year National Program for the Development of Agriculture

VI.   Mao Zedong (excerpts: ([187]: February 16, 1956: 6–8; [193]: 26; [208]: 22; [137]: 241; [273]: 463).

Liao Luyan (text: [70]): explanation of the Draft National Program for Agricultural Development.

Chen Yun: Speech, "Problems That Must Be Paid Attention to in Joint State-Private Ownership," January 25, 1956 (excerpt: [27]: 293–95).

IX.   The Draft Twelve-Year National Program for Agricultural Development was published on the day of this meeting. This draft had been submitted to this meeting by the January 23, 1956, Politburo Meeting (meeting 57).

59

I.   *January 30–February 7, 1956*
II.   **SECOND SESSION OF THE NATIONAL COMMITTEE OF THE SECOND CPPCC**
III. Beijing
VI.   Zhou Enlai: "Political Report," January 30, 1956 (text: [194]: January 31, 1956).

Li Jishen: "Work Report of the Standing Committee of the Second CPPCC," January 30, 1956 (text: [195]: 1957: 206–208).

Guo Moruo: "The Summons to the Intellectuals During the High Tide of the Socialist Revolution," January 31, 1956 (text: [195]: 1957: 208–12).

Chen Boda: "The Socialist Transformation of China's Agriculture," February 2, 1956 (text: [195]: 1957: 213–16).

Chen Shutong: "Report on the Socialist Transformation of Capitalist Industry and Commerce," January 31, 1956 (text: [195]: 1957: 216–19).

Dong Biwu: "Report on the Problem of Wiping Out All Counterrevolutionary Elements," January 31, 1956 (text: [195]: 1957: 219–22).

VII. "Decision on the Second Session of the Second CPPCC on the Political Report," February 7, 1956 (text: [195]: 1957: 206).

"Decision of the Second Session of the Second CPPCC on the Work Report of the Standing Committee of the Second CPPCC," February 7, 1956 (text: [195]: 1957: 208).

IX.   Texts of the documents also available in [277]: II.

60

I.   *March 1956*
II.   **ENLARGED MEETING OF THE MILITARY AFFAIRS COMMITTEE OF THE CC CCP**
V.   Rectification of the PLA
VI.   Peng Dehuai: Report and concluding speech (mention: [273]: 432).

IX.   This conference discussed the need for rectification of various undesir-
able tendencies in the PLA and to decide on new measures to improve the
quality of political work (mention: [115]: October 4, 1956; [85]: 285;
[273]: 432).

The decisions of this meeting provided the basis for a PLA rectification campaign during the spring and summer of 1956 (mention: ibid.).

61

I.   *March–April 1956*
II.   **(A SERIES OF) MEETINGS OF THE POLITBURO OF THE
CC CCP** (see IX below)
III.   Beijing
V.   Administrative strategy; USSR; rectification
VI.   Mao Zedong: Speech to four-day Enlarged Politburo Meeting, April 1956
(texts: [167]: 35–40; [174]: 30–35): main points: need greater economic
and administrative decentralization without sacrificing discipline; appro-
priateness of Soviet model; Sino-Soviet relations; party rectification;
united front policy.
VII.   "On the Historical Dictatorship of the Proletariat" (texts: [14]: 144–51;
[194]: April 5, 1956).
IX.   In the "Ten Great Relationships" (meeting 62), Mao discloses that over
the previous two months the Politburo had listened to reports on the work
of thirty-four departments of the center concerning finance and economics. After further discussions within the Politburo, these had been summarized into the ten contradictions. Also, from Deng Xiaoping's return from
Moscow on March 3, 1956 (following Khrushchev's "Secret Speech" to
the 20th Congress of the CPSU) to April 5, 1956, the Chinese leadership
had to develop their response to Khrushchev's denigration of Stalin.
Clearly, then, the Politburo met repeatedly during March and April and
devoted its attention to both issues in March and to the ten contradictions
after April 5, 1956. Because, with the sole exception noted above, information on these individual meetings is not currently available, they are
treated here as "a series of Politburo meetings."

Although Mao had the primary role in the drafting of the "Ten Great
Relationships," Liu Shaoqi and Zhou Enlai were also involved (mention:
[282]: 170–71; [108]: 126).

62

I.   *April 25–28, 1956*
II.   **ENLARGED MEETING OF THE POLITBURO OF THE CC CCP**
III.   Beijing

IV. Secretaries of provincial and municipal party committees.

V. Ten Great Relationships

VI. Mao Zedong: Speech entitled "On the Ten Great Relationships," April 25, 1956, delivered to a joint meeting of this conference and the Politburo (meeting 61) as disclosed in [167]: 220; [174]: 118 (texts: [25]: 65–85; [271]: 1970: 36–43; [43]: 892: October 21, 1969: 21–34; [163]: 284–307): wide-ranging review of the contradictions in Chinese society, accompanied by appropriate policy recommendations.

Mao Zedong: Speech, April 28, 1956 (mention: [273]: 457; [82]: February 13, 1984: K18; [89]: 243–44): proposes "double hundred" policy (repeated at Supreme State Conference [meeting 64]).

IX. It was officially announced simply that this conference reviewed the important questions for submission to the upcoming Eighth Party Congress (meeting 70) ([176]: September 14, 1956). Chang ([22]: 42) speculates that rural policy and the de-Stalinization issue were also discussed at this conference.

63

I. *May 1956*

II. **CENTRAL MEETING CALLED BY ZHOU ENLAI AND CHEN YUN**

VIII. Must oppose both conservatism and blind advance in economic construction. Approved policy of steady progress in economic construction with overall balance.

IX. The State Council drew up the 1956 annual economic plan on the basis of this policy.

Upon a suggestion by Zhou, *Renmin ribao* published an editorial "Oppose Conservatism, but Also Oppose Impatience," to explain the new policy (mention: [273]: 464–65; text of editorial in [194]: June 20, 1956, tr. in [216]: 1321: 11).

64

I. *May 2, 1956*

II. **SEVENTH SUPREME STATE CONFERENCE**

V. Policy toward the intellectuals

VI. Mao Zedong (excerpt: [25]: 4000: August 14, 1967: 16; mention: [108]: 125): famous speech calling for applying the slogan "Let one hundred flowers bloom, let one hundred schools of thought contend" to policy toward the intellectuals.

IX.   This speech was a rearrangement of one portion of "On the Ten Great Relationships" (mention: [89]: 235). The "double hundred" policy was originally proposed at the enlarged Politburo meeting on April 28 (mention: [273]: 457). On May 26, 1956, Lu Dingyi made a speech entitled "Let One Hundred Flowers Bloom, Let One Hundred Schools of Thought Contend" to a gathering of scientists, social scientists, doctors, writers, and others in Beijing. This speech in all likelihood closely reflected the substance of Mao Zedong's May 2 talk (revised texts: [14]: 151–63; [194]: June 13, 1956; [156]).

65

I.   *Probably early June 1956*
II.   **BEIDAIHE CONFERENCE**
III.   Beidaihe, Hebei
V.   Economic policy
IX.   Mao Zedong subsequently remarked ([167]: 149; [174]: 80) that the opposition to "boldly advancing" at this meeting influenced "the NPC report." This probably refers to Li Xiannian's budget report to the June 15–30, 1956, National People's Congress (meeting 67), delivered on June 15, 1956.

66

I.   *June 5, 1956*
II.   **NATIONAL CONFERENCE OF HEADS OF PUBLIC SECURITY OFFICES AND BUREAUS**
V.   Policy toward the Procuracy and the capitalists
VI.   Peng Zhen: Report (excerpts: [265]; [158]: 83): encouraged public security officials to respect the Procuracy and asserted that capitalists would basically accept reform.

67

I.   *June 15–30, 1956*
II.   **THIRD SESSION OF THE FIRST NPC OF THE PRC**
III.   Beijing
VI.   Li Xiannian: "Report on the 1955 National Budget and the 1956 Draft Budget," June 15, 1956 (text: [195]: 1957: 159–66).
        Liu Lantao: "Investigation Report by the Budget Committee of the

First NPC on the 1955 State Budget and the Draft 1956 State Budget,'' June 28, 1956 (text: [195]: 1957: 166–67).

Liao Luyan: "Explanation of the (Draft) Model Charter for Higher-Level Agricultural Producers Cooperatives," June 15, 1956 (text: [195]: 1957: 169–72).

Wu Xinning: "Investigation Report by the Proposal Committee of the First NPC on the (Draft) Model Charter for Higher-Level Agricultural Producers Cooperatives," June 19, 1956 (text: [195]: 1957: 172–73).

Peng Zhen: "Work Report of the Standing Committee of the NPC of the PRC," June 14, 1956 (text: [195]: 1957: 179–80).

Zhou Enlai, "On the Current International Situation, Our Foreign Policy, and the Liberation of Taiwan," June 28, 1956 (text: [195]: 1957: 182–88).

Guo Moruo: "Scientific Regulations and Planning and Letting a Hundred Schools of Thought Contend," June 18, 1956 (text: [195]: 1957: 188–90).

Li Fuchun: "The Conditions with Respect to Implementing Our First Five-Year Plan for the Development of the National Economy," June 10, 1956 (text: [195]: 1957: 190–94).

Chen Yun: "On the Question of the Socialist Transformation of Private Industry and Commerce," June 18, 1956 (text: [195]: 1957: 194–97; [27]: 307–18).

Deng Zihui: "The Conditions of the Agricultural Cooperativization Movement Over the Past Year and Future Work," June 19, 1956 (text: [195]: 1957: 197–200).

Bo Yibo (mention: [108]: 146).

Chen Yun: Speech, "Overcome Malpractices in the State Monopoly on Purchasing and Marketing," June 30, 1956 (text: [27]: 319–26).

Zhou Enlai: "Closing Speech," June 30, 1956 (summary: [195]: 1957: 200–201).

A total of 164 people addressed this meeting.

VII. "Decision of the Third Session of the First NPC on the 1955 Budget and the Draft 1966 Budget," June 30, 1956 (text: [195]: 1957: 168–69).

"Model Charter for Higher-Level Agricultural Producers Cooperatives," June 30, 1956 (text: [195]: 1957: 173–79).

Other minor resolutions and decisions: (text: [195]: 1957: 180–82).

IX. All documentation of this meeting can also be found in [280].

On the basis of this meeting, and on the suggestion of Zhou Enlai, *Renmin ribao* published "Oppose Conservatism, but Also Oppose Impatience" on June 20, 1956 (mention: [108]: 146; tr. in [216]: 1321: 11).

68

I.   *August 22 and September 8 and 13, 1956*

II.   **SEVENTH PLENUM OF THE SEVENTH CC CCP**

V.   Preparation for the September 15–27, 1956, Eighth Party Congress (meeting 70)

IX.   The "Draft Twelve-Year National Program for Agricultural Development" had anticipated that this plenum would discuss and adopt the Draft ([158]: 120), but there is no documentary evidence that the Draft was in fact discussed at this plenum.

69

I.   *September 1956 (or not long thereafter)*

II.   **NATIONAL WORK ASSIGNMENT MEETING**

V.   Labor contract system

VIII. Proposed that China adopt a labor contract system based on that in use in the USSR ([151]).

IX.   In September 1956 Liu Shaoqi ordered Ma Wenrui and Lai Ruoyu to organize an investigation team and go to the USSR to inspect the labor contract system there. The team wrote a report on the Soviet labor contract system, which Liu Shaoqi then revised and had the Ministry of Labor circulate, after which it became the basis for discussion at this meeting. The labor contract system passed by this meeting was then implemented in Canton and elsewhere ([151]).

    All information on this meeting comes from the single Red Guard source cited above.

    More information on Ma Wenrui's trip to the USSR is given in [206]: 177: April 19, 1967: 18–19.

70

I.   *September 15–27, 1956*

II.   **EIGHTH NATIONAL CONGRESS OF THE CCP**

III.   Beijing

IV.   1,026 delegates representing 10,730,000 party members; representatives of Communist, worker, labor, and people's revolutionary parties from 59 countries, including about 140 foreign delegates and observers representing 56 foreign Communist parties; representatives of China's democratic parties and nonparty people (mention: [108]: 131).

V.   Adopt new party Constitution; elect new Central Committee; Second Five-Year Plan; subjectivisim within the party; relations within the Communist bloc

VI.   The congress heard a total of 133 speeches by 113 delegates, including 43 delegates of other Communist parties (mention: [108]: 131). Delegates also read 45 written reports ([43]: 426: November 9, 1956: i). List of these in ibid.: 9–16; texts: [195]: 1957: 65–158. The most important of these presentations were as follows:

Mao Zedong: Opening address, September 15, 1956 (text: [72]: 5–12; [195]: 1957: 8–9; [163]: 312–33).

Deng Xiaoping: "Report on Revision of the Party Constitution," September 16, 1956 (text: [72]: 169–228; [195]: 1957: 26–37).

Zhou Enlai: "Report on the Second Five-Year Plan," September 16, 1956 (texts: [72]: 261–328; [195]: 1957: 37–49).

Liu Shaoqi: "Political Report of the CC CCP to the Eighth National Congress of the Party," September 15, 1956 (texts: [72]: 13–112; [195]: 1957: 9–27; [144]: 337–408; [147]: *xia*: 202–76).

Chen Yun: Speech, "New Issues Since the Basic Completion of the Socialist Transformation," September 20, 1956 (text: [135]: 7–22; [28]: 1–14): reviews changeover of capitalist industry and commerce into joint state-private enterprises; variety and specifications of goods have decreased because there are only a few wholesale companies and individual shops cannot buy directly from factories; the practice of exclusive state purchasing and marketing of key commodities should continue, but market controls over consumer goods should be reduced; blind amalgamation of production and commercial units must be checked; price policy should facilitate production.

Chen Yun: Speech, "Methods of Solving the Tensions in the Supplies of Pork and Vegetables" (text: ibid.: 23–29): explains main reasons for pork and vegetable shortages; proposes measures to increase fodder, raise procurement prices, and other incentives to increase pig-raising; state monopoly on buying and selling vegetables should not be implemented, and prices must be allowed to fluctuate.

Bo Yibo (summary: [282]: 179): ratio of accumulation to national income should not go below 20 percent; capital construction should not be less than 40 percent of national budget.

Li Xuefeng (summary: [282]: 179): criticism of one-man leadership, advocated factory director responsibility system under leadership of party committee.

Zhu De and Dong Biwu (mention: [108]: 472–73).

VII.   "Constitution of the Communist Party of China" (texts: [61]: 1–30; [72]: 135–68; [195]: 1957: 49–54).

"Resolution of the Eighth National Congress of the CCP on the Political Report of the Central Committee" (texts: [61]: 31–46; [72]: 113–34; [195]: 1957: 55–57).

"Proposals of the Eighth National Congress of the CCP for the Second Five-Year Plan for the Development of the National Economy (1958–1962)" (texts: [61]: 47–70; [72]: 229–60; [195]: 1957: 58–63).

VIII.   Elected a new Central Committee of the CCP (name lists: [43]: 426: November 9, 1956: 2; [61]: 71–75; [195]: 1957: 64).

Created the new positions of party general secretary and Standing Committee of the Politburo.

IX.   A number of specialized meetings held during the summer of 1956 may have served as preparatory meetings for the Seventh Plenum of the Seventh CC (meeting 68) and this congress. These specialized meetings include the following: United Front Work Symposium convened by the United Front Work Department on July 2–4, 1956, and attended by over two hundred people ([195]: 1957: 242–43); Symposium of Directors of the Propaganda, Culture, and Education Departments of thirteen provincial party committees on July 20, 1956 ([238]); and a Work Conference of Higher Level Party Schools in July 1956 ([153]).

A preparatory meeting convened on August 30–September 12, 1956 (mention: [89]: 248).

The Red Guards made a number of assertions concerning the politics of this congress for most of which there is no supporting evidence. Two of the most significant assertions are that (1) Liu Shaoqi's "Political Report" was a product of drafts done by Liu, Deng Xiaoping, and Peng Zhen, in which Peng Zhen drafted the section of the report on the "Political Life of the State" ([250]: June 10, 1967); and (2) Peng Dehuai was the person who proposed that the new party Constitution drop reference to the Thought of Mao Zedong ([107]: 40; [183]).

The *Renmin ribao* editorial on this congress is in ([43]: 426: November 9, 1956: 19–22; [194]: September 29, 1956).

71

I.   *September 28, 1956*
II.   **FIRST PLENUM OF THE EIGHTH CC CCP**
III.   Beijing
IV.   Ninety-six full and seventy alternate members of the CC CCP.
V.   Election of people to central party organs

VII.   "Communique" (texts: [61]: 103–104; [176]: September 28, 1956): Includes name lists for people elected to the following party positions: chairman; vice-chairmen; general secretary; Politburo members, alternate members, and Standing Committee members; Secretariat members and alternate members; Control Committee members, alternate members, secretary, and deputy secretaries.

IX.   The positions of general secretary and Standing Committee of the Politburo are new and were created at the preceding Eighth Party Congress of September 15–27, 1956 (meeting 70).

72

I.   *November 10–15, 1956*

II.   **SECOND PLENUM OF THE EIGHTH CC CCP**

IV.   Eighty-four full and 65 alternate members of the Central Committee; 147 responsible work personnel of the center and localities participated without the right to vote.

V.   Foreign affairs—Egypt, Poland, and Hungary; budget; foodstuffs

VI.   Liu Shaoqi: "Report on the Current Situation" (summaries: [61]: 105–107; [195]: 1957: 147–48; [89]: 257): deals with Poland, Hungary, and Egypt—the policies adopted and the lessons to be learned; raises question of treating capital goods as commodities to be circulated.

    Zhou Enlai: "Report on the Plan of National Economic Development and the Control Figures of the Budget for 1957" (excerpt: [286]: 229–38; summaries: [61]: 105–107; [195]: 1957: 147–48; [273]: 476; [282]: 180–81): reviews 1956 economic performance, proposes control figures for 1957, and calls for "suitable retrenchment in certain fields" in the 1957 plan.

    Chen Yun, "Measures for Solving Tensions in the Supply of Pork and Other Nonstaple Foods," November 11, 1956 (text: [28]: 15–27; summaries: [61]: 105–107; [195]: 1957: 147–48; [273]: 476; [282]: 181): proposes measures for the purchase and sale of grain and for increasing production of pork and edible oil.

    Mao Zedong, "Closing Speech," November 15, 1956 (text: [163]: 332–49): calls for reducing waste and for rectification of subjectivism, sectarianism, and bureaucratism; warns against great Han and great power chauvinism; international situation; Sino-Soviet relations; question of great and small democracy.

VII.   "Communique" (texts: [61]: 105–107; [195]: 1957: 147–48): notes that this conference approved Politburo's analysis of and actions toward the international situation; recognized the righteousness of the USSR's actions toward Hungary; called for a nationwide "increase production and practice economy" campaign.

IX. Mao Zedong subsequently commented that this plenum discussed contradictions among the people ([167]: 51; [174]: 82) and that it devised "seven articles" having to do with opposition to bold advances ([167]: 152; [174]: 83). There is no other information available on the "seven articles."

Mao apparently spoke to a preparatory meeting for this plenum on October 21, 1956 (mention: [137]: 477).

73

I. *November 20, 1956*
II. **SYMPOSIUM OF DIRECTORS OF PROPAGANDA DEPARTMENTS OF PROVINCIAL PARTY COMMITTEES**
V. Role of Mao Zedong (?)
VI. Lu Dingyi (excerpt: [237]): questions how "all merits can go to one individual."
IX. All information on this meeting comes from the single Red Guard source cited above.

74

I. *December 1956*
II. **ENLARGED MEETING OF THE POLITBURO OF THE CC CCP**
III. Beijing
V. The new international and domestic situation (in light of the Soviet Union's 20th Party Congress and disturbances in Eastern Europe)
IX. The December 29, 1956, *Renmin ribao* article "More on the Historical Experience of the Dictatorship of the Proletariat" was written on the basis of this meeting and Mao Zedong's viewpoint. Clearly, this was a precursor to Mao's "On the Correct Handling of Contradictions among the People."

75

I. *December ?-4-?, 1956*
II. **CONFERENCE OF ORGANIZATION DEPARTMENT HEADS OF PROVINCIAL AND MUNICIPAL PARTY COMMITTEES**
V. Party organization work
VI. Liu Shaoqi, December 4, 1956 (excerpts: [98]; [153]; [240]: April 28,

1968): the organs of the state are firmly established and class struggle is easing; must concentrate on organizing social life; the time of leaps forward is past.

76

I.   *December 8, 1956*
II.   **DISCUSSION MEETING ATTENDED BY SOME OF THE DELEGATES TO THE SECOND SESSION OF THE ALL-CHINA FEDERATION OF INDUSTRY AND COMMERCE**
III.   Beijing
IV.   Mao Zedong, Liu Shaoqi, Chen Yun, Lu Dingyi, Bo Yibo, responsible people of various relevant central departments and people's groups, and responsible people from the various provincial and municipal delegations to the Second Session of the All-China Federation of Industry and Commerce ([195]: 1957: 52).
V.   How to make the industrial and commercial circles more active in socialist construction
VI.   Mao Zedong, December 8, 1956 (texts: [167]: 61–72; [174]: 36–45): must continue the alliance with the USSR; domestic counterrevolutionaries are no longer a major problem; capitalists can air ideas without fear; duration of fixed interest should be seven years, with some flexibility; CCP must retain good relations with large, medium, and small capitalists.
IX.   The Second Session of the All-China Federation of Industry and Commerce convened in Beijing for December 10–23, 1956 (detailed information: [195]: 1957: 542–44).

1957 _____

77

I.   *1957*
II.   **NATIONAL INVESTIGATE CADRES WORK CONFERENCE**
        (Quanguo shen gan gongzuo huiyi)
V.   Treatment of cadres who have "problems" in their histories
VIII.   Those cadres who have problems that occurred a long time ago and who have done much good work since need only retell their history and personally accept responsibility for past errors. If they do so, they will not subsequently be considered to have problems in their histories ([196]).

IX.   This meeting was convened by the Organization Department of the CC CCP, under the direction of An Ziwen ([196]).

All information on this meeting comes from the single Red Guard source cited above.

78

I.   *Early 1957*
II.   **MEETING OF THE POLITBURO OF THE CC CCP**
V.   Policy toward Tibet
IX.   Deng Xiaoping and Peng Zhen had drafted a "Draft Decision with Respect to Democratic Reform Work in Tibet," and they circulated it to the authorities in Tibet. This "Draft Decision" produced opposition owing to its "capitulationist" nature. It then came up for discussion at this Politburo meeting, at which time Mao opposed the "Draft Decision" and Deng Xiaoping clashed with the Chairman over this issue ([207]).

All information on this meeting comes from the single Red Guard source cited above.

79

I.   *January ?–18–27, 1957*
II.   **CONFERENCE OF CCP PROVINCIAL AND MUNICIPAL SECRETARIES**
IV.   Mao Zedong, Chen Yun, Zhou Enlai (and other central leaders?) and an unspecified number of provincial and municipal party secretaries.
V.   Hundred Flowers; economic problems; relations with the USSR; foreign policy; *xiafang* ("sending down") of upper-level cadres
VI.   Mao Zedong: Speech, January 18, 1957 (text: [163]: 350–59): propaganda is needed to overcome doubts regarding viability of cooperatives; Khrushchev's secret speech caused some CCP members to doubt superiority of socialism; great democracy is necessary to expose and isolate reactionaries.

Mao Zedong: "Interjections" (texts: [167]: 73–81; [174]: 46–53) and "Summary," January 27, 1957 (texts: [167]: 81–90; [174]: 54–62; [163]: 359–83): must prepare for trouble and not fear it (regarding the Hundred Flowers movement and the repercussions of Hungary); must stress ideological work; the Soviets lack understanding of contradictions; must increase the harvest to demonstrate the superiority of the cooperatives; must pay attention to oils, pork, and food grains; need more small industrial plants; it is necessary to *xiafang* cadres and to pay attention to outsider/local ratios at the *xian* level; brief review of international situation; should liberalize policy toward drama; must cope with the results of the rapid cooperativization; circulation of *Cankao xiaoxi* ("Reference News"—a secret publication on world events) will increase from 2,000 to 400,000 and will circulate among nonparty people.

Chen Yun: "The Scale of Construction Should Be Compatible with National Strength" (text: [135]: 47–57; [28]: 40–49): calls for stabilization of markets, a balanced budget, improved distribution of basic materials and daily necessities, limited expansion of capital construction, and attention to the constraint of agriculture on the scale of economic construction.

IX. The major thrust of this conference seems to have been to inform the provincial and municipal authorities of what to expect and what attitudes to adopt with regard to the Hundred Flowers movement.

Mao Zedong subsequently commented that opposition to "bold advances" had continued to gain ground at this meeting ([167]: 152; [174]: 83).

80

I.   *February 27–March 1, 1957*
II. **ENLARGED ELEVENTH SUPREME STATE CONFERENCE**
IV. 1,800–1,900 people ([195]: 1958: 326).
V.   Contradictions in Chinese society; party rectification
VI. Mao Zedong: "On the Correct Handling of Contradictions Among the People," February 27, 1957 (incorrect date of February 29, 1957, is given in [167]: 150: 82) (revised texts: [14]: 273–94; [162]; [203]: 432–79; [163]: 384–421): wide-ranging discussion of antagonistic and nonantagonistic contradictions in socialist society; suppression of counterrevolution; agricultural cooperation; intellectuals; rectification; the economy; and China's path to industrialization.

Li Jishen, Zhang Bojun, Huang Yanpei, Ma Xulun, Chen Jiayu, Chen Shutong, Guo Moruo, Cheng Qian, Ma Yinchu, Xu Deheng, Da Pusheng, Liu Wenhui, Che Xiangchen, Sheng Pihua, Sun Weiru, and Huang Qixiang addressed a plenary session on March 1, 1957 (mention: [195]: 1958: 326).

Mao Zedong: Concluding speech, March 1, 1957 (text: [167]: 90–100): stresses bureaucratism to the virtual neglect of subjectivism and sectarianism; defines limits of permissible criticism; orders increased circulation (from 2,000 to 300,000) of *Cankao xiaoxi* (Reference News); stresses need for greater efforts to control population growth; announces plans to convene a Central Committee plenum on united front work; previews the March National Conference on Propaganda Work (meeting

82); comments on procedure for transmitting his February 27, 1957, speech to lower levels.

IX.   After hearing Mao's speech on February 27, the delegates discussed its contents in small groups on February 28-March 1 ([195]: 1958: 326), and on the basis of these discussions revisions were made in the text of the speech before it was circulated to lower levels ([167]: 100). The text released to the public in the early summer, however, had been revised again, and this second revised text is the one cited above.

MacFarquhar ([158]: 192, 250–51) argues that Mao Zedong had not sought prior Central Committee or Politburo approval for his speech of February 27 and that this speech met with considerable opposition at the highest levels. For instance, the March 3, 1957, *Renmin ribao* photograph of the rostrum did not include Liu Shaoqi, Zhu De, Lin Biao, Lin Boqu, Luo Ronghuan, and Penq Dehuai, although in all probability some or all of these men were present at this conference.

81

I.   *March 5-20, 1957*
II.   **THIRD SESSION OF THE NATIONAL COMMITTEE OF THE SECOND CPPCC**
III.   Beijing
VI.   Zhou Enlai, "Report on [My] Visit to Eleven Countries in Asia and Europe," March 5, 1957 (text: [195]: 1958: 184–92).
    Chen Shutong: "Work Report of the Standing Committee of the Second CPPCC," March 5, 1957 (text: [195]: 1958: 192–94).
VII.   "Decisions of the Third Session of the Second CPPCC," March 20, 1957 (text: [195]: 1958: 194–96).
IX.   Texts of these documents also available in [277]: III.

82

I.   *March 6-13, 1957*
II.   **NATIONAL CONFERENCE ON PROPAGANDA WORK OF THE CCP**
IV.   More than 380 leading cadres of the party's propaganda, cultural, and education departments at the central and provincial (or municipal) levels; more than 100 nonparty people from various departments and institutions of science, education, literature and art, and the press ([165])—for a total of over 500 people ([158]: 376, n.3).
V.   Intellectuals; rectification

VI. Mao Zedong: Comment (or part of speech?), March 6, 1957 (mention: [71]: 26): "What to publicize in the press depends upon whether or not it benefits the people."

Mao Zedong: Speech, March 12, 1957 (texts: [165]; [163]: 422–35): discusses the issues of the struggle between socialism and capitalism; the situation of intellectuals and remolding this group; and rectification; should convene propaganda conferences in the various localities.

IX. Mao Zedong spoke individually to forums of various delegates to this meeting, as follows: heads of propaganda, cultural, and educational departments of nine provinces and educational departments of nine provinces and municipalities, March 6, 1957; heads of education departments and bureaus of seventeen provinces and municipalities, March 7, 1957; and journalists and publishers attending the conference, March 10, 1957 (mention: [158]: 373, n.39).

In his March 1, 1957, speech to the Enlarged Supreme State Conference (meeting 80), Mao anticipated this meeting and indicated that the major item on the agenda would be the transmittal of his February 27, 1957, speech.

These is no information available concerning the discussion of the February 27, 1957, speech at this meeting. This conference reaffirmed that education must be combined with productive labor ([14]: 446).

83

I.   *April 1957 (probably between April 1 and April 7)*
II. **HANGZHOU CONFERENCE OF THE SHANGHAI BUREAU**
III. Hangzhou, Zhejiang
IV. At least Mao Zedong and members of the Shanghai Bureau of the CCP.
V.   Hundred Flowers Campaign; rectification
VI. Mao Zedong: Speech (texts: [167]: 100–109; [174]: 63–71): focuses on the need for the Hundred Flowers movement and for rectification; touches upon birth control and the question of interest payments; opposes dogmatism, versus the revisionism that he attacked in his March 12, 1957, speech to the CCP National Conference on Propaganda Work (meeting 82); calls for rectification of *Renmin ribao*; recommends that each province have a nonparty newspaper; suggests that one-third of the intellectuals should be party members by 1966.
IX. Mao evidently used this meeting to help build momentum for the Hundred Flowers movement.

84

I.   *April 30, 1957*
II.   **TWELFTH SUPREME STATE CONFERENCE**
III.   Beijing
V.   Rectification campaign against bureaucratism, dogmatism, and subjectivism
VI.   Mao Zedong: Speech (mention: [167]: 158): calls for intellectuals to take root among the proletariat.
VIII.   Transmitted the directive issued by the Central Committee on April 27, 1957, entitled: "A Rectification Campaign for the Entire People" (mention: [158]: 210) (text of directive: [195]: 1958: 29–30): this directive calls for people to study Mao Zedong's February 27, 1957, speech to the Enlarged Supreme State Conference (meeting 80) and his March 12, 1957, speech to the CCP National Conference on Propaganda Work (meeting 82) and launches a rectification campaign to attack the problems of bureaucratism, dogmatism, and subjectivism.
IX.   Mao invited responsible persons of democratic parties and nonparty personages to conduct an informal dialogue on April 30, 1957, presumably at this conference (mention: [273]: 488).

    MacFarquhar ([158]: 210) indicates that Liu Shaoqi and Peng Zhen were out of Beijing when the April 27, 1957, rectification directive was drafted. They were back in time for the April 30, 1957, Supreme State Conference, though, and this directive was issued directly following this conference. The conference thus served to inform key people of the contents of the directive and to discuss its implementation.

85

I.   *June 26–July 15, 1957*
II.   **FOURTH SESSION OF THE FIRST NPC**
III.   Beijing
VI.   Zhou Enlai: "Report on the Government's Work," June 26, 1957 (text: [195]: 1958: 201–14).

    Peng Zhen: "Work Report of the Standing Committee of the NPC of the PRC," June 28, 1957 (text: [195]: 1958: 240–41).

    Li Xiannian: "Report on the 1956 State Budget and the Draft 1957 Budget," June 29, 1957 (text: [195]: 1958: 214–24).

Bo Yibo: "Report on the Results of Implementing the 1956 National Economic Plan and on the Draft of the 1957 National Economic Plan," July 1, 1957 (text: [195]: 1958: 224–33).

Dong Biwu: "Report on the Work of the Supreme People's Court," July 2, 1957 (text: [195]: 1958: 233–35).

Zhang Dingcheng: "Report on the Conditions of Procuracy Work Since 1956," July 1, 1957 (text: [195]: 1958: 235–40).

Ulanfu: "Report of the Establishment of the Guangxi Zhuang Autonomous Region and the Ningxia Hui Autonomous Region," July 5, 1957 (text: [195]: 1958: 241–43).

Zhou Enlai: "Report on the Question of the Sino-Burmese Border," July 9, 1957 (text: [195]: 1958: 244–45; [286]: 239–46).

Zheng Zihua: "Investigation Report of the Budget Committee of the First NPC on the 1956 State Budget and the Draft 1957 State Budget," July 12, 1957 (text: [195]: 1958: 245–47).

Other minor reports: (text: [195]: 1958: 247–48).

VII.   "Decision of the Fourth Session of the First NPC" (text: [195]: 1958: 248–49).

IX.   All documentation of this meeting can also be found in [281].

86

I.   *July 1957*

II.   **QINGDAO CONFERENCE OF SECRETARIES OF PROVINCIAL AND MUNICIPAL PARTY COMMITTEES**

III.   Qingdao, Shandong

V.   Rightism; National Agricultural Program; class contradictions

VI.   Mao Zedong: Speech(es?) (excerpts: [26]: 56; [43]: 891: October 8, 1969: 25 and 38; [129]: 50792: 42; [182]: 43: October 25, 1968: 5; [216]: 4000: August 14, 1967: 18): stresses need for rectification under the firm guidance of the provincial first secretaries; reaffirms the continuing struggle between the two roads in both urban and rural areas; affirms the need to create a political situation conducive to the rapid growth of the Chinese economy.

Mao: "The Situation in the Summer of 1957," article written at and distributed to this conference (text: [163]: 473–82): party rectification; antirightist struggle; supports the immediate initiation of a socialist education movement in rural areas, with emphasis on "educating" middle peasants; cooperativization not enough, also need socialist revolution on political and ideological fronts; working class must train its own intellectuals over ten to fifteen years.

VII.   "The Situation in the Summer of 1957" may be the document Mao

Zedong subsequently referred to as the "Qingdao document," which he asserted was a necessary supplement to his "On the Correct Handling of Contradictions Among the People" ([167]: 123, 125; [174]: 72–74).

IX.   This conference evidently again raised the issue of the Draft National Twelve-Year Program for Agricultural Development, pushed forward the rectification campaign against rightists, raised the issue of class struggle, and marked the beginning of the radicalization that led to the Great Leap Forward.

87

I.   *July 8, 1957*
II.   **NATIONAL TELEPHONE CONFERENCE OF PROVINCIAL SECRETARIES**
V.   Treatment of rightists
VI.   Deng Xiaoping: instructs provincial party secretaries on how to treat rightists in their own organizations ([158]: 283).
IX.   The only evidence MacFarquhar cites for this conference is a Red Guard source ([116]: June 14, 1967) that itself gives the year 1958 (which MacFarquhar asserts must be in error) ([158]: 397, n.60). Thus, the evidence for this conference is very thin.

88

I.   *"After the Antirightist Struggle"*
II.   **STANDING COMMITTEE OF THE POLITBURO OF THE CC CCP**
V.   Liu Shaoqi's Political Report to the Eighth Party Congress (meeting 70).
VIII.   According to Wu Lengxi's confession made during the Cultural Revolution, at this meeting of the Standing Committee of the Politburo Mao Zedong formally told Liu Shaoqi that the standpoint (*guandian*) the latter had taken at the Eighth Party Congress had been in error ([248]).

    All information on this meeting comes from the single Red Guard source cited above.

89

I.   *September 20–October 9, 1957*
II.   **THIRD (ENLARGED) PLENUM OF THE EIGHTH CC CCP**
IV.   Ninety-one full and 62 alternate members of the CC CCP; 416 persons

composed of first secretaries of the provincial, municipal, and autonomous region party committees, first secretaries of the district party committees in the municipalities directly under central control, and responsible personnel in the departments of the Central Committee.

V.   Rectification; administration; wages and labor insurance; Draft Twelve-
Year National Program for Agricultural Development; industrial, commercial, and financial management

VI.   Deng Xiaoping: "Report on the Rectification Movement" (text: [14]:
341–62; [43]: 477: October 25, 1957: 1–28): sections deal with bourgeois
intellectuals; the countryside; the working class; minority nationalities;
the armed forces; and the Communist Party and Young Communist
League.

Zhou Enlai: "Report on Labor Wages and Labor Insurance and Amen-
ities" (mention: [61]: 109–10; [195]: 1958: 182; [282]: 198).

Deng Zihui: "On the Agricultural Cooperatives' Enlargement, Production, and Several Other Problems" (partial texts: [194]: November
14, 1957; [195]: 1958: 520–24): covers measures to increase the production of agricultural cooperatives; calls for increase in labor days devoted
to basic construction in the coops; cites need for improved management
work, fewer cadres separated from production, and lower administrative
overhead costs; argues for greater pig raising as a source of fertilizer;
praises the expansion of state-run markets in the rural areas.

Chen Yun: "Report on the Improvement of the Administrative System
of the State and on the Questions of Agricultural Production Increase,"
September 24, 1957 (mention: [61]: 109–10; [195]: 1958: 182; excerpt:
[135]: 73–75; [28]: 66–68): there should be appropriate decentralization
of authority but simultaneous integration to maintain overall balance,
especially with respect to capital construction; direction of financial investment should be controlled locally; a financial management and inspection system must be established after reform of the fiscal system.

Chen Yun: Speech, "Essential Methods for Solving the Food and
Clothing Problems," September 24, 1957 (excerpt: [28]: 69–77): shortages of food and clothing are due to population increase and the shift of
labor from agriculture to industry; agriculture must get a larger share of
the investment budget; discusses chemical fertilizer, chemical fibers,
combating waterlogging, and expanding irrigated areas.

Mao Zedong: Speech, October 7, 1957 (texts: [167]: 122–26; [174]:
72–76): affirms that the primary contradiction at the current time is that
between the bourgeoisie and the proletariat, as the events since the September 15–27, 1956, Eighth Party Congress (meeting 70) make clear.

Mao Zedong: Speech, "Be Activists in Promoting the Revolution,"
October 9, 1957 (text: [163]: 483–97): rectification should switch from an
antirightist struggle to airing views and making reform; party secretaries

rarely helped run coops in second half of 1956; ten-year plans are needed for four pests, family planning, and to combine political and professional work and create proletarian intellectuals; sets goal of twenty million tons of steel in fifteen or so years; criticizes opposition to rash advance in 1956; line of Eighth Party Congress on principal contradiction is incorrect; differences with the Soviet Union and Khrushchev regarding Stalin, peaceful transition, and Hundred Flowers policy.

VII.   "Communique," October 9, 1957 (texts: [61]: 109–10; [195]: 1958: 182): states that the plenum "basically passed" the following documents:

    —1956–1967 National Program for Agricultural Development (Revised Draft)

    —Draft Regulations on the Improvement of the Industrial Management System

    —Draft Regulations on the Improvement of the Commercial Management System

    —Draft Regulations on the Improvement of the Financial System and the Demarcation of Financial Powers Between Central and Local Governments

    —Draft Regulations Affecting Labor Wages, Labor Insurance, and Welfare Provisions for Workers and Employees

VIII.   Meeting discussed and approved the party center's report on the rectification campaign ([273]: 490).

IX.   This plenum probably took corrective measures in agricultural cooperatives to ease cadre-peasant tensions and closed free markets for the peasants ([14]: 342).

Although the plenum agreed with Mao's viewpoint of the primary contradiction, it did not alter the formal conclusion of the Eighth Party Congress ([273]: 490).

The resolutions on industry, commerce, and finance were later approved by the 61st meeting of the State Council on November 8, 1957, and published on November 15; main points summarized in [282]: 198.

Given the fact that this plenum "basically passed" the Revised Draft 1956–1967 National Program for Agricultural Development, it is remarkable that Deng Zihui's report (cited above) did not mention this program. This address was first published in November 1957 (while Mao Zedong was in Moscow), and it is the only major known speech that was not mentioned in the communique.

This plenum marked the most visible acceleration toward the Great Leap Forward, but it seems to have culminated three months of discussion of the document passed by the Qingdao meeting in July (meeting 86), which marked the beginning of this acceleration. While its relationship to the Qingdao Conference is clear, however, the Third Plenum must also be seen as a turning point. For instance, one week prior to this plenum the

"Directive of the Central Committee of the CCP Concerning Doing Well the Work of Managing Production in Agricultural Cooperatives" was published (mention: [214]: 357, n.64). This directive called for a policy of consolidation of the cooperatives. It undoubtedly reflected the decision reached at a September National Rural Work Conference, mentioned in Deng Zihui's speech ([195]: 1958: 520–21).

The Third Plenum almost certainly discussed the Second Five-Year Plan and also the USSR's launching of Sputnik, the latter of which occurred in the midst of this lengthy meeting.

90

I.   *October 13, 1957*
II.   **THIRTEENTH SUPREME STATE CONFERENCE**
IV.   Sixty-one people, including Zhu De, Liu Shaoqi, Zhou Enlai, and responsible people of the CCP, various democratic parties, nonparty democrats, and people's groups ([195]: 1958: 326).
V.   Rectification; Twelve-Year National Program for Agricultural Development
VI.   Mao Zedong: Speech, "Have Firm Faith in the Majority of the People" (texts: [167]: 126–45; [163]: 498–513): endorses the current rectification campaign and argues that it must be pushed further; endorses the Twelve-Year National Program for Agricultural Development and specifies that its future consideration should follow the following process: within a few days, have a joint meeting of the Standing Committee of the NPC and the Standing Committee of the CPPCC discuss the program and issue a report on it, circulate this report throughout the rural areas, factories, and democratic parties for discussion, around December 1957 convene a CCP National Conference to pass the program, then have the Politburo recommend it to a NPC session to be a convened in December 1957 or January 1958; the 1958 plan and budget should be considered earlier than the usual May or June period; suggest steel target of twenty million tons by end of Third Five-Year Plan.

Deng Xiaoping: Speech (mention: [163]: 501).

VIII.   The meeting announced the following decisions ([195]: 1958: 326):

—Continue to carry out the rectification campaign in a thorough manner.

—Convene a joint meeting of the Standing Committee of the National People's Congress and Political Consultative Conference to discuss the revised draft of the Twelve-Year National Agricultural Development Program.

—Following the above joint meeting, disseminate the program among the people of the whole country for discussion.

IX.   On October 14, 1957, the revised draft was in fact submitted to and "basically" passed by the joint Standing Committee meeting noted above ([194]: October 15 and October 18, 1957).

The 40 Articles set targets of 400 catties of grain per *mu* north of the Yellow River, 500 north of the Huai River, and 800 south of the Huai River; Mao's speech to the Third Plenum (meeting 89) had suggested targets of 800, 1,000, and 2,000, respectively ([163]: 511, 486).

91

I.   *December 9–24, 1957*
II.   **NATIONAL AGRICULTURAL WORK CONFERENCE**
III.   Beijing
VI.   Zhu De (mention: [108]: 164–65): development of agriculture must be speeded up to catch up with industry and meet the developmental needs of national construction.

Huang Jing (given to this meeting? Source only says report given to CC meeting in 1957 and commended by Mao Zedong and Zhou Enlai: [194]: February 23, 1980: in [82]: March 21, 1980: L13): report on agricultural mechanization.

VIII.   Although it is unclear if this decision was made at this meeting, one source says CC CCP decided upon the policies of simultaneous development of industry and agriculture during the Second and Third Five-Year Plans, of paying attention to sideline commodity production, and of attempting to fulfill ahead of schedule some of the targets of the revised draft of the 1956–1967 agriculture development program (mention: [108]: 165).

92

I.   *December 13, 1957*
II.   **CONFERENCE OF HEADS OF UNITED FRONT WORK DEPARTMENTS**
V.   Attitudes toward capitalists after socialist transformation
VI.   Liu Shaoqi (excerpts: [79]; [228]): asserts that it is still proper to refer to the "capitalist class" as long as former capitalists continue to receive interest payments, but that once these payments cease this terminology would be incorrect.
IX.   Interest payments to capitalists were scheduled to end in 1962, with the possibility of an extension to be decided at that time.

1958

93

I.	*January 3–4, 1958*
II.	**HANGZHOU MEETING**
III.	Hangzhou, Zhejiang
V.	Work methods
VI.	Mao Zedong: Speech (mention: [108]: 166; [282]: 205): discusses work to be done after antirightist rectification; criticizes 1956's opposition to rash advance.
IX.	The discussions at this meeting, along with those of the January 11–22, 1958, Nanning Conference (meeting 94), formed the basis for the Sixty Work Methods (text: [26]: 57–76; [43]: 892: October 21, 1969: 1–14). These work methods, which are extremely broad in scope, thus probably accurately define the full range of issues discussed at Hangzhou.

94

I.	*January 11–22, 1958*
II.	**NANNING CONFERENCE**
III.	Nanning, Guangxi
IV.	Some Politburo members and regional party secretaries ([22]: 50, but Chang in turn cites no source for this).
V.	Sixty Work Methods; the General Line
VI.	Mao Zedong: Speeches, January 11 and 12, 1958 (texts: [167]: 145–54; [174]: 77–84): strongly attacks the upper levels of the state apparatus for essentially usurping power through relying on their own expertise to produce documents too technical for members of the Politburo to understand and discuss intelligently; asserts that the Politburo lacks expertise but is the "proletarian" planning council; attacks the lack of perspective of party conservatives in 1956–57, saying that it is necessary to continue to advance boldly while correcting errors; urges experts to become more red and reds to become more expert.
VIII.	Affirmed again the need to combine education with productive labor ([14]: 446).

Adopted the slogan "Basically transform the rural areas after three years of struggle" ([167]: 260; [174]: 141) (this slogan was first proposed by a "comrade from Henan"—probably Wu Zhipu).

Proposed that the provinces make plans on how long it would take—

five, seven, or so many years—for the value of industrial production to catch up with that of agricultural production ([167]: 201; [174]: 103).

Mao Zedong issued an instruction at this conference to unfold a patriotic health campaign centering on the elimination of the "four pests" (text: [257]).

IX. The Sixty Work Methods (texts: [26]: 57–76; [43]: 892: October 21, 1969: 1–14) were made up on the basis of discussions at this meeting (meeting 93). These work methods, which are extremely broad in scope, thus probably accurately define the full range of issues discussed at Nanning.

This meeting was a turning point: afterward, the desire to achieve impressive results and the consequent leftist mistakes developed rapidly (mention: [108]: 166; [282]: 205).

On January 12, 1958, Mao Zedong sent a letter to Liu Jianxun and Wei Guoqing asking particularly the former to take a more direct and active role in editing the Guangxi provincial newspaper and writing editorials (text: [43]: 891: October 8, 1969: 27).

The *Renmin ribao* editorial of January 14, 1958, put forward the slogan "walk on two legs," suggesting that this concept must have been under discussion at Nanning. A two-week National Economic Planning Conference held in early December 1957 laid the groundwork for this strategy ([214]: 337).

At the conclusion of this meeting, Mao convened a rump session on January 22 to discuss the proposal to build a dam at Three Gorges ([143]: 279–80).

95

I. *January 25–February 2, 1958*
II. **FIFTH SESSION OF THE FIRST NPC**
III. Beijing
VII. "Proposal by the Standing Committee of the NPC to Remove Rightists Huang Shaohong and Nine Others from Their Positions in the Nationalities, Proposals, and National Defense Committees," January 31, 1958 (text: [195]: 1958: 323).

Ma Mingfan: "Investigation Report of the Credentials Committee of the First NPC on the Question of the Qualifications of the Representatives Who Were Additionally Elected and of Zhang Naiqi and Thirty-seven Other Rightists," February 1, 1958 (text: [195]: 1958: 322).

VII. "Resolution Approving the Proposal of the Standing Committee of the NPC . . . " (text: [195]: 1958: 323).

96

I.   *January 28–30, 1958*
II.   **FOURTEENTH SUPREME STATE CONFERENCE**
V.   Rectification; Twelve-Year National Program for Agricultural Development; work methods
VI.   Mao Zedong: Speeches, January 28 and 30, 1958 (complete text: [167]: 154–59; partial texts: [170]: 10–14; [206]: 21: April 2, 1968: 2–4; [232]: December 1, 1969: 38–39): highly optimistic, calling for continuing the rectification for six months, most severely within the party and in a milder form among democratic parties, at the conclusion of which efforts should be directed toward carrying out a technical revolution; completing the Draft Twelve-Year National Agricultural Development Program in eight years instead of the almost ten years remaining in the original 1956–1967 program; instituting a regular program of four months of *xiafang* (sending down) of responsible cadres in the party center per year; *xiafang* of nonparty personages as they see fit; affirming the importance of permanent revolution.
IX.   At this meeting Mao indicated the importance of carrying out a *mild* rectification among nonparty people to bring them into the fold in the swelling movement in China to increase production. He recognized clearly the continuing need for technical personnel.

     Mao Zedong signed the Draft Sixty Work Methods (texts: [26]: 57–76; [43]: 892: October 21, 1969: 1–14) one day after the close of this conference, which suggests that this document, which had been drawn up on the basis of the discussions at the Hangzhou and Nanning meetings earlier in the month (meetings 76 and 77), was also discussed at this Supreme State Conference.

97

I.   *February 13–23, 1958*
II.   **ENLARGED MEETING OF THE POLITBURO OF THE CC CCP**
III.   Beijing
IV.   Over 100 people
VI.   Mao Zedong: Speech, February 18, 1958 (mention: [89]: 234): the Ten Great Relationships speech came about during one and a half months of talks in Beijing with comrades from thirty-four departments.
VIII.   Further criticized 1956's opposition to rash advance (mention: [108]: 166).
IX.   Meeting transmitted the spirit of the Nanning Conference. Some of the

Great Leap Forward policies were first raised at this meeting (mention: [273]: 497).

98

I.   *March 8 or 9–26, 1958*
II.   **CHENGDU CONFERENCE**
III.   Chengdu, Sichuan
IV.   Members of the CC CCP and of local party committees ([14]: 553; [43]: 590: September 9, 1959: 23; [194]: September 1, 1959).
V.   Rural policy; the media; industrial administration
VI.   Mao Zedong: Speech, March 9, 1958 (mention: [167]: 163; [201]: 100).

Mao Zedong: Speech, March 10, 1958 (partial texts: [110]: November 1973: 95–98; [167]: 159–65; [201]: 96–103): must retain flexibility and a critical attitude in learning from the USSR; should have proper mix of centralization and decentralization.

Mao Zedong: Speech, March 20, 1958 (texts: [110]: December 1973: 103–107; [167]: 165–72; [201]: 103–13): discusses the mass movement to improve agricultural tools; Draft Twelve-Year National Program for Agricultural Development; pace of agricultural development; pacing of mass movements; and problems of opposition.

Mao Zedong: Speech, March 22, 1958 (texts: [110]: December 1973: 107–12; [171]: 45–52; [167]: 172–80; [201]: 113–24): denigrates bourgeois intellectuals and says not to fear them; promotes having each province run its own publication; lists water conservancy, antirightism, rectification, and mass revolution as the current policies; suggests audience consider Chengdu a rectification meeting that has helped to break through the stale attitudes of the party.

Mao Zedong: Speeches, dates unspecified (summaries: [89]: 236; [273]: 497–98; [87]: February 1, 1985, tr. in [82]: February 12, 1985: K3; [262]: January 25, 1981, tr. in [82]: March 13, 1981: annex, p. 5; [110]: October 1981: 82): opposing rash advance is anti-Marxist; discusses personality cult; two exploiting classes and two working classes continue to exist in China.

Zhou Enlai: Report, "Opinions on the Major Water Conservation Projects at Three Gorges and Planning Regarding the Yangtze Basin" (mention: [194]: March 17, 1979, tr. in [82]: March 22, 1979: L16).

VII. "Opinion Concerning the Question of Agricultural Mechanization" (excerpts: [215]: 80–82)—purportedly proposed by Mao Zedong, passed by this meeting, but then never circulated or implemented ([205]: 610: 1968: 19; [215]: 79 and 82).

Thirty-seven documents were discussed and approved, including a second version of the 1958 annual economic plan and budget; development of local industry; appropriate merging of small coops into large ones (mention: [108]: 166; [273]: 497).

This conference also adopted, but did not announce, a resolution entitled "Opinion on the Three Gorges Water Resources Project and on the Outline Plan for the Yangtze Basin." This is quite likely the same report given by Zhou Enlai and reportedly received Mao's approval. This resolution very cautiously approved the proposal to build a dam at the Three Gorges site. For further discussion, see [143]: 280–84.

VIII.   Have simultaneous development of industry and agriculture ([216]: 1925: 34). Accelerate and expand scope of the administrative decentralization measures (mention: [14]: 435; [22]: 122).

Meeting discussed management of the plan, industry, materials, finance, prices, commerce, and education (mention: [282]: 208).

IX.   This meeting adjourned for participants to make inspection tours of the countryside and then reconvened. The adjournment occurred for a period of days between March 10 and March 21, 1958.

Along with the January 1958 Hangzhou and Nanning meetings (meetings 93 and 94), the Chengdu meeting laid the groundwork and drafted summaries for the May 5–23, 1958, Second Session of the Eighth Party Congress (meeting 103) ([167]: 218, 220; [174]: 117–18).

At this conference, the leadership calculated that the 1958 harvest would be 17 percent to more than 20 percent above that of 1957 ([97]: August 16, 1958: 8).

At this conference, Mao Zedong proposed the appropriate amalgamation of small cooperatives in a planned way, which was subsequently formally approved by the Central Committee ([216]: 1925: January 2, 1959: 34).

The second budget and annual plan approved at this meeting was not published, but set goals that should be fulfilled; the goals of the first budget, which were decided at the National People's Congress in February (meeting 95) and published, had to be fulfilled (mention: [273]: 497).

During this conference, the CC issued a directive regarding expanding the campaign to oppose waste and conservatism (mention: [108]: 166–67).

Peng Zhen made a speech "at a meeting" on March 25, 1958 (excerpt: [265]): unclear whether he made this speech at the Chengdu meeting.

On May 3, 1958, the State Council issued a decision to place agricultural machinery under the direct management of the agricultural producers cooperatives ([75]: 147: 16). This reflected the deliberations at the Chengdu meeting.

Lin Biao, Kang Sheng, and maybe others rejected the principle of opposing cult worship, instead used the slogan "correct cult worship" (mention: [89]: 450–51).

Wang Renzhong said Mao was already aware of the dangers of exaggeration at this conference (mention: [275]: no. 4, 1978, tr. in [82]: December 14, 1978: E14).

99

I.   *March 7, 1958*
II. **SECRETARIAT OF THE CC CCP**
V.   Combining education with productive labor
XII. Deng Xiaoping (excerpt: [94]): while it may be beneficial to introduce some productive labor into the educational process, one must be careful not to go too far and too fast in this direction.
IX. All information on this meeting comes from the single Red Guard source cited above.

100

I.   *April 1958*
II. **NATIONAL CONFERENCE ON EDUCATIONAL WORK**
V.   Relations between party members and intellectuals in the educational field
VI. Lu Dingyi: Speech (excerpts: [157]): stressed the need to maintain liaison with and use of the older and more technically qualified intellectuals in order to do party work in education properly.
IX. This conference was one of two that the CC CCP convened in mid-1958 on educational work. The other met on June 28, 1958 (meeting 109) ([14]: 440).

101

I.   *April 1–6, 1958*
II. **HANKOU CONFERENCE**
III. Hankou, Hubei
V.   Rectification and contradictions among the people
VI. Mao Zedong: Speech, April 6, 1958 (texts: [167]: 180–86; [174]: 85–90): the most anti-Communist classes in China encompass perhaps thirty million members, and there are still more members of the wavering bourgeoisie (including actual bourgeoisie, intellectuals, and former rich peas-

ants); contradictions among the people are very important.

Reports of two provinces regarding fulfilling the Forty Articles in one year and water conservation (mention: [273]: 498).

102

I.   *May 3, 1958*
II.   **FOURTH PLENUM OF THE EIGHTH CC CCP**
V.   Adopt reports to submit to the forthcoming Second Session of the Eighth Party Congress (meeting 103).
VIII.   This plenum adopted reports to be submitted to the May 5–23, 1958, Second Session of the Eighth Party Congress (meeting 103) ([61]: 111; [176]: May 25, 1958).

103

I.   *May 5-23, 1958*
II.   **SECOND SESSION OF THE EIGHTH CONGRESS OF THE CCP**
III.   Beijing
V.   Rectification; Great Leap Forward; General Line; Moscow Conference
VI.   Liu Shaoqi: "Work Report of the CC CCP to the Second Session of the Eighth Party Congress" (texts: [14]: 416–38; [43]: 507: June 2, 1958: 1–25; [195]: 1959: 17–26; [202]: 16–66): reviews the present international situation; the rectification campaign; industrial and agricultural production; the Great Leap Forward; and the General Line for Socialist Construction.

Deng Xiaoping: "Report on the Moscow Meeting of Communist and Workers Parties" (summary: [61]: 79–80): affirms the importance of the two declarations of the November 1957 Moscow Meeting and castigates Yugoslav revisionism.

Tan Zhenlin: "Explanation of the 1956–1967 National Agricultural Development Program (Second Revised Draft)" (texts: [43]: 508: June 4, 1958: 1–8; [195]: 1959: 29–31; [202]: 80–94): explanation of the major revisions and additions to the first revised draft of the 1956–1967 National Program for Agricultural Development.

Delegates from the provinces and autonomous regions of Zhejiang, Gansu, Anhui, Guangxi, Qinghai, Hebei, Guangdong, Xinjiang, Henan, and Shandong reported on the rectification campaign waged by party organizations in these areas against rightist, localist, nationalist, and right-opportunist elements inside the party (mention: [61]: 83; [202]).

Mao Zedong: Speech, May 8, 1958 (texts: [167]: 186–96; [174]: 91–

99): stresses the need to break down superstition and "let the initiative and creativity of the laboring people explode."

Mao Zedong: Speech, May 17, 1958 (texts: [167]: 196–209; [174]: 99–109): discusses the international situation of unity within the socialist camp and disunity among the imperialists; domestically, stresses the Twelve-Year National Agricultural Development Program, deep plowing, close planting, and the need for optimism; positively appraises the possible results of nuclear war.

Mao Zedong: Speech at meeting of heads of delegations, May 18, 1958 (texts: [174]: 119–24; [167]: 220–25): essentially recapitulates the substance of his earlier speeches to the Congress.

Mao Zedong: Speech, May 20, 1958 (texts: [174]: 115–18; [167]: 209–16): stresses optimism and the desirability of unbalanced growth.

Mao Zedong: Concluding speech, May 23, 1958 (texts: [174]: 115–18; [167]: 216–20): expresses great satisfaction with the decisions of the meeting.

117 people presented their views at plenary sessions of this congress, and another 145 circulated their views in writing. Those who addressed plenary sessions included Zhou Enlai, Zhu De, Chen Yun, Chen Yi, Li Xiannian, Ulanfu, Zhang Wentian, Lu Dingyi, Chen Boda, Kang Sheng, Bo Yibo, Wang Jiaxiang, and Li Xuefeng ([61]: 81).

VII.   "Second Session of the Eighth National Congress of the CCP" (texts: [61]: 77–85; [202]: 5–15).

"Resolution of the Second Session of the Eighth Party Congress on the 1956–1967 National Agricultural Development Program" (texts: [61]: 99; [195]: 1959: 29; [202]: 95).

"Resolution of the Second Session of the Eighth Party Congress on the Moscow Conference of Communist and Workers Parties" (texts: [14]: 410–15; [61]: 89–97; [195]: 1959: 26–29; [202]: 69–79).

"Resolution of the Second Session of the Eighth Party Congress on the Work Report of the Central Committee" ([61]: 87–88; [195]: 1959: 17; [202]).

"Name List of Alternate Members Additionally Elected to the Central Committee by the Second Session of the Eighth Party Congress" (texts: [61]: 101; [195]: 1959: 31–32).

IX.   This congress put the seal of approval on the Great Leap Forward strategy for China. It revolved around three themes: the continuing rectification campaign; the Great Leap Forward and the General Line for Socialist Construction; and the greater Communist bloc unity that had resulted from the November 1957 Moscow Conference. As embodied in the above resolutions, the congress approved the General Line for Socialist Construction, approved in principle the Twelve-Year National Program for the Development of Agriculture, and endorsed the results of the November 1957 Moscow Conference.

Twenty-five people were elected as members or alternate members of the CC. The conclusion of the Eighth Congress regarding the primary contradiction facing China was formally changed to "proletariat versus bourgeoisie, socialist road versus capitalist road" (mention: [108]: 168; [173]: 499).

104

I.   *May 25, 1958*
II.   **FIFTH PLENUM OF THE EIGHTH CC CCP**
III.   Beijing
V.   Election of additional people to party leading organs; founding of *Hongqi* (Red Flag)
VIII. Elected Lin Biao as additional vice-chairman of the CC CCP and Standing Committee member of the Politburo; elected Ke Qingshi, Li Jingquan, and Tan Zhenlin as additional members of the Politburo; elected Li Fuchun and Li Xiannian as additional members of the Secretariat of the CC CCP; advanced Yang Xianzhen and Wang Enmao from alternate to full members of the CC CCP ([61]: 111; [176]: May 25, 1958).

Founded fortnightly journal *Hongqi* with Chen Boda as editor. Decided to establish editorial boards for this journal by the CC CCP, the Shanghai Bureau of the CC CCP, and by the CCP committees of the various provinces, municipalities, and autonomous regions (ibid.).

IX.   On this same day, Mao Zedong personally led a group to a reservoir construction site. This group included, among others, all members of the Standing Committee of the Politburo except Chen Yun ([1]: 72).

105

I.   *May 27–July 22, 1958*
II.   **ENLARGED CONFERENCE OF THE MILITARY AFFAIRS COMMITTEE**
IV.   More than 1,000 high-ranking persons (mention: [82]: FE: 145: July 28, 1958: BBB–1; [216]: 1822: July 30, 1958).
V.   Army strategy; party work in army; military rectification
VI.   Mao Zedong: Speech, June 28, 1958 (partial texts: [170]: 15–21; [201]: 125–30; [206]: 21: April 2, 1968: 5–8; summary: [97]: no. 16, August 16, 1981, tr. in [82]: September 17, 1981: K20): cannot use Soviet ordnances in wartime; China must use its own ordnances; should not uncritically study the USSR; must seek Soviet aid but place primary emphasis on self-help; Soviet military operational plans and thinking

focus only on offensive operations, which does not fit China's practical situation; Xiao Ke is guilty of dogmatism to a serious degree; people may be criticized by name, but the resolutions of this conference may not name names; this is a rectification conference aimed at enhancing ideology and destroying slavish acceptance of Soviet experiences.

Zhu De, Lin Biao, Deng Xiaoping, Liu Bocheng, He Long, Chen Yi, Luo Ronghuan, Nie Rongzhen, and Ye Jianying also addressed this conference; Peng Dehuai summed up the conference's discussion (mention: [82]: FE: 145: July 28, 1958: BBB-1; [216]: 1822: July 30, 1958).

VIII.   Decided on the principles for the future development of the People's Liberation Army in view of the experiences of the previous years and adopted decisions concerning national defense work in light of the current international situation. (It is clear that these decisions included a more important role for party committees in the army; less reliance on Soviet strategy; and more stress on the people's militia [mention: ibid.].) Decided to write new military manuals for the PLA (mention: [133]: 651).

IX.   After this conference, rectification meetings were convened at all levels of the army through the remainder of 1958 ([167]: 266; [174]: 146).

Shortly after the conclusion of this conference, Zhu De stated that the meeting had fundamentally overcome the defects of "an exclusive military viewpoint, neglect of political and ideological work, and tendencies toward dogmatism and formalism" ([43]: 514: August 6, 1958: 3).

On July 23, 1958, China commenced its propaganda campaign declaring its willingness to liberate Taiwan at any moment ([176]: July 23, 1958), and this led directly to the bombardment of August-September (the 1958 Taiwan Straits crisis). Almost certainly, therefore, this policy toward the Taiwan question was aired at this conference.

Purportedly, at this conference Mao Zedong also deprecated the current systems of military pay and military ranks in favor of the earlier guerrilla systems of "supply" (*gonggei*) and "Communist life"; asserted that Liu Shaoqi, Gao Gang, and Peng Dehuai had advocated the Soviet system of military pay but that Mao had opposed this all along; attacked Peng Dehuai's "pure technological viewpoint" and advocated having politics take command; and endorsed the militia system and called for having "every man a soldier" (mention: [121]).

106

I.   *May 30, 1958*
II.   **ENLARGED MEETING OF THE POLITBURO OF THE CC CCP**
V.   Part-work, part-study schools
VI.   Liu Shaoqi: Speech (text: [147]: *xia*: 323–27; excerpts: [205]: 653: May

5, 1969: 22, 29; [225]: April 29, 1967; [225]: May 6, 1967; [229]: 3; [239]: April 22, 1967; summary: [89]: 258; [108]: 239–40): if China is going to meet the demands of students for continuing education, it is necessary and correct to set up part-work, part-study schools in addition to the full-time school system; therefore, several types of school systems, including full-time, part-work, part-study, and spare-time education, should be developed.

107

I.   *June 5, 1958*
II.   **MEETING OF THE SECRETARIAT OF THE CC CCP**
V.   Work in the higher party school
VI.   Peng Zhen (excerpts: [94]: 17; [216]: 639: January 6, 1969: 3): advocates the study of the "classics" of communism in the higher party school.

Deng Xiaoping (excerpts: [53]: 6, 43): Mao Zedong's thoughts on philosophy are systematic and concentrated; his thoughts on agricultural economics are rich but not systematic, and we must make efforts to systematize these; the purpose of studying for a year is to imbue an interest in reading and studying theory.

IX.   [216]: 639: January 6, 1969: 3, places this meeting in May 1958. Both sources on Peng Zhen assert that Yang Xianzhen agreed with Peng Zhen's policy recommendation and that the thrust of this recommendation went against Mao Zedong's preference to avoid the sterile study of theory in favor of greater emphasis on the study of actual practice in China.

108

I.   *June 20–24, 1958*
II.   **MEETING OF THE POLITBURO OF THE CC CCP**
V.   Wage system and wage reform, including the contract labor system
VI.   Liu Shaoqi: Speech, June 20, 1958 (excerpts: [114]: April 16, 1967; [149]): there have been policy mistakes, and the orientation has not been well defined; we have not instituted a socialist, proletarian, Marxist-Leninist oriented line (unclear whether this remark applies primarily or exclusively to the labor system).

Liu Shaoqi: Speech, June 21, 1958 (excerpt: [151]): in the new enterprises there is a permanent labor and a contract labor system, and workers in the latter do not enjoy labor insurance benefits; need a reform of the labor system in the direction of the contract labor system.

Liu Shaoqi: Speech, June 24, 1958 (mention: [205]: 616: March 25, 1968: 23): should have different labor insurance for permanent and contract laborers in new enterprises; the labor system must be reformed.

IX. Liu Shaoqi presided over this meeting, which probably indicates that Mao Zedong did not attend ([129]: August 1, 1967).

109

I. *June ?-28-?, 1958*
II. **NATIONAL CONFERENCE ON EDUCATIONAL WORK**
V. Study of the classics in full-time schools
VI. Lu Dingyi: Speech, June 28, 1958 (excerpt: [154]): it is not necessary that a classical work be "of the people" (*you renmin xing*) in order for students in the full-time schools to study it; few classical works could meet this type of qualification.
IX. This was one of two national education conferences convened in mid–1958. The other met in April 1958 ([14]: 440) (meeting 100).

110

I. *July 1958*
II. **MEETING OF THE SECRETARIAT OF THE CC CCP**
V. Party leadership
VI. Deng Xiaoping (excerpts: [77]: July 8, 1967; [216]: 3933: May 5, 1967: 10): the party committee at a given level has the primary responsibility for exercising party leadership at that level; should make clear that it is permissible to wear brightly colored clothes.
IX. All information on this meeting comes from the single Red Guard source cited above.

111

I. *July ?-11-16-?, 1958*
II. **NATIONAL UNITED FRONT WORK CONFERENCE**
V. United Front work; bloc affairs; international relations
VI. Deng Xiaoping: Speech, July 11, 1958 (excerpts: [53]: 17, 26, 49–50): nonparty people now may feel we are cooler toward them—should make efforts to overcome this through continued enthusiastic united front work; should use peaceful competition rather than fighting to defeat U.S. impe-

rialism; our opposition to Yugoslavia is good in that it sets up an "opposite" and therefore facilitates carrying out what amounts to an ideological rectification campaign within the Communist bloc.

Deng Xiaoping, July 15, 1958 (excerpts: [116]: June 14, 1967): socialism is the best guarantee of peace; Tito, American imperialism, and Japanese militarism are impressed only by strength; generally speaking, a third world war is not now in sight.

Deng Xiaoping, July 1958 (excerpts: [54]: 12–13): until now we could not raise some aspects of the question of religion with the Moslems—must wait until there is some popular demand to raise them before these can be settled.

Peng Zhen: Speech, July 16, 1958 (excerpts: [161]; [184]; [42]): we are now in the era of the final abolition of exploiting classes; industrial and commercial capitalists should utilize socialist forms of management but retain the spirit they had as private entrepreneurs; it is sometimes difficult to demarcate class origins—where it is unclear, therefore, a determination should not be made.

112

I.   *Mid- to late July or August 1958*
II.   **NATIONAL TELEPHONE CONFERENCE OF PROVINCIAL PARTY SECRETARIES**
IV.   Provincial party secretaries and some members of the CC Secretariat.
V.   Agricultural tool reform movement
VI.   Tan Zhenlin: Speech (mention: [194]: August 21, 1958): the main link in the current movement to improve farm tools is putting in ball bearings where appropriate, and the leaders of various regions should grasp this and mobilize the masses to effect it.
IX.   This meeting was the first of two telephone conferences with provincial party secretaries convened by the CC Secretariat. No information is available on the second conference. A July 13, 1958, joint CC CCP and State Council instruction to unfold a campaign to improve agricultural implements sparked the two conferences, which were convened to organize this effort and investigate the relevant conditions (mention: ibid.).

After this first telephone conference, Mao Zedong issued an instruction to the effect that each province should draw up a plan and make concrete arrangements regarding the movement to use ball bearings and reform farm tools (ibid.; [205]: 610: January 15, 1968: 20; [205]: 633: November 4, 1968: 12—the latter two sources mistakenly assert that Mao issued his instruction at the telephone conference itself). After Mao issued his instruction, the CC Secretariat convened separate telephone conferences of the provincial party secretaries of North China and of those of South China to hear reports and give instructions (mention: [194]: August 21, 1958).

Peng Zhen presided over this conference, and Tan Zhenlin presided over a subsequent telephone conference of provincial party secretaries devoted to the same subject (mention: ibid.).

113

I. *August 17–30, 1958*
II. **ENLARGED MEETING OF THE POLITBURO OF THE CC CCP ("BEIDAIHE CONFERENCE")**
III. Beidaihe, Hebei
IV. First secretaries of the CCP committees of all provinces, autonomous regions, and municipalities directly under the central government, responsible members of party organs in various relevant government departments, and members of the Politburo ([195]: 1959: 32; [216]: 1846: September 4, 1958: 1–2).
V. Great Leap Forward; people's communes; national economic plan for 1959; problems in current industrial production; commercial work; educational policy; militia work; health work; physical labor for cadres; foreign affairs; population growth
VI. Mao Zedong (mention: [170]: 86): affirms the continuing importance of class struggle under socialism; raises the issue of contradictions; discusses the current situation.

Mao Zedong: a series of talks (text: [289]):

August 17 (pp. 1–8): steel target may not be reached; Chen Yun and Li Xiannian are in charge of water conservation, and Li in charge of commercial purchasing and allocation; international situation: East wind has not yet prevailed over West wind; sets conference agenda.

August 19 (pp. 8–17): management system for industry; decentralize authority but improve planning; fantasizes about near and distant future.

August 21, a.m. (pp. 17–26): importance of fulfilling steel quota; leader-mass relations; replace wage system with former supply system; support of idealism and utopian socialism.

August 21, p.m. (pp. 27–38): grain production and rest time for peasants; better to mediate problems as they occur than to rely on law; every commune should have an airport and every province 100–200 planes (2 per county).

August 30, a.m. (pp. 38–51): collective ownership and the transition to communism; divide land into equal thirds for trees, grain, and fallow; by 1962, China's 700 million people should produce 700 million tons of steel; problems are due to socialism borrowed from Soviet Union and indigenous capitalism; CC members should spend one month per year in labor.

VII.   "Decision of the Party Center on the Question of Establishing People's Communes in the Rural Areas," August 29, 1958 (texts: [14]: 454–56; [194]: September 10, 1958; [195]: 1959: 32–34). "Directive of the Party Center on the Universal Unfolding of the Socialist and Communist Education Campaign in the Rural Areas During This Winter and Spring," August 29, 1958 (texts: [194]: September 11, 1958; [195]: 1959: 34; [216]: 1857: September 19, 1958: 1–3).

"Directive of the Party Center on Water Conservancy Work," August 29, 1958 (texts: [194]: September 11, 1958; [195]: 1959: 35; [216]: 1857: September 19, 1958: 4–6).

"Directive of the Party Center on Deep Plowing and Soil Improvement," August 29, 1958 (texts: [194]: September 11, 1958; [195]: 1959: 35–36; [216]: 1857: September 19, 1958: 7–8).

"Directive of the Party Center on the Fertilizer Question," August 29, 1958 (texts: [194]: September 11, 1958; [195]: 1959: 36–37; [216]: 1857: September 19, 1958: 9).

"Decision of the Party Center on Continuing to Unfold the Movement to Wipe Out the Four Pests," August 29, 1958 (texts: [194]: September 11, 1958; [195]: 1959: 37; [216]: 1857: September 19, 1958: 10).

"Eight-Point Charter in Agriculture" (mention: [166]: 132; [174]: 209): includes irrigation, fertilizer, soil improvement, seeds, close planting, crop protection, reform of farm tools, and field management.

Announcement of the Meeting, August 31, 1958 (texts: [195]: 1959: 32; [176]: August 31, 1958; [216]: 1846: September 4, 1958: 1–2).

IX.   As embodied in the above decisions and directives, this meeting put the sanction of the party center on the movement to form people's communes on a nationwide scale and called for a mass movement to increase production. The meeting decided that agricultural production was forging ahead well and therefore that the main emphasis should fall on increasing industrial output to the point where it could catch up with agricultural production. In the industrial sphere, the main emphasis should be on key projects. The meeting decided that the central issue in industry is iron and steel and machine-building, and the latter depends on the former two. Thus, the leaping development of iron and steel is both necessary and possible.

The Beidaihe meeting was preceded by more specialized conferences convened in preparation for the larger meeting. Several of the known specialized meetings in early August 1958 are:

—National Telephone Conference of the Provincial Party Committee Secretaries (meeting 112)—concerned with the movement to reform farm tools.

—National Conference of Public Security, Procuracy, and the Courts, August 2, 1958 (mention: [152])—a meeting on the political and legal system.

—National Forum on Party School Work, August 13, 1958 (mention: [237]).

On August 25–31, 1958, the Central Committee simultaneously convened a conference on industrial production with the participation of secretaries in charge of industry from the party committees of the various provinces, autonomous regions, and directly administered municipalities (mention: [195]: 1959: 32; [216]: 1846: September 4, 1958: 1–2).

On August 23, 1958, China began a heavy artillery bombardment of Quemoy and on August 28, 1958, Beijing warned of an imminent landing ([93]: 266–67). Mao dealt with this subject while at Beidaihe (mention: [167]: 258; [174]: 138).

Mao's speech on August 19 indicates that China had already sent troops to Vietnam by this time ([289]: 15).

Renmin ribao published an editorial entitled ''First Put Up the Framework of the People's Communes'' on September 10, 1958, to convey the spirit of the Beidaihe Conference.

114

I.   *Early September 1958*
II.   **ENLARGED MEETING OF THE POLITBURO OF THE CC CCP**
III.   Zhongnanhai, Beijing
IV.   Mao Zedong, Liu Shaoqi, Zhou Enlai, Zhu De, Zhang Wentian, Wang Bingnan, and others (Chen Yi did not attend).
V.   U.S.-China relations
VI.   Wang Bingnan: Speech (mention: Wang Bingnan's memoirs in *Shijie zhishi*, no. 5, March 1, 1985, tr. in [82]: March 28, 1985: B6): report on U.S.-China ambassadorial-level talks.
VIII. Meeting decided to appoint some people from the Ministry of Foreign Affairs to draft a new plan for U.S.-China talks, apparently the basis for Zhou's September 6, 1958, statement proposing new talks and an exchange of envoys.

115

I.   *September 5–9, 1958* (see IX below)
II.   **FIFTEENTH SUPREME STATE CONFERENCE**
III.   Beijing

IV.   Additional people attending each day for a total of 101 in attendance by the final session (name lists: [194]: September 6, 1958, September 7, 1958, September 9, 1958).

V.   Results of Beidaihe Conference; Taiwan Straits crisis; and international affairs.

VI.   Mao Zedong: Speech, September 5, 1958 (mention: [194]: September 6, 1958; text: [167]: 226–37): jubilantly assesses the progress and prospects of the Great Leap Forward (will surpass England in all but shipbuilding, cars, and electric power in two years, have already basically completed the 1956–1967 National Program for the Development of Agriculture); analyzes the following problem areas in foreign affairs: who fears war more—the United States or China (answer: United States); the nature of American forces (aggressive, but directed primarily against nationalism); the current tense situation (PRC wants relaxation, but tension is not all bad); withdrawal of U.S. forces from the Middle East; DeGaulle's rise to power in France and implications for the French Communist Party; the blockade of China (beneficial in that it encourages self-reliance); lack of diplomatic recognition of China (also encourages self-reliance); and the need to prepare to defend China against a U.S. war of aggression.

Tan Zhenlin: Report, September 5, 1958 (mention: [194]: September 6, 1958): discusses conditions of agricultural production in China this year, arrangements for agricultural production during this winter and next spring, people's communes, militia, and the patriotic sanitation movement centered on the elimination of the four pests.

Li Fuchun: Report, September 6, 1958 (mention: [194]: September 6 and 7, 1958): discusses this year's leap forward in industrial and agricultural production, the state construction plan for 1959, and the Second Five-Year Plan.

Zhou Enlai: Report, September 6, 1958 (mention: [253]: 18: September 25, 1958: 14; [194]: September 6 and 7, 1958): discusses foreign policy, centering on the current situation in the Taiwan Straits and the PRC's "Statement Concerning the Current Situation in the Taiwan Straits Area."

Mao Zedong: Speech, September 8, 1958 (summary: [194]: September 9, 1958; partial text: [167]: 237–41): Taiwan is now completely in America's grasp, and this includes Quemoy and Matsu; the tension is good for purposes of domestic mobilization; during the Second Five-Year Plan China will catch up to the United States in gross steel output; China should double 1958's grain output in 1959 (see IX below).

Li Xiannian: Report, September 8, 1958 (mention: [194]: September 9, 1958): discusses budget and revenue expenditures this year, presents a preliminary outline of the financial budget for 1959, and analyzes problems in commercial work.

Lu Dingyi: Report, September 8, 1958 (mention: ibid.): discusses work in education and problems of participation in labor by cadres.

Mao Zedong: Speech, September 9, 1958 (text: [167]: 241–45): must combine mental and manual labor; provides year-by-year figures for China's total income and basic investment for 1950–58, showing great increases in both for the Great Leap Forward; are now erecting the scaffolding for the people's communes and will resolve the detailed problems during the coming winter and spring; it is necessary now to grasp both industry (iron, steel, and machinery) and agriculture.

VIII. Authorized Zhou Enlai to issue his September 6, 1958, "Statement [of the PRC] Concerning the Current Situation in the Taiwan Straits Area" (mention: [194]: September 6, 1958; text of statement: [216]: 1851: September 11, 1958: 1–3).

IX. *Renmin ribao* ([194]: September 9, 1958) asserted that this conference concluded at 2:00 p.m. on September 8, 1958. It is unclear whether the September 9, 1958, session that Mao addressed was a secret final session of this conference or in fact amounted to a rump session of some of the people who had attended the formal conference that concluded on September 8.

This conference did not meet on September 7, 1958 (mention: [194]: September 7, 1958).

Li Xiannian's and Lu Dingyi's reports were originally scheduled to be delivered on September 6, 1958 (mention: [194]: September 6, 1958). They were evidently postponed until the September 8 session due to the time taken to discuss Zhou Enlai's September 6 statement mentioned above. The press does indicate that the September 6 session discussed this statement extensively before it was made public (mention: [194]: September 7, 1958).

This meeting was held at the height of the Taiwan Straits crisis. This crisis seems to have taken a turn for the worse on September 4, 1958. On September 6 Zhou Enlai offered to resume ambassadorial talks with the United States; this may have been the real turning point in the crisis ([93]: 267). Relatedly, the summary of Mao's September 8, 1958, speech given in the contemporary media ([194]: September 9, 1958) deviates from the partial text of this talk that became available during the Cultural Revolution ([167]: 237–41) only in the summary's inclusion of a paragraph omitted in the partial text on Mao's hopes about progress in the Warsaw talks in which he stated that these talks might lead to some results provided that both sides have a sincere desire to settle the issue.

116

I.   *November 2–10, 1958*
II.   **FIRST ZHENGZHOU MEETING**
III.   Zhengzhou, Henan
IV.   Some of the leading comrades of the party center and some of the leading comrades of the various localities ([43]: 542: December 29, 1958).
V.   Consolidation of the people's communes

Mao Zedong (excerpt: [167]: 247; [174]: 128): must lead the peasants step by step (instead of all at one stroke) toward ownership by the whole people.

Mao Zedong: Speech on Stalin's *Economic Problems of Socialism* (texts: [166]: 116–20; [167]: 247–51; [174]: 129–32): repeatedly advises caution in making changes in the rural areas and strongly opposes trying to do away with the law of value and the need for commodity exchange; affirms that "it is better to go slow" with respect to the transition to communism.

Mao Zedong (excerpt: [108]: 239): must correct deviations of egalitarianism and excessive centralism.

Mao Zedong (excerpt: [89]: 434): "bourgeois rights" of two kinds: relations among people and within financial and commercial system.

VII.   "Fifteen-Year Program" (mention: [167]: 265; [174]: 145)—this was then dropped at the Sixth Plenum of the Eighth CC CCP in December 1958 (meeting 120).

Formulated some measures to correct the deviations in the commune movement since the August 1958 Enlarged Politburo Meeting at Beidaihe (meeting 113) (mention: [43]: 590: September 9, 1959).

Put forward two slogans: "Big collective and small freedom" and "Grasp production and grasp livelihood" ([174]: 210).

Called on the provinces to study Stalin's *Economic Problems of Socialism*, *Textbook on Political Economy* (third edition), and *Marx, Engels, Lenin, and Stalin on the Communist Society* (mention: [167]: 262; [174]: 143).

IX.   This conference initiated a sustained period of critical examination of the strengths and weaknesses of the major tasks being performed, in reaction against the previous overly rosy attitude ([232]: 70: January 1970: 41). It marked the beginning of the correction of such leftist errors as the "communist wind" ([48]; [232]: 50: May 1968: 35).

This conference was convened personally by Mao Zedong ([43]: 542: December 29, 1958). It was preceded by nationwide inspection trips by the leaders ([1]: 78–79).

Mao vetoed a proposal by Chen Boda and others to eliminate commodity production and monetary exchange and implement allocation of goods without compensation (mention: [108]: 177; [89]: 315).

117

I.   *November 21–27, 1958*
II.   **EXPANDED MEETING OF THE POLITBURO OF THE CCP CC (WUCHANG MEETING)**
III. Wuchang, Hubei
IV.   Some of the leading comrades of the party center and the first secretaries of the party committees of the various provinces, municipalities, and autonomous regions ([43]: 542: December 29, 1958).
V.   Targets for 1959; consolidation of people's communes; Sixth Plenum of Eighth CC CCP
VI.   Mao Zedong: Speech(es?) (excerpts: [108]: 178; [89]: 317; [273]: 508): do not equate science with superstition when doing away with blind faith; Beidaihe resolution has deficiencies and must be corrected, e.g., next year's steel target is too high.

Wang Jiaxiang (mention: [194]: June 10, 1982, tr. in [82]: June 15, 1982: K11): submitted to the CC the correct view of not favoring the tendency to accomplish the transition to communism prematurely in the countryside.

VII. Made preparations for the Sixth Plenum of the Eighth CC CCP, which met immediately afterward (meeting 118) ([43]: 542: December 29, 1958).

Reduced steel output targets for 1959 from the 30 million tons set at Beidaihe in August (meeting 113) to 20 million tons ([166]: 244; [174]: 311).

Resolved to "seek truth from facts" (mention: [167]: 264; [174]: 144).

IX.   Mao Zedong subsequently commented that it was at this conference that he combined the revolutionary fervor of the August Beidaihe meeting (meeting 113) with practical spirit ([167]: 258; [174]: 138). At this meeting, he declared that planned production targets must be lowered (mention: [166]: 133; [174]: 210).

Mao Zedong personally convened this meeting ([43]: 542: December 29, 1958). The meeting clearly set the policy of scaling down the overly enthusiastic targets set in August in view of the intervening experience.

At about the time of this conference, Peng Dehuai toured the Hunan region and upon investigation found that production was decreasing instead of surging ahead there ([107]).

Mao Zedong wrote two letters on November 25, 1958, neither of which pertains directly to this meeting (texts: [167]: 245–47; [174]: 125–27).

118

I.   *November 28–December 10, 1958*
II.   **SIXTH (ENLARGED) PLENUM OF THE EIGHTH CC CCP**
III.   Wuchang, Hubei
IV.   Eighty-four members of the Central Committee and eighty-two alternate members of the Central Committee; leading comrades of various relevant departments of the CC; and first secretaries of party committees of various provinces, municipalities, and autonomous regions who are not themselves CC or alternate CC members ([14]: 483–86; [43]: 42: December 28, 1958; [61]: 113–20; [195]: 1959: 37–38; [213]: 1–11).
V.   People's communes; national economic plan for 1959; Mao Zedong relinquishing the post of chairman of the PRC; rural finance and trade administrative systems; international situation (ibid.)
VI.   Mao Zedong: Speech, December 9, 1958 (texts: [167]: 259–69; [174]: 140–48—mistakenly labeled as December 19, 1958): optimistic speech, but calling for consolidation, rectification, and the need to avoid exaggeration.
VII.   "Communique" (texts: [14]: 483–86; [43]: 42: December 28, 1958; [61]: 113–20; [195]: 1959: 37–38; [213]: 1–11).

        "Resolution on Some Questions Concerning the People's Communes," December 10, 1958 (texts: [14]: 488–502; [43]: 42: December 28, 1958; [61]: 123–48; [195]: 1959: 39–45; [213]: 12–49).

        "Decision Approving Comrade Mao Zedong's Proposal That He Will Not Stand as Candidate for Chairman of the People's Republic of China for the Next Term of Office," December 10, 1958 (texts: [14]: 487; [43]: 42: December 28, 1958; [61]: 121–22; [195]: 1959: 39; [213]: 50–51).

        "Decision on Improvement of the Financial and Trade Administration in the Rural Areas" (mention in "Communique"); on December 20, 1958, passed by CC CCP and State Council (texts: [61]: 619–27; [176]: December 22, 1958).
VIII.   Reduced the 1959 steel production target from thirty million to twenty million tons. This decision had actually been taken at the November 21–27, 1958, Wuchang Meeting (meeting 117). The "Communique" specified a target of eighteen million tons, but Mao noted that the real target figure was twenty million tons ([166]: 59; [174]: 179).

        Noted with satisfaction the great unity of the socialist camp headed by the Soviet Union ("Communique").
IX.   Chen Yun argued against announcing the 1959 targets for steel, coal,

grain, and cotton at this meeting (mention: [89]: 324).

On December 1, 1958, the Politburo held a meeting at Wuchang (meeting 120). This represents one of many instances where a small body meets at the same time as a larger body and serves, in essence, as the steering committee for the larger gathering.

On November 30, 1958, Mao Zedong addressed "Directors of Various Cooperative Areas" (texts: [167]: 251–55; [174]: 133–36). The substance of his remarks closely parallels the documentation of the Sixth Plenum, and it is clear from Mao's comments that this group had already been meeting for some days. Mao addressed the same group again on December 12, 1958 (texts: [167]: 256–58; [174]: 136–39) and discussed the results of the Sixth Plenum.

Convened a telephone conference of the provinces on December 10, 11, or 12, 1958, to explain the reasons for Mao Zedong's resignation as chairman of the PRC ([167]: 258, 268–69; [174]: 138, 148). Li Xiannian wrote an article on the improvement of financial and trade administration in rural areas following this meeting (texts: [75]: 158: March 1959: 27–36; [97]: 2: January 16, 1959: 1–8).

119

I.   *December 1958*
II. **SECRETARIAT OF THE CC CCP**
V.   Party leadership
VI. Deng Xiaoping (excerpt: [94]): asserts there can be no leadership by party committees if those committees fail to assert control over organs at corresponding levels.
IX. All information on this meeting comes from the single Red Guard source cited above.

120

I.   *December 1, 1958*
II.   **MEETING OF THE POLITBURO OF THE CC CCP**
III. Wuchang, Hubei
V.   International situation
VI.   Mao Zedong: Speech, "On the Question of Whether Imperialism and All Reactionaries Are Real Tigers" (text [or excerpt?]: [182]: 37–38: September 13, 1977: 7–8; excerpt: [193]: 72–74): must despise imperialism strategically and respect it tactically.
IX.   This meeting took place during the November 28-December 10, 1958, Sixth Plenum (meeting 118).

1959

121

I.   *Late December 1958–early January 1959*

II.   **ENLARGED MEETING OF THE SECRETARIAT OF THE CC CCP (?)**

V.   Summarize the three-month-long discussion about the rights of the bourgeoisie under the Great Leap Forward

VII.   "Summary" (mention: [248]).

VIII.   Zhang Chunqiao should write up the results of this meeting for publication in *Renmin ribao* (ibid.).

IX.   An article by Zhang Chunqiao on the rights of the bourgeoisie under socialism (text: [194]: October 13, 1958) led Mao Zedong to launch a three-month discussion of this issue. This meeting then convened to sum up this discussion. The meeting decided that the rights of the bourgeoisie could not be summarily abolished under socialism and that the wage system was not necessarily less progressive than is the free supply system. The meeting instructed Zhang Chunqiao to write up the conclusions for publication in *Renmin ribao*, but Zhang subsequently failed to do so ([248]).

Deng Xiaoping convened this meeting, and thus it probably assumed the form of an enlarged meeting of the Secretariat, although this is speculation. Hu Qiaomu also attended and allegedly played an important role (ibid.).

All information on this meeting comes from the single Red Guard source cited above. *Renmin ribao* carried a series of articles discussing the rights of the bourgeoisie under socialism during this period. Those for December 1958-January 1959 appear in [194]: December 3, 6, 12, 24, and 26, 1958, and January 3, 9, 20, 24, and 27, 1959, the last three appearing to resolve the issue along the lines suggested above.

122

I.   *January–March 1959*

II.   **NATIONAL EDUCATIONAL WORK CONFERENCE**

V.   Critical review of 1958 educational policy

VI.   Lu Dingyi: Speeches, February 1959 and March 1, 1959 (excerpts: [157]): need improvement rather than reform in education; the scope of attacks and criticism has been too broad; the party has now made a lot of enemies and has become isolated.

VIII.   "Advanced the principles" of laying emphasis on teaching, manifesting the leading role of teachers in pedagogical work, and establishing normal relationships between teachers and students (mention: [84]).

IX.   The Propaganda Department of the Central Committee convened this conference ([84]).

The conference reviewed the changes that had taken place in education during the course of 1958 and decided that the attack on former teachers had been too broad and not sufficiently focused. It thus decided to try to reestablish to a degree the authority of these teachers. The conference also touched on a wide range of related issues, such as part-work, part-study, as contrasted with full-time study ([157]).

123

I.   *January 12–26, 1959*

II.   **NATIONAL CONFERENCE OF DIRECTORS OF CCP RURAL WORK DEPARTMENTS**

III.   Beijing

IV.   Primarily, directors of people's communes and responsible personnel of CCP rural work departments at the province, municipality, and autonomous region levels; also attended by some central CCP leaders (mention: [216]: 1953: February 13, 1959: 1–3).

V.   Implementation of decisions of the November 28-December 10, 1958, Sixth Plenum of the Eighth CC CCP (meeting 118)

VI.   Tan Zhenlin and Deng Zihui (mention: ibid.): advocate leading the people's communes into a gigantic winter cultivation movement, centered on manure accumulation.

VIII.   All of the following decisions are mentioned in ibid.:

—Must oppose any underestimation of the determination and driving vigor of the masses.

—Must promote a high tide in production and a mass emulation movement of the communist style that tempers competition with mutual concern and assistance.

—Communes should draw up four sets of plans: a three- to five-year long-range construction plan; an annual plan; a quarterly plan; and a short-period or monthly plan.

—Should institute a quota and responsibility system to improve labor productivity.

—The various areas should study, diffuse, and implement the resolutions of the November 28-December 10, 1958, Sixth Plenum of the Eighth CC CCP (meeting 118).

IX.   This conference was convened by the Rural Work Department of the CC CCP.

This conference began with an analysis of the rural conditions following the introduction of the commune system; it then proceeded with discussions on measures to achieve a still greater leap forward in rural work in 1959, emphasizing using the experiences gained in 1958 to strengthen commune management. The conference concentrated on the questions of utilization of manpower, raising of productivity, renovation of techniques, and achievement of the production increases scheduled for grain and cotton with simultaneous regard for the overall development of agriculture, forestry, animal husbandry, subsidiary occupations, and fisheries. It also discussed questions of communal structure, finance, and democratic life (mention: ibid.).

This is likely to be the January 1959 "Beijing Conference" referred to in a number of other sources (e.g.: [170]: 45; [174]: 185, 311). Two nonparty conferences preceded this meeting: the December 25, 1958–January 1, 1959, National Conference of Advanced Units in the Socialist Construction of Agriculture; and the January 2–3, 1959, National Agricultural Work Conference ([195]: 1959: 436–38).

124

I. *February ?–2–?, 1959*
II. **CONFERENCE OF PROVINCIAL AND MUNICIPAL CCP COMMITTEE SECRETARIES**
V. Great Leap Forward in 1959 (also, see IX below)
VI. Mao Zedong: Speech, February 2, 1959 (texts: [167]: 271–79; [174]: 151–58): recognizes the defects of work in 1958 and admits particular ignorance of the questions of "planned and proportionate development"; at the same time, must retain the spirit of 1958 and launch another leap forward in 1959, having learned from past experiences; should now have a speed up after the lull of December–January.
IX. Mao Zedong anticipated this conference in his December 12, 1958, talk with directors of various cooperative areas ([167]: 257; [174]: 137–38), at which time he specified the agenda as examining the two resolutions of the November 28–December 10, 1958, Sixth Plenum of the Eighth CC CCP (meeting 118); reorganizing the state structure (to allow for the existence of people's communes as the basic-level state organs); preparing a report for the mid-April 1959 National People's Congress (meeting 132); and discussing the question of education. It is not possible to tell how many of these things were actually discussed at this conference. Mao anticipated that this conference would convene on February 1, 1959, in either Beijing, Shanghai, or Chengdu. On July 14, 1959, Peng Dehuai referred to this conference as having convened in January 1959 ([216]: 4032: October 2, 1967: 4).

125

I.   *Early February 1959*
II.   **NATIONAL CONFERENCE ON COMMUNICATIONS WORK**
V.   Communications work during 1959
VIII.   Passed a four-point program—concentrating on technological innovation, organization, construction, and revamping and consolidation of the building corps for communication and postal services—to cope with the tasks imposed by the Great Leap Forward for 1959 (mention: [43]: 593: September 22, 1959: 18; [216]: 1964: March 3, 1959: 3–4).
IX.   This conference was convened by the Communications Work Department of the CC CCP and met at the same time as a National Conference of Directors of Communications, convened by the Ministry of Communications to deal with the same set of issues (mention: ibid.).

   This conference also studied a series of other questions dealing with the role the party plays in the guidance of transportation enterprises. It emphasized applying the concept that "the whole nation is a single chessboard" (mention: [216]: 1964: March 3, 1959: 4).

   This conference was followed up by a telephone conference on April 10, 1959, addressed by Zeng Shan, director of the CC CCP Communications Work Department ([216]: 2003: April 30, 1959: 20).

126

I.   *February 27–March 5, 1959*
II.   **ENLARGED MEETING OF THE POLITBURO OF THE CC CCP ("SECOND ZHENGZHOU MEETING")**
III.   Zhengzhou, Henan
IV.   Twenty central leaders and twenty-seven provincial, municipal, and autonomous region party secretaries.
V.   Rectification of commune organization and policy
VI.   Mao Zedong: Speeches, February 27, 1959 (twice); February 28, 1959; March 1, 1959; March 5, 1959; and March 1959 (texts: [166]: 8–49; text of second February 27, 1959, speech also in [167]: 279–88; brief and misleading excerpts: [170]: 22–24): these speeches so greatly overlap and interweave that they are best summarized together. The three speeches of February 27 and 28 are so repetitious that they were probably made to separate small groups at Zhengzhou. The basic analysis is as follows: Regardless of the claims for an outstanding 1958 harvest, state purchases were in fact quite poor, and shortages appeared from November 1958 to February 1959. After investigation, it is clear that the problem lies in the ownership system in the communes. Currently, the commune and higher

levels appropriate too much in the form of labor and goods, thus making basic-level cadres unhappy and alienating the peasants, thereby creating an incentive for both to connive to cheat the state. The basic-level cadres and peasants are completely correct. The situation can be remedied by making the team the basic level for accounting and allocation of work and pay; decreasing the range of areas in which communes and higher levels have authority, including the amount of industry they run; insisting on fair compensation for all requisitioned goods and making less use of corvée labor; demanding less for accumulation and paying out more in wages; and stressing the need for continuing income inequality and continuing use of material incentives. Twelve slogans ([166]: 35) sum up Mao's program. Mao clearly is arguing against strong opposition at this conference, as indicated by such remarks as "I am speaking for 10 million cadres at the level of production team head and for 500 million peasants. If you do not join me in firmly and thoroughly carrying out right opportunism [as opposed to the left adventurism against which he is arguing], I will carry it out thoroughly alone, even to the point of giving up my party membership" ([166]: 41). Still, Mao's speeches continue to be suffused with an air of great optimism about the Great Leap Forward and the communes in terms of basic line and production possibilities.

Mao: written remarks (mention: [89]: 321): some of 1958's mistakes were due to left adventurism (written in response to Shanxi's criticism of localism regarding the consolidation of communes).

VIII. Meeting drafted "Some Provisions on the Management System of the People's Communes" (mention: [108]: 182; [283]: 239); approved the policy of consolidation and establishment of communes, summarized by fourteen slogans (mention: [89]: 321-22).

Circulated the minutes of this meeting, called for the immediate convening of six-level cadre conferences at the provincial, municipal, and special district levels by the respective party committees to study and discuss these documents, and scheduled another enlarged Politburo meeting to convene in Shanghai (it met on March 25-April 1, 1959 [meeting 129]) to further this discussion on the basis of the results of the local meetings that had been held ([166]: 104-105; [174]: 164-65). Additional information on these local meetings is available in [166]: 50, 106-107; [174]: 163, 166-67.

127

I.   *March ?-7-?, 1959*
II.   **FOREIGN AFFAIRS CONFERENCE**
V.   Foreign affairs; ownership system in agriculture

VI.   Chen Yi: Speech, March 7, 1959 (excerpt: [67]): neglect of the small collective ownership system in favor of ownership by the whole people wrongs the peasants and sets them against the production teams—peasants are still peasants with a two-faced nature to a degree, just as foreigners are still foreigners.

   All information on this meeting comes from the single Red Guard source cited above.

   It is not clear that this is a party meeting.

   This meeting convened in the midst of the February 27–March 10, 1959, Enlarged Meeting of the Politburo at Zhengzhou (meeting 126), although it seems likely that this meeting convened in Beijing.

128

I.   *"Not long after the Second Zhengzhou Meeting"* (*probably mid-March 1959*).
II.   **SECRETARIAT OF THE CC CCP**
V.   Problems in communes
VI.   Deng Xiaoping (mention: [248]): the communes still have many problems in production and construction and are plagued by confusion, empty boasting, blind command, and numbers inflation at all levels. The budget and economics committees should do research to better specify these problems and suggest solutions for discussion at the next Central Work Conference.
VIII.   Directed Wu Lengxi to have the New China News Agency collect materials on the problems of the communes and publish these in the *Cankao ziliao* (Internal Reference Materials) for cadres (ibid.).
IX.   All information on this meeting comes from the single Red Guard source cited above.

129

I.   *March 25–April 1 or 2, 1959*
II.   **ENLARGED MEETING OF THE POLITBURO OF THE CC CCP**
III.   Shanghai
IV.   First secretaries of provincial, municipal, and special district party committees (among others?) ([166]: 104; [174]: 164]).
V.   Preparations for the April 2–5, 1959, Seventh Plenum of the Eighth CC CCP (meeting 130); 1959 economic targets; policy toward communes
VI.   Mao Zedong: Speech (mention: [43]: 851: April 26, 1968: 13).

   Mao: Speech (summary: [89]: 323): must settle old accounts to satisfy the masses in communes; should study Hai Rui; suggests policy of giving production teams some ownership.

Zhang Wentian: Speech (mention: [249]: 296): discusses the problem of abnormal inner-party work style.

VIII. Further reduced the 1959 steel production target from the 20 million tons that had de facto been set at the Sixth Plenum of the Eighth CC CCP (meeting 118) to 16.5 million tons ([166]: 244; [174]: 311).

Adopted eighteen articles, criticized the "Mazheng" report, and determined that the state would make reimbursement and indemnification [for items requisitioned by the communes?], according to a subsequent statement by Mao Zedong ([166]: 263; [174]: 242).

IX. "Many comrades" discussed the need to speak the truth about the experience of the Great Leap Forward (mention: [89]: 363).

This conference followed a series of meetings in the provinces that had been called for by the Enlarged Politburo meeting at Zhengzhou on February 27-March 5, 1959 (meeting 126). Its agenda focused on discussing and resolving the problems that had arisen in these meetings so as to hammer out a unified line that could then serve as the basis for a major leap forward commencing in April 1959. There is little concrete information on what actually transpired at this conference, other than that it continued the process of rectifying the communes (e.g., [232]: 70: January 1, 1970: 46). This conference prepared for the Seventh Plenum of the Eighth CC CCP (meeting 130), which convened in Shanghai on April 2-5, 1959, and the actions of the plenum presumably were decided at this preceding conference.

Purportedly, at this meeting Bo Yibo argued for higher steel targets in a covert attempt to wreck the Great Leap Forward. Similar assertions were made about Bo's activities at the November 21-27, 1958, Wuchang Meeting (meeting 117) ([102]). At this conference, Peng Dehuai attacked Mao Zedong's assuming command in person, asserting that such command meant disregarding the Standing Committee of the Politburo (mention: [43]: 851: April 26, 1968: 13).

Xue Muqiao and Sun Yefang convened a follow-up conference for discussing economic theories. This conference met in Shanghai on April 3-22, 1959 ([217]: 206: October 6, 1967: 26). This conference, attended by some central leaders, presages the more regular use of "brain trusts" during the early 1960s to work on specific aspects of policy.

130

I. *April 2-5, 1959*
II. **SEVENTH (ENLARGED) PLENUM OF THE EIGHTH CC CCP**
III. Shanghai
IV. Eighty-one members and eighty alternate members of the CC CCP; lead-

ing comrades of various departments of the CC and first secretaries of the party committees of the various provinces, municipalities, and autonomous regions who are not either full or alternate members of the CC.

V.   The 1959 Economic Plan; nominations for leading positions in state organs; overhaul of the people's communes

VI.   Mao Zedong: Speech (partial text: [166]: 51–53; [174]: 175–77; [216]: 4000: August 14, 1967: 22): on work methods: stresses the need for planning, for allowing a reserve and slack resources, and for continuing to foster criticism.

Mao: Speech (mention: [194]: December 26, 1981, tr. in [82]: January 4, 1982: K9; mention: [108]: 260; [273]: 511): emphasizes resourcefulness over decisiveness, but opposes arbitrary decisions without analysis of overall situation; criticizes boastfulness of cadres and fear of speaking truth in 1958; should study Hai Rui.

Mao Zedong (mention: [194]: October 3, 1980, tr. in [82]: October 6, 1980; [9]: December 21, 1978, tr. in [82]: December 27, 1978: E21): criticism of patriarchal tendencies in the party.

Zhang Wentian: Speech (summary: [249]: 309): develop inner-party democracy; study Hai Rui; dare to speak out, do not fear admonition, demotion, loss of face, expulsion from party, divorce, or death.

VII.   "Communique" (texts: [61]: 149–50; [194]: April 8, 1959; [195]: 1959: 45; [216]: 1991: April 13, 1959: 5–6): mentions the following decisions taken:

—Adopted and decided to submit to the April 18–28, 1959, First Session of the Second NPC (meeting 132) a draft plan for the development of the national economy in 1959.

—Laid down specific measures for the continued overhaul of the people's communes.

—Decided on nominations for leading posts in state organs to be submitted to the First Session of the Second NPC (meeting 132).

IX.   The nominations to leading state posts included Liu Shaoqi's replacement of Mao Zedong as Chairman of the People's Republic of China.

Li Fuchun's report on the draft plan for development of the national economy in 1959 presented at the First Session of the Second NPC gives the essential details of that plan (text: [195]: 1959: 101–106). It seems clear that this plenum sanctioned and legitimized the series of policy proposals that had been raised at the February 27–March 5, 1959, Second Zhengzhou Meeting (meeting 126), discussed in local meetings, and then reviewed at the March 25–April 1, 1959, Enlarged Politburo meeting in Shanghai (meeting 129). The final proposal that emerged regarding the communes evidently made production brigades the basic accounting units instead of the teams Mao Zedong had proposed at Second Zhengzhou. It also, however, included Mao's stress on the need for a closer fit between labor and remuneration and on the need to concentrate more on agriculture within the communes (analysis in [1]: 86–87).

Before this meeting, Mao issued four inner-party circulars to oppose leftist tendencies such as boasting and exaggeration (mention: [194]: December 26, 1981, tr. in [82]: January 4, 1982: K9).

131

I.   *April 15, 1959*
II.   **SIXTEENTH SUPREME STATE CONFERENCE**
IV.   106 persons, comprising leaders of the state, members of the National Committee of the Chinese Communist Party, the various democratic parties and people's organizations, and prominent figures from various circles.
V.   Appointments to government positions; foreign affairs; internal unity
VI.   Mao Zedong: Speech (texts: [166]: 54–57; [167]: 289–92): discusses the 1958 Taiwan Straits crisis and the current Tibet crisis; calls for greater unity in the country, less criticism of rightists, and greater respect for teachers in the schools—overall, asserts that the situation is better than in 1957 and thus that there need not be the tensions of that year in handling the question of rightism.

Xerab Gyaco (vice-chairman of Qinghai government, member of CPPCC, and other posts): Speech (mention: [194]: December 19, 1980, tr. in [82]: January 13, 1981: L12): expresses support for suppression of Tibet rebellion.
VIII. Agreed that the list of candidates for state positions would be submitted as recommendations to the joint meeting of the Presidium of the current NPC session and heads and vice-heads of groups of deputies.

132

I.   *April 18–28, 1959*
II.   **FIRST SESSION OF THE SECOND NPC**
III.   Beijing
VI.   Zhou Enlai: "Report on the Government's Work," April 18, 1959 (text: [195]: 1959: 89–101).

Li Fuchun: "Report on the Draft of the 1959 National Economic Plan," April 21, 1959 (text: ibid.: 1959: 101–106).

Li Xiannian: "Report on the 1958 State Budget and the 1959 Draft State Budget," April 21, 1959 (text: ibid.: 107–10).

Peng Zhen: "Work Report of the Standing Committee of the NPC of the PRC," April 20, 1959 (text: ibid.: 110–11).

Zeng Shan: "Investigation Report of the Budget Committee of the Second NPC on the 1958 State Budget and the Draft 1959 State Budget" (text: ibid.: 111–12).

Other minor reports: (texts: ibid.: 112).

VII. "Decisions of the First Session of the Second NPC of the PRC on the Government Work Report, the 1959 National Economic Plan, the 1958 State Budget, and the Draft 1959 State Budget," April 28, 1959 (text: ibid.: 112–13).

"Decision on the Question of Tibet," April 28, 1959 (text: ibid.: 113).

"Decision on the Abolition of the Ministry of Justice and the Procuracy Ministry," April 21, 1959 (text: ibid.: 114).

Other minor decisions: (texts: ibid.: 114).

VIII. Elected people to leading state organs—including the selection of Liu Shaoqi to replace Mao Zedong as Chairman of the PRC ([216]: 2003: April 30, 1959: 1–3).

IX. The April 2–5, 1959, Seventh Plenum of the Eighth CCP (meeting 130) decided to nominate Liu Shaoqi to replace Mao Zedong as Chairman of the PRC.

133

I. *April 17–29, 1959*
II. **FIRST SESSION OF THE THIRD CPPCC**
III. Beijing
VI. Li Weihan: "Work Report of the Standing Committee of the Second CPPCC" (text: [195]: 1959: 122–23).

Other minor reports: (texts: ibid.: 124).

VII. "Political Decision of the First Session of the Third CPPCC," April 29, 1959 (text: ibid.: 124–25).

VIII. Elected Mao Zedong as honorary chairman, Zhou Enlai as chairman, thirteen others as vice-chairmen (mention: [273]: 513; [108]: 184).

IX. This meeting was held simultaneously (and to a large extent jointly) with the First Session of the Second NPC (meeting 111).

134

I. *April 29–30, 1959*
II. **MEETING OF THE SECRETARIAT OF THE CC CCP**
VIII. Instructed the Central Financial and Economics Small Group to study

three issues: divide the steel target into a reliable one and one to strive for; steel distribution for 1959 should be on the basis of the reliable target; if the amount of distributed steel decreases, some production items will have to be reduced (mention: [135]: 117).

135

I.   *May 11, 1959*
II.   **MEETING OF THE POLITBURO OF THE CC CCP**
IV.   Mao Zedong apparently absent.
V.   Steel, Great Leap Forward
VI.   Chen Yun: Speech, ''The Problem of Making Practicable the Steel Target,'' May 11, 1959 (text: [135]: 117–26; [28]: 120–29): discusses plans to reduce the steel target set at April's Seventh Plenum (meeting 130) and to establish a reliable target as well as an ideal target; describes technical and supply problems that make current target unreasonable.
IX.   Chen Yun's proposal was also contained in a letter (text: [135]: 127–28; [28]: 130–31) to Mao Zedong (which implies his absence); CC and Mao accepted Chen's advice.

       [89]: 324 describes an almost identical meeting but says Chen proposed lowering the steel target from 16.5 million tons (the precise target set at the Seventh Plenum was 18 million tons, of which 16.5 million tons was to be of good quality).

       [273]: 513 also mentions that Chen proposed at a Politburo meeting that the steel target be lowered to 13 million tons, but does not specify when he made the proposal.

136

I.   *May 28, 1959*
II.   **SECRETARIAT OF THE CC CCP**
V.   Decline in the quality of products
VI.   Bo Yibo (excerpt: [5]): laments the decline in quality of light industrial production and decline in quality of periodicals.
IX.   The only information on this meeting comes from the Red Guard source cited above, and this source is somewhat ambivalent about whether Bo Yibo made his comments at this or another meeting of the Secretariat of the CC.

137

I.   *June 18–23, 1959*
II.   **CONFERENCE ON NONSTAPLE FOOD AND HANDICRAFT PRODUCTION IN THE CITIES**
        (convened by the CC CCP)
III.   Shanghai
IV.   165 people, including responsible persons of the interested departments of the CC CCP and the State Council, secretaries of the CCP municipal committees of thirty-seven big and medium-sized cities, and responsible persons of relevant departments (mention: [216]: 2049: July 7, 1959: 14–15).
V.   Nonstaple food and handicraft production in the cities
VI.   Li Xiannian (mention: ibid.). Ke Qingshi: Speech (mention: ibid.).
VIII.   Adopted a directive calling for self-reliance supplemented by outside help in solving the supply of nonstaple food in cities (summary: ibid.): called for cultivation of vegetables in nearby suburban areas and for a wider variety of nonstaple foods in the more outlying suburban areas. Adopted a directive on energetically restoring and developing handicraft production in respect to variety, quality, and quantity of products (summary: ibid.): called for strengthening leadership over handicraft production through transferring back a part of the cadres who have previously been transferred out of this field of work.
IX.   Li Xiannian presided over this conference. The conference was convened because the supply of nonstaple foods in the cities had been insufficient recently (mention: ibid.).

138

I.   *July 2–August 1, 1959*
II.   **LUSHAN CONFERENCE**
III.   Lushan, Jiangxi
IV.   Deng Xiaoping and Chen Yun were absent ([1]: 88–97); Peng Dehuai may have absented himself for most of the period after July 14, 1959 ([188]: 59).
V.   Rectification of communes; the Peng-Huang-Zhang-Zhou rightist clique
VI.   Mao Zedong: "Important Instructions," June 29 and July 2, 1959 (texts: [166]: 63–65; [174]: 182–84): need better balance, less anarchy, higher quality, and less egalitarianism; should pursue an agriculture first policy.
        Mao Zedong: Opening Speech, July 2, 1958 (summaries: [273]: 515; [108]: 186; [89]: 326–27): accomplishments are bountiful, problems are

not few, the future is bright; main lesson of Great Leap Forward is that it is unbalanced; affirms Chen Yun's proposal first to handle markets and then to handle capital construction; cadres at prefect level and above should study the Soviet Union's "Textbook on Political Economy" to understand the problems of socialist economic development and the laws of economic development.

Peng Dehuai: Comments at meetings of the Northwest Group, July 3–4 and 6–10 (excerpts: [19]: 1–5, 393–95; [41]; [46]: 24–26; [232]: 50: May 1, 1968: 31–32; [273]: 515–16): Mao Zedong's leadership style and errors are the source of much of the difficulty that the Great Leap Forward has encountered.

Liu Shaoqi: (mention: [136]: 63; [181]: 97: June 1, 1985, tr. in [82]: June 3, 1985: W26): too much talk of accomplishments when a thorough discussion of shortcomings is needed; central authorities and *Renmin ribao* each deserve half the blame for problems encountered.

Mao Zedong: Speech, July 10, 1959 (partial texts: [170]: 44–45; [206]: 21: April 2, 1968: 10): it is necessary to have an accurate view of errors; the General Line has been and remains correct.

Zhu De: Speech to Central China delegates (mention: [194]: August 1, 1983, tr. in [82]: August 8, 1982: K12); [194]: December 4, 1984, tr. in [82]: December 13, 1984: K7): supports allowing peasants to engage in family sideline production as a means of getting rich.

Peng Dehuai: "Letter of Opinion," July 14,1959 (texts: [185]; 281–87; [19]: 7–13, 397–401; [43]: 851: April 26,1968: 19–23; [216]: 4032: October 2, 1967: 1–5; [48]; [232]: 48: March 1, 1968: 42–44): addressed personally to Mao Zedong; critically reviews the Great Leap Forward to date and contains a number of subtle jibes at Mao's leadership itself.

Mao Zedong: written comments on Peng's letter (excerpts: [273]: 517): orders Peng's letter copied and distributed to all attending conference.

Huang Kecheng: Speech, July 17 or 19, 1959 (mention: [273]: 517; [89]: 331): commune system is excellent but last year it was not handled well from a short-term point of view.

Zhou Xiaozhou: Speech, July 19, 1959 (mention: [273]): this conference should stress summing up experience after affirming accomplishments; expresses support for Peng Dehuai's letter.

Zhang Wentian: Speech, July 21, 1959 (text: [265]: 480–506; mention: [46]; [273]: 517; [89]: 331–32): long speech to a meeting of North China Bureau: affirms accomplishments of Great Leap Forward and analyzes causes of mistakes: subjectivism and onesidedness; politics and economics; relationship between three kinds of ownership; democracy and centralism; supports Peng Dehuai's opinions; criticizes the way the Lushan meeting is being run.

Ke Qingshi: Speech, July 21, 1959 (mention: [249]: 315): supports Zhang Wentian's speech at same meeting Zhang addressed.

Mao Zedong: Speech, July 23, 1959 (partial texts: [19]: 15–26, 405–12; [110]: 6: 7: April 1970: 80–86; [166]: 67–71; [167]: 294–305; [201]: 131–46; [232]: 50: May 1, 1958: 32–35, 40–41; [170]: 27–43—p. 42 in the last-named source mistranslates "may take twenty five-year plans" to read "may take a twenty-five year plan"; some additional excerpts in [33]: I: 20: July 24, 1968: 28–30; [46]; [273]: 517; [89]: 332): strident and aggressive, this speech cuts out the middle ground, asserts that all must take a stand either for or against the Great Leap and the communes, and declares that some people have committed right opportunist errors and that others must now separate themselves from the erring few; after this, meeting shifts to criticism of Peng, Huang, Zhang, and Zhou.

Mao Zedong: "Comment on a Letter of Opinion from Li Zhongyun," July 26, 1959 (texts: [170]: 47–51; [166]: 72–75; [232]: 70: January 1, 1970: 41–42): Mao regards this "comment" as a supplement to his July 23, 1959, speech; responding to a very critical letter from Li, Mao asserts that Li, like many others, overestimates the errors of the Great Leap Forward but that, unlike most others, Li is at least open in his criticism; the center and the provincial, municipal, and autonomous region party committees should discuss this letter. Mao Zedong: "Comment on Three Documents," July 29, 1959 (text: [166]: 76): calls for circulation of Khrushchev's July 18, 1959, denunciation of the communes and two other documents and for discussion and evaluation of Khrushchev's prediction.

Mao Zedong: "Critique of Peng Dehuai's July 14, 1959, Letter of Opinion" (excerpts: [170]: 25–26): scathing critique of Peng's letter as right opportunist and antiparty.

VII. Revised draft of "On the Situation and Tasks—Minutes of the July 2, 1959-? Lushan Meeting" (mention: [273]: 517).

VIII. Decided to convene the Eighth Plenum of the Eighth CC CCP (meeting 141). Decided to launch a nationwide antirightist campaign (inferred from [13]: 96–97; [19]: 323, 491).

IX. Mao gave a talk on June 29, 1959, that was very similar to his opening address (mention: [89]: 328).

A detailed chronology of this meeting is contained in [273]: 515–17. For additional details on informal discussions that took place during this conference, see: [136].

It appears that the party center originally convened this meeting to review the results of the new initiatives that were decided upon in April 1959 with a view to continuing the consolidation work in the communes (mention: [216]: 3937: May 11, 1967: 2). Mao Zedong was evidently taken aback when he read the minutes of many of the small group meetings and when he received Peng Dehuai's July 14 letter. He decided that this amounted to an attack on his personal leadership and decided to draw the line clearly. This in turn forced the Chairman to turn his attention at least partly away from antileftism and consolidation of the communes (although the latter continued on his agenda) and to launch an antirightist campaign, allegedly to his chagrin ([166]: 259, 265; [174]: 238, 243).

There is a substantial body of unverified statements about the preparations for this conference by various individuals and the actions of major figures during the course of the meeting. The most important are:

—Liu Shaoqi, at one of the small group meetings early in the conference, criticized NCNA and *Renmin ribao* for reporting statements by central leaders as they toured the provinces—these statements were not mature and should not have been publicized ([248]). This criticism clearly reflected upon Mao Zedong's famous statement that "people's communes are good," which he said on a tour of Henan and which then received national publicity.

—Wu Lengxi supported Peng Dehuai by collecting information for him before Lushan and by expressing essential agreement with him at one of the small group meetings after Peng's July 14 Letter of Opinion was circulated. Wu was criticized and had to make a self-examination ([206]: 196: August 3, 1967: 22).

—Bo Yibo went to Lushan prepared to give a speech against the Three Red Banners, which Xue Muqiao and Sun Yefang had drafted for him. He dropped this, however, in favor of a speech supporting the Three Red Banners when he saw Peng Dehuai being crushed at this meeting ([206]: 207: October 17, 1967: 13).

—He Long supported Peng Dehuai at Lushan ([225]: January 28, 1967).

—Jin Ming, at that time the minister of finance, supplied Huang Kecheng with the materials that Huang used to attack the Great Leap Forward at Lushan ([69]). The Lushan Conference specified the existence of an antiparty "military clique" led by Peng Dehuai, Huang Kecheng, Zhang Wentian, and Zhou Xiaozhou. Peng Dehuai's confession at the August 2–16, 1959, Eighth Plenum of the Eighth CC CCP (meeting 139) illuminates the roles of the latter three during the course of the Lushan Conference (partial texts: [19]: 31–38, 417–21; [46]; [232]: 50: May 1, 1968: 38–40). One source ([43]: 851: April 26, 1968: 14) also places Tan Zheng in this clique.

Short excerpts from Peng Dehuai's July 14, 1959, "Letter of Opinion" that do not appear in the "complete texts" cited above are given in several sources (e.g.: [217]: 220: March 8, 1968: 27).

Ye Jianying later recalled that he, Liu Shaoqi, Zhou Enlai, and Deng Xiaoping all originally supported Peng but were persuaded by Mao to join him in attacking "the hapless Peng" (speech to Third Plenum, December 1978: [110]: May 1980: 77). For Peng's own recollections on this meeting, see [185].

During the Lushan Conference, the Central Committee received and disseminated a report from the Anshan Steelworks that advocated the Great Leap Forward, opposed rightist tendencies, and proposed high targets. Anshan had previously stayed aloof from the Great Leap Forward, and thus Mao received this report with considerable satisfaction ([166]: 249; [174]: 230; [194]: March 22, 1977, in [82]: March 22, 1977: E1).

139

I.   *August 2–16, 1959*

II.   **EIGHTH (ENLARGED) PLENUM OF THE EIGHTH CC CCP**

III.   Lushan, Jiangxi

IV.   Seventy-five full and seventy-four alternate members of the CC CCP and fourteen or fifteen others working in relevant departments of the CC CCP and in provincial, municipal, and autonomous region party committees ([14]: 533–36; [61]: 151–56; [73]).

V.   Peng-Huang-Zhang-Zhou rightist clique; the economy; consolidation of communes; foreign affairs

VI.   Mao Zedong: Speech, August 2, 1959 (partial (?) texts: [19]: 27–30, 413–15; [170]: 60–63; [232]: 50: May 1, 1968: 35–36): calls again for doing away with unrealistic targets; explains the right opportunist attack during the previous month.

Mao Zedong: "Letter to Zhang Wentian," August 2, 1959 (text: [170]: 54–55): chides Zhang and asserts Mao will not meet with him for a while yet; calls on Zhang to "rectify painfully."

Mao Zedong, "Comment on the Document 'The Status of Tens of Mess Halls of Daozhu Brigade, Danling Commune, Pingjiang Xian, Hunan, Which Have Been Dissolved and Then Restored,'" August 5, 1959 (texts: [19]: 317–18, 485–86; [170]: 64–65): notes that the moral is that one must not capitulate in the face of difficulties.

Mao Zedong: "Comments on 'The Status of Wang Guofan Commune Has Always Been Good' and 'Who Are the People in Rural Villages Who Have More Complaints?'" August 6, 1959 (texts: [19]: 319, 487; [170]: 66): each special district should find one or more communes that can serve as models like the Wang Guofan commune and then study and propagate their experiences; the latter document is related to "those people who have made more complaints at Lushan now."

Mao Zedong: "Comment on the 'Report' Concerning the Dissolution of Wuwei Xian Mess Halls by Order of Zhang Kaifan, Secretary of the Secretariat of the Anhui Party Committee," August 10, 1959 (texts: [19]: 321–22, 489; [170]: 67–68): Zhang Kaifan is an example of a provincial-level rightist.

Mao Zedong: Instruction, August 10, 1959 (text: [166]: 85; [167]: 306–307); There are right opportunists in the Central Committee (e.g., the "Military Club") and in the provinces (e.g., Anhui's Zhang Kaifan), and they organize intraparty factions to spread their influence; these people have connections with Gao Gang; they must be quickly exposed but can be saved through thought reform (because they have a dual nature—reactionary and revolutionary); must be stern in criticism and lenient in treatment—i.e., must give them a way out.

Mao Zedong: "Comment on the Report on Liaoning Province Carrying Out the CC CCP's Directive to Oppose Right Deviation," August 12, 1959 (partial texts: [19]: 323, 491): details Liaoning's rapid and concrete steps to carry out an antirightist campaign.

Mao Zedong, Speech, August 15, 1959 (excerpt: [194]: March 12, 1971).

Mao Zedong: "Forward to *Empiricism or Marxism-Leninism*," August 15, 1959 (texts: [19]: 325–27, 493–94; [170]: 72; [166]: 87): calls for cadres to read the third edition of *The Small Dictionary of Philosophy* and the *Textbook of Political Economy* during the coming two years.

Mao Zedong: "Comments on 'How a Marxist Should Correctly Deal with the Revolutionary Mass Movement,'" August 15, 1959 (text: [170]: 70–71): a bitter attack on his accusers.

Mao Zedong: "Concerning Mei Cheng's 'Qifa,'" August 16, 1959 (texts: [170]: 56–59; [167]: 310–12; [232]: 50: May 1, 1968: 37–38): this poem should be circulated; it illustrates well the utility of the CCP's practice of rectification (Mao had referred to this poem in his August 2, 1959, letter to Zhang Wentian).

Mao Zedong: "The Origins of Machine Guns and Mortars, Etc.," August 16, 1959 (texts: [170]: 73–76; [167]: 307–10; [217]: 191: July 14, 1967: 21–22): Peng Dehuai and the others can be completely cured under the proper circumstances.

Mao Zedong: Speech, August 16, 1959 (texts: [170]: 45–56; [170]: 185; [232]: 69: December 1, 1969: 43): asserts that the right opportunists had to attack at Lushan for soon after this meeting there would have been no more problems to attack at all.

Peng Dehuai: Self-criticism (excerpts: [19]: 31–38, 417–21; [46]; 215]: 50: May 1, 1968: 38–40): reviews Peng's opposition to Mao's policies during the 1920s–1940s and then analyzes in detail his own behavior and that of Zhang Wentian and Huang Kecheng at the July 2–

August 1, 1959 Lushan Conference (meeting 138).

VII.   "Communique," August 16, 1959 (texts: [14]: 533–35; [19]: 291–96; [61]: 151–56; [73]): contains the following decisions:

—Lowers the targets set earlier in 1959 for steel, coal, grain, and cotton.

—Provides corrected (lowered) figures for 1958 production.

—Production of steel by indigenous methods will be removed from the state plan and will be carried out by local authorities as conditions warrant (to relieve the current shortage of agricultural labor power).

—Expresses support for the USSR's efforts at the Geneva Foreign Ministers Conference and for the agreement by the United States and USSR to exchange visits by their heads of state.

—Brands the "emergence of right opportunist ideas among some comrades" as the "principal danger now facing the achievement of a continued leap forward this year" and calls for party committees at all levels to criticize and overcome resolutely such right opportunism.

"Resolution of the CC CCP Concerning the Antiparty Clique Headed by Peng Dehuai" (partial texts: [19]: 39–44, 423–27; [61]: 167–72; [97]: 13: 1967: 18–20; [182]: 34: August 18, 1967: 8–10): calls on Peng Dehuai, Huang Kecheng, Zhang Wentian, Zhou Xiaozhou, "and others" to admit and disclose their mistakes before the party and rectify them; announces that these same people are relieved of their posts other than their Central Committee and Politburo memberships.

"Resolution on Developing the Campaign for Increasing Production and Practicing Economy," August 16, 1959 (texts: [14]: 536–39; [19]: 297–305; [61]: 157–66; [73]; [195]: 1960: 100–102): the proper commune form is three-level ownership with the brigade as the basic unit; must immediately begin an increase-production-and-practice-economy campaign.

"Struggle to Defend the General Line and Oppose Right Opportunism," August 16, 1959 (mention: [108]: 188; [273]: 577).

IX.   This plenum convened to develop more fully the case against Peng Dehuai and other "rightists" (including Lu Dingyi and Deng Tuo ([194]: March 8, 1979, tr. in [82]: March 16, 1979: E7, [176]: July 10, 1980, tr. in [82]: July 11, 1980: L2]) and to have the Central Committee formally take action against them. In this sense, its purpose was to formalize and legitimize the decisions of the July 2-August 1, 1959, Lushan Conference (meeting 138). Evidently, Mao Zedong personally insisted on convening this plenum to seal the fate of Peng et al. (mention: [43]: 851: April 26, 1968: 14). Some people attended the Lushan Plenum who had not been present at the Lushan Conference (mention: [170]: 61; [232]: 50: May 1, 1968: 35). Deng Xiaoping attended the conference but not the plenum (mention: [43]: 851: April 26, 1968: 14).

Mao Zedong fully utilized the technique of making marginal notations on documents and then circulating these documents for study during the course of this plenum. All of Mao's "Comments" cited in VI above were circulated to the people attending this plenum (and some were in addition circulated to lower levels of the party). While this plenum produced a formal decision to launch a nationwide antirightist campaign, evidently the July 2-August 1, 1959, Lushan Conference (meeting 138) had already produced a Central Committee directive to carry out such a campaign (for Guangdong: [13]: 96–97; for Liaoning: [19]: 323, 491; for Shanxi: [216]: 2141: November 23, 1959: 14–38).

Hong Xuezhi seems to be one of the "others" who were branded as "rightists" at this conference ([232]: 3: March 1, 1965: 7).

140

I.   *August 24, 1959*
II.   **ENLARGED SEVENTEENTH SUPREME STATE CONFERENCE**
IV.   Attended by representatives of the following units: CCP Politburo and CC; Standing Committee of the NPC; Kuomintang Revolutionary Committee; China Democratic League; Chinese Association for the Promotion of Democracy; China Peasants and Workers Democratic Party; Chinese Zhigong Party; Jiu-san Society; Democratic Autonomy League of Taiwan; All-China Federation of Trade Unions; Central Committee of the Chinese Youth League; PRC Scientific and Technical Association; Federation of Chinese Literary and Art Circles; State Council; *Renmin ribao*; Political Research Office of the CC CCP; Premier's Office; and by nonparty personages. For a complete name list, see ([195]: 1960: 278).
V.   Economy; the antirightist campaign
VI.   Zhou Enlai: "Report" (mention: [195]: 1960: 278): reviews the degree of fulfillment of the national economic plan during January-June 1959; reports on the increase-production-and-practice-economy campaign mandated by the Eighth Plenum of the Eighth CC on August 16, 1959 (meeting 139); asserts the need to oppose rightist conservatism.

Liu Shaoqi: "Summary Speech" (mention: ibid.): an "important" speech that reviewed the domestic and foreign situations.

Nine others (names listed) spoke and called for vigorously carrying out an increase-production-and-practice-economy campaign and for meeting the 1959 production targets (mention: ibid.).
VIII. Decided to bring up the points made in Zhou Enlai's report at the next meeting of the Standing Committee of the NPC (mention: ibid.).
IX.   This meeting clearly served primarily to communicate the substance of the decisions of the August 2–16, 1959, Eighth Plenum of the Eighth CC (meeting 139) to key leaders in various fields in China.

141

I.   *August 18–September 12, 1959*
II.   **ENLARGED MEETING OF THE MILITARY AFFAIRS COMMITTEE OF THE CC CCP**
III.   Beijing
IV.   Lin Biao, Mao Zedong, Liu Shaoqi, Peng Dehuai, and others.
V.   The purge of Peng Dehuai ([194]: August 17, 1967); criticism of Huang Kecheng (mention: [273]: 518)
VI.   Peng Dehuai: "Letter to Mao Zedong," September 9, 1959 (texts: [166]: 96; [174]: 188): notes the criticism already received at this meeting; recognizes his errors; asks to be allowed to undergo several years of study or labor.

Mao Zedong: "Comment on Peng Dehuai's Letter," September 9, 1959 (texts: [166]: 95; [174]: 187): welcomes Peng's letter and orders it circulated to all people attending this meeting and the concurrent Conference on Foreign Affairs (meeting 142); indicates that Peng can probably fully reform after several years of study and that labor would probably be inappropriate for someone of Peng's age; suggests that Peng be allowed to undertake investigations of factories and rural areas.

Mao Zedong: "Speech to a Joint Session of the Enlarged MAC Meeting and the Foreign Affairs Conference" (meeting 142), September 11, 1959 (partial texts: [170]: 79–84; [166]: 97–101; full text: [201]: 147–57): deems this meeting successful; several comrades in the party are not Marxists but are merely fellow travelers; in order to have solidarity it is necessary to have discipline; Peng Dehuai and Zhang Wentian have violated discipline in the past; erring comrades must correct their errors; everyone must study; I have also erred; we will succeed through unity and perseverance.

Lin Biao: Speech, September 1959 (excerpt: [101]: May 25, 1967: 3): studying Mao Zedong Thought is the essence of studying Marxism-Leninism.

Lin Biao: Speech, October 12, 1959 (should be September 12, 1959?) (partial text: [217]: 218: February 20, 1968: 19–20): harsh, face-to-face attack on Peng Dehuai, admonishing him that he had better rectify his errors.

Liu Shaoqi (excerpts: [124]: 1967; [150]: 3–4; reprinted in [258]: November 23–28, 1967; [152]): scattered and unsystematic remarks.

IX.   Lin Biao convened this conference (mention: [194]: August 17, 1967). It confirmed Peng Dehuai's errors and all but determined that he would undergo several years of study (the final determination would be made by the Central Committee). During the course of this conference, background documents on the Peng Dehuai case were being assembled, printed, and distributed (mention: [170]: 80; [232]: 70: January 1, 1970: 44). Lin Biao reportedly stressed a plan at this meeting to build China into one of the strongest socialist countries in the world (mention: [133]: 419).

The Conference on Foreign Affairs (meeting 142) met at the same time as this meeting, but it is not clear if the dates are identical (mention: [273]: 518).

After this meeting, a half-year campaign to oppose right opportunism began (mention: ibid.).

From the time of this meeting, Lin Biao assumed responsibility for the work of the Military Commission of the CCP (mention: [270]: 301).

142

I.   *September ?-9-12-?, 1959*
II. **CONFERENCE ON FOREIGN AFFAIRS**
III. Beijing
V.   Criticism of Peng Dehuai and Zhang Wentian; foreign affairs
VI. Mao Zedong: "Speech to a Joint Session of the Conference on Foreign Affairs and the Enlarged Meeting of the Military Affairs Committee" (meeting 141), September 11, 1959 (partial texts: [170]: 79–84; [166]: 97–101; full text: [201]: 147–57): several comrades in the party are not Marxists but are merely fellow travelers; to have solidarity it is necessary to have discipline; Peng Dehuai and Zhang Wentian have violated discipline in the past; erring comrades must correct their errors; everyone must study; I have also erred; we will succeed through unity and perseverance.

Chen Yi: Report, September 12, 1959 (brief excerpt: [67]): Zhang Wentian's attitude is better than that of Peng Dehuai—should not beat Zhang to death with a club.
IX. The people at this conference received copies of Peng Dehuai's September 9, 1959, letter to Mao Zedong and of Mao's September 9, 1959, comment on this letter (texts: [166]: 95–96; [174]: 187–88). Peng's letter recognizes his errors and asks for a period of several years of study or labor to reform, and Mao's comment indicates that he welcomes this communication from Peng.

143

I.   *Between October 1 and October 15, 1959*
II. **TELEPHONE CONFERENCE**
V.   Grain production
IX. The Secretariat of the CC CCP convened this conference to urge all

communes to fulfill their targets for grain production ([194]: December 28, 1959; [176]: October 16, 1959).

144

I.   *October ?–29, 1959*
II.   **NATIONAL INDUSTRIAL PRODUCTION, COMMUNICATIONS, AND TRANSPORT CONFERENCE** (convened by the CC CCP and State Council)
IV.   Industrial secretaries of the various provincial, municipal, and autonomous region party committees, responsible members of the industrial production commissions, and responsible members of the central industrial and communications departments (mention: [216]: 2134: November 12, 1959: 4–6).
V.   How to fulfill 1959 industrial production, communications, and transport targets and lay the groundwork for 1960 work in this sphere
VIII.   The conference reached the following conclusions (mention: ibid.):
        —Must thoroughly stamp out rightist tendencies in this sphere.
        —Must change the present practice of having production slow down at the beginning of each month and the beginning of each year.
        —Must further and more extensively launch the "increase production and practice economy" campaign, and should promote the communist style of cooperation and coordination, mutual aid, and mutual benefit in this campaign.
        —Enterprise management must be strengthened.
        —The party committees must strengthen their leadership over production.
IX.   This conference also made concrete provisions for industrial production in the first quarter of 1960 (mention: ibid.).
        Bo Yibo presided over this conference, and other CCP leaders, including Zhou Enlai, Peng Zhen, and Li Fuchun, attended to hear reports and give important directives (mention: ibid.).

145

I.   *November 9–28, 1959*
II.   **CONFERENCE OF PROVINCIAL AND MUNICIPAL CULTURE AND EDUCATION SECRETARIES OF THE CCP**
V.   Long-term development plan and theoretical work in educational institutions; antirightist movement in the cultural and educational system
VI.   Lu Dingyi (excerpt: [157]): in some places it is better not to construct simple primary schools.

IX.   This meeting was convened by the Central Culture and Education Small
        Group (mention: [274]: 941).

146

I.   *December 8–?, 1959*
II.   **NATIONAL CULTURAL WORK CONFERENCE**
V.   Criticize bourgeois literature and art
VIII.   Indicated that it is necessary to launch a movement to criticize thoroughly
        bourgeois literature and art, revisionism, and nineteenth-century Europe-
        an literature (mention: [270]: 302).
IX.   This meeting was convened by the Propaganda Work Department of the
        Central Committee. It is possible that this is the same meeting as the
        following entry.

147

I.   *December ?–27–30, 1959*
II.   **NATIONAL LITERATURE AND ART WORK CONFERENCE**
V.   Themes of work; USSR
VI.   Chen Yi: Report, December 27, 1959 (excerpt: [67]): can put on works
        about enemies, deceased people, contemporary people, the people of
        antiquity, Chinese, and foreigners.
            Chen Yi: Speech, December 27, 1959 (excerpt: ibid.): Khrushchev has
        his logic.
            Deng Xiaoping: Speech, December 27, 1959 (excerpt: [53]: 50): in
        criticizing Soviet revisionism, must use research and care and not simply
        launch a general attack; in criticizing revisionism in literature and art, the
        method is to criticize ourselves.
            Lu Dingyi, December 30, 1959 (excerpts: [194]: August 7, 1967;
        [237]: 5): should not divide literary and art works into simply the two
        categories of beneficial and harmful—rather, should have the three cate-
        gories of beneficial, harmless, and harmful; should not throw out harm-
        less things just because we want to promote useful things.
            Zhou Yang: Summary Report, December 30, 1959 (excerpt: [116]:
        May 6, 1967): can divide literature and art into the three categories of
        beneficial, harmless, and harmful; the harmless category is for those
        things that are not harmful politically and that have some benefit for life—
        e.g., landscape paintings.
IX.   This conference was convened by the CC CCP Propaganda Department
        (mention: [53]: 50).

1960

148

I.   *January 1960*
II.   **MEETING OF THE POLITBURO OF THE CC CCP**
V.   Relations with the capitalists
VI.   Liu Shaoqi (excerpt: [6]): the capitalists are now coming closer to us and we should likewise get a bit closer to them.
IX.   All information on this meeting comes from the single Red Guard source cited above.

149

I.   *January 7–17, 1960*
II.   **ENLARGED MEETING OF THE POLITBURO OF THE CC CCP**
III.   Shanghai
V.   Foreign affairs, probably primarily Sino-Soviet relations; 1960 national economic plan
VIII.   Proposed tentative plan to convert communes from team ownership to commune ownership (mention: [108]: 189; [273]: 520). Agreed to a 22 percent increase in industrial and agricultural production over 1959 (26 percent for industry and 16 percent for agriculture). Advocated public cafeterias and urban peoples' communes within the year ([273]: 519–20).
IX.   Mao Zedong subsequently commented that the Central Committee devoted so much attention to foreign affairs at this time that local cadres were adversely affected. In the same speech, Mao made specific reference to this meeting ([166]: 259; [174]: 238).

150

I.   *Between January and August 1960*
II.   **ENLARGED CONFERENCE(S) OF THE MILITARY AFFAIRS COMMITTEE OF THE CC CCP**
IX.   Between January and August 1960, either one or two Enlarged Conferences of the Military Affairs Committee were convened (mention: [85]: 286; [133]: 263, 605). There is no available information on the substance of these meetings.

151

I.   *February 1960*
II.   **CONFERENCE OF THE CC CCP**
III.   Canton
V.   Foreign affairs, probably primarily Sino-Soviet relations
IX.   Mao Zedong subsequently commented that the Central Committee devot-
       ed so much attention to foreign affairs at this time that local cadres were
       adversely affected. In the same speech, Mao made specific reference to
       this meeting ([166]: 259; [174]: 238).

152

I.   *March 7–12 and May 16–21, 1960*
II.   **CONFERENCE OF CULTURE AND EDUCATION SECRETARIES
       OF PROVINCIAL AND MUNICIPAL CCP COMMITTEES**
V.   Education reform; production enterprises run by cultural and education
       departments; academic criticisms; student participation in productive
       labor (mention: [274]: 941)
IX.   At this conference, Lu Dingyi tried to slow down and establish some
       prudence in the criticism and repudiation of academic thought. He also
       advocated spending a longer time on experimentation in teaching reforms
       (mention: [84]: 17).

153

I.   *March ?–22–?, 1960*
II.   **CONFERENCE OF THE CC CCP**
III.   Hangzhou
V.   Foreign affairs, probably primarily Sino-Soviet relations
VI.   Mao Zedong: Speech, March 22, 1960 (texts: [167]: 316–19; [174]: 226–
       28): focuses on anti-China sentiment in the international community and
       affirms that it is limited to less than 10 percent of the people; asserts that
       Chinese unity and achievements will reduce this animosity still further.
IX.   Mao Zedong subsequently commented that the Central Committee devot-
       ed so much attention to foreign affairs at this time that local cadres were
       adversely affected. In the same speech, Mao made specific reference to
       this meeting ([166]: 259; [174]: 238).
       Chen Boda subsequently noted that "at Hangzhou" Mao Zedong had
       worked out his own (versus Deng Xiaoping's) twenty-five-rule antirevi-
       sionist program (mention: [205]: 651: April 22, 1969: 5). Chen may have
       been referring to this meeting.

154

I.   *March 29–April 10, 1960*
II.   **SECOND SESSION OF THE SECOND NPC**
III.   Beijing
VI.   Li Fuchun: "Report on the Draft of the 1960 National Economic Plan,"
        March 30, 1960 (text: [195]: 1960: 173–82).

   Li Xiannian: "Report on the 1959 State Budget and the Draft 1960
State Budget," March 30, 1960 (text: ibid.: 182–87).

   Tan Zhenlin: "Struggle to Bring to the Fore the National Agricultural
Development Program," April 6, 1960 (text: ibid.: 187–91).

   Lu Dingyi: "Education and Study Must Be Reformed," April 9, 1960
(text: ibid.: 191–94).

   Zhou Enlai: "Speech on the Question of the Current International
Situation and Our Foreign Relations," April 10, 1960 (summary: idib.:
194–96).

   "Work Report of the Standing Committee of the NPC of the PRC"
(text: ibid.: 196).

   Zeng Shan: "Investigation Report of the Budget Committee of the
Second NPC of the PRC on the 1959 State Budget and the Draft 1960 State
Budget," April 10, 1960 (text: ibid.: 197). Other minor reports: (texts:
ibid.: 198).

VII.   "Decisions of the Second NPC of the PRC on the 1960 National Economic Plan, the 1959 National Budget, and the Draft 1960 State Budget,"
April 10, 1960 (text: ibid.: 198).

155

I.   *March 29–April 11, 1960*
II.   **SECOND SESSION OF THE THIRD CPPCC**
III.   Beijing
VI.   Chen Shutong: "Work Report of the Standing Committee of the National
        Committee of the Third CPPCC," March 29, 1960 (text: [195]: 1960:
        214–15).

   Chen Zhengren: "Report on the Examination of Proposals by the
Proposal Examination Committee of the Second Session of the Third
CPPCC," April 11, 1960 (summary: ibid.: 216).

VII.   Summary of resolutions passed (ibid.: 215–16).
IX.   Representatives at this meeting also participated in a nonvoting capacity
        in the March 29-April 10, 1960, Second Session of the Second NPC
        (meeting 154).

156

I.   *April 22, 1960*
II.   **MEETING OF THE CC CCP**
III.   Beijing
V.   Commemorate the ninetieth anniversary of Lenin's birth
VI.   Lu Dingyi: "Report: Unite under Lenin's Revolutionary Banner!" (text: [155]: 85–105): review of the essentials of Leninism and of Mao Zedong's development of Leninist doctrine; attack on revisionism.
IX.   Earlier, in April 1960, the Chinese had published a long, scathing attack on Yugoslav (read: Soviet) revisionism, entitled "Long Live Leninism" (text: [97]: 8: April 16, 1960; [155]: 1–56). Lu Dingyi's speech largely reiterated the major themes in this earlier essay.

157

I.   *May 1960*
II.   **CONFERENCE OF THE CC CCP**
III.   Shanghai
V.   Foreign affairs, probably primarily Sino-Soviet relations
IX.   An unusual amount of foreign travel during this month: Zhou Enlai and Chen Yi visited Cambodia, North Vietnam, and Mongolia; Bo Yibo toured Poland for May 10–31.

Mao Zedong subsequently commented that the Central Committee devoted so much attention to foreign affairs at this time that local cadres were adversely affected. In the same speech, Mao made specific reference to this meeting ([166]: 259; [174]: 238).

158

I.   *June 1960*
II.   **SHANGHAI CONFERENCE**
III.   Shanghai
V.   Anshan Steel Charter
IX.   Wu Lengxi commented that around the time of this June conference he asked Deng Xiaoping for instructions on how to publicize the "Anshan Steel Charter," which Mao Zedong had authorized in March. Deng responded that at that time strength must be concentrated to oppose revisionism and thus there was no hurry with the "Anshan Steel Charter." He also mentioned that Anshan Steel itself still had many problems

([248]; [194]: March 22, 1977, tr. in [82]: March 22, 1977: E1).

It is unclear whether the above comments actually apply to the Shanghai meeting itself.

159

I.   *June 14–18, 1960*
II.   **ENLARGED MEETING OF THE POLITBURO OF THE CC CCP**
III. Shanghai
V.   International situation; supplement to Second Five-Year Plan
VI.   Mao Zedong (mention: [283]: 273): in 1958 and 1959 we emphasized quantity, now we must emphasize quality; production targets should be lowered slightly; less talk, more action.

Mao Zedong talk entitled "Ten-Year Summary," which discussed the need to learn better the laws governing socialist revolution and construction (mention: [270]: 306).

IX.   One source ([270]: 306) notes that this conference discussed the international situation but provides no details. The Bucharest Conference of Communist and Workers Parties convened for June 24–26, and this meeting apparently discussed this upcoming conference.

160

I.   *July 5–August 10, 1960*
II.   **CONFERENCE OF THE CC CCP**
III. Beidaihe, Hebei
IV.   All provincial party secretaries, among others ([22]: 269).
V.   Economic priorities; foreign affairs (probably primarily Sino-Soviet relations); regional party bureaus
VI.   Mao Zedong: Speech (mention: [283]: 274): three-level system of ownership with production brigade as the basic accounting unit will not change for at least five years; give individuals a degree of ownership and allow commune members to keep private plots.

Li Fuchun and Bo Yibo: Report (mention: [108]: 194; [273]: 522): main measures in industrial and communications production in third quarter of 1960.

Li Fuchun: Speech (mention: [108]: 194; [273]: 522): 1961 plan to be prepared on basis of "readjustment, consolidation, and raising standards" (does not include "filling out").

Zhou Enlai: Speech, "The Communist Internationale and the CCP," July 14 and 15, 1960 (excerpt: [286]: 300–12): discussion of the Comintern's policies and activities from its founding in 1919 to its dissolution in 1943, with particular reference to its "shortcomings and mistakes" in 1927–1935; all revolutions must rely on the practice of that country's people and the independence of its party.

VII. "Targets for the Whole Party's Engaging in Agriculture and Grain in a Big Way" (mention: [283]: 274; [108]: 194–95; [273]: 522).

VIII. Placed renewed emphasis on the "agriculture as the base, industry as the leading factor" policy first articulated by Mao Zedong in 1959 ([43]: 884: July 18, 1969: 18; [97]: 17: September 1, 1960: 1).

Possibly reestablished party bureaus at the regional level ([22]: 269–70).

Possibly identified the "five (erroneous) styles" among local cadres: communism, commandism, privileged behavior, blind direction, and exaggeration ([1]: 101–102).

IX. The Sino-Soviet dispute escalated sharply in June-July, with a bitter clash between Khrushchev and Peng Zhen at the Bucharest Conference in June and the sudden pullout of all Soviet advisers in China in July. Mao Zedong subsequently commented that the leaders devoted most of their energies to foreign affairs at this conference, and undoubtedly the deterioration in Sino-Soviet relations and the need to cope with the disruption engendered by the withdrawal of Soviet advisers figured prominently in these deliberations ([166]: 259; [174]: 238).

Mao, probably mistakenly, later mentioned that this conference had convened in September 1959 ([166]: 259; [174]: 238).

161

I. *July 6, 1960*
II. **MEETING OF THE POLITBURO OF THE CC CCP**
V. Party leadership in the fields of literature and art; "Fourteen Articles on the Work of Scientific Research Organizations"
VI. Liu Shaoqi (excerpt: [120]): attacks the party's leadership in literature and art.
IX. This meeting discussed the "Fourteen Articles on the Work of Scientific Research Organizations" (mention: ibid.).

All information on this meeting comes from the single Red Guard source cited above.

162

I. *August 1, 1960*
II. **FOREIGN AFFAIRS CONFERENCE**
V. Struggle against revisionism (USSR) and U.S. imperialism

VI.   Chen Yi: Report (excerpt: [67]): to concentrate on antirevisionism is not good, for the main opponent is U.S. imperialism.

IX.   All information on this meeting comes from the single Red Guard source cited above. It is not certain that this meeting was convened by the CCP.

163

I.   *September 12–October 20, 1960*

II.   **ENLARGED MEETING OF THE MILITARY AFFAIRS COMMITTEE OF THE CC CCP**

IV.   Luo Ronghuan did not attend this conference (mention: [133]: 227).

V.   Strengthening political and ideological work in the armed forces

VI.   Lin Biao: Speech, September 12, 1960 (mention: [273]: 523): on the "four firsts" policy.

VII.   "Resolution on the Strengthening of Political and Ideological Work Among the Armed Forces," October 20, 1960 (texts: [61]: 345–88; [133]: 66–94).

IX.   This conference, convened by Lin Biao, marked the beginning of a great intensification of political work in the army and the reassertion of party control down to the company level. This work heavily stressed the study and application of Mao Zedong Thought. A number of sources note that Lin Biao personally formulated the "Resolution" cited above (e.g.: [43]: 894: October 27, 1969: 24). Lin Biao published a major article, "The Victory of the Chinese People's Revolutionary War Is the Victory of Mao Zedong Thought" (text: [97]: 19: October 1, 1960: 1–12), on October 1, and this piece contained many of the central ideas embodied in the October 20, 1960, "Resolution" cited above.

It is possible that two meetings took place: one on September 12, the other from September 13 to October 20 ([273]: 523).

164

I.   *September 17, 1960*

II.   **CENTRAL PROPAGANDA WORK SYMPOSIUM**

V.   Using Mao Zedong Thought

VI.   Lu Dingyi (excerpt: [154]): should not use Mao Zedong Thought indiscriminately, e.g., in the teaching of natural sciences.

All information on this meeting comes from the single Red Guard source cited above.

165

I.	*November 1960*
II.	**FOREIGN AFFAIRS CONFERENCE**
V.	Khrushchev
VI.	Chen Yi (excerpt: [67]): Khrushchev is not entirely wrong—we should support him when he is correct and oppose him when he is in error.
IX.	All information on this meeting comes from the single Red Guard source cited above. It is not certain that this conference was convened by the CCP.

166

I.	*November 24–December 12, 1960*
II.	**NATIONAL CONFERENCE ON CULTURE AND EDUCATION WORK**
V.	Applying the policy of readjustment, consolidation, filling out, and raising standards to the educational system.
VIII.	The documents of this meeting called for the following (mention: [84]: 17): better implementation of the policy of letting a hundred flowers bloom; institutions of higher education should give priority to improving the quality of teaching; existing full-time schools should allow adequate time for teaching and should control the time spent in labor; the Ministry of Education should quickly finish revising the teaching plans and compiling important materials of instruction for the main departments and courses; there should be appropriate mergers, adjustments, abolition, etc., in the newly established institutions of higher learning; the number of new schools set up during the mass movement should be decreased; should not push the mass line too far in scientific education; should pay attention to improving the quality of teachers and cultivating postgraduates.
IX.	The Central Culture and Education Small Group convened this conference ([274]: 942). Following this conference, the Central Culture and Education Small Group wrote "Report on Arrangements for Education Work in 1961 and Beyond," which was approved and transmitted by the CC CCP on February 7, 1961. The report pointed out that "the current cultural and educational work must implement the policy of adjustment, consolidation, filling out, and raising standards" and "emphasize the filling out of contents, energetic raising of quality, and suitable control of development" (mention: ibid.).

167

I.   *December 1960* (? see IX below)
II.   **ENLARGED MEETING OF THE MILITARY AFFAIRS COMMISSION**
VII. "Resolution on Political Work" (mention: [137]: 127; [91]: December 20, 1981, tr. in [82]: January 13, 1982: K7).
IX.   Mao Zedong included a statement in the above resolution that Mao Zedong Thought had developed in the collective struggle of the party and the people. Mao's note was made in December, but the Military Affairs Commission meeting referred to probably took place in September-October 1960 (meeting 163).

168

I.   *December ?–14–?, 1960*
II.   **NATIONAL PROPAGANDA CONFERENCE**
V.   Propaganda regarding the United States and USSR
VI.   Chen Yi (excerpt: [67]): after the Moscow Conference our propaganda should change; in the struggle against America, we can tolerate differences in tone (between our propaganda and that of the USSR) without affixing blame to anyone; from now on we can unite, as struggle is not beneficial to us; this is a question of contradictions among the proletariat, and we cannot think in terms of a split.
IX.   This meeting was convened by the Propaganda Department of the CC CCP (mention: [67]). All information on this meeting comes from the single Red Guard source cited above.

1961

169

I.   *1961*
II.   **CENTRAL WORK CONFERENCE**
V.   Free markets
VI.   Zhu De (excerpt: [263]: February 24, 1967; [217]: 172: April 3, 1967:

23): actively supports free markets that can again enliven commerce; these markets can include products of handicrafts industry and even of some state-run industries.

IX.   All information on this meeting comes from the single Red Guard source cited above.

170

I.   *January 1961*
II.   **MEETING OF THE SECRETARIAT OF THE CC CCP**
V.   Length of school curriculum
VI.   Deng Xiaoping (excerpt: [124]: March 8, 1967): objects to Mao Zedong's instruction to shorten the school curriculum; asserts that actually Jiang Nanxiang and others prefer the five-year curriculum but have not been able to maintain their support for it owing to too much outside pressure.
IX.   All information on this meeting comes from the single Red Guard source cited above.

171

I.   *December 1960–mid-January 1961*
II.   **EXPANDED CENTRAL WORK CONFERENCE**
III.   Beijing
V.   Classes in socialist society
VI.   Mao Zedong (excerpts and mention: [166]: 258; [174]: 237; [205]: 635: December 2, 1968: 21; [89]: 279–80; [194]: December 27, 1983, tr. in [82]: January 9, 1984: K21): condemned the Soviet declaration of a ''state of the whole people'' and a ''party of the whole people''; discusses investigation and study.

    Mao Zedong: January 13, 1961 (mention: [89]: 280): the importance of investigative work.

    Liu Shaoqi (excerpt: [205]: 635: December 2, 1968: 21).

    Chen Yun: Speech, ''Must Give Wrongdoers a Way Out [*wang kai yi mian*] in Arranging Markets,'' January 19, 1961 (text: [28]: 132–36): discusses the issues of importing grain and the lack of consumer goods.

VIII.   Reviewed and decided to expand the campaign to rectify the communes (mention: [283]: 287–88).

Approved several concrete policies for rural work, on the basis of the Twelve Points (mention: ibid.: 288–89):

    —Raise procurement prices of rural sideline products and settle accounts by returning or paying compensation for illegally seized property and possessions.

—Allow commune families to engage in sideline industry, handicrafts, and small private plots.

—Enliven the village markets, but do not create chaos.

IX.   This conference was followed directly by the January 14–18, 1961, Ninth Plenum of the Eighth CC CCP (meeting 172) and thus probably in part prepared for the convening of that meeting.

172

I.   *January 14–18, 1961*
II.   **NINTH (ENLARGED) PLENUM OF THE EIGHTH CC CCP**
III.   Beijing
IV.   Eighty-three full and eighty-seven alternate members of the CC CCP; twenty-three other comrades from the departments concerned of the CC and from party committees of various provinces, municipalities, and autonomous regions ([82]: January 25, 1961: FE: BBB1–5; [194]: January 21, 1961; [195]: 1961: 11–12; [176]: January 20, 1961).
V.   November 1960 Moscow Conference; economic policy; regional party bureaus
VI.   Deng Xiaoping: "Report on the Meeting of Representatives of Communist and Workers Parties Held in Moscow in November 1960" (mention: ibid.; [273]: 526).

Li Fuchun: "Report on the Fulfillment of the 1960 National Economic Plan and the Main Targets for the 1961 National Economic Plan" (mention: [82]: January 25, 1961: FE: BBB1–5; [194]: January 21, 1961; [195]: 1961: 11–12; [176]: January 20, 1961; [283]: 294; [108]: 196–97; [273]: 525).

Mao Zedong: Speech, January 18, 1961 (texts: [166]: 258–66; [174]: 237–45): stresses the importance of agricultural production, the need to concentrate on consolidation and rectification, and the significance of supporting the Moscow Declaration.

VII.   "Communique" (texts: [61]: 173–76; [82]: January 25, 1961: FE: BBB1–5; [194]: January 21, 1961; [195]: 1961: 11–12; [176]: January 20, 1961): mentions the following decisions:

—Decided on a policy of all-around support for agriculture, concentration on light industry, and reduction in investment in heavy industry, and directed the State Council to draw up a 1961 National Economic Recovery Plan that reflects these priorities and to submit that plan to the National People's Congress for adoption.

—Must carry out on a nationwide scale the rectification campaign (against leftist excesses) that has already begun in some places.

—Decided to establish six regional party bureaus—Northeast, North, East, Central-South, Southwest, and Northwest—to strengthen leadership over party committees in provinces, municipalities, and autonomous regions.

"Resolutions on the Meeting of Representatives of Communist and Workers Parties in Moscow" (texts: [61]: 179–84; [194]: January 21, 1961; [195]: 1961: 12–13).

VIII.   Approved the September 1960 decision of the Politburo to establish six regional bureaus ([108]: 198).

IX.   Overall, this plenum formalized the policies of readjustment, consolidation, filling out, and raising standards and of agriculture as the base and industry as the leading factor. Most of these policies had been decided upon at the July-August 1960 Central Committee Conference at Beidaihe (meeting 160).

After this plenum, Mao led an investigation of Zhejiang, Hunan, and Guangdong (mention: [89]: 280; [194]: December 27, 1983, tr. in [82]: January 9, 1984: K21).

173

I.   *January 20–26, 1961*
II.   **MEETING OF THE MILITARY AFFAIRS COMMITTEE OF THE CC CCP**
III.   Beijing
V.   Training of the armed forces
VI.   Ye Jianying: Talk and summary speech (summary: [133]: 249–55): wide-ranging review of work in training during 1960 and the future tasks in this sphere.
VII.   "Summary" (text: ibid.: 217–24): reviews training during 1960 and emphatically urges the training policy of "compactness and quality" for 1961.
IX.   This conference essentially evaluated the changes in training procedures that Lin Biao had implemented since assuming the position of minister of defense in the late summer of 1959.

174

I.   *February 1961*
II.   **MEETING OF THE SECRETARIAT OF THE CC CCP**
V.   Teaching materials
VI.   Peng Zhen (mention: [84]: 18): rejects the idea of reforming the content of teaching and compiling new teaching materials collectively by the masses; assigns Jiang Nanxiang responsibility for compilation and selec-

tion of teaching materials for the departments of science, engineering, agriculture, and medicine, and gives Zhou Yang this responsibility for the department of arts.

IX.   Peng Zhen convened and presided over this meeting (mention: ibid.).

All information on this meeting comes from the single Red Guard source cited above.

175

I.   *February 5, 1961*
II.   **FOREIGN AFFAIRS CONFERENCE**
V.   Khrushchev
VI.   Chen Yi: Report (excerpt: [67]): Khrushchev also has a number of good opinions.
IX.   All information on this meeting comes from the single Red Guard source cited above. This meeting may not have been convened by the CCP.

176

I.   *March 13 or 14 or 15-23, 1961* (see IX below)
II.   **CENTRAL WORK CONFERENCE ("CANTON CONFERENCE")**
III.   Canton
V.   People's communes; investigation and study
VI.   Deng Xiaoping (excerpt: [94]: 20): asserts that communes were developed too quickly and with inadequate prior investigation work.

Mao Zedong: private conversation with Wang Renzhong (excerpt: [176]: December 10, 1978, tr. in [82]: December 14, 1978: E14): we have been wrong in overemphasizing rural public mess halls; investigative team from the Chinese Academy of Sciences was labeled right opportunist for reaching this same conclusion.

Mao Zedong: (mention: [89]: 281): on investigative work.

Zhou Enlai: Speech to the Central-South and North China Small Groups, March 9, 1961 (excerpt: [286]: 313-14): discusses the need for investigations; oppose both rightism and leftism when they appear. appear.

VII.   "An Open Letter from the Central Authorities of the Chinese Communist Party to All Comrades with Regard to the Draft Rules and Regulations Concerning Work in the Rural People's Communes" (mention: [133]: 405).

"Rules and Regulations Concerning Work in the Rural People's Communes (Draft)" (mention: ibid.: text available at Columbia University, according to [22]: 281; see also [89]: 281–82; [283]: 300; [273]: 527).

"An Open Letter of the Central Authorities of the Chinese Communist Party to the Various Central Bureaus and the Party Committees of the Various Provinces, Cities, and Districts Regarding the Faithful Carrying Out of Investigation Work," March 22, 1961 (mention: [133]: 405, 498; [273]: 527).

"On Investigation Work" (written by Mao Zedong in 1930) (mention: [133]: 405, 498; [89]: 281).

VIII. Discussion over whether leftist mistakes had been overcome, with an improvement in production and people's lives, or whether the problem of relief and compensation was not yet solved and the rural situation still serious. Mao emphasized the need for investigations because of this disagreement ([194]: December 13, 1985 tr. in [82]: December 20, 1985: K1).

IX. The different starting dates are given in three different sources: ([273]: 527; [89]: 281; [283]: 300, respectively).

This meeting decided to circulate the first two of the above documents to rural party branches and rural commune members for study and discussion, which they should complete by April 1961. They should then be ready to make suggestions for improvements. The latter two documents were dispatched to cadres of the higher and middle levels for study. These cadres were to discuss the educational value of the actual experiences during the previous two years and carry out rectification (mention: [133]: 405). Mao Zedong's personal defense concerning the Great Leap Forward, as articulated in his January 30, 1962, speech to the Enlarged Central Work Conference (meeting 192), asserted that while mistakes were made, the Leap provided a great learning experience for the party and the revolution. This meeting seems to mark the beginning of Mao's stressing this approach to the setbacks of 1960–61.

Mao Zedong anticipated this conference in his January 18, 1961, speech to the Ninth Plenum of the Eighth CC CCP (meeting 172).

Deng Xiaoping prepared in advance some materials for this conference that offended Mao, who in turn chided both Deng and Peng Zhen, asserting that "without investigation, there is no right to speak" (mention: [129]: 41202: May 29, 1967: 121; [66]: 20: February 18, 1967). Deng and Peng purportedly then twisted the meaning of Mao Zedong's call at this conference for more investigation work. They organized an investigation of a county in suburban Beijing with the intent of gathering materials critical of the Great Leap Forward rather than with the purpose of learning new lessons from the experience (mention: [74]).

The program set up within the armed forces to study the four documents that emerged from this meeting is outlined in an April 4, 1961, speech by Liu Zhijian (text: [133]: 405–11).

Prior to this conference, Mao Zedong was already in Canton meeting separately with local leaders from the Central-South, Southwest, and West regions and from the Northeast, North, and Northwest; these two meetings then joined the Canton conference ([89]: 280–81; [273]: 526–27).

During the three months following this conference, Liu Shaoqi, Deng Xiaoping, Peng Zhen, Chen Yun, and other central leaders spent several weeks carrying out "on-the-spot" investigations in rural areas (details, with bibliographic references, in [22]: 284–85).

Not long after this conference, the Central Committee issued the "Twelve Articles," which emphasized the problem of settling of accounts regarding the seizure of land without compensation by production teams, instead of the problem of solving the problem of egalitarianism, as emphasized at the Canton conference ([89]: 282).

177

I.   *April 11–25, 1961*
II.   **PLANNING CONFERENCE FOR THE COMPILATION AND SELECTION OF TEACHING MATERIALS FOR THE ARTS FACULTY IN INSTITUTIONS OF HIGHER LEARNING**
IV.   Two hundred participants, among whom eighty were bourgeois specialists from around the country (mention: [206]: 155: September 25, 1966: 1).
V.   Educational reform
VI.   Zhou Yang (excerpts and summary: ibid.; [84]: 19–20): calls for reducing student participation in political activities and labor; reducing collective compilation of teaching materials by the masses; stressing the training of specialized personnel for the various trades, albeit only for people who are patriotic and who will work for socialism and communism; exposing defects; expressing views freely.
       Lu Dingyi (mention: [208]).
VIII. The conference brought forward a "teaching scheme" for literature, history, philosophy, economics, political science, pedagogy, and foreign languages (mention: [206]: 155: September 28, 1966: 2; [274]: 943). The conference decided to rewrite more than 130 kinds of textbooks, 140 kinds of reference books, and 100 kinds of foreign language teaching materials (mention: [206]: 155: September 28, 1966: 2).
IX.   This meeting was convened by Lu Dingyi under the auspices of the Propaganda Department of the CC CCP and presided over by both Zhou Yang and Lin Mohan (mention: [91]: August 11, 1967). One source ([84]: 19–20) asserts that the principles laid down at this conference produced a restoration of the curriculum, goals, and teaching methods of the pre-1958 teaching system in liberal arts. A February 1961 meeting of the

Secretariat of the CC CCP (meeting 174) had given Zhou Yang responsibility for the compilation and selection of teaching materials in the department of arts.

178

I.   *May 21–June 12, 1961*
II.   **CENTRAL WORK CONFERENCE**
III.   Beijing
V.   Finish work of Canton conference, specifically: collect opinions of cadres and masses regarding the communes; revise the Sixty Articles; discuss the five unhealthy winds (contained in a letter from Mao Zedong to Deng Xiaoping: mention: [97]: no. 24, December 16, 1982, tr. in [82]: January 11, 1983: K7).
VI.   Liu Shaoqi: Speeches, May 30, 31, 1961 (excerpts: [194]: August 15, 1967; [182]: 34: August 18, 1967: 18; [206]: 25: May 13, 1968: 21–35; [231]): gives a bleak appraisal of the current situation in the country.

 Liu Shaoqi: Speech, "Causes of the Current Economic Difficulties and Methods for Their Solution," May 31, 1961 (text: [147]: *xia*: 335–41): food shortages are the most severe problem: after local consumption, not enough is left to be sent to the cities; the problems encountered in agriculture, industry, and education are primarily the result of shortcomings and mistakes in our work; solutions include expanding private plots and sideline production, sending urban residents to the countryside, and cutting back on heavy industry.

 Chen Yun: Speech, May 31, 1961 (text: [135]: 144–54; [28]: 151–60): on reductions in staff and mobilizing urban residents to go to the rural areas.

 Deng Xiaoping: June 1961 (mention: [94]: 9): attributes the failure of the Great Leap Forward 30 percent to natural calamities and 70 percent to human failings.

 Mao Zedong: Self-criticism, June 12, 1961 (mention: [167]: 406; [201]: 166–67; [97]: 3: March 6, 1979, tr. in [82]: April 13, 1979: L11): talks about his own shortcomings and mistakes; asks to have this self-criticism disseminated (it was later learned that this request was not complied with).

 Mao Zedong: June 1961 (mention: [94]: 22): asserts that the most important thing to do at this point is to issue a new set of directives for launching a new study movement and for the reeducation of cadres.

 Zhou Enlai and Li Xiannian also spoke (mention: [273]: 528).
VII.   "Rules and Regulations Concerning Work in the Rural Peoples' Communes (Revised Draft)" (mention: [273]: 528; [283]: 306; [108]: 286).

"Some Provisions for Improving Commercial Work (Draft for trial use)," June 19, 1961 (mention: [273]: 528; [283]: 306; [108]: 200–201).

"Provisions for Some Policy Problems Regarding the Urban and Rural Handicraft Industry (Draft)," June 19, 1961 (mention: [273]: 528; [283]: 306; [108]: 201).

"Some Policy Provisions for Setting Forestry Rights, Protecting the Forests, and Developing the Forestry Industry (Draft)" (mention: [273]: 529).

"Nine Measures for Reducing the Urban Population and Reducing the Amount of Urban Grain Consumption" (mention: [273]: 529; [108]: 204).

"Circular on Some Problems in the Work of Reducing Staff Size" (mention: [273]: 529).

IX.   A Beidaihe Planning Conference convened in July 1961 and addressed by Liao Luyan was concerned with specifying the new conditions and policies in the countryside in view of the discussion at this Central Work Conference ([24]: 23; [216]: 4001: August 15, 1967: 10–11).

This conference called for a reduction in urban population of more than twenty million people in the face of severe food shortages. These people were sent back to the countryside over the following months.

179

I.   *?–June 2–19–?, 1961*

II.   **NATIONAL FORUM ON LITERATURE AND ART WORK**

V.   Role and degree of politics in literature and art work; "Ten Articles on Literature and Art"

VI.   Zhou Yang: Speeches, June 2 and 16, 1961 (excerpts: [237]: 12,15; [238]): the policy of letting one hundred schools of thought contend is not being carried out thoroughly enough.

Zhou Enlai: Speech, June 19, 1961 (text: [286]: 323–48; mention: [194]: December 19, 1978, tr. in [82]: December 29, 1978: E29; [30]: September 18, 1981, tr. in [82] September 18, 1981: K6): criticizes leftist practices; says Marxism has wide permissible boundaries; democracy is needed to overcome one-man rule.

VIII.   Revised the original draft of the "Ten Articles on Literature and Art" and circulated the revised draft for further modifications.

IX.   At this meeting, Zhou Yang and Lin Mohan explained and discussed the Draft "Ten Articles on Literature and Art." This meeting played an important role in the ongoing process of drafting what finally became known as the "Eight Articles on Literature and Art." Reviews of this process are in [1]: 128–29; [261]: 25, with some disagreement on particulars between these two sources. Due to strong resistance, these articles could not be implemented ([194]: December 19, 1978, tr. in [82]: December 29, 1978: E29). The Propaganda Department of the CC CCP convened a preparatory meeting before this conference on May 27, 1961. Zhou Yang addressed this earlier gathering (excerpt: [237]: 18). On June 23, 1961, Zhou Yang addressed the National Conference on the Making of Movies with Story Lines, at which he seems to have applied the general principles discussed at the National Forum on Literature and Art Work (excerpts: [116]).

180

I.	*July 6, 1961*
II.	**MEETING OF THE POLITBURO OF THE CC CCP**
V.	Scientific work
VI.	Deng Xiaoping (excerpt: [101]: May 23, 1967): supports the "Fourteen Articles for Work in Scientific Research Organs"; asserts these articles should be modified and supplemented in practice and that they should become the "constitution" for work in scientific research; admonishes party cadres to serve the vital needs of the scientists.
IX.	All information on this meeting comes from the single Red Guard source cited above.

181

I.	*July 8, 1961*
II.	**MEETING OF THE SECRETARIAT OF THE CC CCP**
III.	Beidaihe, Hebei
IV.	At least Deng Xiaoping, Peng Zhen, Lu Dingyi, Wang Jiaxiang, Luo Ruiqing, Bo Yibo, Lin Feng, Yang Shangkun, and Jiang Nanxiang ([208]).
V.	Drafting the "Sixty Articles on Higher Education"
VI.	Deng Xiaoping (excerpts: [1]: 134; [124]; [84]: 20–21; [4]; [208]): expresses strong support for the thrust of the "Sixty Articles on Higher Education," which are in the process of being drafted.
IX.	Somewhat differing reviews of the process of drafting the "Sixty Articles on Higher Education" are given in [1]: 134–35; [84]: 20–21; [208].

This meeting occurred in the midst of a July 3–15, 1961, conference convened by the Ministry of Education to map plans for reducing the scale of the educational system during the ensuing three years ([274]: 943).

182

I.   *July 26, 1961*
II.   **SECRETARIAT MEETING**
V.   Industry
VI.   Deng Xiaoping (mention: [89]: 270): report on work conditions in Beijing; suggested readjusting industry and consolidating enterprises.
VII.   "(Draft) Work Regulations for State-Run Industrial Enterprises (Seventy Articles on Industry)" (summary: [89]: 270–71).
IX.   The Seventy Articles document was drafted by a small group headed by Bo Yibo ([89]: 270).

    An August 10–15, 1961, Secretariat meeting (meeting 183) chaired by Deng Xiaoping further discussed and revised the Seventy Articles ([89]: 270).

183

I.   *August 10–15, 1961*
II.   **SECRETARIAT MEETING**
V.   Seventy Articles on Industry
VIII.   Discussed and revised the "(Draft) Work Regulations for State-Run Industrial Enterprises" (Seventy Articles on Industry).
IX.   This meeting was chaired by Deng Xiaoping ([89]: 270).

184

I.   *Late August–mid-September 1961*
II.   **LUSHAN CENTRAL WORK CONFERENCE ("SECOND LUSHAN CONFERENCE")**
III.   Lushan, Jiangxi
V.   Adjusting the communes; industry; grain production; commerce; education; cadre training
VI.   Deng Xiaoping: September 1961 (excerpt: [116]: March 26, 1967): presents a bleak assessment of the current situation and places most of the responsibility on human errors.

    Deng Xiaoping (mention: [89]: 271): industrial enterprises must be strengthened.

VII.   Approved the final version of "Draft Regulations on State-Run Industrial Enterprises," which had been revised by Deng Xiaoping, Bo Yibo, and others ([108]: 200; [283]: 314; [273]: 529–30).

VIII.   "Instructions on Current Problems in Industry" ([283]: 314; [273]: 530).

"Provisional Work Regulations for Institutes of Higher Education Directly under the Ministry of Education" (known as the Sixty Articles on Higher Education) ([273]: 530; [283]: 314).

"Decision on Cadre Training" ([273]: 530).

IX.   The "Sixty Articles on Higher Education" had been most recently modified by the July 8, 1961, meeting of the Secretariat of the CC CCP (meeting 181). A number of other sources mention this conference without providing any information about what transpired (e.g.: [272]: II: 1969: 550; [74]; [105]; [205]: 640: January 13, 1969: 19). One source ([1]: 120) indicates that further adjusting the communes was the main agenda item.

185

I.   *September 1961*
II.   **CENTRAL WORK CONFERENCE**
V.   "Sixty Articles on Higher Education"
VII.   "Sixty Articles on Higher Education" (mention: [208]).
IX.   The "Sixty Articles" had been most recently modified by the July 8, 1961, meeting of the Secretariat of the CC CCP (meeting 181).

All information on this meeting comes from the single Red Guard source cited above.

186

I.   *October 18–November 11, 1961*
II.   **ALL-PLA POLITICAL WORK CONFERENCE**
III.   Beijing
IV.   Political commissars or directors of political departments at and above the level of army of the PLA and some divisional political commissars or directors of divisional political departments (mention: [216]: 2620: November 16, 1961: 9–10).
V.   Review of 1961 work; discussion of creation of more "four-good" companies.
VI.   Zhou Enlai: Report (mention: ibid.).

Deng Xiaoping: Report (mention: ibid.).

Lin Biao: Directive (mention: ibid.): on the question of strengthening company-building and the methods of work.

Xiao Hua: Report (mention: ibid.): on the continual creation of "four-good" companies.

Luo Ruiqing: Speech (mention: ibid.).

Luo Ronghuan: Summing-up speech (mention: ibid.).

VIII. Adopted four work regulations drafted by the General Political Department for the company political commissars, party branches, YCL branches, and committees of revolutionary servicemen (mention: ibid.).

Pointed out that company-building consisted mainly in achieving the "four-goods" (mention: ibid.).

Leading organs must undertake investigations so that their work always proceeds from knowledge of the actual situation (mention: ibid.).

Must place on a firm basis, consolidate, and raise the work of creating "four-good" companies; consolidate and strengthen the fighting strength of the army; and strengthen the revolutionary and modern construction of the army (mention: ibid.).

IX. Mao Zedong, Liu Shaoqi, Zhou Enlai, Zhu De, Lin Biao, Deng Xiaoping, Luo Ronghuan, and Luo Ruiqing greeted the conference participants at a reception (mention: ibid.).

The General Political Department of the PLA convened this conference (mention: ibid.).

187

I. *October ?–22–?, 1961*

II. **CONFERENCE TO BAN BACKDOOR DEALINGS IN COMMODITIES**

V. Black markets and free markets

VI. Liu Shaoqi: Speech, October 22, 1961 (excerpts: [116]: April 16, 1967; [250]: February 25, 1967; [206]: 652: April 28, 1969: 4; [217]: 180: May 1, 1967; [217]: 193: July 21, 1967: 30; [49]): calls for easing restrictions on rural free markets to cut down on the black market problem (essentially, a policy of making the illegal legal); plays down the difficulty of dealing with the inevitable increase in capitalist methods and thought that this more lenient policy will engender.

IX. Following the meeting, provincial authorities began to extend free markets and private plots ([1]: 121).

188

I. *Mid-November 1961*

II. **CHANGGUANLOU MEETING**
(named after the building in which it was convened)

III. Beijing's western suburbs

IV.   Deng Tuo, Lu Yu, Zheng Pu, Wan Yi, Song Rufen, Zhang Mingyi, Li Qi, Song Shuo, Xiang Ziming, Wang Hanbin, Xiao Jia, Zhu Qiming, Lan Guangying, Zhao Xuezheng, and Jia Tingsan—the official positions of almost all of these participants are given in [74]: 29.

V.   Review of Great Leap Forward with respect to the following policy areas: national economic planning; capital construction; finance and trade; culture, propaganda, and health; education and science; party work; mass work; work of the control committees; and the impact of important or questionable documents that did not fit the above categories (mention: ibid.).

VII.   "Report" of more than thirteen thousand characters summarizing the results of this critical review of work (mention: ibid.: 34).

IX.   Xiao Jia wrote the meeting's "Report." This document was then forwarded to Peng Zhen (ibid.).

This meeting was convened under orders of Peng Zhen and was kept secret from Mao Zedong and other central leaders. It culminated an ongoing process of investigation and critical review of the policies of 1958–1961 undertaken under the auspices of Peng Zhen and Deng Xiaoping in 1961. This review had included earlier on-site investigations into agriculture (May 1961), industry (February-August 1961), culture and education, and finance and trade. This investigation also included perusal of CC CCP documents to pinpoint those that had been most important in causing the subsequent dislocations. Deng Tuo took charge of the Changguanlou Meeting himself, and participants brought to the meeting all CC CCP documents issued to party committees at *xian* (county) level and above during 1958–1961. Peng Zhen allegedly planned to use the materials analyzed at this meeting to launch a general attack on Mao Zedong's leadership and on the whole policy of the Three Red Banners at the January 11–February 7, 1962, Enlarged Work Conference of the CC CCP (meeting 192), but the political climate at that meeting made him decide not to follow through with this plan ([74]). All information on this meeting comes from the single Red Guard source cited above.

189

I.   *Between December 1 and December 10, 1961*

II.   **CONFERENCE OF PARTY SECRETARIES IN INDUSTRY**

III.   Beijing

V.   "Seventy Articles in Industry"

VI.   Deng Xiaoping (excerpt: [116]): need several years of adjustment following the Great Leap Forward.

VII.   Probably the "Seventy Articles in Industry" (summary of text: [61]: 689–94).

190

I.   *December ?-21-?, 1961*
II. **CENTRAL WORK CONFERENCE**
V.   Mass line
VI. Deng Xiaoping: December 21, 1961 (excerpt: [5]): large-scale mass meetings and mass campaigns are not suited to resolving all types of problems; rather, the mass line includes more subtle and flexible types of communications.
IX. All information on this meeting comes from the single Red Guard source cited above.

1962

191

I.   *1962*
II. **HANGZHOU CONFERENCE**
III. Hangzhou, Zhejiang
V.   Commercial work
IX. During this conference, Yao Yilin reported to Mao Zedong on commercial work. Mao then questioned Yao very closely and sharply about conditions in the field of commerce. After Yao returned to Beijing, he reported all of this to Li Xiannian, who had not attended the Hangzhou Conference (mention: [10]: May 26, 1967).

All information on this meeting comes from the single Red Guard source cited above.

192

I.   *January 11-February 7, 1962*
II. **ENLARGED WORK CONFERENCE OF THE CC CCP**
III. Beijing
IV. Over seven thousand cadres from five levels: center, province, district, *xian*, and commune or urban enterprise.
V.   Review of Great Leap Forward; rectification and rehabilitation; administrative problems
VI. Mao Zedong (mention: [89]: 236): unite the universal truth of Marxism-

Mao Zedong (mention: [194]: November 23, 1977, tr. in [82]: December 6, 1977: E12): Sixty Articles on Higher Education needs further testing and revision.

Deng Xiaoping: Speech "Party Building and Inner Party Life" (mention: [89]: 346–47; [108]: 208; [273]: 535): self-criticism of the Secretariat; democratic centralism has been weak recently; leaders and deputy leaders must unite with the majority.

Zhou Enlai: Speech, "Socialist Construction in Recent Years" (mention: [74]: 34–35; [108]: 208; [273]: 535): sums up the achievements made under the Three Red Banners and evaluates Mao Zedong's leadership during this period in a positive light.

Peng Zhen (mention: ibid.): supports Mao Zedong. Liu Shaoqi: January 26, 1962 (excerpt: [206]: 25: May 13, 1968: 26): criticizes the extent of the antirightist campaign after the August 2–16, 1959, Lushan Plenum (meeting 139).

Liu Shaoqi: "Report," January 27, 1962 (text: [147]: *xia*: 349–417; mention: [171]: 48; [167]: 410; [5]; [201]: 171–72; [283]: 324; [89]: 343–44): excerpt titled "The Style of Seeking Truth from Facts" in [194]: December 9, 1985, tr. in [82]: December 13, 1985: K5–7): sums up positively but critically the experiences of the previous four years and points out defects in four areas: production targets and scale of capital construction were too high; boundary between collective and public ownership was obscured, causing errors of "communist wind" and egalitarianism; excessive decentralism; mistakes of Politburo. Over past several years, those who have spoken the truth have been punished, while those who submitted false reports and hid defects were not punished.

Liu Shaoqi: Oral summary of "Report," January 27, 1962 (text: [147]: *xia*: 418–43; excerpts: [123]: April 18, 1967; [124]: January 1967; [205]: 652: April 28, 1969: 22; [206]: 25: May 13, 1968: 23–27; [217]: 162: February 14, 1967: 4; [89]: 551–52; [108]: 205–207; [194]: December 13, 1985, tr. in [82]: December 20, 1985: K1): there should be some reversals of verdicts on those struck down during the antirightist campaign; the failures of the Great Leap Forward were 30 percent owing to natural calamities and 70 percent owing to human error; main reason for mistakes is insufficient knowledge of economics; discussion of mass line. Mao Zedong: Speech, January 29, 1962 (mention: [273]: 534): develop democracy and communication between levels, solve problems in relations between organizations at different levels.

Lin Biao: Speech, January 29, 1962 (mention: [74]: 34–35; [82]: June 20, 1967: ddd16-ddd21; [89]: 347–48; [273]: 535): strongly supports Mao Zedong and the Three Red Banners; calls for all to study Mao Zedong Thought.

Mao Zedong: Speech, January 30, 1962 (text: [97]: 7: July 1, 1978; [176]: June 30, 1978, in [82]: June 30, 1978: E1-38; partial texts: [171]: 39-58; [167]: 399-423; [201]: 158-87; additional excerpts: [167]: 673; [174]: 456: less complete texts: [43]: 891: October 8, 1969: 37-40; [232]: 72: March 1, 1970: 42-43; mention: [108]: 207-208; [89]: 346, 515; [137]: 375; [273]: 534; [194]: April 13, 1978, tr. in [82]: April 26, 1978: E18): wide-ranging talk reviewing the following major areas: how this conference has been run; the problem of democratic centralism; united front questions; understanding the objective world; the international communist movement; and the need to unite the whole party and the whole people. This speech touches on a very wide range of subjects, including substantial information on party history.

Zhu De: Talk at a Shandong panel discussion, "Correct the 'Left' Deviation and Restore and Develop Production," February 1962 (mention: [89]: 343-45; [108]: 205-207; [273]: 535; [176]: July 31, 1978, tr. in [82]: August 1, 1983: K8).

Zhou Enlai: Speech to the Fujian group, February 3, 1962 (excerpt: 286: 349-52): on the need to speak the truth and do practical work.

Deng Xiaoping: Speech, February 6, 1962 (text: [97]: 4: February 15, 1987, tr. in [82]: February 17, 1987: K1-14): assesses the strengths of the party (above all, Mao Zedong Thought), but points out the current degeneration of traditional work style and the trend toward decentralization; specifies guidelines for improving democratic centralism and ideological unity; discusses the problems of a party in power; calls for reversal of verdicts; notes that responsibility for errors resulting from mass movements resides first with the center and second with the provincial level; a cadre should be judged by his whole career's work and not by short-term performance.

Zhou Enlai: Speech, February 7, 1962 (mention: [89]: 347): errors in government work mainly the responsibility of the State Council and its offices; offers methods for overcoming problems in current economic life.

Liu Shaoqi: February 8, 1962 (excerpt: [182]: 34: August 18, 1967: 15, 18): calls for "open opposition" both within the party and among the people.

Lu Dingyi (excerpt: [194]: November 9, 1967): agrees with Liu Shaoqi's February 8, 1962, call for an opposition group.

Chen Yun: Talk to Shaanxi delegation, February 8, 1962 (partial text: [135]: 181-84; [28]: 178-81; mention: [108]: 208): describes abnormal internal party life in recent years; leading cadres must be open to different opinions; party center is primarily responsible for mistakes in recent years; must obey objective laws.

VIII. Most of those labeled as "rightists" had their labels removed ([89]: 24).

IX.   This conference marked a major effort to determine what lessons should be drawn from the experience of the Great Leap Forward. Liu Shaoqi's report was originally submitted to the conference in draft form, circulated, revised by a twenty-one member drafting committee presided over by Liu, and then resubmitted—all in the early part of the conference. Mao Zedong expressed approval both with the substance of the revised "Report" and with the procedure by which revisions had been effected (mention: [171]: 39, 58; [167]: 399–400, 410; [201]: 158–59, 171–72). Mao suggested to Liu that he not read the written report but instead give an informal talk ([194]: December 13, 1985, tr. in [82]: December 20, 1985: K1). Although evidence in the form of texts of speeches is missing, Cultural Revolution materials assert strongly that Mao Zedong and Liu Shaoqi clashed sharply over the question of rehabilitating Peng Dehuai and other rightists. Purportedly, Lin Biao and Zhou Enlai sided with Mao, with Peng Zhen also giving support (see below), while Deng Xiaoping sided with Liu. On the initial clash, see [121]; [97]: 13: August 17, 1967.

Peng Zhen purportedly went to this meeting prepared to give a negative assessment of Mao Zedong's previous leadership based on the work done at the November 1961 Changguanlou meeting (meeting 189) but then changed his stance after seeing how the wind was blowing at this conference ([74]: 34–35).

The Secretariat of the CC CCP wrote a report to the center that analyzed its own shortcomings and errors. This report was circulated at this Enlarged Work Conference (mention: [5]).

Mao Zedong purportedly asked Chen Yun to report to the conference on the situation in finance and trade, but Chen demurred on the basis of inadequate investigation having been done ([10]: March 14, 1967).

This conference, as many others, met both in plenary sessions and in small groups. The latter were defined primarily by province at this meeting ([171]: 44; [167]: 406; [201]: 166).

Red Guards allege that when Mao Zedong asserted at this conference that the period of difficulties had ended and the country would grow stronger from then on, Liu Shaoqi responded that while the political situation had become better, the economic situation remained very bad ([10]: May 26, 1967).

Liu Shaoqi was encouraged to publish his collected works by those attending this meeting and to publish individual articles to tie in with the transmittal and implementation of the meeting's guidelines ([194]: January 15, 1982, tr. in [82]: January 25, 1982: K20–21).

The Central Committee published "Circular on the Work of Reexamining Party Members and Cadres" (April 27, 1962) on the basis of this meeting ([89]: 352).

Responsible members of some departments and commissions, regions, and provinces gave self-criticisms ([89]: 347).

193

I.   *February 21–23, 1962*

II.   **ENLARGED MEETING OF THE STANDING COMMITTEE OF THE POLITBURO ("XILOU MEETING")**
        (Named after the building in Zhongnanhai in which it convened)

III.   Beijing

IV.   Liu Shaoqi, Chen Yun, Deng Xiaoping, Li Xiannian, and others. Mao Zedong was absent ([38]: 361).

V.   The current financial situation; individual farming; the budget

VI.   Chen Yun: "Report on the Current Financial and Economic Conditions and Certain Measures for Overcoming Difficulties" (mention: [13]: 139–40; [217]: 172: April 3, 1967: 10; [18]; [108]: 210): stresses the dangers of inflation; notes the budget deficit; calls for distribution of land to the household; presents a bleak overall assessment.

        Deng Xiaoping (mention: [38]: 361): discusses the merits of Anhui's "farm responsibility system" and recommends this for broader application.

        Liu Shaoqi (excerpts and mention: [13]: 139–40; [10]: May 26, 1967; [10]: March 14, 1967): criticizes the state budget as being inaccurate in showing a surplus; calls for a new set of figures and for self-criticism among finance people; calls for "guaranteed production at the household level" and for "individual farming"; asserts that both industry and agriculture must retrench.

        Li Xiannian (mention: [10]: May 26, 1967): accepts Liu Shaoqi's criticism of past finance work.

VIII.   Approved Chen Yun's report for circulation to the provinces for discussion (mention: [38]: 361).

IX.   Liu Shaoqi presided over this meeting in Mao Zedong's absence. Liu later stated that directly following this meeting he went to Mao and reported on its contents ([210]).

        The Standing Committee of the Politburo discussed and approved Chen Yun's speech in March 1962 (meeting 195) ([108]: 210).

        Chen Yun made a report on the financial situation to a conference of the members of party committees in the ministries and commissions of the State Council that convened on February 26, 1962 (meeting 196), and he based his speech to this conference on his remarks at the Xilou Meeting; in particular, he called for a three- to five-year period of readjustment (text: [135]: 185–201; [28]: 182–97; mention: [272]: IV: 1: January 10, 1970: 125; [89]: 268). Li Xiannian and Li Fuchun also spoke at the party members of the State Council meeting; on March 28, 1962, the Central Committee authorized the issuance of these three speeches ([108]: 210–11; [89]: 374).

Chen Yun had refused Mao Zedong's request to report on the financial situation at the January 11–February 7, 1962, Enlarged Work Conference of the CC CCP (meeting 192), declaring that inadequate investigation had been done ([10]: March 14, 1967).

More specialized conferences were also convened around this time, at which it seems that the leaders tried to grapple with the problems of moving away from the mass mobilization system, e.g., see Deng Xiaoping's remarks at a February 1962 Conference on Industry and Communications (excerpts: [94]: 11).

194

I.   *February 26, 1962*
II.   **CONFERENCE OF MEMBERS OF PARTY GROUPS IN THE MINISTRIES AND COMMISSIONS OF THE STATE COUNCIL**
V.   Free markets and profits from speculation
VI.   Chen Yun: Speech, "The Current Financial and Economic Situation and Some Measures for Overcoming Difficulties," February 26, 1962 (text: [135]: 185–201; [28]: 182–97): discusses the range of opinions regarding free markets; analyzes declining grain production, excessive scope of capital construction, inflation, and declining standards of living; suggests a three- to four-year period of economic readjustment.

        Li Xiannian (mention: [273]: 211).

        Li Fuchun (mention: [273]: 211).

VIII.   On Liu Shaoqi's and Deng Xiaoping's authority and in the name of the center, decided to circulate Chen Yun's speech to the various localities (mention: ibid.).
IX.   Liu Shaoqi, following Chen Yun's speech, ordered the Ministry of Finance to draft supplementary tax regulations to deal with profits made from speculation. Allegedly, the regulations that emerged de facto allowed speculators to avoid the additional levy on their profits (mention: [18]).

Chen Yun's speech was approved by the Standing Committee of the Politburo in March (meeting 197); Chen's speech, the speeches of Li Xiannian and Li Fuchun, and other relevant documents were issued on March 18 ([108]: 210–11).

195

I.   March 1962
II.   **ENLARGED MEETING OF THE STANDING COMMITTEE OF THE POLITBURO OF THE CC CCP**
VIII.   Approved Chen Yun's speech to meeting of party members of the State

Council (meeting 194); Chen's speech, the speeches of Li Xiannian and Li Fuchun also given at that meeting, and other related documents were issued on March 18 (mention: [108]: 210–11).

196

I.   *March 3–26, 1962*
II.   **NATIONAL CONFERENCE FOR THE CREATION OF DRAMAS AND OPERAS**
III.   Canton
IV.   Over two hundred participants from throughout the country ([205]: 635: December 2, 1968: 22).
V.   Revive the enthusiasm of artists and writers for their work
VI.   Tao Zhu: March 5, 1962 (excerpts: [25]; [189]: May 26, 1967; [217]: 166: March 13, 1967: 33, 36; [217]: 203: September 15, 1967: 35–37; [222]): the CCP has erred to the left during the previous few years; the authorities have not given the writers sufficient freedom and incentives; writers should be allowed to write what they perceive and feel; the subject matter in writing should be broadened.

Lin Mohan (excerpts: [217]: 203: September 15, 1967: 37–38): the primary requisite of art is not education but rather artistic appeal; writers should be allowed to decide their own topics; works should show both the light and dark in life; good plays should be put on the stage regardless of whether they are modern, ancient, Chinese, or foreign; there is so much political pressure now that whenever three or more people are together everything they say is untrue; should compile a complete collection of Chinese and foreign classical plays of outstanding representative value.

Qi Yanming (excerpts: ibid.: 38–39): the antirightist movement has been a main factor in generating defects and mistakes; Wu Han has been asked to distribute copies of the eighty history works that he has written as they are published in the press.

Tian Han (excerpts: ibid.: 39): everyone should speak freely at this meeting without holding back; should avoid portraying wholly good or wholly evil characters; should learn more about European culture.

Yang Hansheng (excerpts: ibid.: 39–40): reviews the ten official dogmas (his own enumeration) about creative work and disputes them; asserts it will be necessary to fight anyone who calls this conference a rightist undertaking.

Chen Yi: "Report" of forty thousand characters (excerpts: [205]: 635: December 2, 1968): it is impermissible to put the label of bourgeois intellectual on all intellectuals; the CCP must take care not to condemn people improperly for their writings; thought reform need not assume the form of campaigns in the future; the participants in this conference should freely air their grievances. Zhao Huan (excerpts: [205]: 635: December 2, 1968: 27): the 1957 Hundred Flowers campaign was a trap set by Mao Zedong.

VII.   "Conference Report" written by the secretary general of the meeting, Zhao Xin (mention: ibid.: 30): called, inter alia, for less stringent party leadership over literature and art; abrogation (because they are "meaningless") of the PLA movements for three reconciliations and three check-ups, the four-good companies, and the five-good soldiers; ceasing propagation of Mao Zedong Thought, opposition to experts, opposition to things foreign, and opposition to things ancient and famous (branding these "oversimplification" and "one-sidedness"); and reversal of verdicts on rightists who had been criticized.

IX.   This conference played a major role in promoting the thaw in literature and art during the early 1960s. It was followed by a similar type of conference, albeit on a more modest scale, in Dairen ʲin August 1962 (meeting 205).

The Secretariat of the Party Group of the Theatrical Association began to prepare for this conference in 1961 through the publication (by January 1962) of nineteen issues of brief bulletins concerning the conference. On the eve of the conference, the leaders in literature and art circles convened a meeting in the Xinjiang Room of the Great Hall of the People in Beijing to make further preparations (mention: ibid.: 19). Tao Zhu had hosted a National Conference on Scientific and Technological Work in Canton during February 1962 which, as this meeting, sought to revive the enthusiasm of specialists for work in their fields.

197

I.   *March 21, 1962*
II.   **EIGHTEENTH SUPREME STATE CONFERENCE**
       (number of the conference given in [182]: 34: August 18, 1967: 18)
IV.   158 people, including Song Qingling, Dong Biwu, Zhu De, Zhou Enlai, and "other personages from relevant areas" ([195]: 1962: 49).
V.   Preparations for Third Session of Second NPC (meeting 198)
VI.   Liu Shaoqi and Zhou Enlai made "important speeches" on the current situation and on important problems in work (mention: ibid).
IX.   This meeting discussed the preparations for the upcoming Third Session of the Second NPC (mention: ibid.).

198

I.   *March 22–April 16, 1962*
II.   **THIRD SESSION OF THE SECOND NPC**
III.   Beijing
VI.   Zhou Enlai: "Government Work Report," March 27 and 28 (excerpt: [286]: 370–87; summary: [195]: 1962: 3–4; [89]: 262).
        Zhou Enlai: "Speech," April 16, 1962 (mention: [195]: 1962: 4).
        Altogether, 164 people addressed this meeting (mention: ibid.).
VII.   "Work Report of the Standing Committee of the NPC" (text: ibid.: 5–6).
        "Examination Report of the Budget Committee" (texts: ibid.: 5).
        "Decision of the Third Session of the Second NPC on the Government Work Report" (text: ibid.).
        "Other minor reports on credentials and proposals" (texts: ibid.: 6–7).

199

I.   *March 23–April 18, 1962*
II.   **THIRD SESSION OF THE THIRD CPPCC**
III.   Beijing
VI.   Chen Shutong: "Work Report of the Standing Committee of the National Committee of the Third CPPCC," (text: [195]: 1962: 10–12).
        Zhou Enlai: "New Developments in China's Democratic United Front," April 18, 1962 (text: [286]: 388–402).
        Altogether 223 people addressed this meeting.
VII.   Summary of decisions passed ([195]: 10). Texts of minor resolutions ([195]: 12).
IX.   The representatives attending this meeting also participated in a nonvoting capacity in the March 22–April 16, 1962, Third Session of the Second NPC (meeting 198) where they listened to and discussed Zhou Enlai's Government Work Report.

200

I.   *May 1962*
II.   **(ENLARGED) WORK CONFERENCE OF THE BEIJING MUNICIPAL PARTY COMMITTEE**
III.   Friendship Guest House in Beijing

V.   Transmit information on the January 11-February 7, 1962, Enlarged
         Work Conference of the CC CCP (meeting 192).
VI.   Peng Zhen and Liu Ren addressed this meeting (mention: [74]: 35-36):
         strongly defended Beijing Municipality's actions in the past, asserting
         that the city's leaders had avoided "blowing the five kinds of wind"
         (essentially, extreme leftism). The exceptions within Beijing, according
         to Peng Zhen, occurred because some people did not obey the Beijing
         municipal party committee ([11]).
IX.   Other people attending this meeting strongly disagreed with Peng Zhen
         and Liu Ren's assessment as stated above (mention: [74]: 35-36).

201

I.   *May 7-11, 1962*
II.   **WORK MEETING CONVENED BY STANDING COMMITTEE OF
         THE POLITBURO OF THE CC CCP**
III.   Beijing
IV.   Liu Shaoqi, Zhou Enlai, Zhu De, Deng Xiaoping, some members of the
         Politburo and Secretariat, secretaries of all central bureaus, responsible
         persons of all central and State Council departments, and others (105
         people in all) (mention: [273]: 537).
V.   Economic readjustment
VI.   Deng Zihui (mention: ibid.: 538): advocates expanding private plots.
             Zhu De (mention: ibid.): advocates development of sideline industries
         by families belonging to communes.
             Deng Xiaoping (mention: ibid.): should admit that mistakes were
         made since 1958 below the county level, and these mistakes must be
         corrected at once.
             Zhou Enlai: Speech, May 11, 1962 (excerpt: [286]: 403-11): acknowl-
         edges recent political and economic difficulties; although the country has
         passed the worst period, the situation is still serious; the central tasks at
         present are to streamline the administration, increase production and
         practice economy, guarantee the markets, and reestablish order.
             Liu Shaoqi: Speech, "How Is the Current Economic Situation?" May
         11, 1962 (text: [147]: *xia*: 444-49): the current economic situation is very
         difficult and the worst is not yet over for the cities and industry; underes-
         timating the difficulties will allow greater dangers to emerge.
VII.   "Report on the Discussion of the 1962 Readjustment Plan," drafted by
         the Central Financial and Economic Group (summary: [108]: 211-12;
         [273]: 537-38); report published by CC on May 12, 1962.

202

I.   *Summer 1962*
II.   **MEETING OF THE SECRETARIAT OF THE CC CCP**
V.   Individual farming
VI.   Deng Xiaoping (excerpt: [124]: March 8, 1967): defends the policy of *dangan* (individual farming) with his famous quote: "It does not matter whether a cat is black or white, so long as it catches mice."
IX.   All information on this meeting comes from the single Red Guard source cited above. [182]: 16: April 16, 1976: 18 dates Deng's speech to 1961.

203

I.   *August 6–September 23, 1962*
II.   **CENTRAL WORK CONFERENCE**
III.   Beidaihe, Hebei (August 6-late August) and Beijing (August 26–September 23) (mention: [273]: 543).
V.   Agriculture, commerce, industry and planning, solidarity within the party, and international affairs
VI.   Mao Zedong: Speech, August 6, 1962 (mention: [89]: 348; [273]: 543): the problem of classes, the national situation, and contradictions. Mao also spoke six times to meetings of the central small group.

Zhu De (excerpt: [217]: 172: April 3, 1967: 23; [66]: February 11, 1967): supports individual farming (*dangan*), free markets in the rural areas, and no production teams in the mountainous areas.

Chen Yun (mention: [210]): calls for the "three freedoms and one guarantee" (*sanzi yibao*).

Mao Zedong: Speech, August 9, 1962 (partial text: [167]: 423-29; excerpts: [182]: 17: April 24, 1970: 7; [182]: 26: June 23, 1967: 28; [182]: 39: September 26, 1969: 5; [137]: 27, 170, 207): although mistakes were made in 1958-1960, those mistakes began to be corrected in second half of 1960; full of biting sarcasm, Mao stresses the need for continuing class struggle in China, the continuing possibility of capitalist and feudal restoration, and the need for a blistering attack on the Ministry of Finance; Mao also thoroughly denounces the program of individual farming and calls for socialist education (text contains an interjection by Kang Sheng).

Mao Zedong (mention: [89]: 359; [268]: 34: August 1980: 45): novels have been used for antiparty activities.

Kang Sheng (ibid.): criticizes the novel *Liu Zhi Dan* for having serious political problems, namely, reversing the verdict on Gao Gang and Rao Shushi.

Mao (mention: [89]: 351): opposes individual farming; raises the question of agricultural cooperativization; criticizes Deng Zihui.

Chen Boda: "Report on Agriculture" (mention: [170]: 86; [167]: 430; [201]: 188).

Li Fuchun and Bo Yibo?: "Report on Industry and Planning" (mention: ibid.).

Li Xiannian (mention: [10]: April 27, 1968; [89]: 351): advocates the unified supply of commodities under state control, but Chen Boda objects.

Chen Yi: "Report on the International Situation" (mention: [170]: 90; [167]: 433; [201]: 192).

IX.   On August 5, 1962, the day before this conference began, Mao told responsible members of the Central-South and East regions that he was fairly clear about Peng Dehuai and was unable to criticize him (mention: [89]: 352).

In preparation for this conference, Tao Zhu and Jin Ming had Wu Nansheng carried out investigations of individual farming in several *xian*. Wu sent reports to Tao and Jin on his findings, and the latter two brought these to the conference (mention: [221]).

Mao Zedong subsequently commented that this conference had resolved the important problems of agriculture and commerce and the secondary problems of industry, planning, and party unity ([170]: 85; [167]: 430; [201]: 188).

This conference formed the prelude to the September 24–27, 1962, Tenth Plenum of the Eighth CC CCP (meeting 206). All people who attended the Tenth Plenum also attended this meeting (and vice versa?) (mention: [170]: 86; [167]: 430; [201]: 188).

Liu Shaoqi subsequently commented that he had "inclined to the Right" at this conference and did not begin to correct himself until the Tenth Plenum ([38]: 361). The revised edition of Liu's *How to Be a Good Communist* came out during this meeting (in August 1962).

204

I.   *August 1962*
II.   **MEETING OF THE SECRETARIAT OF THE CC CCP**
V.   Examination of cadres
VI.   Deng Xiaoping (excerpt: [94]: 22): deals with the examination of cadres.
IX.   All information on this meeting comes from the single Red Guard source cited above.

205

I.   *August ?-3-8-?, 1962*
II.   **DALIAN CONFERENCE ON SHORT NOVELS ABOUT THE COUNTRYSIDE**
III.   Dalian, Liaoning
V.   Content of short novels about the countryside
VI.   Zhou Yang: "Report" (mention: [265]).

Kang Zhuo: Speeches, August 3, 7, and 8, 1962 (excerpts: [216]: 3750: August 1, 1966: 2-3): the General Line is wrong; must slow down, the important thing is to write about the painful lessons.

Shao Quanlin: Speech (excerpts: [260]; [243]): advocates the portrayal of "middle" characters in novels.

IX.   Zhou Yang convened this two-week conference to discuss the writing of short novels about the countryside. Some of those attending argued strongly for depicting the Great Leap Forward as a major mistake that had produced a virtual disaster in the rural areas (mention: [86]: 286).

This conference was one of several convened in 1962 to encourage free and lively expression among creative writers. Its predecessor was the March 3-26, 1962, National Conference for the Creation of Dramas and Operas (meeting 196).

206

I.   *September 24-27, 1962*
II.   **TENTH (ENLARGED) PLENUM OF THE EIGHTH CC CCP**
III.   Beijing
IV.   Eighty-two full and eighty-eight alternate members of the CC CCP; thirty-three others from departments concerned of the CC CCP and the various provincial, municipal, and autonomous region party committees ([43]: 691: October 5, 1962: 1; [61]: 185); Peng Dehuai, Xi Zhongxun, Zhang Wentian, Huang Kecheng, and Jia Tafu did not attend (absence approved by CC: mention: [273]: 543).
V.   International situation; collective economy of the communes; agricultural production; commercial work; administrative problems; party control work; positions in the Secretariat of the CC CCP; socialist education; rehabilitation of rightists
VI.   Mao Zedong: Speech, September 24, 1962 (texts: [170]: 85-93; [167]: 430-36; [201]: 188-96): stresses international revisionism and class struggle; favors selective—but not blanket—rehabilitation of rightists;

asserts that cadres should not permit class struggle to divert them from improving their work methods, as happened following the August 2–16, 1959, Eighth Plenum of the Eighth CC CCP (meeting 139).

Kang Sheng ([108]: 220; [89]: 359; [273]: 547; [268]: no. 34, August 1980: 45): criticizes the novel *Liu Zhi Dan* for major political problems, namely, reversing the verdicts on Gao Gang and Rao Shushi, and criticizes Xi Zhongxun for being associated with the novel.

Liu Shaoqi: self-criticism (mention: [194]: January 15, 1982, tr. in [82]: January 25, 1982: K22).

VII.   "Communique" (texts: [43]: 691: October 5, 1962: 1–5; [61]: 185–92; [195]: 1963: 1–2): notes the following documents passed and decisions taken:

—"Resolution on the Further Strengthening of the Collective Economy of the People's Communes and Expanding Agricultural Production," September 27, 1962 (text: [61]: 193–205).

—"Resolution on the Question of Commercial Work."

—"Decision on the Planned Interchange of Important Leading Cadres of Party and Government Organizations at Various Levels."

—Decided to strengthen the work of party control commissions at all levels and elected additional members to the Central Control Commission.

—Elected Lu Dingyi, Kang Sheng, and Luo Ruiqing as additional members of the Secretariat of the CC CCP and decided to dismiss Huang Kecheng and Tan Zheng from their posts on this body.

—"Regulations on the Work of the Rural People's Communes (Revised Draft)" (text: [61]: 695–725).

—"Resolution on the Unfolding of Class Struggle Throughout the Country" (mention: [176]: May 28, 1967).

VIII.   Established a group, headed by Kang Sheng, to investigate Xi Zhongxun, Jia Tafu, and Liu Jingfan, and another group to investigate Peng Dehuai (mention: [273]: 547; [108]: 220).

IX.   Peng Dehuai submitted an eighty-thousand-character "Letter of Opinion" to this plenum that argued for a reversal of the verdict on him (mention: [19]: 207, 390–92, 481; [91]: August 16, 1967; [183]). He also wrote letters to the CC and Mao on June 16 and in August ([108]: 219; [89]: 352).

Liu Shaoqi subsequently commented that Mao Zedong personally had returned to Beijing from Beidaihe and drafted the decisions on further developing and consolidating the collective economy and on commerce passed by this plenum (mention: [272]: IV: 1: January 10, 1970: 126).

Mao revised a paragraph of the communique to emphasize class struggle (cited in full: [89]: 348–49).

Red Guards assert that at this plenum it was discovered that twenty-nine people, including Deng Xiaoping and Liu Lantao, had written a history of the party that essentially reversed the verdict on Gao Gang ([250]; [258]: December 1, 1967).

This plenum directly followed the August 6-September 23, 1962, Central Work Conference (meeting 203), and it seems clear from the number and range of documents passed by the four-day plenum that it in fact served primarily to legitimate the decisions taken by this earlier work conference. All people attending this plenum had also attended the previous Central Work Conference ([170]: 86; [167]: 430; [201]: 188). Although this plenum is most famous for Mao Zedong's call to "Never forget class struggle," it actually considered a very broad range of economic, administrative, and foreign policy issues. In agriculture, for instance, it clearly foreshadowed both the Socialist Education Movement and the major efforts commencing in 1963 to effect a technical transformation of agriculture.

Three more specialized meetings seem to be clear follow-ons to the decisions taken at the Tenth Plenum: an October 1962 meeting of party secretaries in industry (mention: [65]: February 15, 1966); a November 12, 1962, Organization Work and Control Conference of the CC CCP (meeting 208); and the February 8–March 31, 1963, National Agricultural Science and Technology Conference (meeting 216).

207

I.   *October ?–22–?, 1962*
II.   **NATIONAL CULTURE AND EDUCATION WORK CONFERENCE**
VI.   Full-time schools
VII.   Lu Dingyi (excerpt: [208]): expresses support for state-run full-time primary and secondary schools.
IX.   All information on this meeting comes from the single Red Guard source cited above.

208

I.   *November ?–12–29–?, 1962*
II.   **ORGANIZATION WORK AND CONTROL CONFERENCE OF THE CC CCP**
IV.   Directors of organization departments of the various CC CCP bureaus, as mentioned in [152]: 20.

V.   Organization Department control over cadres; cadre training; regulations for cadres; registration of cadres.

VI.   An Ziwen: "Report" (mention: [288]: 16): advocates registration of party members; stipulates regulations governing the basic-level work of the party in industry, commerce, and the rural districts.

Liu Shaoqi (excerpts: ibid.: 15): the CC CCP Organization Department should exercise tighter control over cadres.

Deng Xiaoping: Report, November 26, 1962 (excerpt: [53]: 1): people do not now all dare to speak out, but speaking out is better than keeping things secret.

Deng Xiaoping (excerpts: [94]: 13, 17): everyone should practice the "three nos" (no grabbing of pigtails, no hitting with sticks, no pasting of labels); must continue to distinguish party schools and short-term rotation training classes from each other.

VIII. Decided to set up experimental points for the registration of party members (mention: [152]: 21).

IX.   Liu Shaoqi and An Ziwen convened this conference ([288]: 15).

Mao Zedong's August 9, 1962, speech (partial text: [167]: 423–29) to the August–September 23, 1962, Central Work Conference (meeting 203) raised some of the key issues with which this meeting dealt.

209

I.   *October 22–November 27, 1962*
II.   **NATIONAL PROPAGANDA AND EDUCATION CONFERENCE**
V.   Position of teachers; propaganda, culture, and education work.
VI.   Lu Dingyi: November 27, 1962 (excerpt: [208]: 47): good teachers and principals should have their salaries raised and may be praised at some rallies.

Zhou Yang: November 1962 (excerpt: [116]: May 6, 1967): on the whole, the major events in the ideological sphere (Hu Shi, antirightist campaign, etc.) during the past thirteen years have produced active results; only a portion of them have been too leftist.

VIII. Discussed gradual reduction in the number of schools with two part-time shifts; proper running of keypoint schools; salaries of elementary school teachers; and the quality of teaching (mention: [274]: 944).

210

I.   *December ?–21–?, 1962*
II.   **CENTRAL WORK CONFERENCE**
V.   USSR

VI.   Deng Xiaoping: December 21, 1962 (excerpt: [5]): none of Khrushchev's contradictions has been resolved, and he cannot obtain help from America; it is possible that Khrushchev will turn toward China for assistance.

IX.   All information on this meeting comes from the single Red Guard source cited above.

1963

211

I.   *1963*

II.   **ENLARGED CONFERENCE OF THE MILITARY AFFAIRS COMMITTEE**

V.   Party recruitment in the PLA

VIII.   Decided to recruit "x" (specific figure omitted) percentage of soldiers as party members to insure that each platoon had a party fraction and each squad party members (in line with Mao Zedong's directive to build party branches in companies) (mention: [288]: 17).

IX.   All information on this meeting comes from the single Red Guard source cited above.

212

I.   *1963*

II.   **NATIONAL POLITICAL WORK CONFERENCE**

VI.   Bo Yibo (mention: [141]): discusses economic struggle and opposes class struggle.

IX.   All information on this meeting comes from the single Red Guard source cited above.

213

I.   *1963*

II.   **CENTRAL WORK CONFERENCE**

V.   Problems in industry

IX.   Purportedly, at this conference Chen Boda drafted a document on the problems in industry. Deng Xiaoping and Li Jingquan opposed this document, and their opposition succeeded in preventing the meeting from passing it (mention: [45]).

All information on this meeting comes from the single Red Guard source cited above.

214

I. *January 1963*
II. **SYMPOSIUM ON LITERATURE AND ART**
V. Unclear
VI. Liu Shaoqi (excerpts: [122]; [148]: 18): capitalist works have some artistic nature; agrees with Zhou Yang's remarks at this symposium.
   Zhou Yang (excerpt: [148]: 19): too short to be meaningful.
IX. Liu Shaoqi, Deng Xiaoping, Zhou Yang, and Peng Zhen convened this symposium in the name of the party center in response to an instruction of Mao Zedong earlier in January 1962 concerning literature and art. They allegedly used this symposium to undermine Mao's instruction (mention: [122]).

215

I. *Mid- to late February 1963*
II. **MEETING OF THE CC CCP**
III. Beijing
V. Socialist Education Campaign in the rural areas
VI. Mao Zedong (mention: [8]: 63; [108]: 221): introduces the experiences of Hunan and Hubei provinces as models to follow in the Socialist Education Movement; lays great stress on the need to focus attention on class struggle as an integral part of this campaign.
VII. Approved "CC Targets for Strictly Enforcing 'Increase Production and Practice Economy' and for Opposing Graft and Embezzlement, Profiteering, Extravagance and Waste, Decentralization, and Bureaucratism," published on March 1, 1962 (mention: [273]: 553; [108]: 221; [89]: 355).
VIII. Made concrete plans for the Socialist Education Campaign and a large-scale "five anti" campaign in urban and rural areas (mention: [288]: 16; [108]: 221; [89]: 355; one source says a "five anti" campaign in some urban basic units and a "four clean-ups" campaign in some villages: [273]: 553).
IX. This meeting studied reports from various locales about the conduct of the Socialist Education Campaign, with the objective of improving the conduct of this campaign ([1]: 248; [167]: 441; [174]: 319). Mao Zedong

subsequently commented that this meeting helped to clarify matters with respect to this campaign but that some district committee secretaries after this meeting still did not understand things thoroughly—they were able to clear things up only after making on-the-spot investigations ([167]: 441; [174]: 319).

This meeting very likely convened during the course of the February 8–March 31, 1963, National Agricultural Science and Technology Conference (meeting 217), which focused on the technical transformation of agriculture.

216

I.   *February 2–27, 1963*
II.   **ALL-PLA CONFERENCE ON POLITICAL WORK**
IV.   Political commissars, directors of political departments from army and navy units, public security forces, army schools and scientific research organs in the army, and a number of political commissars and directors of political departments of the divisional level ([216]: 2936: March 12, 1963: 1–4).
V.   Review of work in 1962 and specification of 1963 tasks
VI.   Zhou Enlai: Report (mention: ibid.).
      Peng Zhen: Report (mention: ibid.).
      Xiao Hua: Report entitled "Bring the Movement for Creating Four-Good Companies to a Higher Stage and Incessantly Increase the Fighting Strength of Our Army" (summary: ibid.): discusses twelve basic experiences (enumerated in the summary) concerning the building of companies.
      Reports by representatives of the frontier garrison forces who fought on the Sino-Indian border (mention: ibid.).
      Luo Ronghuan: Speech (mention: ibid.).
      Luo Ruiqing: Speech (mention: ibid.)
VIII. The conference used three phrases to sum up the future requirements of the work in the forces: grasp the actual situation; lay the foundation; and improve the quality (mention: ibid.).
IX.   This conference reviewed the results of the strengthening of political and ideological work in the whole army in 1962, summed up the basic experiences in the creation of "four-good" companies in the recent two years, studied the future political tasks, and discussed the draft of the amended regulations of political work (mention: ibid.).
      The participants in this conference were greeted at a reception by Mao Zedong, Liu Shaoqi, Zhu De, Deng Xiaoping, He Long, Nie Rongzhen, Xu Xiangqian, and Luo Ruiqing (mention: ibid.).

The General Political Department of the PLA convened this conference (mention: ibid.).

217

I.   *February 8–March 31, 1963*
II. **NATIONAL AGRICULTURAL SCIENCE AND TECHNOLOGY CONFERENCE**
III. Beijing
IV. Over 1,200 scientists, leading members of departments and organizations concerned, from throughout the country (mention: [216]: 2918: February 13, 1963: 14).
V.   Improve agricultural technology and help formulate a long-term program in this sphere
VI. Nie Rongzhen: Speech, February 8, 1963 (mention: ibid.): the purpose of this conference is to strengthen the work of agricultural technology and pool wisdom for the technical transformation of China's agriculture.

Tan Zhenlin: Speech, February 8, 1963 (mention: ibid.: 15): raises the following problems that must be solved: water conservancy, fertilizer, utilization of land, seeds, plant protection, farming systems, agricultural machinery, electrification, livestock breeding and veterinary science, afforestation and management, fuller utilization of water resources, and meteorological research.

Nie Rongzhen: Speech (mention: [43]: 711: September 4, 1963: 10): calls upon agronomists to center their research on soil improvement, rational application of fertilizer, irrigation, improved seed strains, rational close-planting, plant protection, field management and improvement of farm implements.

VIII. This conference worked out a program for the development of agricultural science and technology, with three thousand topics of research (mention: ibid.).
IX. The CC CCP and the State Council jointly sponsored this conference and Nie Rongzhen presided over it (mention: ibid.; [216]: 2918: February 13, 1963: 14).

The February 1963 Meeting of the Central Committee (meeting 215), which focused on class struggle in the countryside, convened at about the time of this conference.

The authorities were also laying out long-term plans in other fields at this time. For instance, a March 16–17, 1963, National Conference on Medical Science produced a ten-year plan for the development of medical science. Mao Zedong and other top party leaders held a reception for the delegates to this conference ([191]: 14: June 20, 1967; [43]: 711: September 4, 1963: 11).

218

I.   *April 1963*
II.   **NATIONAL ORGANIZATION WORK CONFERENCE**
V.   Party-building
VIII.   Specified the "ten standards" for reregistration of party members (mention: [250]: June 14, 1967).
IX.   One source (ibid.) asserts that Liu Shaoqi, Deng Xiaoping, Peng Zhen, and An Ziwen convened this conference, while another source ([288]: 16) says that Liu Shaoqi directed An Ziwen to convene it (Liu was abroad April 12–May 6, 1963). This conference was part of an effort to expand party membership.

219

I.   *April 3–25 or 26, 1963*
II.   **MEETING OF HEADS OF CCP CULTURAL BUREAUS**
IV.   Heads of CCP cultural bureaus.
V.   Subject matter of plays and literary works
VI.   Xia Yan: Speeches, April 18 and 25, 1963 (excerpts: [57]): our literature and art ranks are now good and can overcome any danger of revisionism.
VII.   "Circular on Suspending the Performance of Ghost Plays" (mention: [124]: March 21, 1968; [217]: 227: June 4, 1968: 14).
IX.   The circular mentioned above was issued at Jiang Qing's prodding (mention: ibid.).

At this meeting, Zhou Yang, Lin Mohan, and Shao Quanlin attacked the idea that artistic work should focus exclusively on events since 1949 (mention: [261]: 30).

On April 27, 1963, an Enlarged Meeting of the All-China Federation of Literary and Art Circles convened, and the contents of this meeting reflected the discussions of the April 3–26, 1963, meeting, according to ibid. The contemporary media indicate that this meeting of the federation, attended by 380 people, stressed the need to reflect class struggle in literary and art works and condemned the degeneration in literature and art works in other socialist countries ([216]: 2986: May 24, 1963: 2–5).

220

I.   *May 2–12, 1963* (as given in [108]: 221; [273]: 553; [89]: 376)
II.   **CENTRAL WORK CONFERENCE**
III.   Hangzhou, Zhejiang
IV.   Some Politburo members, regional secretaries (small-scale meeting).
V.   Directive for the Socialist Education Movement
VI.   Mao Zedong: Speech early in the conference (texts: [167]: 436–40; [174]: 314–17): the Socialist Education Movement is the greatest class struggle in China since land reform and is comparable with the nationwide liberation struggle in its scope and significance; must assume a basically lenient posture toward those who have erred.

      Mao Zedong: Discussions, May 7, 8, and 11, 1963 (summary: [167]: 440–46; [174]: 318–24): discusses in some detail four major problems:

      Mao Zedong: Discussions, May 7, 8, and 11, 1963 (summary: [167]: 440–46; [174]: 318–24): discusses in some detail four major problems: the state of affairs; where understanding comes from; the ten major points in the Socialist Education Movement; and the methods to be used.

VII.   "Draft Resolution of the Central Committee of the Chinese Communist Party on Some Problems in Current Rural Work," May 20, 1963 (texts: [8]: 58–71; [61]: 735–52): this document is frequently referred to as the "Former Ten Points."
VIII.   Decided to circulate for reference the twenty reports from various levels of local units that had formed the basis of study at this meeting (mention: [8]: 59).
IX.   Several Red Guard sources erroneously date portions of Mao Zedong's speeches at this conference to "June" 1963 ([43]: 842: December 8, 1967: 10; [216]: 4000: August 14, 1967: 22).

      Yang Shangkun called for Mao Zedong to "quit the stage" at a meeting in May 1963 (mention: [264]; [206]: 27: July 8, 1968: 57). It is unclear whether this occurred at the Hangzhou conference.

221

I.   *July 1963*
II.   **FORUM ON LITERATURE AND ART**
V.   Reform of traditional operas and plays.
VI.   Liu Shaoqi (excerpt: [148]: 19): must stress the new in traditional operas and plays; traditional operas and plays and foreign plays should be placed in a secondary position.

IX.   All information on this meeting comes from the single Red Guard source cited above.

This meeting came at a time when Jiang Qing was calling for reform in operas and plays from her temporary residence in Shanghai.

222

I.   *July 5, 1963*
II.   **MEETING OF CENTRAL BUREAUS**
V.   The Socialist Education Movement
VI.   "Report on Socialist Education in Industrial and Transportation Enterprises" (mention: [205]: 652: April 28, 1969: 38).

Liu Shaoqi (excerpts: ibid.: 35, 38): should follow a policy of giving people hope; many landlords have properly reformed and can change their class labels; children of landlords should be judged by their own actions; it is necessary to apply efforts to production and construction.

IX.   Mao Zedong anticipated this meeting in his speech to the May 2–12, 1963, Hangzhou Conference (meeting 220) ([167]: 438; [174]: 316), at which time he specified that in July the Central Bureaus should meet to sum up experiences and to handle the situation.

223

I.   *September 1963*
II.   **CENTRAL WORK CONFERENCE**
III.   Beijing
V.   Industry, agriculture, reform of operas and plays
VI.   Mao Zedong: September 27, 1963 (excerpt: [26]: 85; [43]: 891: October 8, 1969: 41; [216]: 4000: August 14, 1967: 23; [273]: 558): must develop new things from the old in drama.
VIII. Approved a three-year economic readjustment ([273]: 564; [283]: 366); this may have been done at a separate work conference held at the same time.
IX.   In September 1963, the Central Committee issued the "Provisions of Certain Concrete Policies of the CC CCP Concerning the Socialist Education Movement in the Rural Areas (Draft)" (frequently called the "Later Ten Points") (texts: [8]: 72–94; [61]: 753–86). It is unclear whether a single Central Work Conference covered all the agenda items listed in V above and thereby provided the forum for discussion of this document, or whether several conferences were held at the same time. One source

places Mao's speech in the context of the Socialist Education Movement ([273]: 558).

There was a symposium on opera work convened for August 29– October 4, 1963, at which Zhou Yang expressed sentiments quite different from those Mao articulated in his talk cited above (excerpts from Zhou Yang: [104]; [237]: 14, 15).

224

I.   *October ?–23–?, 1963*
II.   **CENTRAL WORK CONFERENCE**
V.   Big-character posters
VI.   Deng Xiaoping (excerpts: [53]: 19): during tranquil periods people do not write big-character posters; the vast upsurge in these posters during a campaign thus involves the elements of competition and formalism.
IX.   All information on this meeting comes from the single Red Guard source cited above.

225

I.   *November 15–16, 1963*
II.   **SUPREME STATE CONFERENCE**
IV.   155 people, including leaders of the state, responsible people of the CCP, various democratic parties, and people's groups, personages of various circles in society, and other relevant personages.
V.   Prepare for the November 17–December 3, 1963, Fourth Session of the Second NPC (meeting 226).
VI.   Liu Shaoqi and Zhou Enlai: Reports on the current international and domestic situations and our tasks (mention: [195]: 1964: 273).

      Peng Zhen: Report on major problems confronting the Fourth Session of the Second NPC (meeting 226) (mention: ibid.).

226

I.   *November 17–December 3, 1963*
II.   **FOURTH SESSION OF THE SECOND NPC**
III. Beijing
VI.   Li Fuchun: "Report on the Conditions for Investigating the 1963 National Economic Plan and the Draft of the 1964 National Economic Plan" (mention: [195]: 1964: 6).

Li Xiannian: "Report on the Draft State Budget for 1963 and an Estimate of the Conditions for Implementing It and the Initial Arrangements for 1964 State Budget" (mention: ibid.).

Peng Zhen: "Explanation of the Quotas for Representatives and the Election Question for the Third NPC" (mention: ibid.).

A total of 248 people addressed this meeting (ibid.).

Zhou Enlai: Speech, December 2, 1963 (mention: ibid.): on the current domestic and foreign situations and tasks.

VII.   "Communique" (text: ibid.: 6–8).

"Decisions of the Fourth Session of the Second NPC of the PRC on the 1963 National Economic Plan and 1964 National Economic Plan, on the 1963 State Budget and the Initial Preparations for the 1964 State Budget," December 3, 1963 (text: ibid.: 8).

"Decision of the Fourth Session of the Second NPC of the PRC on the Delegate Quotas and Election Question of the Third NPC," December 3, 1963 (text: ibid.: 8–9).

IX.   The delegates to the Fourth Session of the Third CPPCC (meeting 227) attended this meeting in a nonvoting capacity (ibid.: 6).

227

I.   *November 17–December 4, 1963*
II.   **FOURTH SESSION OF THE THIRD CPPCC**
III.   Beijing
VI.   Chen Shutong: "Work Report of the Standing Committee of the Third CPPCC" (mention: [194]: December 5, 1963; [195]: 1964: 12).
VIII.   Approved of Chen Shutong's Report ([194]: December 5, 1963; [195]: 1964: 13).
IX.   Entire meeting attended the simultaneous Fourth Session of the Second NPC (meeting 226) in a nonvoting capacity ([194]: December 5, 1963; [195]: 1964: 12).

228

I.   *December 24–26, 1963* (see IX below)
II.   **REPORT MEETING**
IV.   Bo Yibo, Liu Shaoqi and presumably others.
V.   Management of industry
VI.   Bo Yibo: Report on conditions in industry and on the situation at an industrial conference (mention: [118]).

Liu Shaoqi (excerpts: ibid.; [215]: 265–66, which in turn cites a wide range of sources for these same excerpts): should not have administrative management of enterprises; should have national, unified trusts; must manage the economy by economic methods.

IX.   Liu Shaoqi's remarks cited above were made on December 24 and 26, 1963, each time at a "report meeting with Bo Yibo." It is unclear whether these were two separate meetings or two days of a longer meeting.

Liu Shaoqi, at "a meeting" in December 1963, gave specific instructions that a trust should be formed in agricultural mechanization departments (mention: [215]: 268). It is unclear whether this occurred at this report meeting.

Bo Yibo participated in another report meeting on January 6, 1964, that was also concerned with trusts. At this, he argued for combining scientific research with production to obtain the fastest results ([5]). There is no other information on this January 6, 1964, meeting.

1964

229

I.   *Beginning of 1964*
II.   **ENLARGED MEETING OF THE MILITARY AFFAIRS COMMITTEE OF THE CC CCP**
V.   Summary of the work of 1963
VIII.   Directed the "drafting group" (*qizao zu*) to draft the summary of military work during 1963 and discussed the substance of this summary (mention: [169]).
IX.   All information on this meeting comes from the single Red Guard source cited above.

230

I.   *January 3, 1964*
II.   **LITERATURE AND ART SYMPOSIUM**
        (convened in the name of the Politburo of the CC CCP) ([101]: 4: May 10, 1967; [217]: 205: September 29, 1967: 36–37).
III.   Huairen Hall, Beijing

IV.   Liu Shaoqi, Deng Xiaoping, Peng Zhen, Kang Sheng, Jiang Qing, and Zhou Yang, among others.

V.   Degree to which literature and art should be cleansed of old things

VI.   Zhou Yang: "Report" (excerpts: [43]: 842: December 8, 1967: 11–12; [261]: 32): asserts that the Ministry of Culture committed errors of understanding, but this does not amount to an error in line.

Liu Shaoqi (excerpts: [101]: 4: May 10, 1967; scattered excerpts in numerous other sources): China's culture has now progressed from being a "new democratic" culture to being a "socialist" culture (the former is not antipathetic to capitalism while the latter is); should give second place to historic plays and foreign plays; cultural workers who are antiparty should be subjected to criticism, but not to such rigorous treatment as during the antirightist movement; it is permissible to write about weaknesses in people and errors in our work; Mao Zedong's Yan'an Forum talk and *On New Democracy* are now out of date since China now has a socialist culture.

Deng Xiaoping (mention: [43]: 842: December 8, 1967: 12; [94]: 27).

Peng Zhen (mention: [101]: 4: May 10, 1967; [217]: 205: September 29, 1967: 36).

VIII.   Deng Xiaoping instructed Zhou Yang to work out a "Plan for Development of Socialist Literature and Art" (mention: [94]: 27).

Criticized certain operas for attacking the party through innuendo ([273]: 559).

IX.   Liu Shaoqi and Deng Xiaoping convened this meeting in response to Mao Zedong's December 12, 1963, comment on a report by Ke Qingshi. This comment (texts: [26]: 86; [43]: 891: October 8, 1969: 41; [182]: 23: June 2, 1967: 8) expresses chagrin that more effort has not been put into the development of socialist art.

Kang Sheng and Jiang Qing allegedly argued with the others at this symposium, accusing them of undermining the spirit of Mao Zedong's December 12, 1963, comment (mention: [111]; [194]: August 28, 1969; [91]: July 25, 1967; [217]: 227: June 4, 1968: 14).

The center convened another meeting on problems in literature and art on February 19, 1964 (meeting 234). Liu Shaoqi addressed this meeting and argued that historical plays must be made to serve the present. A literary and art forum of the armed forces also convened in January 1964 (mention: [205]: 604: December 4, 1967: 2–3).

231

I.   *February 13, 1964*

II.   **SPRING FESTIVAL FORUM**

IV.   Mao Zedong, Kang Sheng, Zhang Shizhao, Huang Yanpei, Xu Deheng, and other party and nonparty people drawn from the CC CCP and the Academy of Sciences.

V.   Sino-Soviet relations; educational reform; emulating the army and Daqing

VI.   Mao Zedong: Speech (text, including interjections by others: [167]: 455–65; [174]: 326–36; [201]: 197–211; text of Mao's comments on education alone, and excluding interjections by other: [26]: 93–97): discusses Sino-Soviet relations; affirms the need to emulate the PLA and Daqing; emphasizes the need to change methods in education, especially along the lines of shortening the time spent in school, less intense studies, less demanding examinations, and greater flexibility and liveliness in education.

IX.   This forum assumed the format of a somewhat rambling symposium on domestic and international problems. Although there is no record of actual "decisions," "instructions," or "resolutions," some subsequent writings treat Mao Zedong's remarks at this symposium as de facto "instructions," and a meeting of leading cadres from institutions of higher learning was convened to transmit these "instructions" (mention: [84]: 26–27).

During subsequent months, the leadership convened more specialized meetings to deal with the issues that Mao had placed on the educational agenda at this symposium, e.g., the National Conference on Political Classes in Higher and Middle Schools that convened in June–July 1964 ([84]: 27; [68]).

232

I.   *February 19, 1964*

II.   **CONFERENCE TO DISCUSS PROBLEMS IN LITERATURE AND ART**

V.   Reform of historical plays

VI.   Liu Shaoqi (excerpt: [104]): in reforming historical plays, must make the past serve the present; some historical plays have been revised properly and some have not (lists examples of both).

IX.   This conference was convened by the Central Committee. All information on this meeting comes from the single Red Guard source cited above.

233

I.   *March 1964*

II.   **REPORT MEETING**

V.   Sino-Soviet relations; domestic politics; revolutionary successors

VI. Mao Zedong: Remarks (texts: [167]: 471–79; [174]: 339–46): wide-ranging discussion of struggle with the USSR; current campaign to study the *Selected Works of Mao Zedong*; Socialist Education Movement; lessons learned from the Great Leap Forward; need to study the PLA and the Ministry of Petroleum; need for revolutionary successors; and on dividing one into two (including a substantial review of inner-party history).

234

I. *March 3, 1964*
II. **MEETING OF THE SECRETARIAT OF THE CC CCP**
V. Socialist Education Movement at Beijing University
VI. Deng Xiaoping (mention: [4]): criticizes the way the Socialist Education Movement is being carried out at Beijing University because the people carrying out the movement have a wrong idea of the character of the problem, did not seek to carry out a three-way alliance, and carry the struggle to excess.
IX. All information on this meeting comes from the single Red Guard source cited above.

235

I. *March ?-28-?, 1964*
II. **HANDAN FORUM**
III. Handan, Hebei
V. Four Clean-ups campaign
VI. Mao Zedong: Speech, March 28, 1964 (partial text: [167]: 480–81; [174]: 337–38): the current Four Clean-ups campaign should be a class struggle (the first since 1957) that will take at least three or four years to complete.

236

I. *April 28, 1964*
II. **REPORT MEETING**
III. Beidaihe, Hebei
IV. Mao Zedong, Xie Fuzhi (and others?).
V. Application of the Former and Later Ten Points to labor reform
VI. Mao Zedong and Xie Fuzhi (texts: [167]: 493–94; [174]: 347–48): discuss the application of the Former Ten Points and the Later Ten Points to the problem of labor reform.

237

I.   *May 1964*
II.   **CENTRAL WORK CONFERENCE**
III.   Beidaihe, Hebei
V.   Revolutionary successors; contract labor; two-track educational system
VI.   Mao Zedong (mention: [152]: 19); stipulates five requirements for the training of revolutionary successors.

Liu Shaoqi (mention: [205]: 616: March 25, 1968: 24): advocates maintaining the system of both temporary and permanent workers.

Liu Shaoqi (mention: [1]: 362): discusses the two-track educational system of full-time and part-work, part-study schools.

IX.   All three of the above discussions are said to have taken place at "Central Work Conference(s)" in May 1964. It is unclear whether they occurred at the same conference, or at two or even three such meetings. Only [205]: 616: March 25, 1968: 24 refers to the meeting having convened at Beidaihe.

One source ([250]: March 13, 1967) indicates that Liu Shaoqi made the remarks noted above at a Central Work Conference that convened in April 1964.

238

I.   *May 15–June 17, 1964*
II.   **WORK CONFERENCE OF THE CC CCP**
III.   Beijing
IV.   Mao Zedong, Zhou Enlai, Liu Shaoqi, Zhu De, Dong Biwu, Deng Xiaoping, Peng Zhen, Chen Yi, He Long, Li Xiannian, Li Jingquan, Tan Zhenlin, Ulanfu, Lu Dingyi, Kang Sheng, Bo Yibo, Li Xuefeng, Liu Lantao, Yang Shangkun, Nie Rongzhen, Luo Ruiqing, Xiao Jingguan, Xu Guangda, and leading members of various bureaus of the CC CCP, provincial party committees, municipal and autonomous region party committees, party committees of various departments under the CC CCP, and various mass organizations (mention: [216]: 3242: June 22, 1964: 1–2).

V.   Education; Sino-Soviet affairs; military work and revolutionary successors; Third Five-Year Plan; Socialist Education Movement; dual track labor and education systems; revisionism
VI.   Mao Zedong (mention: [152]: 19): stipulates five requirements for the training of revolutionary successors.

Liu Shaoqi: Speech(es?) (mention: [205]: 616: March 25, 1968: 24;

[1]: 362; [89]: 240): advocates maintaining the system of both temporary and permanent workers; discusses the two-track educational system of full-time and part-work, part-study schools.

Mao Zedong (mention: [8]: 120): specifies six standards for evaluating the Socialist Education Movement.

Mao Zedong: Speech, June 6, 1964 (texts: [167]: 497–99; [174]: 353–55): on the Third Five-Year Plan: stresses need to get away from Soviet planning techniques; affirms importance of agricultural self-sufficiency; must have better training of cadres.

Mao Zedong: Speech June 8, 1964 (excerpt: [21]: 13–14): teachers should print and distribute their lectures; must place greater emphasis on self-learning. Mao Zedong: Speech, June 16, 1964 (texts: [167]: 500–504; [174]: 356–60): on having military work meet the need for training revolutionary successors: local party committees should pay more attention to military work; militia work must be improved; specifies five requirements for training proper successors to the revolution.

State Planning Commission: Report on the Third Five-Year Plan (mention: [283]: 378).

Mao Zedong (ibid.): agriculture and national defense are both fists, but for those fists to have a punch, they must rest on the butt of basic industry; learn from Dazhai.

Liu Shaoqi: June 16, 1964 (excerpts: [250]: March 18, 1967): too brief to be meaningful.

VII.   "Organizational Rules of Poor and Lower Middle Peasant Associations (Draft)," June 1964 (text: [8]: 95–101)—passed at this conference or reflects the decisions at this meeting?

VIII.   Approved Liu Shaoqi's proposal for dual track labor and education systems (regular labor and temporary and contract labor, full-time schools and part-work, part-study schools) ([89]: 240).

IX.   It was the belief of this meeting that revisionism had already appeared in China: one-third of the basic units were not controlled by the party. This finding resulted in the revision of the Later Ten Points by Liu Shaoqi, which was further corrected by Mao Zedong and approved by a Central Work Conference on September 18, 1964 ([89]: 356, 377; [108]: 223; [273]: 555).

The evidence does not indicate clearly whether this was one or several meetings. The various documents cited above refer to an Enlarged Meeting of the Standing Committee of the Politburo, a Meeting of the Standing Committee of the Politburo, and a Central Work Conference, in addition to a Work Conference of the CC CCP. The decision to treat these all as one meeting under the last rubric is, therefore, arbitrary.

Oliver [pseud.] ([180]: 486) asserts that a June 1964 Central Committee Work Conference set off the shrill antirevisionist tone evident since the summer of 1964 and also formulated the program to cultivate revolutionary successors.

239

I.   *August 2, 1964*
II.   **CENTRAL CONFERENCE ON EDUCATIONAL SYSTEM**
V.   Part-work, part-study
VI.   Liu Shaoqi (excerpts: [81]: 15): touches upon implementation of part-work, part-study and its relationship to contract labor and apprentice systems in the urban areas.
IX.   All information on this meeting comes from the single Red Guard source cited above.

240

I.   *August 10, 1964*
II.   **CONFERENCE OF CADRES OF PARTY CENTRAL DEPARTMENTS AND OF BEIJING MUNICIPAL CADRES**
V.   Socialist Education, Four Clean-ups, and Five-Anti movements
VI.   Liu Shaoqi: "Report on Problems of the Socialist Education Movement, the Four Clean-ups, and the Five-Anti Campaign" (excerpts: [205]: 652: April 28, 1969: 34, 37): the Later Ten Points did not place enough emphasis on freely mobilizing the masses—they should be revised; 33 percent of basic-level cadres in North China, 60–70 percent in Hebei, and almost 100 percent in Shanxi are under the control of class enemies; probably one-third of all basic-level units are not in our hands—must carry out investigation to determine the real proportions; even those who genuinely engage in building socialism should sweat and undergo arduous struggle.
IX.   All information on this meeting comes from the single Red Guard source cited above.

     Liu stressed the same theme in his report to the August 18–24, 1964, conference (meeting 242).

241

I.   *Mid-August 1964*
II.   **MEETING CONVENED BY SECRETARIAT**
V.   Development of the interior

VI. Mao Zedong: Speeches, August 17 and 20, 1964 (mention: [283]: 379): it is important to develop the interior to counter the present concentration of factories and schools in large cities and coastal areas, which is harmful to national defense.

VIII. Set provisions that gave priority to development of interior over next few years (mention: ibid.).

242

I. *August ?-18-24-?, 1964*
II. **CONFERENCE**
IV. Mao Zedong, Kang Sheng, Chen Boda, Lu Ping, and a number of intellectuals (among others?).
V. Class struggle; dialectics; Socialist Education Movement
VI. Mao Zedong: "Talk on Problems of Philosophy," August 18, 1964 (texts: [201]: 212–30; [167]: 548–61; [174]: 384–96): stresses importance of having intellectuals go to the countryside to gain firsthand experience of conditions there and of class struggle; castigates Yang Xianzhen's theory of "two combines into one" and emphasizes the universality of "one divides into two"; asserts that at present approximately one-third of the power is in the hands of the enemy or sympathizers of the enemy; calls on people to study history from the point of view of class struggle.

Liu Shaoqi: "Report," August 18, 1964 (excerpts: [205]: 652: April 28, 1968: 35, 37): the targets of the Socialist Education Movement in the countryside have already devised means of foiling the work teams—thus, must be prepared for a very sharp and complicated struggle in this endeavor; it is necessary to carry out secret work for one or two months; should take root, exchange experiences, and mobilize the masses—the past methods of convening investigation meetings are no longer adequate.

Mao Zedong: "Talk on Sakata's Article," August 24, 1964 (partial texts: [167]: 561–67; [174]: 397–402): discussion of an article on basic particles by Sakata Shiyouchi; emphasis on problems of cognition, perpetual change, and the inevitability of death.

Mao Zedong: "Talk on Methods of Solidarity," August 1964 (texts: [167]: 545–48; [174]: 403–405): should adopt a method of first struggling with and then presenting a way out for errant cadres so that they can rectify their errors; must popularize dialectics.

IX. It is unclear whether the four presentations noted above were made at the same conference. Mao's August 18, 1964, talk includes a number of interjections by Kang Sheng and contains hints that he is addressing a largely nonparty audience of intellectuals, primarily people concerned with philosophy. Liu's August 18, 1964, speech, by contrast, seems to be directed to an audience of work team members. Mao's August 24, 1964, talk includes interjections by unnamed others but clearly is not a complete text of the discussion. His August 1964 talk on methods of solidarity contains hints that his audience consisted exclusively of party members. Since all concern an interrelated set of issues and there is no firm basis for assigning them to separate meetings, they are presented together here.

The degree of class struggle in the countryside and how to handle errant cadres is a theme that runs throughout these pieces. Liu stresses here, as he did in his report to an August 10, 1964, meeting (meeting 240), the inadequacy of present methods in the Socialist Education Movement and the need to take a harder line. This stronger approach was embodied in the "Revised Later Ten Points," promulgated in September 1964. Mao, on the other hand, agrees with Liu's August 10, 1964, assessment (repeated at this conference [116]: April 25, 1967) that one-third of the party units are in the hands of the enemy, but he seems more concerned to rectify and achieve unity with the erring cadres.

Attacks on Yang Xianzhen's theory of "two combines into one" began in earnest in the Chinese press in July 1964.

243

I.   *September 4, 1964*
II.   **REPORT MEETING**
V.   Sino-Soviet relations
VI.   Mao Zedong (excerpts: [167]: 577–78; [174]: 406–407): stresses that China must be prepared for a break with the USSR; comments on Sino-Romanian and Soviet-East European relations.

244

I.   *September 23, 1964*
II.   **MEETING CONVENED BY PENG ZHEN**
V.   Rectification in literature, art, philosophy, and social science
VI.   Lu Dingyi: "Report" (mention: [237]: 8): deals with rectification in literature and art work and in philosophy and social science.
IX.   All information on this meeting comes from the single Red Guard source cited above.

245

I.   *October 15, 1964*
II.   **CONFERENCE OF LEADING CADRES OF THE CC ORGANIZATION DEPARTMENT, CC CONTROL COMMISSION, MINISTRY OF PUBLIC SECURITY, AND OTHER UNITS**
V.   Four clean-ups
VI.   Liu Shaoqi (excerpts: [206]: 25: May 13, 1968: 29, 33): the four clean-ups has not succeeded; many problems of class struggle can no longer be solved by holding investigation meetings.
IX.   All information on this meeting comes from the single Red Guard source cited above.

246

I.   *October (probably the third week) 1964*
II.   **MEETING OF THE POLITBURO OF THE CC CCP**
V.   USSR
VI.   Liu Shaoqi (excerpt: [148]: 18): assessment of the CPSU has taken a 30 degree turn compared with the past.
IX.   This meeting convened in the wake of Khrushchev's ouster on October 14, 1964. The Chinese quickly sent the new Soviet leaders their greetings and hopes for improved relations (mention: [177]: October 29, 1964).

247

I.   *December 15, 1964–January 14, 1965* ([273]: 557)
II.   **CENTRAL WORK CONFERENCE**
III. Beijing
V.   Socialist Education Movement
VI.   Mao Zedong and Chen Boda: Discussion, December 27, 1964 (texts: [167]: 597–98; [174]: 427–28): the principal contradiction is between socialism and capitalism; the four cleans and four uncleans do not explain the nature of the problem; there are at least two factions in the CCP—the socialist faction and the capitalist faction.
      Mao Zedong: Speech, December 28, 1964 (texts: [167]: 598–602; [174]: 429–32): reviews two of the Twenty-three Points: the nature of the problem and work attitudes (Mao refers to the latter as Article 16, while

in the Twenty-three Points adopted in January 1965 this was Article 21, thus indicating that Mao was still discussing a draft of this document).

Liu Shaoqi: Speech at the Northwest Group Meeting, December 1964 (excerpt: [130]: 18): on differentiating classes in the pastoral areas.

Liu Shaoqi (mention: [272]: IV: 1: January 10, 1970: 126; [182]: 3: January 14, 1977: 12): affirms that the nature of the Socialist Education Movement is the contradiction between the four cleans and the four uncleans and that is also the intersection of the contradictions between those inside and outside the party and between contradictions among the people and between the enemy and ourselves; promotes the "experience of Taoyuan."

Mao Zedong: Speech, January 3, 1965 (texts: [167]: 606–14; [174]: 437–44): disparages the work done to date by the Socialist Education Movement work teams and calls for bringing the masses into the process of party rectification in the villages.

VII.   "Some Problems Currently Arising in the Course of the Rural Socialist Education Movement" (frequently called the "Twenty-three Points"), January 14, 1965 (text: [8]: 118–26).

IX.   Mao Zedong at this meeting criticized An Ziwen's tendency toward "closed-doorism" in the recruitment of new party members (mention: [288]: 17). He also criticized Liu Shaoqi and Wang Guangmei for the latter having taken too large a work team with her when she went down to Xincheng *xian* in November 1964 (her team consisted of 1,500 people for work in a *xian* with a population of 280,000) (mention: [65]: May 7, 1967).

Mao Zedong is reported to have drawn up the "Twenty-three Points" at this conference on January 1, 1965 (mention: [206]: 32: November 25, 1968: 14).

There is evidence of Central Work Conferences of one sort or another in session either continuously or sporadically from as early as December 1, 1964. [205]: 639: January 6, 1969: 21 refers to a Central Work Conference on December 2, 1964. Also, the December 20, 1964, Central Work Symposium (meeting 249) refers to a meeting that had been going on among the central leaders for some time previously. Thus, this is most likely one of several meetings of central leaders designed to work out in detail the targets and methods of the Socialist Education Movement, including both the rural four clean-ups and the urban five-antis.

248

I.   *December 18, 1964*
II.   **SUPREME STATE CONFERENCE**
IV.   187 people, including Song Qingling, Zhu De, Zhou Enlai, Liu Shaoqi,

Dong Biwu, responsible people in the CCP, the various democratic parties, and people's groups, and relevant personages from various fields (mention: [195]: 1965: 125).

V.   Preparation for the December 20, 1964–January 4, 1965, First Session of the Third NPC (meeting 251) and the December 20, 1964–January 4, 1965, First Session of the Fourth CPPCC (meeting 250)

VI.   Zhou Enlai (mention: ibid.): explains the main contents of the report on government work he will deliver to the First Session of the Third NPC (meeting 251).

Peng Zhen (mention: ibid.): explains problems in the agenda of the First Session of the Third NPC and the First Session of the Fourth CPPCC (meeting 250).

249

I.   *December 20, 1964*
II.   **CENTRAL WORK SYMPOSIUM**
IV.   Mao Zedong, Zhou Enlai, Kang Sheng, Li Xiannian, Xie Fuzhi, Liu Xiufeng, Li Weihan, Zhang Zhiyi, Li Xuefeng, Gao Yangwen, Wang Haoshou, and the first secretaries of the Anhui, Guizhou, Qinghai, and Gansu party committees (among others?).
V.   Four clean-ups; five-antis
IX.   The stenographic record of this symposium is available ([167]: 578–97; [174]: 408–26), with the characters for the names of a number of speakers represented by x's. This symposium followed more extensive discussions carried out during previous days and focused on the four clean-ups in the countryside and the five-antis in the cities. Mao Zedong stressed strongly the need to rectify party cadres first in the countryside, thereby keeping the target of the four clean-ups relatively narrow and not letting corrupt cadres slip through. At the same time, he opposed the idea of demanding repayment of 100 percent of the money gained through corruption. The discussion of the urban five-antis concentrated on the demand for training good cadres.

This symposium should be viewed in the context of the December 1964 Central Work Conference (meeting 247).

250

I.   *December 20, 1964–January 5, 1965*
II.   **FIRST SESSION OF THE FOURTH CPPCC**
III.   Beijing

VI. Guo Moruo: "Work Report of the Standing Committee of the Third CPPCC," December 20, 1964 (text: [195]: 1965: 34–36).

VII. "Decisions of the First Session of the Fourth CPPCC," January 5, 1965 (text: ibid.: 36–37).

IX. On December 21–22, 1964, the delegates to this meeting attended the First Session of the Third NPC (meeting 251) in a nonvoting capacity (ibid.: 32).

251

I. *December 20, 1964–January 4, 1965*
II. **FIRST SESSION OF THE THIRD NPC**
III. Beijing
VI. Zhou Enlai: "Government Work Report," December 21–22, 1964 (excerpt: [286]: 439–42; summary: [195]: 1965: 9–16; [108]: 233–35).

Xie Juezai: "Work Report of the Supreme People's Court," December 26, 1964 (summary: [195]: 1965: 16–17).

Zhang Dingcheng: "Work Report of the Supreme People's Procuracy," December 26, 1964 (summary: ibid.: 17–18).

There were also other minor written reports and speeches.

VII. "Decisions of the First Session of the Third NPC of the PRC on the Government Work Report, the Major Indicators of the 1965 National Economic Plan, and the Initial Preparations for the 1965 State Budget," January 4, 1964 (text: ibid.: 18–19).

"Decision of the First Session of the Third NPC of the PRC on the Work Reports of the Supreme People's Court and the Supreme People's Procuracy," January 4, 1965 (text: ibid.: 19).

"Decision of the First Session of the Third NPC of the PRC on the Work Report of the Standing Committee of the NPC," January 4, 1965 (text: ibid.).

VIII. Election of state and government leaders (summary: [108]: 235).
IX. Many of the documents from this meeting are also available in [282].

Zhou Enlai's work report formally proposed the "Four Modernizations" policy at Mao's suggestion ([137]: 131). Zhou's work report and the 1965 economic plan were approved "after heated debate" ([108]: 235). Zhou reportedly used this report to oppose Liu Shaoqi's December 1964 speech to the Central Work Conference on the Socialist Education Movement (meeting 247), which "painted a bleak picture of the socialist new countryside" (mention: [182]: 3: January 14, 1977: 12).

252

I.   *December 30, 1964*
II.   **SUPREME STATE CONFERENCE**
IV.   177 people, including Song Qingling, Dong Biwu, Liu Shaoqi, Zhu De, Zhou Enlai, responsible people of the CCP, democratic parties, people's groups, provinces, municipalities, and autonomous regions, and other relevant personages (mention: [195]: 1965: 125).
V.   Items related to the December 20, 1964–January 4, 1965, First Session of the Third NPC (meeting 251) and the December 20, 1964–January 5, 1965, First Session of the Fourth CPPCC (meeting 250).
VI.   Liu Shaoqi: Speech (mention: ibid.): on the current international and domestic situation and some important problems in work.
IX.   This conference also continued discussion of the Government Work Report that Zhou Enlai delivered to the December 20, 1964–January 4, 1965, First Session of the Third NPC (meeting 251) and consulted on name lists for alternate members and state leaders to be proposed at the First Session of the Third NPC and on name lists of political consultative leaders and alternate members to be proposed at the December 20, 1964–January 5, 1965 First Session of the Fourth CPPCC (meeting 250).

Two Red Guard sources ([123]: April 18, 1967; [126]) assert that at ''a December 1964 Supreme State Conference'' (almost undoubtedly referred to this December 30, 1964, conference rather than the December 18, 1964, Supreme State Conference [meeting 248]) Liu Shaoqi proposed to propagate the Later Ten Points (this must in fact be the Revised Later Ten Points, Liu's program for carrying out the Socialist Education Movement) throughout the country. To the extent this charge is true, Liu utilized this meeting to advocate his own views on this issue at almost the same time that Mao Zedong was working out his own version (the Twenty-three Points) at a December 1964 Central Work Conference (meeting 247).

1965

253

I.   *1965*
II.   **NATIONAL RURAL PART-FARMING, PART-STUDY EDUCATIONAL CONFERENCE**
V.   Part-farming, part-study system

VI.   Liu Shaoqi: Speech (exerpts: [81]; [252]: 11: April 27, 1967; [149]):
promotes the part-farming, part-study system in the rural areas, touching
specifically on curriculum, enrollment, length of semesters, teaching
staff, study materials, and the need to formalize this type of educational
system.

IX.   He Wei participated in a "report meeting" on this conference on April 3,
1965 (excerpts: [149]; [229]).

Liu Shaoqi in July 1965 issued an instruction concerning this type of
educational system (excerpt: [149]).

Lu Dingyi addressed a Part-Farming, Part-Study Work Conference
convened by the Ministry of Education in April 1965 (excerpt: [157]). Liu
Shaoqi also addressed this meeting, and the summary of the proceedings
is available in [216]: 3470: June 3, 1965: 20–21.

254

I.   *March–April 1965*
II.   **NATIONAL URBAN PART-WORK, PART-STUDY
EDUCATIONAL CONFERENCE**
V.   Urban part-work, part-study system
VI.   Liu Shaoqi: Speech (excerpts: [81]; [252]): promotes the two-track (full-
time and part-work, part-study) school system as a way to prevent capital-
ist restoration; discusses variants of work-study in terms of different
balances between work and study and the wage implications involved.

Lu Dingyi: "Report," early April (mention: [239]: May 15, 1967).

He Wei: "Summary Report" (summary: ibid.): major points are as
follows: the conference proceeded in three stages, viz.: study of the
instructions of the center, Mao Zedong, and Liu Shaoqi; exchange of
experiences; and discussion of some methods; conference convened under the impetus of the Politburo and Liu Shaoqi; Liu Shaoqi addressed the
conference twice, advocating the "four-four" system of half-work, half-
study and stressing the need to proceed slowly (five years of experimenta-
tion) and to emphasize consolidation; Lu Dingyi made an important
report, also stressing the need to proceed cautiously; the conference as a
whole stressed the importance of a two-track educational system in order
to prevent capitalist restoration and revisionism.

IX.   He Wei mentioned that this conference was preceded by an enlarged
meeting of the Politburo that was convened to deal with the part-work,
part-study system's problems. He gave no date for this enlarged Politburo
meeting (mention: ibid.).

255

I.   *March 3, 1965*
II.   **MEETING OF THE SECRETARIAT OF THE CC CCP**
III. Beijing
V.   Cultural Revolution at Beijing University; rectification in literature and art circles
VI.   Deng Xiaoping (mention: [120]; [94]: 14; [250]: March 21, 1967; [96]: 9–10; [101]: May 23, 1967; [217]: 162: February 14, 1967: 9–10; [55]; [273]: 560): some people are using the rectification campaign in literature and art circles to gain recognition for themselves by criticizing others; criticizes the implementation of the Socialist Education Movement at Beijing University; admits Lu Ping and Peng Peiyun to the leadership group of the work team at Beijing University; insists, in effect, that the "three unifications" called for in the "Twenty-three Points" be carried out instantly instead of the gradual process specified in that document, thus assuring that the leading members of a unit would be able quickly to establish relations with the incoming work team, to the disadvantage of rebellious students and others in the unit.

   Peng Zhen (mention: [250]: April 22, 1967): joins with Deng Xiaoping in attacking the implementation of the Socialist Education Movement at Beijing University.
IX.   The official summary of the meeting pointed out that the criticism campaign as carried out since 1964 had been excessive, which prevented creativity from flourishing, and therefore should be quickly stopped ([273]: 560).

256

I.   *March 9–19, 1965*
II.   **FIRST INTERNATIONAL HOTEL CONFERENCE**
III. Beijing
V.   Socialist Education Movement at Beijing University
IX.   Wan Li convened this meeting at Deng Xiaoping's request (mention: [96]: 8–10).

   At this conference, Wan Li attempted to influence the course of the Socialist Education Movement at Beijing University by casting a favorable light on Lu Ping, but he was not completely successful in this effort (mention: ibid.; [250]: April 22, 1967; [217]: 165: March 10, 1967: 8–9).

257

I.   *April 1965*
II.   **MEETING OF THE POLITBURO OF THE CC CCP**
V.   "Hai Rui Dismissed from Office"
VI.   Mao Zedong (mention: [124]: May 25, 1967): clearly points out that the major problem in Wu Han's "Hai Rui Dismissed from Office" is the problem of dismissal (i.e., that this play must be treated as a political question related to the rightist attack at the Lushan Conference in July 1959 [meeting 138] rather than as an academic question) and that Wu Han's problem is a political problem.
IX.   All information on this meeting comes from the single Red Guard source cited above.

258

I.   *April 2, 1965*
II.   **NATIONALITIES HOTEL CONFERENCE**
III.   Beijing
V.   Composition of work team at Beijing University
VIII.   Decided to replace Zhang Panshi (the former team leader) with Xu Liqun and to add Chang Xiping to the nine-man leading group of the Socialist Education Movement Work Team at Beijing University (mention: [96]: 9–10).

    Added Lu Ping and Peng Peiyun to the nine-man leading group of the Beijing University work team (mention: [250]: April 22, 1967).
IX.   On the basis of information given to him by Chang Xiping, Deng Xiaoping convened the meeting to change the composition of the work team at Beijing University (mention: [96]: 9–10).

259

I.   *June 1965*
II.   **MEETING CONVENED BY LIU SHAOQI**
V.   Dictatorship of the proletariat
IX.   Liu Shaoqi argued that the Four Clean-ups campaign in the cities should not be followed by implementing measures of education through labor. He and Deng Xiaoping also advocated a longer period of peaceful coexistence with religious elements in the cities (mention: [123]: April 18, 1967; [126]).

260

I.   *July 13, 1965*
II.   **(ENLARGED) MEETING OF THE FIVE-MAN CULTURAL REVOLUTION GROUP**
IV.   Peng Zhen, Kang Sheng, Lu Dingyi, Lin Feng, Zhou Yang, Wu Lengxi, Jiang Nanxiang, Deng Tuo, Lin Mohan, Xu Liqun, Xiao Wangdong, Shi Ximin, Liu Baiyu, and others (mention: [120]; [101]: 4: May 10, 1967; [194]: August 13, 1967).
V.   Sending opera troupes to the countryside
VI.   Xiao Wangdong: Report on ''An Outline Report to the Central Committee from the Ministry of Culture Party Committee on Some Problems in Current Cultural Work'' (excerpts: [120]): advocates sending down opera troupes to the countryside and curtailing traditonal opera; calls for further investigations with respect to films.

      Kang Sheng (excerpt: ibid.): urban-oriented cultural products are not suited for the rural areas; rather should look at some of the work done by the CCP in the rural areas during the Anti-Japanese War to develop ideas concerning how to produce cultural events appropriate to the rural areas.

      Peng Zhen, Lu Dingyi, Xu Liqun (mention: ibid.): support Xiao Wangdong's recommendations.
IX.   Xiao Wangdong's report was next considered at a September 6, 1965, meeting of the Politburo of the CC CCP (meeting 265).

261

I.   *August ?-3-21, 1965*
II.   **NATIONAL CONFERENCE ON POLITICAL WORK IN AGRICULTURE AND FORESTRY**
III.   Beijing
V.   Political work in agriculture and forestry
VI.   Tan Zhenlin, August 3, 1965: Remarks (mention: [256]).
VIII.   This conference reached the following conclusions (mention: [216]: 3526: August 26, 1965: 1):

      —The question of strengthening ideological and political work is fundamental.

      —Ideological and political work must be carried out in line with the special characteristics of China's rural areas.

      —Must study Chairman Mao's works, learn from the PLA, and acquire the Dazhai and Daqing spirit of self-reliance.

      —Farming units that set examples in stable and high yields can become pacesetters in the Three Great Revolutionary Movements (class struggle, struggle for production, and scientific experimentation).

IX.   This conference also studied ways of strengthening ideological and political work among the staff of state-owned agricultural and forestry farms and enterprises (mention: ibid.).

The "Department of the CC CCP in charge of ideological and political work in agricultural and forestry units" convened this conference (mention: ibid.).

Mao Zedong and Liu Shaoqi received the delegates attending this conference (mention: ibid.).

262

I.   *August 9 (?), 1965* (see IX below)
II.   **MEETING OF THE SECRETARIAT OF THE CC CCP**
V.   Study of Mao Zedong Thought
IX.   This meeting focused on the "living study and application of Mao Zedong Thought." Liu Shaoqi and Deng Xiaoping circulated a summary of the meeting that cautioned against the rigid, formalistic study of Mao's works. This summary in turn purportedly influenced a *Zhongguo qingnian bao* (Chinese Youth) editorial entitled "Taking Reality as the Starting Point, Guide the Study of Mao Zedong's Works" (mention: [250]: March 21, 1967; text of editorial: [276]).

While [250]: March 21, 1967, places this meeting in August 1965, a snippet of a quotation from Deng Xiaoping's remarks to a meeting of the Secretariat on August 9, 1965 ([94]: 2) is in line with the theme of this meeting.

There was a CC CCP Conference on the Youth League, also attended by Deng Xiaoping, on this same day (meeting 263).

263

I.   *August 9, 1965*
II.   **CONFERENCE OF THE CC CCP**
V.   Communist Youth League work
VI.   Deng Xiaoping (excerpts: [94]: 4–5; [205]: 639: January 6, 1969: 4; [47]): opposes too much concentration on the dogmatic study of Mao Zedong's works.

Peng Zhen (excerpts: ibid.): agrees with Deng's opposition to the dogmatic study of Mao Zedong's works. Luo Ruiqing (excerpts: ibid.): too brief to be meaningful.

IX.   On this same day, the Secretariat of the CC CCP met to discuss the study of Mao Zedong Thought (meeting 262).

264

I.   *September 1965*

II.   **(ENLARGED) MEETING OF THE STANDING COMMITTEE OF THE POLITBURO OF THE CC CCP**

IV.   Attended by, among others, the leading comrades of all the regional bureaus of the CC CCP (mention: [182]: 21: May 19, 1967: 6).

V.   The problem of revisionism within the CCP

VI.   Mao Zedong (mention and excerpts: [115]: June 6, 1966; [84]: 18; [159]; [182]: 21: May 19, 1967: 6; [182]: 33: August 11, 1967: 7; [205]: 640: January 13, 1969; [246]): asserts there is a need to subject bourgeois reactionary ideology to criticism; notes the possibility of revisionism in the CC CCP; orders (on September 10, 1965) that Wu Han's "Hai Rui Dismissed from Office" be criticized and directs Peng Zhen to make certain this criticism is carried out.

IX.   This meeting seems to have marked an important turning point for Mao Zedong in his thinking about the measures necessary to rectify the problem of revisionism in the higher levels of the CC CCP. There is, however, extremely little concrete information on this meeting.

    A National Conference of the Heads of Cultural Departments and Sections convened on September 9–27, 1965, and was addressed by prominent national leaders such as Peng Zhen. There is a great deal of scattered information on this conference (e.g.: [194]: August 13, 1967; [241]).

265

I.   *September 1965*

II.   **MEETING OF THE POLITBURO OF THE CC CCP**

V.   Public health work

VIII.   Liu Shaoqi directed (mention: [191]: May 4, 1967; [191]: June 26, 1967; [217]: 209: November 3, 1967: 20):

    —Send doctors and nurses from the large hospitals to the outpatient departments of government organs and street organizations so as to put the latter on a sound footing.

    —Send doctors and medicines to the doorsteps of the patients.

IX.   Discussion at this meeting centered on the urban-rural distribution of health services. It also touched on the need for health workers to participate in labor (mention: [191]: May 4, 1967).

This meeting was convened after Mao Zedong issued his June 26, 1965, directive (texts: [167]: 615–16; [201]: 232–33) on "placing the focal point of medicine and health work in the countryside." Red Guards subsequently viewed this Politburo meeting as a means of deflecting the force of Mao's directive by focusing on other—urban—aspects of the health care delivery problem ([191]: June 26, 1967; [217]: 209: November 3, 1967: 20).

266

I.   *September 6, 1965* (see IX below)
II.   **MEETING OF THE POLITBURO OF THE CC CCP**
IV.   Liu Shaoqi, Deng Xiaoping, Peng Zhen, Lu Dingyi, Bo Yibo, Zhou Yang, Xiao Wangdong (mention: [1]: 408).
V.   Discuss Ministry of Culture Party Group's Report
VI.   Liu Shaoqi (excerpts: [101]: 4: May 10, 1967; [169]; [217]: 205: September 29, 1967: 38): scattered remarks on various aspects of cultural work.

Xiao Wangdong (mention: [120]; [101]: 4: May 10, 1967; [194]: August 13, 1967): presents the "Outline Report to the Central Committee from the Ministry of Culture Party Committee on Some Problems in Current Cultural Work," which he had previously presented to the five-man Cultural Revolution Group for discussion on July 13, 1965 (meeting 260).

VIII.   Liu Shaoqi instructed that:

—Work to carry out Mao Zedong's policy line in literature and art should not be pushed "too urgently" (mention: [194]: August 18, 1967).

—Xia Yan and Qi Yanming can serve as deputy team leaders in carrying out the four clean-ups (mention: ibid.).

—Xiao Wangdong should transmit this report to the National Conference of Heads of Cultural Bureaus and Sections for discussion (this conference convened for September 9–27, 1965: [241]) (mention: ibid.).

—the Ministry of Culture should begin to produce short stories, movies, operas, etc., that take as their general theme the Four Clean-ups movement and can be made public at some time in the future (there had been a ban on such materials until this date) (mention: [99]).

IX.   The following sources mistakenly give the date of this meeting as September 9, 1965: ([1]: 408; [217]: 205: September 29, 1967: 38).

Xiao Wangdong's report laid the basis for the subsequent February Outline Report (see the February 3, 1966, Five-man Cultural Revolution Group meeting [meeting 279] and the February 5, 1966, Standing Committee of the Politburo meeting [meeting 280]), which in turn crystallized the differences between Jiang Qing and Peng Zhen on cultural matters on the eve of the Cultural Revolution.

267

I.   *November 1965* (see IX below)

II.   **NATIONAL URBAN PART-WORK, PART-STUDY CONFERENCE**

IV.   Representatives of the central and local departments dealing with planning, industry, communications, finance and trade, labor, and education; representatives of schools of various types; central party leaders and representatives of the Ministry of Education (mention: [216]: 3598: December 15, 1965: 13–16).

V.   Setting policy toward urban part-work, part-study schools

VI.   Liu Shaoqi (mention: ibid; excerpts: [153]): there are only three ways to prevent revisionism and capitalist restoration: the Socialist Education Movement, the two-track school systems, and cadre participation in labor.

       Lu Dingyi: Report (mention: [216]: 3598: December 15, 1965: 13–16; excerpts: [157]); reiterates Liu's remarks just noted; stipulates expectations about the spread of education in China over the coming one hundred years; reviews some problems in the 1958 effort to establish a system of part-work, part-study schools.

       Deng Xiaoping (excerpt: [94]: 18): need not develop the part-work, part-study system too quickly.

       Zhou Enlai (mention: [216]: 3598: December 15, 1965: 13–16): gives important instructions at the conference. Representatives of Daqing (mention: ibid.): give accounts of Daqing's self-reliance and experience in running schools with industry and thrift.

VIII.   The conference reached the following conclusions (all from ibid.):

       —Development of full-time and part-work, part-study systems is one of the important guarantees for preventing the restoration of capitalism in China.

       —Must persist in the principle of "five years of experimentation and ten years of popularization"—should neither vacillate in determination nor enforce this system too rapidly.

       —Major current tasks are to strengthen leadership (especially party leadership); make overall planning; actively carry out experiments; and consolidate gains already made.

       —The "four-four" system (four hours a day of work and four hours a day of study) is generally the best form of part-work, part-study system.

IX.   This conference was called "under the direct leadership of the Party

Central Committee and Chairman Liu Shaoqi and was presided over by the Ministry of Education'' (mention: ibid.).

A November 6, 1965, Enlarged Meeting of the Politburo of the CC CCP (meeting 268) dealt with this same subject.

A December 5, 1965, NCNA dispatch (ibid.) noted that this conference had met ''recently.''

268

I.   *November 6, 1965*
II.   **ENLARGED MEETING OF THE POLITBURO OF THE CC CCP**
V.   Two-track educational system
VI.   Liu Shaoqi (excerpts: [123]: April 18, 1967; [124]: January 1, 1967; [149]: 26–27; [225]: May 6, 1967 and April 29, 1967; [227]: April 29, 1967; [229]): suggests the Ministry of Higher Education and the Ministry of Education study further and make preparations concerning the reform of the full-time schools; advocates the ''four hours of work, four hours of study'' system for the part-work, part-study schools.
IX.   In November 1965 Liu Shaoqi purportedly convened, in the name of the Politburo, a symposium attended by responsible people of the various CCP central departments and the ministries of the State Council, at which he promoted his own ideas on the part-work, part-study system (mention: [126]). It is unclear whether this is the same meeting as the November 6, 1965, Enlarged Politburo meeting or is a preliminary or follow-up meeting. It is probably the latter since there is independent confirmation of a symposium on this subject on November 10, 1965 ([132]: May 22, 1967, and June 2, 1967). One month later Liu wrote an outline report on this same subject (excerpt: [225]: April 29, 1967).

The meetings that set a precedent for this one are the March 1965 National Rural Part-Farming, Part-Study Educational Conference (meeting 253) and the March–April 1965 National Urban Part-Work, Part-Study Educational Conference (meeting 254).

269

I.   *November 15, 1965*
II.   **ENLARGED MEETING OF THE POLITBURO OF THE CC CCP**
V.   Two-track school system
VI.   Liu Shaoqi (excerpt: [208]: 54): should not give blind commands with respect to reform of the full-day school system.
IX.   All information on this meeting comes from the single Red Guard source cited above.

270

I.   *November 28, 1965*
II.   **MEETING CONVENED BY ZHOU ENLAI**
III. Beijing
IV.   Zhou Enlai, Peng Zhen, Deng Tuo (and others?). Not attended by Wu Han.
V.   Failure of Beijing press to reprint Yao Wenyuan's article
VIII. Decided the Beijing press would reprint Yao Wenyuan's November 10, 1965, *Wenhui bao* article criticizing Wu Han's "Hai Rui Dismissed from Office" (mention: [125]; [246]: 3).
IX.   The November 29, 1965, *Beijing ribao* (Beijing Daily) reprinted Yao Wenyuan's article, with an editor's note that was in fact penned by Peng Zhen (mention: ibid.).

271

I.   *December 1965*
II.   **MEETING OF THE HEADS OF ORGANIZATION DEPARTMENTS OF THE PARTY COMMITTEES OF THE VARIOUS PROVINCES AND MUNICIPALITIES**
V.   Class struggle and proletarian dictatorship
VI.   Liu Shaoqi (excerpt: [116]: April 16, 1967): class struggle in China has been basically concluded and the level of criminal activity has fallen off; can therefore deemphasize the organs of proletarian dictatorship.
IX.   All information on this meeting comes from the single Red Guard source cited above.

272

I.   *December 8–15, 1965*
II.   **ENLARGED MEETING OF THE STANDING COMMITTEE OF THE POLITBURO OF THE CC CCP**
III. Shanghai
IV.   Luo Ruiqing did not attend (mention: [90]: 287).
V.   Luo Ruiqing affair
VI.   Lin Biao, Ye Qun, Wu Faxian, and Li Zuopeng (mention: [108]: 264) all criticize Luo Ruiqing.
VIII. Luo Ruiqing was transferred out of his leading post for military affairs. Yang Chengwu appointed chief of general staff (ibid.).

IX.   This meeting convened to criticize Luo Ruiqing's errors, with Lin Biao launching the most vociferous attack against Luo here (mention: [43]: 894: October 27, 1969: 22; [258]: April 22, 1968; [90]).

The proceedings of this meeting were circulated, following which the PLA's political work conferences among high-level party and army cadres further exposed Luo Ruiqing's "many and serious wrongdoings" (mention: [90]: 287).

This meeting marked the first major overt step by Lin Biao to purge Luo Ruiqing—a process that culminated in the March 4–April 8, 1966, meeting that resolved the Luo Ruiqing issue (meeting 281).

273

I.   *December 20–22(?), 1965* (see IX below)
II.   **HANGZHOU CONFERENCE**
III.   Hangzhou, Zhejiang
IV.   Lin Biao but not Liu Shaoqi (mention: [59]: 74). Also attended by Mao Zedong, Chen Boda, Ai Siqi, Guan Feng, Tao Zhu, and others.
V.   Mass line and *xiafang*
VI.   Mao Zedong: Speech, December 21, 1965 (texts: [26]: 103–11; [43]: 891: December 21, 1965: 51–55; [171]: 1–6; [167]: 624–29; [201]: 234–41; [232]: 66: September 1, 1969: 41–43): philosophers must engage in labor; students must go down to the countryside; higher education should be shortened; philosophical articles should be written in a way that is easier for all to understand.
IX.   Mao Zedong also conversed with Ai Siqi and Chen Boda on December 21, 1965 (text: [167]: 630): stressed the degree to which the twenty-year-old youths of today will hold the fate of the revolution in their hands two or three decades hence; affirmed the importance of carrying out the mass line. Mao Zedong is reported to have conversed with Peng Zhen, Kang Sheng, and Yang Chengwu on December 22, 1965, at which time he stressed that the crux of the matter in Wu Han's "Hai Rui Dismissed from Office" is the question of "dismissal" (i.e., that this play must be treated as a political question related to the rightist attack at the Lushan Conference in July 1959 [meeting 138] rather than as an academic question). Peng Zhen defended Wu Han ([125]: 21).

An official Beijing source ([182]: 23: June 2, 1967: 22) asserts that on December 21, 1965, Mao Zedong stressed the "dismissal" aspect of "Hai Rui Dismissed from Office," but the available texts of his speech and conversation that day do not confirm this. Mao Zedong is reported to have ordered at this conference that work teams should not be dispatched hurriedly (mention: [217]: 166: March 13, 1967: 24). Dittmer ([59]: 74) notes that this conference lasted three days and that Liu Shaoqi, who remained in Beijing, learned about the substance of the proceedings via a telephone call to Lin Biao.

274

I.   *"End of"* 1965
II.   **MEETING OF THE SECRETARIAT OF THE CC CCP**
V.   Part-work, part-study system
VI.   Deng Xiaoping (excerpt: [94]: 18): should not undertake part-work, part-study schools too rapidly, as they will produce too many people who expect jobs from the state; at least some graduates of these schools will have to work as laborers.

Jiang Nanxiang: "Report on a Part-Work, Part-Study Conference to Be Convened by the Ministry of Higher Education" (mention: ibid.).
IX.   All information on this meeting comes from the single Red Guard source cited above.

The conference on which Jiang Nanxiang reported convened in January 1966 (meeting 275).

1966

275

I.   *January 1966*
II.   **NATIONAL PART-WORK, PART-STUDY CONFERENCE FOR HIGHER SCHOOLS**
V.   Part-work, part-study system for higher schools (including universities and certain technical schools)
VI.   Lu Dingyi (excerpt: [157]).
IX.   This is one of a continuing series of meetings on the part-work, part-study system of education during 1965–66. Other meetings on this subject convened in March 1965 (meeting 253), March-April 1965 (meeting 254), November 1965 (meeting 267), November 6, 1965 (meeting 268), end of 1965 (meeting 274), and a meeting of the Secretariat of the CC CCP in January 1966 (meeting 276).

276

I.   *January 1966*
II.   **MEETING OF THE SECRETARIAT OF THE CC CCP**
V.   Part-work, part-study system
VI.   Jiang Nanxiang (mention: [94]: 18): reports on the part-work, part-study system.

Deng Xiaoping (excerpt: ibid.): Beijing University will remain a full-time school; it will be good if a thorough reform of the arts faculties can be accomplished at the beginning of the Third Five-Year Plan.

IX.   All information on this meeting comes from the single Red Guard source cited above.

Jiang Nanxiang's report probably concerned the results of the National Part-Work, Part-Study Conference for Higher Schools, which convened in January 1966 (meeting 275).

277

I.   *January 2, 1966*
II.   **MEETING CONVENED BY PENG ZHEN**
III.   Beijing
IV.   Responsible people from cultural and educational circles, newspapers and magazines, the Beijing Municipal administration, and the armed forces (mention: [125]: 21).
V.   Wu Han's "Hai Rui Dismissed from Office"
VI.   Hu Sheng reports Mao Zedong's views on Wu Han's play but neglects to stress the question of "dismissal," which Mao had emphasized at the Hangzhou Conference of December 20–22, 1965 (meeting 273). Kang Sheng challenges Hu on this point, bringing Peng Zhen to Hu's defense (mention: ibid.: 21–22).

Lu Dingyi (excerpt: [237]: 9): stresses the need to deal with academic problems before turning attention to political problems.

VIII.   Peng Zhen instructed Deng Tuo to send all articles criticizing Wu Han's "Hai Rui Dismissed from Office" to Lu Dingyi for prior perusal and revision (mention: ibid.).

278

I.   *February 2-20, 1966*
II.   **FORUM ON THE WORK IN LITERATURE AND ART FOR THE ARMED FORCES**
III.   Shanghai
V.   The two-line struggle in literature and art and present tasks
VI.   Jiang Qing (mention: [182]: April 28, 1978: 7): literature and art have been under the dictatorship of a sinister line for seventeen years.

Zhang Chunqiao (mention: [194] and [176]: May 18, 1978, tr. in [82]: May 24, 1978: E3).

VII.   "Forum Summary" (texts: [113]: 4-16; [123]: May 25, 1967; [182]: 23: June 2, 1967: 10-16—the last source includes a ten-point concluding portion of measures to be taken in the armed forces that is missing from the first two sources): analyzes the past developments in literature and art and specifies the tasks for the future.

IX.   Jiang Qing was entrusted by Lin Biao to convene this forum. It served as a counterweight to the February 3 and 5, 1966, meetings (meetings 279 and 280), which produced the "February Outline Report."

The "Forum Summary" was revised three times by Mao Zedong before being finalized (mention: [182]: 23: June 2, 1967: 21; [273]: 562). It was then approved by a meeting of the Military Affairs Committee of the CCP on March 30, 1966 (meeting 284), transmitted by the CC on April 10, 1966, and formally affirmed as the preferred document over the "February Outline Report" by the May 4-26, 1966, Enlarged Meeting of the Politburo of the CC CCP (meeting 289). Chen Boda also commented on the summary, but it is not clear if his comments were incorporated into the final version ([194] and [176]: May 18,1978, tr. in [82]: May 24, 1978: E3).

279

I.   *February 3, 1966*
II.   **ENLARGED MEETING OF THE FIVE-MAN CULTURAL REVOLUTION GROUP**
III.   Beijing
IV.   Xu Liqun and Hu Sheng, in addition to the regular members of the group.
V.   Treatment of leftists in the educational sphere

VII.   "Summary Report on the Current Scientific Debate" (February Outline), drafted at this meeting and distributed by the CC CCP on February 10, 1966 ([273]: 561).

VIII. Decided to submit a report to members of the Standing Committee of the Politburo who were in Beijing at that time (mention: [125]: 23).

IX.   Peng Zhen allegedly distributed seven items of printed materials prepared by Xu Liqun and Yao Zhen. These called for rectification of leftists in the educational sphere and for more freedom of expression in that sphere. Xu Liqun objected to linking "Hai Rui Dismissed from Office" to the Lushan meetings of the summer of 1959 (meetings 138 and 139), as Mao Zedong had demanded. Lu Dingyi and Peng Zhen supported this view, while Kang Sheng clashed with all of them, arguing that it is necessary to protect the leftists (such as Guan Feng and Qi Benyu) and direct fire against Wu Han (mention and excerpts: [263]: January 19, 1967; [124]: May 27, 1967; [125]: 22–23; [252]).

At the conclusion of this meeting, Peng Zhen directed Xu Liqun to draft the report noted in VIII above (mention: [125]: 23).

This proved to be a key meeting in the development of the "February Outline Report," a document that came under severe fire from Mao Zedong during the May 4–26, 1966, Enlarged Meeting of the Politburo of the CC CCP (meeting 289). On the evening of February 3, 1966, Xu Liqun and Yao Zhen visited Peng Zhen's home to discuss the drafting of the report from the day's meeting, and at this time they decided to have the report ignore the views expressed by Kang Sheng earlier in the day. Xu and Yao then drafted the report on February 4, 1966, and submitted it to the February 5, 1966, meeting of the Standing Committee of the Politburo (meeting 280).

280

I.   *February ?–5–7–?, 1966*
II.   **MEETING OF THE STANDING COMMITTEE OF THE POLITBURO OF THE CC CCP**
III. Beijing
IV.   Mao Zedong did not attend.
V.   Treatment of leftists
VI.   Peng Zhen: February 5, 1966 (mention: [217]: 195: July 31, 1967: 12): makes a report during which he attacks the leftists and presents the "February Outline," which had been drafted following the February 3, 1966, Enlarged Meeting of the Five-man Cultural Revolution Group (meeting 279). Another source ([246]: 7) says Xu Liqun, and not Peng Zhen, presented the substance of the "February Outline Report" to this

meeting. Still another ([125]: 24) asserts that both Xu Liqun and Yao Zhen presented this report to the meeting, albeit with frequent interruptions by Peng Zhen.

VIII.   Approved the "February Outline Report" after it was revised by Peng Zhen ([108]: 266).

Decided to submit a report to Mao Zedong that reflected the substance of the draft of the "February Outline Report" ([125]: 24).

IX.   Liu Shaoqi presided over this meeting in Mao Zedong's absence. Directly following the February 5 meeting, Peng Zhen directed Xu Liqun, Hu Sheng, Yao Zhen, and Wu Lengxi to make another revision of the "February Outline Report." After approval by the Politburo Standing Committee, it was cabled to Mao in Wuhan on February 7 ([108]: 266). On February 8, 1966, Peng Zhen, Xu Liqun, Hu Sheng, and Wu Lengxi traveled to Wuchang to present the revised report to Mao Zedong (some sources say Peng Zhen, Kang Sheng, and Lu Dingyi reported to Mao: [273]: 561; [108]: 267). Red Guards assert that Peng never actually showed Mao the text of the report, instead simply raising some of the issues with him. Furthermore, even though Mao did not agree with Peng on these issues, Peng reportedly returned to Beijing and said that Mao had approved of distribution of the report to the entire party. He then had Xu Liqun and Hu Sheng make some final amendments and draft the "Comments by the Party Center," after which he submitted the revised report to Liu Shaoqi and Deng Xiaoping for distribution to lower levels of the party (mention: [125]: 4). The report was distributed on February 12, 1966 (texts: [34]: 7–12; [216]: 3952: June 5, 1967: 1–4). A number of points in the May 16 Circular passed by the May 4–26, 1966, Enlarged Meeting of the Politburo of the CC CCP (meeting 289) support this Red Guard account of the events of February 5–12, 1966.

All this occurred while Jiang Qing was convening her February 2–20, 1966, Forum on the Work in Literature and Art for the Armed Forces (meeting 278), which produced a "Forum Summary" in sharp contrast to the "February Outline Report."

281

I.   *March 4–April 8, 1966* (with a hiatus in the middle)

II.   **CENTRAL COMMITTEE WORK GROUP MEETING**

IV.   During the first thirteen days, attended by responsible cadres in each general department of the Military Affairs Committee of the CCP, the Ministry of Public Security, the Office for National Defense Industry, the Committee of National Defense Science, the Academy of Military Science, most military districts and services, and by Luo Ruiqing. After a hiatus and beginning on March 22, 1966, attended in addition by representatives of various CC CCP departments, related concerned ministries of the State Council, and responsible cadres of the CCP bureaus. These additional people attended the second session of this meeting at the instruction of the CC CCP (mention: [90]: 287–88).

V.   Luo Ruiqing affair
VI.   Luo Ruiqing: Confession, March 12, 1966 (mention: [90]: 311): this is deemed to be inadequate.

Peng Zhen (mention: [90]: 314): defends Luo Ruiqing.

Jin Ming (mention: [69]): representing Tao Zhu and the Central-South at this meeting, strongly opposes criticism of Peng Zhen.

VIII. Made the following recommendations to the CC CCP (mention: [90]: 313–14):

—Luo Ruiqing should be dismissed from all his duties in the military affairs system.

—Luo should be dismissed from his duties as vice-minister of the State Council.

—Luo should be dismissed from his duties as member of the Standing Committee of the Politburo of the CC CCP.

—A political and organizational summing up should be made of Luo's mistakes.

—The report of the CC Work Group and the documents it has produced should be circulated to the proper levels in order to eradicate Luo's influence.

IX.   During the first thirteen days of this meeting Luo Ruiqing underwent severe criticism, with Lin Biao leading the attack (mention: [43]: 894: October 27, 1969: 22). On March 18, 1966, Luo attempted suicide by leaping from a window, leaving behind a note that repudiated his March 12, 1966, confession. This suicide attempt came during the middle of a March 17–20, 1966, Enlarged Standing Committee Meeting of the Politburo of the CC CCP (meeting 282), and Mao Zedong's March 20, 1966, address to that meeting seems particularly relevant to the CC Work Group meeting. The CC Work Group then reconvened on March 22, 1966, and passed the recommendations noted in VIII above (mention: [90]: 288, 313).

This meeting culminated a strong attack on Luo Ruiqing that Lin Biao had launched at the December 8, 1965, Central Committee Conference (meeting 272). The decisions taken at this CC Work Group meeting were subsequently approved by the May 4–26, 1966, Enlarged Meeting of the Politburo of the CC CCP (meeting 289).

This CC Work Group meeting designated Ye Jianying, Xiao Hua, Liu Zhijian, and Yang Chengwu to write a report on Peng Zhen's mistakes and submit this report to the CC CCP for approval (mention: [90]: 314).

They submitted this report on April 28, 1966, and it was circulated down to the *xian* level and to regimental party cadres on May 16, 1966 (mention: [43]: 852: May 6, 1968: 7).

282

I. *March 17–20, 1966* (mention: [125]: 26; [246]: 9)
II. **ENLARGED STANDING COMMITTEE MEETING OF THE POLITBURO OF THE CC CCP**
III. Hangzhou
IV. Mao Zedong, Zhou Enlai, Zhu De, Lin Biao, Liu Shaoqi, Peng Zhen, Tao Zhu, Yu Qiuli, and Chen Boda, among others.
V. Military strategy; revolutionary successors; Sino-Soviet affairs; economic administration
VI. Mao Zedong: Speech, March 17, 1966 (partial texts: [167]: 640; [174]: 381): should carry out sincere criticism of bourgeois academic authorities; must cultivate youths and let them have their head; bourgeois authorities are holding real power in academic and intellectual circles (an excerpt from this speech in [(231): 9] substitutes "cultural departments" for "academic and intellectual circles").

Mao Zedong, with interjections by others, March 20, 1966 (texts: [167]: 634–40; [174]: 375–80): wide-ranging discussion, touching on the following main topics: the Chinese refusal to attend the 23d Congress of the CPSU; policies toward intellectuals and the natural sciences; the need to develop proper revolutionary successors (including a very sharp jibe by Chen Boda aimed at Liu Shaoqi); the necessity of adopting a highly decentralized strategy of fighting if China is attacked; and the concomitant need for decentralization of economic administration.

Mao Zedong (excerpt: [273]: 563): the propaganda department must not become the rural work department.
IX. Mao Zedong's tone at the March 20, 1966, session is acerbic. He repeatedly and sharply disagrees with Peng Zhen, and his remarks are very important for understanding the dispute over military strategy that contributed to the downfall of Luo Ruiqing. This meeting convened between the two sessions of the March 4–April 8, 1966, Central Committee Work Group meeting to handle the case of Luo Ruiqing (meeting 281), and Luo himself attempted suicide on March 18, 1966 (mention: [90]).

On March 22, 1966, the Chinese sent the "Letter of the Central Committee of the CCP in Reply to the Letter of the Central Committee of the CPSU Dated February 24, 1966" (text: [182]: 13: March 25, 1966: 5–6), which explains China's refusal to attend the 23d Congress of the CPSU.

This meeting in all likelihood also discussed Jiang Qing's "Forum Summary," for on March 22, 1966, Lin Biao circulated that document to members of the Military Affairs Committee, which met on March 30, 1966, to approve it (meeting 284).

283

I.   *March 28–30, 1966* (mention: [59]: 75)
II.   **CENTRAL COMMITTEE WORK CONFERENCE**
III. Shanghai
V.   Peng Zhen affair
VI.   Mao Zedong: March 28, 1966 (excerpts: [125]: 26; [167]: 640–41; [174]: 382; [205]: 640: January 13, 1969: 9): attacks Peng Zhen, Wu Han, the Ministry of Propaganda, and the Beijing Municipal Committee; threatens to disband the Beijing Municipal Committee, Ministry of Propaganda, and the Five-man Cultural Revolution Group headed by Peng Zhen; castigates the "February Outline Report" that grew out of the meetings of February 3 and 5, 1966 (meetings 279 and 280), which Peng Zhen had played a major role in formulating.
IX.   Kang Sheng informed Mao Zedong during this meeting that Peng Zhen had investigated Yao Wenyuan for issuing a document without the approval of the Central Propaganda Department ([273]: 563).

At this time, Peng Zhen was coming under attack in the Central Committee Work Group meeting of March 4–April 8, 1966 (meeting 281).

At this time, Jiang Qing's "Forum Summary," which disagreed sharply with the "February Outline Report," was under consideration by members of the Military Affairs Committee and was passed by a meeting of that body on March 30, 1966 (meeting 284).

284

March 30, 1966
II.   **MEETING OF THE MILITARY AFFAIRS COMMITTEE OF THE CCP**
V.   "Forum Summary"
VIII. Approved the "Forum Summary" (texts: [123]: May 25, 1967; [182]: 23: June 2, 1967: 10–16—the latter source includes a ten-point concluding portion on measures to be taken in the armed forces that is missing from the former source) of the February 2–20, 1966, Forum on the Work in Literature and Art for the Armed Forces (meeting 278) and sent it to the CC CCP and Mao Zedong for approval (mention: [246]: 10).

IX.   Lin Biao had circulated this "Forum Summary" to members of the Military Affairs Committee on March 22, 1966 (mention: [182]: 23: June 2, 1967: 9).

The "Forum Summary" represents Jiang Qing's views as against those expressed in the "February Outline Report" that grew out of the meeting of February 3 and 5, 1966 (meetings 279 and 280). The "Forum Summary" received official approval over the "February Outline Report" at the May 4–26, 1966, Enlarged Meeting of the Politburo of the CC CCP (meeting 289).

285

I.   *April 6, 1966*
II.   **JOINT MEETING OF THE BEIJING MUNICIPAL COMMITTEE AND THE FIVE-MAN CULTURAL REVOLUTION GROUP**
III.   Beijing
V.   Peng Zhen's record
IX.   Peng Zhen convened this meeting and then used it to make a strong defense of his past record, stating that he had erred only in getting a late start in the Cultural Revolution (mention: [246]: 10).

All information on this meeting comes from the single Red Guard source cited above.

286

I.   *April 9–12, 1966*
II.   **MEETING OF THE SECRETARIAT OF THE CC CCP**
IV.   Zhou Enlai attended this meeting.
V.   Peng Zhen affair
VI.   Kang Sheng (mention: [124]: May 27, 1967; [125]: 27; [205]: 640: January 13, 1969: 12; [246]: 10–11): conveys Mao Zedong's instructions and systematically criticizes Peng Zhen's serious mistakes during the Cultural Revolution.

Chen Boda (mention: ibid.): criticizes Peng Zhen's mistakes in political line during the democratic and socialist revolutions.

Peng Zhen (mention: ibid.): defends his record, affirming his continuing support of Mao Zedong and asserting that he had erred only during the Cultural Revolution.

Deng Xiaoping and Zhou Enlai (mention: [246]: 10–11): "finally" point out that Peng Zhen's mistakes were those of opposing Mao Zedong.
VIII.   Resolved to abolish the Five-man Cultural Revolution Group, to dismiss

the "February Outline Report," and to establish a Drafting Committee for the Cultural Revolution (mention: [205]: 640: January 13, 1969: 12; [246]: 11).

IX.   This meeting of the Secretariat seems to be implementing the instructions Mao Zedong gave on March 28 at the March 28–30, 1966, Central Committee Work Conference (meeting 283).

287

I.   *April 16–20, 1966* (see IX below)
II.   **ENLARGED MEETING OF THE STANDING COMMITTEE OF THE POLITBURO OF THE CC CCP**
III.   Hangzhou
V.   Peng Zhen; February Outline Report; Five-man Cultural Revolution Group
VI.   Mao Zedong (mention: [246]: 11): announces the dismissal of the Five-man Cultural Revolution Group.

Mao Zedong (mention: [131]: 119–20): disagrees with Lin Biao's assessment of Mao's abilities.

IX.   Mao Zedong personally convened this meeting (mention: [124]: May 27, 1967; [125]: 27; [252]; [246]: 11). On April 20, 1966, Mao personally sent to all members of the Beijing Municipal Party Committee seven documents and called on Beijing Municipality to expose the question of Peng Zhen (mention: [226]: 56; [272]: September 10, 1976: 54). Most sources give April 16, 1966, alone as the date for this meeting. One source ([205]: 640: January 13, 1969: 13), however, notes that Peng Zhen could not attend another meeting on April 16–20, 1966, because he was tied up at this Politburo meeting. This and the fact that Mao sent seven documents to the Beijing Municipal Party Committee on April 20, 1966, indicates that this meeting probably lasted from April 16 to 20, 1966. Peng Zhen allegedly arranged for *Beijing ribao* (Beijing Daily) to carry a false criticism, embodying essentially his own viewpoint, on April 16, 1966. This was broadcast by NCNA but then withdrawn later that same evening (mention: [246]: 11).

288

I.   *April 21, 1966*
II.   **MEETING OF THE STANDING COMMITTEE OF THE POLITBURO OF THE CC CCP**
V.   Peng Zhen

IX.   This meeting was convened by Liu Shaoqi to discuss a document criticizing Peng Zhen that was written by Mao Zedong (mention: [159]: April 27, 1967).

All information on this meeting comes from a single Beijing wall poster read by a Japanese correspondent.

289

I.   *May 4–26, 1966*
II.   **ENLARGED MEETING OF THE POLITBURO OF THE CC CCP**
III.   Beijing
IV.   Mao did not attend this meeting because he was out of town. Seventy-six people did attend, including Liu Shaoqi, Kang Sheng, Jiang Qing, Zhang Chunqiao, Guan Feng, Qi Benyu, and the others who formed the Cultural Revolution Group after this meeting.
V.   Purge of Peng Zhen, Luo Ruiqing, Lu Dingyi, and Yang Shangkun (and related issues); economic issues
VI.   Lin Biao: Speech, May 18, 1966 (texts: [35]: II: 4: Winter 1969–70: 42–62; [271]: 1970: 50–55; [272]: IV: 5: May 10, 1970: 123–31; [110]: VI: 5: February 1970: 81–92): the Luo Ruiqing problem has already been solved; problems of Lu Dingyi and Yang Shangkun have been exposed and will be solved; the Peng Zhen problem is the most serious of all; Mao Zedong has taken practical security measures against a coup by Peng Zhen, and the danger of a coup is very great and very real; the chief danger is from within the upper levels inside the party; "this time" have struggled against Luo Ruiqing, Peng Zhen, Yang Shangkun, Lu Dingyi, and Lu Dingyi's wife; must place great emphasis on Mao Zedong Thought, as Mao is more experienced than were Marx, Engels, and Lenin.

Kang Sheng (excerpt: [97]: no. 18, September 16, 1980, tr. in [82]: October 10, 1980; [89]: 388): whether one agrees with the statement that political power grows out of the barrel of a gun determines whether one is revolutionary or counterrevolutionary.

VII.   "May 16, Circular" (texts: [26]: 105–13; [97]: 7: May 20, 1967: 1–6; [194]: May 17, 1967; [182]: 21: May 19, 1967: 6–9): explains in detail the critique of the "February Outline Report" and enumerates the following decisions:

—Formally revokes the "Outline Report on the Current Academic Discussion Made by the Group of Five in Charge of the Cultural Revolution" (the "February Outline Report").

—Dissolves the Five-man Group in Charge of the Cultural Revolution and its offices.

—Sets up a new Cultural Revolution Group directly under the Standing Committee of the Politburo of the CC CCP.

VIII. This meeting raised the question of Peng Zhen's attacking Mao Zedong and Mao Zedong Thought; issued the April 30, 1966, "Report on Luo Ruiqing's Mistakes"; and on May 24, the CC issued an "Explanation of Lu Dingyi's and Yang Shangkun's Mistakes" ([273]: 578–79).

On May 23, Peng Zhen, Lu Dingyi, and Luo Ruiqing were removed from the Secretariat and Yang Shangkun was removed as an alternate member of that body (this action later was approved by the full CC); Peng was removed as first secretary and mayor of Beijing; Lu was removed as head of the Propaganda Department; Tao Zhu was transferred to the Standing Committee of the Secretariat [*sic*]; Ye Jianying was transferred to the Secretariat and appointed secretary-general of the Military Affairs Commission; Li Xuefeng was appointed first secretary of Beijing ([273]: 579).

On May 24, the Politburo Standing Committee established a special investigative committee to handle the cases of Peng Zhen, Lu Dingyi, Luo Ruiqing, and Yang Shangkun ([108]: 265).

This meeting also decided to cancel state grants to a large number of industrial enterprises, concentrating future state aid on heavy industrial enterprises related to the manufacture of armaments and munitions (mention: [60]).

IX. On May 8, 1966, this meeting took up specifically the question of Lu Dingyi (mention: [191]: 9: May 19, 1967). Zhou Enlai subsequently commented that this meeting debated the issue of Peng Zhen for twelve days before he admitted his errors (mention: [59]: 77). In dealing with Luo Ruiqing, people at this meeting received copies of the April 13, 1966, report of the Central Committee Work Group, which had met during the March 4–April 8, 1966 (meeting 281) to consider Luo's errors; Luo's March 12, 1966, self-examination; the four major speeches of Ye Jianying, Xie Fuzhi, Xiao Hua, and Yang Chengwu (to the March 4–April 8, 1966, meeting); and the April 24, 1966, report Ye, Xiao, Yang, and Liu Zhijian wrote to Chairman Mao and the Central Committee. On May 16, 1966, these documents, along with an accompanying explanation (text: [43]: 852: May 6, 1968: 7) were circulated down to the level of *xian* and regimental party cadres.

On May 7, 1966, Mao Zedong sent Lin Biao a letter (text: [26]: 103–105) regarding a May 6, 1966, document Lin had given Mao concerning agricultural work by the Rear Services Department of Military Affairs Committee. Mao asked that this document be circulated, discussed, and made the basis for future directives.

Kang Sheng and Chen Boda reportedly revised Lin Biao's speech on coups ([176]: December 21, 1980, tr. in [82]: December 24, 1980: L23).

Lin Biao reportedly threatened to shoot Lu Dingyi at one point in this meeting ([194]: November 29, 1980, tr. in [82]: December 1, 1980: L23). The May 16, 1966, circular was drafted by Mao Zedong ([273]: 579).

This was a key meeting for formalizing a number of decisions that had been taken less formally during the preceding month or so—especially with respect to Peng Zhen and Luo Ruiqing, the Five-man Cultural Revolution Group, and the "February Outline Report."

290

I. *Early June 1966*
II. **ENLARGED MEETING OF THE STANDING COMMITTEE OF THE POLITBURO OF THE CC CCP**
IV. Mao Zedong did not attend.
V. Work teams
VIII. Decided to send work teams from central departments to Beijing University and institutes of higher education, and from the central Communist Youth League to Beijing's high schools; set eight criteria to guide them in running the Cultural Revolution (mention: [273]: 582).
IX. On June 3, 1966, Mao Zedong personally approved the dispatch of work teams to Beijing University and other units. Liu Shaoqi and Deng Xiaoping went to Hangzhou to report on the situation and asked Mao to return to Beijing to take charge of the work. Instead, Mao put Liu in charge of the campaign. Liu presided over this meeting (mention: [218]: December 7, 1980, tr. in [82]: December 9, 1980: U1).

291

I. *June 4, 1966*
II. **ENLARGED MEETING OF THE POLITBURO OF THE CC CCP**
IV. Xu Bing, among others (mention: [211]).
IX. No direct information on this meeting is available, other than the presence of Xu Bing, allegedly at the invitation of Liu Shaoqi (mention: ibid.). On June 7, 1966, however, Tan Zhenlin is reported to have conveyed the spirit of an Enlarged Meeting of the Politburo, at which time he said that the comrades in the audience should forge ahead resolutely and courageously defend the party center, consisting of Mao Zedong, Liu Shaoqi, Zhou Enlai, Deng Xiaoping, and Lin Biao—whoever opposes them will be destroyed (excerpt: [217]: 178: April 24, 1967: 29).

292

I.   *June 8, 1966*
II.   **CONFERENCE OF THE PROPAGANDA DEPARTMENT OF THE CC CCP**
V.   Criticism of high-level cadres in the propaganda and culture realm.
VI.   Tao Zhu (excerpts: [246]: 16): comments on the past performance of Lu Dingyi, Zhou Yang, Xu Liqun, Lin Mohan, and Dong Yalin.
IX.   All information on this meeting comes from the single Red Guard source cited above.

293

I.   *June 9, 1966*
II.   **HANGZHOU CONFERENCE**
III. Hangzhou, Zhejiang
V.   Work teams
VI.   Mao Zedong (mention: [246]: 16): suggests caution in sending out work teams.
IX.   Tao Zhu went to Beijing following this meeting and dispatched work teams in seeming violation of Mao Zedong's sentiments as expressed at the Hangzhou Conference (mention: [116]: January 11, 1967; [192]; [246]: 17).

In October 1966 Deng Xiaoping noted that at a Central Conference in mid-June 1966 Chen Boda (and evidently others) had argued for withdrawing the work teams ([35]: III: 4: Winter 1970–71: 278–89). This may well have occurred at the Hangzhou Conference.

294

I.   *June 21, 1966*
II.   **MEETING CONVENED BY LIU SHAOQI AND DENG XIAOPING**
III. Beijing
V.   Exposing the ''seemingly Left and actually Right.''
VI.   Tao Zhu (excerpt: [189]: March 4, 1967): should write a *Renmin ribao* editorial exposing the ''seemingly Left but actually Right''; Xian Communications College, Beijing University, and Nanking University are not the same—it is a question of ''seemingly Left but actually Right.''
IX.   All information on this meeting comes from the single Red Guard source cited above.

295

I.   *July 13, 1966*
II.   **MEETING CONVENED BY LIU SHAOQI AND DENG XIAOPING**
V.   Cultural Revolution in Beijing Middle Schools
VI.   Liu Shaoqi (excerpts: [246]: 24): asserts that party branches should lead the Cultural Revolution in the middle schools; directs that the movement should focus on examining the teachers and school staff members.
IX.   This meeting convened to discuss the "Preliminary Plan for the Great Cultural Revolution in Beijing Middle Schools" (mention: ibid.).

    All information on this meeting comes from the single Red Guard source cited above.

296

I.   *July 18, 1966*
II.   **EDUCATIONAL REFORM CONFERENCE**
III.   Huairen Hall, Beijing
IV.   Liu Shaoqi, Tao Zhu, Bo Yibo, Zhang Pinghua, Yong Wentao, Hu Keshi, He Wei, and others (mention: [246]: 27).
V.   Work teams; educational reform
IX.   This meeting was convened by Liu Shaoqi and covered the topics of the further dispatch of work teams and the educational reform question (mention: ibid.). This same meeting is mentioned in [84]: 31.

297

I.   *July 19–21, 1966*
II.   **MEETING OF REGIONAL PARTY SECRETARIES AND MEMBERS OF THE CULTURAL REVOLUTION GROUP**
III.   Beijing
V.   Cultural Revolution; work teams; simplification of organs
VI.   Mao Zedong: Speech, July 21, 1966 (excerpts: [26]: 24–26; [43]: 891: October 8, 1969: 58–59): young people are the main force of the Cultural Revolution; Beijing is too quiet; Nie Yuanzi's big-character poster is excellent; using as a pretext the difference between inside and outside of the party shows fear of the revolution.

    Mao Zedong: Speech, July 21, 1966 (two somewhat different texts are available, one in [26]: 26–30; [43]: 892: October 21, 1969: 35–37; [232]: 66: September 1, 1969: 44, and the other in [26]: 30–34; [171]: 32–34):

decries the methods of the work teams and declares they must cease obstructing the Cultural Revolution; calls on his audience to go to the universities themselves to see what is happening; asserts that students must be allowed to make revolution, banning only physical violence; calls for simplification of government and party organs through reductions in staff. According to the second version of this talk cited above, this conference has already met for two days; on July 19, 1966, Mao stated that the work teams are useless and that the former Beijing Municipal Committee and the Ministry of Higher Education are corrupt; *Renmin ribao* is no good. On July 20, 1966, Mao declared that the policy of sending work teams must be changed.

VIII. Mao Zedong produced a draft of the "Sixteen Articles and Communique" (undoubtedly referring to the Sixteen Points and Communique issued by the Eleventh Plenum of the Eighth CC, which convened for August 1–12, 1966 [meeting 300] [mention: (246): 28]).

Decided to change the methods used by the work teams (mention: ibid.).

IX. This was the first meeting convened by Mao Zedong after he returned to Beijing following a long stay in East and Central-South China.

298

I.   *July 22, 1966*
II.   **REPORT MEETING**
III.   Beijing
IV.   Liu Shaoqi, Bo Yibo, Tao Lujia, Chen Boda, and others.
V.   Work teams
VI.   Tao Lujia: "Report of the Academy of Sciences" (mention: [246]: 28).
Bo Yibo (mention: ibid.): about the experiences of work teams.

Mao Zedong: Speech (text: [201]: 256–59): sending work teams to the schools obstructs the unfolding of the Cultural Revolution; must rely on those within the schools, the majority of whom are revolutionary.

VIII.   Liu Shaoqi decided against withdrawing the work teams (mention: [246]: 28; [44]).

IX.   This meeting lasted five hours, of which Tao Lujia's and Bo Yibo's contributions lasted three hours. Members of the Central Cultural Revolution Group were perturbed that they were not allowed to speak more. Liu Shaoqi presided (mention: ibid.).

299

I.   *July 24, 1966*
II.   **ENLARGED MEETING OF THE CULTURAL REVOLUTION GROUP**
III.   Beijing
IV.   Mao Zedong, Liu Shaoqi, Li Xuefeng, and others (mention: [246]: 29).
V.   Withdrawal of the work teams
VIII.   Decided to withdraw the work teams (mention: ibid.; [272]:IV: 1: January 10, 1970: 126–27).
IX.   This morning meeting was followed on the same day by a work conference, which finalized the drafting of the Sixteen Articles and Communique of the forthcoming August 1–12, 1966, Eleventh Plenum of the Eighth CC CCP (meeting 307) (mention: [246]: 29). This drafting had begun with the meeting Mao Zedong convened on July 19–21, 1966 (meeting 297).

   Several sources ([78]: 12; [44]) assert that Bo Yibo left this meeting and convened an enlarged meeting of the party committees for industry and communications at which, instead of transmitting Mao's decisions to withdraw the work teams, Bo urged others to discuss this problem and dispatched people to various schools and institutes to collect materials on the experiences of the work teams to date—materials that Liu Shaoqi and Deng Xiaoping could use at the next central meeting to discuss this issue.

   According to Liu Shaoqi's October 23, 1966, confession ([272]: IV: 1: January 10, 1970: 127), after this meeting the authorities convened a Central Work Conference attended by the responsible cadres of various locales, and this work conference was in turn followed by the August 1–12, 1966, Eleventh Plenum of the Eighth CC CCP (meeting 300). [273]: 584 and [89]: 391 also mention a July 27–30, 1966, preparatory meeting for the plenum, but provide no other information.

300

I.   *August 1–12, 1966*
II.   **ENLARGED ELEVENTH PLENUM OF THE EIGHTH CC CCP**
III.   Beijing
IV.   Seventy-four members and sixty-seven alternate members of the CC

CCP, comrades from the regional bureaus of the CC CCP and from the provincial, municipal, and autonomous region party committees, members of the Cultural Revolution Group of the CC CCP, comrades from relevant departments of the CC CCP and the government, and representatives of revolutionary teachers and students from the institutions of higher learning in Beijing—altogether forty-seven extra participants (mention: [40]; [89]: 391 [108]: 273).

V. Launching the Cultural Revolution; domestic and foreign policy since the Eighth Party Congress; approval of the ouster of Peng Zhen, Lu Dingyi, Luo Ruiqing, and Yang Shangkun

VI. Liu Shaoqi: Work Report, August 1, 1966 (mention: [89]: 391–92; [273]: 584): lists major work in domestic and foreign affairs since the Eighth Party Congress; accepts responsibility for sending work teams.

Mao Zedong: Interjection (to Liu's report?) ([273]: 584): 90 percent of work teams committed errors of orientation.

Deng Xiaoping: August 1, 1966 (mention: ibid.).

Zhou Enlai: August 1, 1966 (mention: ibid.).

Chen Yi: Speech, August 4, 1966 (excerpt: [95]: 6): assumes responsibility for sending the work teams.

Mao Zedong: Interjection, August 4, 1966 (texts: [167]: 650–51; [174]: 449–50): attacks the suppression of the student movement and Li Xuefeng's prohibition on putting up wall posters in public (note: this interjection was purportedly made at an ''Enlarged Meeting of the Standing Committee of the CC'' on August 4, 1966).

Mao Zedong: Speech to Politburo Standing Committee, August 4, 1966 (mention: [273]: 584): criticizes Liu Shaoqi's repression of students, equating it with White Terror emanating from the CC.

Lin Biao: Speech to Cultural Revolution Group, August 8, 1966, published August 11, 1966 (mention: [273]: 585): the ultimate headquarters in this Cultural Revolution is Chairman Mao.

Lin Biao: Speech (partial text: [171]: 16–18): adherence to Mao Zedong Thought is the criterion for staying in office.

Mao Zedong: Speech (excerpt: [262]: December 14, 1966): let the confusion continue for a few months before reaching a conclusion.

Mao Zedong: Closing Speech, August 12, 1966 (texts: [26]: 34–35—mistakenly dates this speech as August 1, 1966; [43]: 891: October 8, 1969: 64; [232]: 66: September 1, 1969: 45–46): calls for carrying out the decisions of the Eleventh Plenum and for convening the Ninth Party Congress during 1967.

VII. ''Communique,'' August 12, 1966 (text: [40]): notes the following decisions of the plenum:

—Approved the May 20, 1963, ''Decision of the CC CCP on Some Problems in Rural Work (Draft)''—this was passed by the May 2–12,

1963, Central Work Conference (meeting 220).

—Approved the January 14, 1965, "Some Current Problems Raised in the Socialist Education Movement in the Rural Areas"—passed by the December 14, 1964–January 14, 1965, Central Work Conference (meeting 247).

—Approved the major economic, organizational, and military policies advocated by Mao Zedong during the previous four years.

—Agreed to the measures already taken and endorsed any future measures decided by the CC CCP with respect to aid to North Vietnam.

—Endorsed the CCP's comprehensive criticism of Khrushchev's revisionism over the previous few years.

"Decision of the CC CCP Concerning the Great Proletarian Cultural Revolution" (frequently called the "Sixteen Points"), August 8, 1966 (texts: [34]: 33–54; [61]: 207–17; [182]: 33: August 12, 1966: 6–11).

VIII. Removed Liu Shaoqi's title as vice-chairman of the CCP, made Lin Biao a vice-chairman, and dropped Liu's rank in the Politburo from second to eighth place (mention: [80]: March 10, 1967: 112; [108]: 274); [273]: 585; [89]: 393).

Approved the ouster of Peng Zhen, Lu Dingyi, Luo Ruiqing, and Yang Shangkun and appointment of Ye Jianying and Guan Feng ([273]: 586).

IX. A preparatory meeting was held July 27–30, 1966, for this plenum, which was only scheduled to last for five days ([273]: 584; [89]: 391). This is likely the same meeting referred to in Liu Shaoqi's confession ([272]: IV: 1: January 10, 1970: 127).

On August 5, 1966, the CC issued document no. 395, which declared that the June 28, 1966, CC document "Bulletin on the Cultural Revolution at Beijing University" was a mistake; this amounted to approving the practice of seizures and beatings (mention: [273]: 273).

The personnel changes were made during the latter part of the plenum (mention: [246]: 32).

A large number of "outside" activities by participants in this plenum took place during the course of the meeting and may have influenced the deliberations at the plenum itself. Some of the more significant of these "outside" activities were:

—Mao Zedong wrote a letter to the Red Guards of the middle school subordinate to Qinghua University on August 1, 1966 (texts: [26]: 115–16; [43]: 891: 63; [182]: 29: July 14, 1967: 29).

—Liu Shaoqi attended meetings at the Beijing College of Building Construction on the evenings of August 2, 3, and 4. Li Xuefeng, Gu Mu, and Qi Benyu accompanied Liu to these (mention: [206]: 35: October 21, 1969: 27).

—Mao Zedong wrote the big-character poster "Bombard the Headquarters" (text: [182]: 33: August 11, 1967: 5) on August 5, 1966.

—Mao Zedong personally greeted the masses who went to the reception center near the headquarters of the CC CCP to greet the promulgation of the "Sixteen Points" on August 10, 1966 (mention: [182]: 34: August 19, 1966: 9–11).

—Tao Zhu on August 11, 1966, addressed the 101 Middle School Red Guards (mention: [192]).

Mao Zedong purportedly recognized that Tao Zhu was giving support to Liu Shaoqi and Deng Xiaoping at this plenum but wanted to give Tao a chance to "come over" (mention: [127]).

Zhou Enlai and Tao Zhu reportedly revised the "Sixteen Points" to soften it a little ([30]: January 8, 1986, tr. in [82]: January 8, 1986: K2).

Xie Fuzhi reportedly took the lead in criticizing Deng Xiaoping ([176]: December 22, 1980, tr. in [82]: December 29, 1980: L14).

Mao Zedong later observed that at the Eleventh Plenum, "After some debate I gained the endorsement of a little over half the comrades. There were still many comrades who did not agree with me, including Li Qingquan and Liu Lantao" ([167]: 674–75; [174]: 457–58). Mao also said in retrospect that it was at this plenum that he abolished the division of the Politburo into the first and second fronts ([167]: 657).

301

I. *August 12, 1966*
II. **MEETING OF THE CULTURAL REVOLUTION GROUP**
V. Implementation of the "Sixteen Points"
VIII. All schools and units should conscientiously study the "Sixteen Points" passed by the August 1–12, 1966, Eleventh Plenum of the Eighth CC CCP (meeting 300), and *Renmin ribao* should continue to carry editorials on this (mention: [171]: 35).

Some technical units in the natural sciences should concentrate on the Cultural Revolution, while other such technical units should continue their work as originally planned. Particularly, "the advanced scientific sectors [should] continue to carry on their work; they cannot stop their work midway" (ibid.).

IX. The above comes from Chen Boda's report on this meeting (text: ibid.), which received Mao Zedong's approval on August 15, 1966.

All information on this meeting comes from the single Red Guard source cited above.

302

I.   *August ?-13-?, 1966*
II.   **CENTRAL WORK CONFERENCE**
VI.   Lin Biao: Speech, August 13, 1966 (mention: [108]: 275): this Cultural Revolution is a movement to dismiss people from office.

303

I.   *August ?-23-?, 1966*
II.   **CENTRAL WORK CONFERENCE**
V.   Policy toward the emerging chaos
VI.   Mao Zedong: Speech (texts [partial?]: [26] 35–36; [43]: 891: October 8, 1969: 68; [171]: 35–36; [173]: 46: October 1969: 84; [232]: 66: September 1, 1969: 46): let the chaos develop for a while yet and stop interfering; permit the students to put up big-character posters in the streets; should wait another four months before deciding the question of the reorganization of the Center of the Youth League.
IX.   As early as March 12, 1966, a Central Work Conference had been scheduled for August or September 1966, at which agricultural mechanization was to have been one of the items on the agenda (mention: [167]: 632; [174]: 373).

304

I.   *October 9–28, 1966*
II.   **CENTRAL WORK CONFERENCE**
III.   Beijing
V.   Cultural Revolution strategy; criticism of Liu Shaoqi and Deng Xiaoping
VI.   Lin Biao: Remarks at a Group Meeting, October 12, 1966 (excerpts: [171]: 74): the fundamental problem now is that there is too much "fear" and not enough "dare."

    Chen Boda: Summary Report of the Cultural Revolution Over the Past Two Months, October 16, 1966 (partial text: [205]: 651: April 22, 1969: 3–4): some people have used work teams to impose their views on the masses; my September 15, 1966, statement that only very good and popular children of senior cadres may hold leading positions has been twisted by others into an absolute prohibition on having these children hold leading positions; some people failed to heed Mao's warning in his August 5, 1966, big-character poster.

Chen Boda: "The Two Lines of the Great Proletarian Cultural Revolution" ([108]: 276; [273]: 587): criticizes the "capitalist reactionary line" and capitalist counterrevolutionary line of Liu Shaoqi and Deng Xiaoping.

Xie Fuzhi ([176]: December 22, 1980, tr. in [82]: December 29, 1980: L14): accuses Liu Shaoqi and Deng Xiaoping of opposition to Mao Zedong.

Deng Xiaoping: Self-criticism, October 23, 1966 (texts: [35]: III: 4: Winter 1970–71: 278–91; [271]: 1970: 33–36; [272]: III: 11: November 10, 1969: 90–94): accepts (along with Liu Shaoqi) responsibility for the mistaken policy of dispatching work teams; notes that he mistakenly had not very frequently made reports to, and sought instructions from, Mao Zedong; declares that he does not understand Mao Zedong Thought well enough; endorses the decisions of the August 1–12, 1966, Eleventh Plenum of the Eighth CC CCP (meeting 300); affirms that he should take Lin Biao as a model.

Liu Shaoqi: Self-criticism, October 23, 1966 (most complete texts: [271]: 1970: 29–33; [272]: IV: 1: January 10, 1970: 123–27; less complete texts: [3]; [160]): accepts some responsibility for mistaken policies during the previous fifty days; reviews his history of mistaken policies going back as far as 1946.

Mao Zedong: Written comments ([240]: March 8, 1980, tr. in [82]: March 28, 1980: L9; [87]: December 5, 1980, tr. in [82]: December 31, 1980: L14): gives positive appraisal of Liu Shaoqi's self-criticism (this appraisal was deleted from published version of Liu's self-criticism).

Mao Zedong: Comment, October 24, 1966 (texts: [26]: 132; [43]: 891: October 8, 1969: 74; [129]: 43249: August 25, 1967: 51—mistakenly dates this as October 25, 1966): this letter to Chen Boda praises Chen's October 16, 1966, Report, suggests several insertions, and calls for wide circulation of the report in pamphlet form.

Mao Zedong: Speech at a General Report Conference (same as supra?), October 24, 1966 (texts: [26]: 40–42; [43]: 892: October 21, 1969: 38; [171]: 12–13; [173]: 45: September 1969: 14; [232]: 66: September 1, 1969: 46): criticizes the way Deng Xiaoping ran the Secretariat; brands Bo Yibo, He Changjing, Wang Feng, and Li Fanwu as "antiparty and antisocialist"; lauds Henan's handling of the Cultural Revolution.

Lin Biao: Speech, October 25, 1966 (texts: [35]: I: 1: Spring 1968: 13–31; [272]: III: 10: October 10, 1969: 96–103; [110]: VI: 2: November 1969: 93–98; [171]: 52–64; [232]: 65: August 1, 1969: 41–46): primarily an explanation and justification for launching the Cultural Revolution; notes that most cadres have been guilty of no worse than misunderstanding Mao's line rather than being anti-Mao.

Chen Boda: Speech, October 25, 1966 (significantly varying texts: [205]: 651: April 22, 1969: 4–6; [217]: 167: March 4, 1967: 1–3): a strong attack on Deng Xiaoping, noting that people generally are not aware of his mistakes; notes Deng's role in Sino-Soviet relations in the early 1960s.

Zhou Enlai: Speech, October 25, 1966 (mention: [246]: 51).

Mao Zedong: October 25, 1966 (texts: [33]: II: 9: February 19, 1969: 25–27; [35]: I: 1: Spring 1968: 7–12; [43]: 891: October 8, 1969: 75–77; [171]: 13–16; [173]: 46: October 1969: 84–85; [201]: 270–74; [232]: 48: March 1, 1968: 41, 47; [232]: 67: October 1, 1969: 37–38): indicates that many cadres came to this meeting with substantial criticisms of the Cultural Revolution to date; concedes that much of this criticism is well-founded, for Mao had proceeded too hastily, before proper political/ideological work had been carried out; advises the cadres to handle things better after they return to their local areas following this conference.

Chen Peixian ([236]: 104, n. 1): review of Cultural Revolution in Shanghai.

Xiao Wangdong: Speech (excerpts: [194]: August 13, 1967): asserts that only a minority in the Cultural Ministry are good; warns of a possible counterattack by people still influenced by Peng Zhen, Lu Dingyi, and others.

VIII. A discussion meeting was held October 24, 1966, to discuss the developments at the Central Work Conference and what people should do after returning to their posts (texts: [25]: 91–97; [43]: 891: October 8, 1969: 70–73; [171]: 8–12; [201]: 264–69; [232]: 67: October 1, 1969: 36–37); it was a wide-ranging discussion attended by at least the following: Mao Zedong, Liu Lantao, Zhou Enlai, Li Jingquan, Li Xiannian, Tao Zhu, and Kang Sheng).

IX. This conference convened to review thoroughly the party strategies and policies during the Cultural Revolution, make clear the nature of Liu Shaoqi's and Deng Xiaoping's transgressions, and thus make better preparations for implementing the decisions of the August 1–12, 1966, Eleventh Plenum of the Eighth CC CCP (meeting 300). The conference originally convened for three days but was extended to nineteen days as the scope and depth of the problems became clearer (mention: [35]: I: 1: Spring 1968: 14). The conference began with considerable disagreement and anger among the participants but in its latter stages, according to Mao, went fairly smoothly ([43]: 891: October 8, 1969: 75).

Xie Fuzhi may have given a rundown on the Cultural Revolution in terms of arrests and political cases, confiscated arms and ammunition, and confiscated property as of October 3, 1966 (summary: [2]: January 9, 1967). It is not certain that Xie made his report to this conference. There is some evidence that at this conference an eight-article supplement to the regulations for handling case materials during the Cultural Revolution was passed but then underwent further revision before being disseminated ([103]).

A number of leaders who either definitely or almost certainly attended this conference made other appearances during October 8–25, 1966. These include the following: Guan Feng—October 12, 1966, speech at the CCP Propaganda Department; Qi Benyu and Guan Feng—other speeches of October 12, 1966; Guan Feng, Wan Li, and Qi Benyu—October 17, 1966, speeches at the auditorium of the Political Consultative Conference; Tao Zhu—October 24, 1966, speech in Beijing; Zhou En-lai—October 24, 1966, instructions; and Chen Boda—October 25, 1966, speech (texts: [206]: 15: May 8, 1967: 3–29).

One source ([37]) asserts that during this conference members of the Cultural Revolution Group argued for unfolding the Cultural Revolution in an all-around way in the factories and villages but that Tao Zhu object-ed, stating that the Cultural Revolution should be carried out among different groups at different times. Tao also asserted that there was no two-line struggle during the Four Clean-ups campaign.

The cadres attending this conference were instructed to return to their local areas and convene three-level meetings (mention: [246]: 52).

There is some confused evidence to the effect that another Central Work Conference convened for several days after the conclusion of this meeting (ibid.). No specific information is available on this other meet-ing, however.

305

I.   *October 24, 1966*
II.   **POLITBURO OF THE CC CCP REPORT MEETING**
VI.   Mao Zedong: Speech (mention: [272]: October 10, 1976: 22): the neces-sity of successors: Malenkov was inexperienced because he was not given authority when Stalin was alive; I will cultivate the prestige of my succes-sors before I die so that they will not consider taking the opposing path.

Lin Biao: Interjection (mention: ibid.): power has fallen into the wrong hands.

306

I.   *Late November or early December 1966*
II.   **CENTRAL COMMITTEE CONFERENCE**
IV.   Central and regional leaders
V.   Problems in production due to the Cultural Revolution
VII.   Document issued on December 9, 1966, warning against disorders caused by workers' organizations ([236]: 32–33).
IX.   This meeting saw a "full-scale debate" between regional leaders, who believed that workers' organizations were the cause of disruption in factories, and the Central Cultural Revolution Group, which felt that the organizations were instead the result of those disturbances. The result of the conference confirmed principles of allowing workers' organizations.

307

I.   *December 3, 1966*
II.   **MEETING OF THE STANDING COMMITTEE OF THE POLITBURO OF THE CC CCP**
V.   Industry and communications work
VI.   Lin Biao: (mention: [283]: 419): criticizes rightist deviation in industry and communications, particularly the November conference and the "Fifteen Points" on industry and communications.
IX.   Lin's speech refers to the National Conference on Industry and Communications, held in November 1966, in which Zhou Enlai said that the Cultural Revolution in industry and communications must be carried out under the leadership of party committees, in groups and at different times, in accordance with the eight-hour work day, and workers must not leave their work stations without authorization nor link up with other areas (mention: ibid.). On the basis of this speech, the State Council's Vocational Work Group organized relevant departments to draft "Some Regulations for Carrying Out the Cultural Revolution in Industry and Communications (The Fifteen Points)" (ibid.: 419–20).

1967

308

I.   *January ?–8–9–?, 1967*
II.   **CENTRAL CULTURAL REVOLUTION GROUP**
V.   Report on the current situation
VI.   Mao Zedong: Remarks, January 8, 1967 (texts: [43]: 892: October 21, 1969: 46; [171]: 16; [173]: 46: October 1969: 86; [232]: 67: October 1, 1969: 38): comments about Tao Zhu.

      Mao Zedong: Speech, January 9, 1967 (texts: [26]: 45–47; [43]: 892: October 21, 1969: 47–48; [171]: 38–39; [173]: 46: 86; [201]: 275–76; [232]: 67: October 1, 1969: 38–39): lauds the January 4, 1967, takeover of *Wenhui bao* and the January 6, 1967, takeover of *Jiefang ribao* (Liberation Daily); praises events in Shanghai as of national significance; affirms the necessity of combining revolution with production, asserting that the two cannot be separated.

309

I.   *January–February, 1967*
II.   **ENLARGED MEETING OF THE MILITARY AFFAIRS COMMITTEE OF THE CC CCP**
V.   January 23, 1967, directive for the PLA to intervene in support of the Left
VI.   Mao Zedong: Speech, January 27, 1967 (texts: [26]: 47–48; [43]: 892: October 21, 1969: 49; [171]: 40; [232]: 67: October 1, 1969: 39) (addresses relayed by Zhou Enlai): the PLA must intervene in support of the Left; power should be seized before anything else is done; it is necessary to support the Left resolutely.

      Lin Biao (excerpt: [171]: 18–19) (probably from this meeting): presents four criteria for evaluating leftists: general orientation, organizational purity, masses' views about the organization, and political principle.
VII. "Directive of the Central Military Committee Reiterating the Carrying Out of the Great Revolution Stage by Stage and Group by Group in Military Regions," January 28, 1967 (text: [34]: 215–16). Ye Jianying communicated a similar but abbreviated text on January 27, 1967 (text: [232]: 67: October 1, 1969: 39).

"Order of the Central Military Committee," January 28, 1967 (texts: [34]: 209–13; [217]: 174: April 10, 1967: 4–5): consists of eight articles.

IX.   Mao Zedong's January 21, 1967, instruction (text: [232]: 67: October 1, 1969: 39) to Lin Biao that the latter should order the army to intervene in support of the Left set the stage for this meeting. Lin made this instruction operational in the January 23, 1967 "Decision of the CC CCP, the State Council, the Military Committee of the CC, and the Cultural Revolution Group of the CC on Resolute Support for Revolutionary Masses of the Left" (texts: [39]: 49; [66]: 18: January 31, 1967).

Nie Rongzhen, Xu Xiangqian, and Ye Jianying vainly argued against the army's role in the Cultural Revolution decided by this meeting ([89]: 394–95).

310

I.   *February 1967*
II.   **MEETING OF THE POLITBURO OF THE CC CCP**
V.   Party leadership in the Cultural Revolution
VI.   Tan Zhenlin: ([97]: no. 16, August 16, 1980 tr. in [82]: September 8, 1980: L40): Lin Biao, Kang Sheng, and Jiang Qing are conspiring to liquidate the party's leadership; the mass line is receiving too much attention (relative to party leadership).

Kang Sheng: (ibid.): Mao leads the party and is personally leading the Cultural Revolution, so how can it be said that there is no party leadership?

311

I.   *February 13 and 16, 1967*
II.   **JOINT MEETING OF THE POLITBURO AND THE CENTRAL CULTURAL REVOLUTION GROUP** ("Huairen Hall Meetings")
III.   Huairen Hall, Beijing
IV.   Zhou Enlai, Chen Yi, Ye Jianying, Xu Xiangqian, Li Fuchun, Li Xiannian, Tan Zhenlin, Yu Qiuli, Nie Rongzhen, Gu Mu, Chen Boda, Kang Sheng, Zhang Chunqiao, Yao Wenyuan, Wang Li, Guan Feng, Qi Benyi, and others.
V.   Conduct of Cultural Revolution
IX.   Beginning in February 1967, enlarged meetings of the Standing Committee of the Politburo were held every two or three days to handle the problems emerging from the Cultural Revolution. According to *Nanjing*

xinhua ribao (October 21, 1984, tr. in [82]: November 6, 1984: K22), these meetings were chaired by Zhou Enlai.

These two particular meetings, which are discussed in tandem in all sources, had Zhou Enlai at the head of a table and the two opposing groups (veteran comrades and the supporters of the Cultural Revolution) facing each other across the table. The sources describe a sharp and acrimonious debate, in which the veteran comrades raised three central issues: the mistreatment of veteran comrades during the Cultural Revolution, whether or not the campaign was to be led by the party, and whether or not it should be allowed to disrupt the army ([108]: 280–81; [89]: 395–97; [273]: 592–93).

After the Huairen Hall meetings, Zhang Chunqiao, Wang Li, and Yao Wenyuan briefed Jiang Qing, who approved their compilation of materials on the meeting; they then reported to Mao Zedong ([108]: 281; [89]: 395).

These meetings were the peak of the "February Adverse Current" and the cause of its rapid demise.

312

I.   *February 15, 1967*
II.   **MEETING OF THE PARTY CENTER**
III. Beijing
V.   Zhou Enlai's work load
VIII. Evidently decided that Zhou Enlai might retain the services of such ministers of the government as could be salvaged (mention: [197]: 329).
IX.   The agenda of this meeting focused on how to keep the burdens of Zhou Enlai within reasonable bounds (mention: ibid.).

All information on this meeting comes from ibid., which cites no primary sources for these data.

313

I.   *February 18, 1967*
II.   **(PARTIAL) MEETING OF THE POLITBURO OF THE CC CCP**
V.   "February Adverse Current" and Huairen Hall meetings
VI.   Mao Zedong (mention: [89]: 397; [108]: 281): criticism of veteran comrades.
IX.   This meeting is unusual in its designation as a "partial" (*bufen*) meeting of the Politburo. This meeting set the stage for seven "Political Life Meetings" held over the next few weeks.

314

I.   *February ?–22–?, 1967*
II.   **MEETING OF THE STANDING COMMITTEE OF THE POLITBURO OF THE CC CCP**
V.   Liu Shaoqi and others
IX.   This meeting "completely defeated" Liu Shaoqi, Deng Xiaoping, Tao Zhu, Zhu De, and Chen Yun. It also branded Liu and Deng as "three-point counter elements" (mention: [2]: April 11, 1967).

All information on this meeting comes from the translation of a Japanese account of a Beijing wall poster.

315

I.   *February 25–March 18, 1967*
II.   **POLITICAL LIFE MEETINGS**
III.   Huairen Hall, Beijing
IV.   Jiang Qing, Kang Sheng, Chen Boda, Xie Fuzhi, and others.
V.   Criticism of Tan Zhenlin and the "February Adverse Current"
VI.   Kang Sheng (mention: [108]: 281; [273]: 593): the Huairen Hall meetings were a serious antiparty incident and a preview of a coup d'etat.

Jiang Qing (mention: ibid.): protecting old comrades protects traitors, spies, and capitalist roaders.
IX.   A total of seven "political life" meetings were held during this period.

316

I.   *March 14–18, 1967*
II.   **JOINT MEETING OF THE POLITBURO AND THE MILITARY AFFAIRS COMMITTEE OF THE CC CCP**
III.   Beijing
V.   Measures to overcome the "February Adverse Current"
IX.   The struggle during this meeting focused on the issue of Tan Zhenlin, with a group supporting Tan and opposing Lin Biao (mention: [197]: 333–34, which in turn cites a host of other sources).

Three documents, all concerned with maintaining order and economic production, were issued during the period when this meeting was in session, although none was explicitly linked with the meeting itself. These documents are "Circular of the CC CCP, the State Council, and the Central Military Committee Concerning the Protection of State Property and the Practice of Economy While Making Revolution," March 16, 1967 (text: [34]: 367–68); "Letter from the CC CCP to Revolutionary Workers and Staff and Revolutionary Cadres in Industrial and Mining Enterprises Throughout the Country," March 18, 1967 (text: [34]: 369–75); and "Circular of the CC CCP Concerning the Suspension of the Big Exchange of Revolutionary Experience All Over the Country," March 19, 1967 (text: [34]: 377–78).

317

I. *Late March–early April 1967* (one source [178] provides the dates of March 27–28, 1967)
II. **CENTRAL WORK CONFERENCE (OR MEETING OF THE STANDING COMMITTEE OF THE POLITBURO OF THE CC CCP?)**
III. Beijing
IV. Two sources assert that this meeting was attended only by members of the Standing Committee of the Politburo ([2]: April 12, 1967; [262]: April 10, 1967).
V. Final defeat of Liu Shaoqi, Deng Xiaoping, et al.
VIII. Officially branded Liu Shaoqi and Deng Xiaoping as revisionists (mention: [177]: April 10, 1967; [262]: April 10, 1967).
IX. This meeting saw a showdown with Liu Shaoqi, Deng Xiaoping, Zhu De, Chen Yun, and Tao Zhu opposing the Cultural Revolution, as against Mao Zedong, Lin Biao, Zhou Enlai, Kang Sheng, Li Fuchun, and Chen Boda. The latter group won with a bare majority, branded Liu and Deng as revisionists, and left a decision on Tao Zhu pending. During the course of this meeting, there were demonstrations against Liu and Deng arranged by Chen Boda directly outside of the building (mention: ibid.: [2]: April 12, 1967; [159]; [178]).

318

I. *April 12–18, 1967*
II. **ENLARGED MEETING OF THE MILITARY AFFAIRS COMMITTEE OF THE CC CCP**
V. PLA should support the Left
VI. Jiang Qing: Speech, April 12, or 13, 1967 (identical texts giving different dates: [110]: VI: 10: July 1970: 83–91; [217]: 192: July 17, 1967: 7–15): reveals considerable personal information about her past and duties;

encourages the PLA in support of the Left, reviews the history of the struggle in culture during the early 1960s; admonishes her audience concerning the proper attitudes to assume toward their children.

Lin Biao, Chen Boda, Kang Sheng, and Zhang Chunqiao also spoke and criticized the "crimes" of Liu Shaoqi and Deng Xiaoping ([270]: 360; [108]: 286).

IX.   Participants voiced their anger over the search of the homes of senior military leaders, including the theft of top secret documents; cf. *Nanjing xinhua ribao*, October 22, 1984, tr. in [82]: November 6, 1984: K24.

319

I.   *April 29–May 1, 1967*
II.   **CONFERENCE OF THE CC CCP**
III.   Beijing
IV.   Attended by the Politburo and the Central Cultural Revolution Group.
V.   Mass line and three-way alliances
VI.   Mao Zedong: Speech (mention and excerpt: [199]: May 25, 1967; [199]: May 30, 1967; [230]): discusses the problems of mass line and three-way alliances; predicts a revival of party structure within a half year to a year; asserts that Liu Shaoqi, Gao Gang, and Peng Dehuai tried to copy the USSR.
IX.   Xie Fuzhi conveyed the contents of this conference to a May 9, 1967, Plenary Session of the Beijing Municipal Revolutionary Committee (mention: [2]: May 30, 1967; [230]).

All information on this meeting from the various Japanese sources cited above may have originated with the same Beijing wall poster.

320

I.   *May (7?), 1967* (see IX below)
II.   **ENLARGED MEETING OF THE STANDING COMMITTEE OF THE POLITBURO OF THE CC CCP**
VII.   "Crucial Points of 'Self-Cultivation' Betray the Dictatorship of the Proletariat" (mention: [108]: 283).
IX.   The document referred to Liu Shaoqi's "On the Self-Cultivation of Communist Party Members." The document was published by *Renmin ribao* and *Hongqi* on May 8, 1967, after being discussed and approved by the Standing Committee of the Politburo.

321

I.   *July 26, 1967*
II.   **ENLARGED CONFERENCE OF THE PARTY CENTER**
III. Beijing
IV. CC CCP members in Beijing, Standing Committee members of the Military Affairs Committee of the CC CCP, responsible comrades from the various large military regions (mention: [247]).
V.   Chen Zaidao affair
IX. Chen Zaidao had just led a mutiny in Wuhan (for details see [198]), and he was brought to this meeting and struggled against ([232]: 94: January 1, 1972: 29–30; [247]).

322

I.   *August 1967* (see IX below)
II.   **MEETING OF THE CENTRAL CULTURAL REVOLUTION GROUP**
III. Beijing
V.   Current situation and tasks in the Cultural Revolution
VI. Mao Zedong: Speech (text: [245]): a wide-ranging talk focused on the following issues: review of the Cultural Revolution to date and nature of the current stage; calls for revolutionary great alliances and for three-in-one combinations (including a section on party rebuilding); need for revolutionary rebels to improve their ideological understanding; comment on the notion that China should become a military factory for the world.
IX. All information on this meeting comes from the single Red Guard source cited above. Zhao Zong (ibid.) uses internal information in the document to specify the date of the meeting as August 1967. The Red Guard document itself, published in January 1968, said only that the meeting occurred "very recently."

323

I.   *August 9, 1967*
II.   **MEETING OF HIGH CENTRAL AND REGIONAL MILITARY AND POLITICAL LEADERS**
III. Beijing

IV.   Lin Biao, Zhou Enlai, Chen Boda, Kang Sheng, Jiang Qing, Xie Fuzhi, Wan Li, Guan Feng, Qi Benyu, Zeng Siyu, Chen Xilian, Liu Feng, Huang Yongsheng, Zheng Weishan, Liu Peishan, Wu Faxian, and other comrades (mention: [287]).

V.   Repercussions of Chen Zaidao affair

VI.   Lin Biao: Speech (summary: ibid.): it is possible to carry out the Cultural Revolution only because of the prestige of Chairman Mao and the strength of the PLA; had previously worried about the Beijing and Wuhan military regions, but the Cultural Revolution has solved the problems in these two areas; should not overreact to being attacked unjustly; should consult extensively with the CC CCP and the Central Cultural Revolution Group.

    Chen Boda and Kang Sheng (mention: ibid.): stress the importance of Lin Biao's speech and assert that this speech should be studied by all from the top to the bottom levels.

IX.   This meeting was part of the continuing reaction by the central leadership to the Wuhan incident of the previous month.

    All information on this meeting comes from the single Red Guard source cited above.

1968

324

I.   *July 28, 1968*

II.   **CENTRAL MEETING**

III.   Beijing

IV.   Mao Zedong, Jiang Qing, Lin Biao, Chen Boda, Zhou Enlai, Kang Sheng, Xie Fuzhi, Yao Wenyuan, Huang Yongsheng, Ye Qun, Wen Yucheng, Wang Dabing, Wu De, Kuai Dafu, Nie Yuanzi, Tan Houlan, Han Aiqing, Huang Zuozhen (and others?) (mention: [167]: 687–717; [174]: 469–97).

V.   Continuing problem of factionalism in Beijing schools

VI.   This meeting assumed the form of a discussion (nearly complete stenographic text: ibid.). Mao Zedong asserted that he was the "black hand" that had sent in the workers to end the armed struggle in the schools. He also demanded an end to future factionalism—a view supported by other senior officials present. Mao castigated Kuai Dafu of Qinghua University. Overall, this conversation includes a very wide-ranging discussion of current and recent problems and tasks of the Cultural Revolution.

325

I.   *October 13-31, 1968*
II.   **ENLARGED TWELFTH PLENUM OF THE EIGHTH CC CCP**
III.   Beijing
IV.   Only forty of the eighty-seven living members of the Eighth Central Committee could attend this meeting; 71 percent of the Central Committee alternate members had been declared enemies during the Cultural Revolution (mention: [270]: 367).

Liu Shaoqi did not attend ([194]: May 15, 1980, tr. in [82]: May 15, 1980: L3). Attendees included the members of the Central Cultural Revolution Group, main responsible members of newly established revolutionary committees of the provinces, municipalities, and autonomous regions and of the Work Group of the Military Affairs Commission. Altogether, 133 people attended ([273]: 601; [89]: 379; [108]: 291–92): see IX below.

V.   Review of Cultural Revolution; purge of Liu Shaoqi; new party constitution; plans for Ninth Party Congress
VI.   Mao Zedong: Opening Speech, October 13, 1968 (mention: [108]: 292; [273]: 601): review of the Cultural Revolution; asserts that the Cultural Revolution is necessary to consolidate the proletarian dictatorship.

Mao Zedong: Speech (mention: [182]: 44 [Supplement]: November 1, 1968: v–viii; excerpts: [16]; [26]: 159—mistakenly dated April 28, 1969; [182]: 51: December 17, 1971: 7): discusses the Cultural Revolution since the August 1–12, 1966, Eleventh Plenum of the Eighth CC CCP (meeting 300): proclaims the victory of the Cultural Revolution but warns of continuing class struggle.

Mao Zedong: October 14, 1968 (mention: [200]: 55): in the future, the Cultural Revolution will seem like a brief interlude; hopes that more Central Committee members will attend the next meeting.

Mao Zedong: October 16, 1968 (excerpts: [26]: 156; [182]: 43: October 25, 1968: 2): comments on the need to get rid of the stale and take in the fresh.

Xie Fuzhi (mention: [176]: December 22, 1980, tr. in [82]: December 29, 1980: L15; [273]: 601–602): criticizes Liu Shaoqi, Deng Xiaoping, Chen Yun, and Zhu De; proposes Liu be judged at an open trial by the masses.

Kang Sheng (mention: [273]: 601): accuses some old comrades of wanting to oppose Mao, negate Yan'an rectification, and reverse the verdict on Wang Ming's line.

Jiang Qing (mention: [273]: 601): criticizes Chen Yi, Ye Jianying, and Xu Xiangqian for disrupting the army.

Huang Yongsheng: (mention: [273]: 602): Zhu De is an old right opportunist element, has wild ambitions, and assumes leadership authority.

Wu Faxian (mention: [273]: 602): criticism of Zhu De for opposing Mao.

Lin Biao: to whole meeting (mention: [273]: 602): criticism of February Adverse Current of 1967.

Mao Zedong: Speech, October 30, 1968 (excerpts: [26]: 156–57; [182]: 44 [Supplement]: November 1, 1968: v–viii): the Cultural Revolution has been absolutely necessary. Lin Biao: Speech (mention: [271]: I: 1969: 2–4; [61]: 227–34; [82]: November 1, 1968: B1-B6; [182]: 44 [Supplement]: November 1, 1968: v–viii).

Mao Zedong: Closing Address, October 31, 1968 (mention: [273]: 602): several old comrades are Politburo members and should be allowed to attend the Ninth Party Congress; eliminate class ranks; do not give credibility to coerced confessions; do not get carried away regarding academic authority.

VII.   "Communique" (texts: [271]: I: 1969: 2–4; [61]: 227–34; [82]: November 1, 1968: B1-B6; [182]: 44 [Supplement]: November 1, 1968: v–viii): mentions the following decisions of the Twelfth Plenum:

—Endorsed the actions of the August 1–12, 1966, Eleventh Plenum of the Eighth CC CCP (meeting 300) and the subsequent Cultural Revolution.

—Decided that "ample ideological and organizational conditions have been prepared" for convening the Ninth Party Congress, and that this Congress would be convened at "an appropriate time."

—Ratified the "Report on the Examination of the Crimes of the Renegade, Traitor, and Scab Liu Shaoqi" submitted by the special group under the CC CCP for the examination of his case (partial texts: [32]: 37: January–March 1969: 175–80; [33]: II: 7: January 22, 1969: 21–26; [271]: I: 1969: 7–9; [61]: 243–50; [80]: III: 1: January 10, 1969: 149–56).

—Adopted a resolution to expel Liu Shaoqi from the party, strip him of all posts inside and outside the party, and continue to settle accounts with him and his accomplices.

"Decision of the Enlarged Twelfth Plenary Session of the Eighth CC CCP on the (Draft) Constitution of the Communist Party of China," October 31, 1968 (texts: [61]: 235–42; [216]: 4334: January 9, 1969: 1–5): decided to circulate this draft to the whole party to serve as the basis of discussion, after which the center would make further revisions and submit it to the Ninth Party Congress.

VIII.   Criticized again the February Adverse Current and "persistent rightists," including Chen Yi, Ye Jianying, Li Fuchun, Li Xiannian, Xu Xiangqian, Nie Rongzhen, Zhu De, Chen Yun, and Deng Zihui ([270]: 368; [89]: 379; [108]: 293): the plenum divided into separate groups to discuss the

February Adverse Current and persistent rightists ([273]: 601–602).

IX.   Because only forty of the ninety-seven Central Committee members attended this plenum, ten alternate members were elected as full members to reach a legal quorum ([89]: 379; [270]: 367).

A special group to investigate Liu Shaoqi had been established on December 18, 1966, and was under the control and guidance of Jiang Qing, Kang Sheng, and Xie Fuzhi ([89]: 378; [108]: 292).

Lin Biao and Jiang Qing reportedly advocated that Deng Xiaoping be stripped of his party membership, but Mao Zedong successfully opposed this ([270]: 368).

1969

326

I.   *March 15, 1969*
II.   **CULTURAL REVOLUTION BRIEF MEETING**
V.   International situation
VI.   Mao Zedong (mention: [270]: 369): recent Sino-Soviet border clashes demonstrate that war cannot be avoided. It is necessary to prepare for war.

327

I.   *April 1–24, 1969*
II.   **NINTH NATIONAL CONGRESS OF THE CCP**
III.   Beijing
IV.   1,512 delegates; not all delegates were party members, and others had been admitted to the party immediately prior to the congress ([108]: 295).
V.   Lin Biao's Political Report; revision of the party constitution; election of a new CC CCP
VI.   Mao Zedong: Opening speech, April 1, 1969 (texts: [272]: IV: 3: March 1970: 118–19; [110]: March 1970: 92–93): briefly reviews party history; calls for party unity.

Lin Biao: Political Report on Behalf of the CC CCP, April 1, 1969 (text: [182]: 18: April 30, 1969: 16–35): presents a general background to the Cultural Revolution itself; stresses the continuing need for struggle and transformation; affirms need to provide an opportunity for rehabilitation for those who have erred in the past; notes importance of promoting increased production; contains a section on party consolidation and party building; has a section on foreign affairs, stressing the United States and USSR.

Mao Zedong: April 11, 1969 (mention: [273]: 603): the key problem at present is that one tendency may conceal another (i.e, apparent leftism may conceal real rightism).

Mao Zedong: April 13, 1969 (mention: [89]: 434): capitalist influences remain.

Mao Zedong: Speeches on April 14, 1969 (mention: [182]: 18: April 30, 1969: 43, 45; [273]: 604): mentions clash with Soviet Union on Zhenbao Island.

Lin Biao: Speech, April 14, 1969 (mention: [182]: 18: April 30, 1969: 43).

Zhou Enlai, Chen Boda, Kang Sheng, Huang Yongsheng, Wang Hongwen, Sun Yuguo, Wei Fengying, Ji Dengkui, and Chen Yonggui: Speeches on April 14, 1969 (mention: ibid.; [273]: 604).

Mao Zedong: (mention: [194]: November 28, 1977, tr. in [82]: November 29, 1977: E10): overwhelming majority of public security cadres are good.

Mao Zedong: many speeches (mention: [182]: 18: April 30, 1969: 43, 45; [108]: 295).

VII.   "Constitution of the Communist Party of China," April 14, 1969 (text: [182]: 18: April 30, 1969: 36–39).

VIII.   Adopted Lin Biao's Political Report, April 14, 1969 (mention: ibid.: 42).

Elected a new CC CCP (name list: ibid.: 47–48).

IX.   The text of Lin Biao's Political Report cited above had been revised through discussions at this congress before being published ([182]: 18: April 30, 1969: 43). The version read by Lin was reportedly written by Kang Sheng and Zhang Chunqiao ([200]: 57, 39).

This congress marked the conclusion of the mass-action stage of the Cultural Revolution (the official CC CCP history ends the Cultural Revolution at the 11th Party Congress in 1977) and convened in the wake of fighting between China and the USSR around Zhenbao Island.

A preparatory meeting was convened by the Central Cultural Revolution Group March 9–27, 1969 ([273]: 603), during which Jiang Qing insisted that Lin Biao's name be inserted into the constitution to avoid misunderstanding ([176]: December 28, 1980, tr. in [82]: December 28, 1980: L2).

The proceedings of the Congress were as follows: convened in plenary session in the late afternoon of April 1, 1969, to hear Mao Zedong's opening speech and Lin Biao's Political Report and to receive texts of the new constitution; met in small groups for April 2–13, 1969, to discuss Mao's opening speech, party history, Lin's report, and the draft constitution (making changes in wording in the latter two documents); convened in plenary session on April 14, 1969, to adopt Lin's Political Report and the Constitution, hearing the speeches noted above for that day; for April 15–24, 1969, concerned primarily with election of the new CC CCP, although delegates also met in small groups organized according to localities, fields of work, and units to discuss further how to implement the decisions of the congress (gleaned from documents in [182]: 18: April 30, 1969).

Lin Biao and the Gang of Four are said to have conspired to forge the histories of fourteen central leading comrades and to have accused them of opposing Mao Zedong ([182]: no. 6, February 4, 1977: 8).

A group had been established to compile materials on Ye Jianying, Chen Yi, Li Xiannian, Li Fuchun, Tan Zhenlin, Chen Yun, and Nie Rongzhen. These materials were presented to this party congress ([9]: December 2, 1980, tr. in [82]: December 4, 1980: L8). The group was arranged by Zhang Chunqiao, and its leading group included Wang Hongwen, Wang Shaoying, and Xu Jingxian ([176]: November 20, 1980, tr. in [82]: November 20, 1980: L12).

The party contained twenty-two million members at this time ([108]: 295).

328

I.   *April 28, 1969*
II.   **FIRST PLENUM OF THE NINTH CC CCP**
III.   Beijing
IV.   All full and alternate members of the CC CCP.
V.   Election of leading organs of the party
VI.   Mao Zedong: Speech (texts: [271]: 1970: 3–5; [110]: VI: 6: March 1970: 94–98; [129]: 50564: May 21, 1970: 3–8): the revolution has not yet ended; in some places, too many people were arrested—they should be allowed to work and participate in mass movements; must consolidate the proletarian dictatorship in each unit; must prepare against war but China will not invade others, even under provocation; the masses should participate in party rebuilding.
VII.   "Communique" (text: [182]: 18: April 30, 1969: 48–49): notes the following actions:
        —Elected Mao Zedong Chairman of the CC CCP.
        —Elected Lin Biao sole vice-chairman of the CC CCP.
        —Elected the Standing Committee of the Politburo and the Politburo itself (name lists included in the "Communique").

329

I.   *April 28, 1969*
II.   **MEETING OF THE POLITBURO OF THE CC CCP**
III. Beijing
VIII. Approved appointments to the forty-two-member Military Affairs Commission, as follows: chairman: Mao Zedong; vice-chairmen: Lin Biao, Liu Bocheng, Chen Yi, Xu Xiangqian, Nie Rongzhen, and Ye Jianying; director of General Office: Huang Yongsheng; deputy director: Wu Faxian; members of General Office: Ye Qun, Liu Xianquan, Li Tianyu, Li Zuopeng, Li Desheng, Qiu Huizuo, Wen Yucheng, Xie Fuzhi ([273]: 606).
IX.   Note that four of the vice-chairman (Chen, Xu, Nie, and Ye) were under political attack before and at the Ninth Party Congress.

1970 _____

330

I.   *March-April 1970*
II.   **PARTY RECTIFICATION AND PARTY-BUILDING FORUM**
VI.   Kang Sheng (mention: [220]: 62): only by differentiating classes on the basis of politics and ideology is it possible to understand the emergence of capitalist roaders within the party.
VIII. Introduced the Qinghua University experience with combining production with schooling. Stressed that this rectification should emphasize the four areas of big study, big criticism, big discussion, and big conclusions. Further discussion summarized in ibid.

331

I.   *March 17–20, 1970*
II.   **CENTRAL WORK CONFERENCE**
V.   Plans for the Fourth National People's Congress and constitutional revisions.
VIII. Majority of participants agreed with Mao Zedong's opinion on convening

the Fourth National People's Congress and not reestablishing the post of state chairman (mention: [108]: 298; [273]: 613; [176]: November 24, 1980, in [82]: November 24, 1980: L15).

332

I.   *Late April 1970*
II.   **MEETING OF THE POLITBURO**
VI.   Mao Zedong (mention: [273]: 613): repeats that he does not want to be named state chairman, nor should that post be created.
IX.   Mao Zedong originally made this proposal in March, and the March 17–20 Central Work Conference approved his proposal.

333

I.   *August 22, 1970*
II.   **MEETING OF THE STANDING COMMITTEE OF THE POLITBURO OF THE CC CCP**
III.   Lushan, Jiangxi
VI.   Mao Zedong (mention: [108]: 299; [273]: 613–14): hopes the Second Plenum will be one of unity and victory, not of divisiveness and defeat.
        Lin Biao (mention: [108]: 298; [273]: 614): proposes creation of post of state chairman and that Mao fill the post.
        Chen Boda (mention: [273]: 614): repeats Lin Biao's proposal.
IX.   Mao Zedong opposed Lin's and Chen's proposal ([108]: 298; [273]: 614).
        This meeting took place on the eve of the Second Plenum.

334

I.   *August 23–September 6, 1970*
II.   **SECOND PLENUM OF THE NINTH CC CCP**
III.   Lushan, Jiangxi
IV.   155 full and 100 alternate members of the CC CCP.
V.   1970 economic plan; draft constitution; preparations against war; party building
VI.   Zhou Enlai: Speech, August 23, 1970 (mention: [108]: 299; [273]: 614): explains agenda for the plenum.
        Lin Biao: Opening speech, August 23, 1970 (excerpts: [108]: 300): proposes Mao Zedong be named state chairman; offers his theory of genius.

Chen Boda: Speech at North China Section Meeting (mention: [270]: 375): supports Lin Biao and attacks Zhang Chunqiao. (This speech was given before August 25).

Mao Zedong: Speech (mention: [194]: September 10, 1970; [182]: 37: September 11, 1970: 5–7). Lin Biao: Speech (mention: ibid.).

Mao Zedong: Article, "My Views," August 31, 1970 (mention: [270]: 375; excerpts: [108]: 301; [273]: 616): criticizes Chen Boda and refutes Lin Biao and his supporters.

Mao Zedong: Speech, September 6, 1970 (mention: [108]: 301; [273]: 616).

Zhou Enlai: Summary speech, September 6, 1970 (mention: [108]: 301; [273]: 616).

VII. "Communique" (texts: [194]: September 10, 1970; [182]: 37: September 11, 1970: 5–7): noted that the plenum called for and approved:

—Convening the Fourth National People's Congress (and instructed the NPC Standing Committee to make appropriate preparations).

—Continuation of the various political movements and efforts at party building and consolidation that had been going on prior to the plenum.

—The State Council's report on the National Planning Conference and the National Economic Plan for 1970.

—The report of the Military Affairs Committee of the CC CCP on strengthening work for preparedness against war.

Approved the draft constitution (text: [82]: November 5, 1970: B1-B6) for further discussion and eventual adoption at the Fourth NPC.

IX. The drafting of the constitution considered at this plenum had begun in March 1970, when Mao Zedong raised the need to convene the Fourth NPC, to pass a new constitution, and to abolish the position of chairman of the state. A drafting committee with Mao as Chairman and Lin Biao as vice-chairman was established on July 12, 1970, and in light of opinions collected throughout the country, revised the original draft of this constitution. This committee then presented the revised draft to the Second Plenum on August 23, 1970 (mention: [272]: VI: 2: February 10, 1972: 119).

Mao Zedong convened an enlarged meeting of the Standing Committee of the Politburo on August 25, which decided to recall the North China Sections No. 2 Brief Bulletin and to have Chen Boda critically examine himself (mention: [270]: 375).

Zhongfa (Central Committee Document) #12 issued on March 12, 1972 (text: [35]: V: 3–4: 1972–73: 31–42) noted that Mao Zedong had, during an August–September 1971 tour of the provinces, depicted the Second Plenum as a struggle between two headquarters. He made the following specific remarks about what transpired at this plenum:

—On August 23–25, 1970, Lin Biao and his collaborators launched a "sneak attack" calling for the appointment of a head of state and advocating the theory of genius; Lin had not shown his speech to Mao in advance.

—Lin's collaborators included Ye Qun, Chen Boda, Huang Yongsheng, Wu Faxian, Li Zuopeng, Qiu Huizuo, Li Xuefeng, and Zheng Weishan.

—Lin also wanted to reverse the line of the April 1–24, 1969, Ninth Party Congress (meeting 327) (with respect to party building?) and to revoke the three items on the agenda of this plenum (probably referring to three of the following four: the 1970 economic plan; the preparations against the war; the draft constitution; and party building).

—During this plenum, Mao wrote a 600-word document entitled "My Views," in which he raised the question of whether history is created by heroes or slaves (and evidently came down in favor of the latter).

—Lin et al. panicked when their views went awry and, among other things, withdrew the transcript of a speech made by Ye Qun at a session of the Central-South Group during this plenum.

—The no. 6 brief prepared by the North China Group (evidently at this plenum) was counterrevolutionary.

—Mao repeatedly stated that he did not want to be head of state.

—This plenum decided to protect Lin rather than overthrow him. The latter had been the practice in all previous struggles between the two lines in the party.

—Some comrades were deceived and hoodwinked at this plenum.

The plot of Lin Biao and his supporters is discussed in detail in ([108]: 299–302; [273]: 614–16; [176]: November 23, 1980, tr. in [82]: November 25, 1980: L7–8). Reportedly, Chen Boda's speech at the North China Section meeting made evident the growing struggle for power between the Lin Biao and the Jiang Qing groups, and Chen's speech caused considerable turmoil when it was circulated to other participants in the form of the Second Bulletin of the North China Group (issued on August 6) (mention: [270]: 375).

The Central Propaganda Department was ordered to conduct an investigation of Chen Boda during this plenum ([108]: 301).

335

I.   *August 23, 1970*
II.   **MEETING OF THE POLITBURO**
III. Lushan, Jiangxi
V.   National economic plan

VI.   Wu Faxian (mention: [108]: 300): suggests that the plenum then in session discuss Lin Biao's speech given earlier that day and that the agenda of the plenum be changed accordingly.

336

I.   *August 25, 1970*
II.   **ENLARGED MEETING OF THE STANDING COMMITTEE OF THE POLITBURO OF THE CC CCP**
III.   Lushan, Jiangxi
VI.   Mao Zedong (mention: [108]: 300): criticizes Chen Boda for spreading fallacies and supporting Lin Biao's speech.
VIII. Decided to halt discussion of Lin Biao's August 23 speech to the Second Plenum and to recall the no. 2 report of the North China Bureau (mention: [108]: 300; [273]: 616).
IX.   This meeting convened during the Second Plenum. On the same day, Jiang Qing and Zhang Chunqiao told Mao Zedong of Lin Biao's plot ([273]: 616).

337

I.   *December 22, 1970–January 24–?, 1971*
II.   **ENLARGED POLITBURO MEETING OF THE CC CCP ("NORTH CHINA CONFERENCE")**
III.   Beidaihe, Hebei
V.   Criticism of generals and of Chen Boda
VI.   Zhou Enlai: Speech, January 24, 1971 (mention: [273]: 618): criticism of Chen Boda.
IX.   This conference was chaired by Zhou Enlai ([108]: 302) and witnessed self-criticisms by seven generals who were Lin Biao's supporters on the Military Affairs Committee of the CC CCP, which Mao Zedong had called for (mention: [35]: V: 3–4: 1972–73: 12, 45). Its purpose evidently was to extend the ongoing criticism of Chen Boda so that it encompassed some of Lin Biao's chief supporters.

       This conference was convened by Zhou at Mao's request. At the conference, there was renewed criticism of Chen Boda's crimes. Also, at the conference the center announced its decision to reorganize the Beijing Military Region (mention: [270]: 376).

1971

338

I.   *1971*
II. **NATIONAL CONFERENCE ON AGRICULTURAL MECHANIZATION**
VII. Apparently set the goal of basically achieving agricultural mechanization by 1980 (mention: [194]: May 30, 1977, tr. in [82]: June 1, 1977: E14).
IX. This conference was convened by the State Council and presided over by Hua Guofeng.

    The spirit of the conference was conveyed in a *Renmin ribao* editorial "The Fundamental Way out for Agriculture Lies in Mechanization" (mention: [9]: January 17, 1977, tr. in [79]: January 19, 1977: E1). One source says the editorial was reviewed, revised, and approved by Hua Guofeng but suppressed by Yao Wenyuan ([194]: May 30, 1977), in [82]: June 1, 1977: E4).

339

I.   *January 9–?, 1971*
II. **MILITARY AFFAIRS COMMISSION FORUM**
IV. 143 people attended.
VI. Mao Zedong (mention: [108]: 302): Huang Yongsheng, Wu Faxian, Ye Qun, Li Zuopeng, and Qiu Huizuo must criticize Chen Boda and make self-criticisms.
IX. Under the direction of Lin Biao, Huang, Wu, Ye, Li, and Qiu refused Mao's order (mention: [108]: 302; [273]: 619).

    On February 19, 1971, the Politburo transmitted Mao Zedong's order that this forum should not be studied by local areas because it met for one month without criticizing Chen Boda ([273]: 619).

340

I.   *Spring 1971*
II. **NATIONAL CONFERENCE ON PUBLIC SECURITY**
VI. Zhou Enlai (excerpt: [182]: March 17, 1978: 33): Chairman Mao's line has always been dominant in our public security work; refutes notion that a sinister line has dominated.

Mao Zedong (at this conference?) (mention: [194]: November 28, 1977, tr. in [797]: November 29, 1977: E3): public security work; should be viewed from the viewpoint of one dividing into two.

IX.   Lin Biao and the Gang of Four charged that "a sinister line" was dominant in public security work in the seventeen years prior to the Cultural Revolution ([182]: March 17, 1978: 33).

341

I.   *April 15–29, 1971*
II.   **REPORT MEETING OF THE "CRITICIZE CHEN BODA, RECTIFY WORK STYLE" MOVEMENT**
IV.   Ninety-nine people, including leading cadres from Beijing, the provinces, and the PLA.
V.   Rectification of Chen Boda; self-criticism by generals
VI.   Zhou Enlai: Summary Speech, April 29, 1971 (mention: [35]: V: 3–4; 1972–73: 39; [108]: 303): gives the confessions of Huang Yongsheng, Wu Faxian, Ye Qun, Li Zuopeng, and Qiu Huizuo and makes public the confessions of Li Xuefeng and Zheng Weishan.
IX.   The thrust of this meeting was to extend the criticism of Chen Boda to Lin Biao's supporters. Mao Zedong later commented that this meeting had been convened to resolve the problems that had been raised at the August 23–September 6, 1970, Second Plenum of the Ninth CC CCP (meeting 334) but that in fact these problems did not end with this meeting (mention: [35]: V: 3–4; 1972–73: 39).

At this meeting, Huang, Wu, Ye, Li Zuopeng, and Qiu actually made self-criticisms that Mao Zedong ostensibly personally approved. They, Zheng, and Li Xuefeng continued to make public appearances but were ordered to make further self-examinations and held their official positions in name only ([64]: no. 25, October 16, 1980, tr. in [82]: October 23, 1980: U4). Lin Liguo had feared that his father, Lin Biao, might also have to make a self-criticism at this meeting, but this fear was not warranted (mention: [35]: V: 3–4; 1972–73: 56–57).

342

I.   *September 26–October ?, 1971*
II.   **CENTRAL FORUM**
IV.   Mao Zedong, Zhou Enlai, Li Fuchun, Chen Yi, Xu Xiangqian, Deng Yingchao, Cai Chang, Wang Zhen, Zhang Dingcheng, Zhang Yunyi, Deng Zihui, Zeng Shan, Nie Rongzhen, and others?

V.   Lin Biao
IX.   Li Fuchun presided over this forum.
        Forum was held to analyze Lin Biao's history and past mistakes in order to explain his rapid transition from Mao Zedong's comrade-in-arms and successor to national traitor.
        All information on this meeting is contained in *Nanjing xinhua ribao*, October 17, 1984 (tr. in [82]: October 26, 1984: K17).

343

I.   *December 1971*
II.   **MEETING OF SENIOR CCP CADRES**
V.   Foreign affairs
VI.   Zhou Enlai (summary: [1]: February 23, 1977, in [82]: February 23, 1977: E25): explanation of President Nixon's visit; relations with the United States and the Soviet Union.

1972_____

344

I.   *1972*
II.   **THIRD PLENUM OF THE NINTH CC CCP**
VI.   Mao Zedong, letter to Zhou Enlai, read by Zhou to plenum (mention: [194]: April 4, 1984, tr. in [82]: April 10, 1984: K8): positive appraisal of Wang Jiaxiang.

345

I.   *May 20–late June 1972*
II.   **REPORT MEETING ON THE CAMPAIGN TO CRITICIZE LIN BIAO AND RECTIFY WORK STYLE**
III. Beijing
IV.   312 people from central departments, provinces, municipalities, and autonomous regions.
VI.   Zhou Enlai: Speech, May 21, 1972 (mention: [273]: 625): recounts the struggle with the Lin Biao clique.

Zhou Enlai: Report, June 10, 11, 12, 1972 (partial text of June 10 report: [194]: January 17, 1985, tr. in [82]: January 24, 1985: K9–11; mention: [273]: 626): describes six inner-party line struggles during the democratic revolution period, including an examination of his own actions with regard to Wang Ming.

Zhou Enlai: Report, "The True Story of the 'Wu Haoqi Affair' Cooked up by the Guomindang" (mention: ibid.).

Mao Zedong (at this meeting?) (mention: ibid.): will not tolerate false allegations against Zhou Enlai in the future.

VII. Mao Zedong letter to Jiang Qing expressing doubts about Lin Biao as far back as 1966 was the main document circulated at this conference; the letter was explained by Politburo members at individual group meetings (ibid.).

The Central Committee issued a document to high-ranking cadres to explain Zhou Enlai's report on Wu Haoqi, and also enclosed firsthand information (ibid.).

1973

346

I.   *March 1973*
II. **MEETING OF SENIOR CCP CADRES**
V.   Foreign affairs
VI. Zhou Enlai (mention: [1]: February 23, 1977, in [82]: February 23, 1977: E25, 27): deployment of Soviet troops suggests their threat is directed against the West; predicts the Soviet Union and the United States will give priority to the Middle East problem after the Vietnam War is over.

347

I.   *April 1973*
II. **MEETING OF THE POLITBURO OF THE CC CCP**
III. *Xiafang* policy
IX. In April 1973, Mao Zedong issued a directive on solving problems associated with the policy of having educated youths settle in the countryside.

Zhou Enlai immediately called a Politburo meeting to discuss implementation of Mao's directive. One result was a national conference on this issue in June 1973 ([176]: January 31, 1977, in [82]: February 1, 1977: E9).

348

I.   *May 20–31, 1973*
II.   **CENTRAL COMMITTEE WORK CONFERENCE**
III.   Beijing
V.   Rehabilitation of veteran leaders, discussion of the "criticize Lin Biao, rectify work style" campaign, preparations for the Tenth Party Congress
VI.   Zhou Enlai (mention: [283]: 512): conveyed Mao Zedong's instructions on economic work.
VII.   "Report on Problems in the National Economic Planning" (prepared by State Planning Commission, mention: ibid.).
VIII.   Under Mao Zedong's instructions, this conference announced the rehabilitation of thirteen veteran cadres, including Tan Zhenlin and Li Jingquan; allowed Wang Hongwen, Hua Guofeng, and Wu De to attend Politburo meetings as nonvoting members and to participate in the work of the Politburo ([108]: 312; [273]: 628).

Approved the method for selecting representatives to the Tenth Party Congress and the principles and methods for revising the party constitution ([273]: 628; [283]: 511).

Discussed the campaign to criticize Lin Biao and rectify work style ([283]: 511).

349

I.   *July 1973*
II.   **MEETING(S?) OF THE POLITBURO**
V.   Preparations for the Tenth Party Congress
VIII.   Discussed revisions of the "Political Work Report," "Party Constitution," and "Report on the Revision of the Party Constitution"; in early June, Mao's approval was sought and he wrote that he "agreed in principle" ([273]: 628).
IX.   The three documents cited above were drafted by Zhang Chunqiao, Yao Wenyuan, and Wang Hongwen (ibid.).

350

I. *August 24–28, 1973*
II. **TENTH NATIONAL CONGRESS OF THE CCP**
III. Beijing
IV. 1,249 delegates.
V. Elect new CC CCP; adopt new party constitution; ratify Lin Biao purge
VI. Zhou Enlai: "Report" (text: [182]: 35–36: September 7, 1973: 17–25): presents the case against Lin Biao; briefly reviews China's recent foreign policy; wide-ranging commentary on the current international situation; specifies the current tasks, stressing the importance of strengthening the centralized leadership of the party; mentions that the CCP now has a membership of twenty-eight million.

Wang Hongwen: "Report on the Revision of the Party Constitution" (text: ibid.: 29–33): explains the basis for the changes in wording that have been made in the party constitution.
VII. "Constitution of the Communist Party of China," August 28, 1973 (text: ibid.: 26–29).

"Press Communique," August 29, 1973 (text: ibid.: 5–8).
VIII. Elected a new CC CCP of 195 full and 124 alternate members (name list: ibid.: 9–10).
IX. This congress confirmed the meteoric rise of Wang Hongwen into the highest levels of the party, reflected by Wang's appointment as vice-chairman of the party at the August 30, 1973, First Plenum of the Tenth CC CCP (meeting 351).

A major purpose of this congress was to remove Lin Biao's name from the party constitution and to specify the line concerning his downfall and how it affected (or did not affect) the decisions of the April 1–24, 1969, Ninth Party Congress (meeting 327).

The newly elected Central Committee reduced the component of military men in general, and those from Lin Biao's Fourth Field Army in particular, and included some important civilians—such as Deng Xiaoping and Tan Zhenlin—who had been targets during the Cultural Revolution.

A preparatory meeting was held August 12–19, 1973, at which the majority of delegates expressed approval for the "Report to the Tenth Party Congress," "Report on the Revision of the Constitution," and the "Party Constitution (Revised Version)." These reports were drafted by Zhang Chunqiao, Yao Wenyuan, and Wang Hongwen ([273]: 628).

351

I.   *August 30, 1973*
II.   **FIRST PLENUM OF THE TENTH CC CCP**
III.   Beijing
V.   Elect central organs of the CC CCP
VII.   "Communique" (text: [182]: 35–36: September 7, 1973: 10): notes from
        this plenum:
            —Elected Mao Zedong Chairman of the CC CCP.
            —Elected four vice-chairmen of the CC CCP (name list in ibid.).
            —Elected a Standing Committee of the Politburo of nine members and
        a Politburo of twenty-one full and four alternate members (name lists in
        ibid.).

352

I.   *November 1973*
II.   **MEETING OF THE POLITBURO OF THE CC CCP**
V.   Criticism of Zhou Enlai
VI.   Jiang Qing (mention: [273]: 632): accuses Zhou Enlai of miscalculation
        in foreign affairs; declares this to be the eleventh two-line struggle.
        Mao Zedong (mention: ibid.): affirms the good work of the meeting, but
        criticizes and rejects both of Jiang Qing's assertions.
IX.   Drawing his conclusions on the basis of unreliable sources, Mao Zedong
        thought Zhou Enlai had spoken incorrectly on some unspecified foreign
        affairs activity and therefore called this meeting to criticize Zhou (men-
        tion: ibid.).

353

I.   *December 12–15, 1973*
II.   **MEETING OF THE POLITBURO OF THE CC CCP**
V.   Rehabilitation of Deng Xiaoping
VI.   Mao Zedong: December 12, 1973 (mention: [108]: 321; [89]: 411; [283]:
        519; [273]: 632): proposes that Deng Xiaoping be appointed a full mem-
        ber of the Politburo and the Military Affairs Commission; criticizes work
        of Politburo and Military Affairs Commission; warns of civil and foreign
        wars; suggests rotation of military region commanders.
            Mao Zedong: December 14, 1973 (mention: [283]: 519; [270]: 386):

discusses transfer of military region commanders; proposes Deng Xiaoping as chief of General Staff.

IX. One source says Mao's proposal to rehabilitate Deng Xiaoping was also made by Ye Jianying ([89]: 411).

On December 22, 1973, the Central Committee issued a directive confirming Deng Xiaoping as full member of the Politburo and Military Affairs Commission ([283]: 519; [273]: 633).

354

I. *December 21, 1973*
II. **MILITARY AFFAIRS COMMISSION MEETING**
VI. Mao Zedong (mention: [*Nanjing xinhua ribao*]: October 20, 1973, tr. in [82]: November 6, 1973: K20; [273]: 633): warns of reemergence of revisionism in China; makes self-criticism for listening to Lin Biao with regard to He Long, Luo Ruiqing, Yang Chengwu, Yu Lijin, and Fu Chongbi; the "Yang-Yu-Fu" incident was a mistake concocted by Lin Biao; reaffirms his support for Zhu De.
IX. On December 22, 1973, the Military Affairs Commission announced the rotation of eight military region commanders (mention: [273]: 633).

At a meeting of leaders from various military regions, held about this time, Mao Zedong warned of revisionism and recommended that those present study the biography of Zhou Bo of the Han dynasty, who defeated an attempt by Empress Lu's followers to usurp the throne; this suggestion was interpreted by those present as allegorical support for Zhou Enlai against Jiang Qing (mention: [176]: September 7, 1978, tr. in [82]: September 8, 1978: E3–4).

1974

355

I. *June 26, 1974*
II. **MILITARY AFFAIRS COMMISSION MEETING**
IX. On September 15, 1973, Ye Jianying sent samples of materials from the planned "Selected Works on Military Affairs" and "Quotations on Military Affairs" to Wang Hongwen, Zhang Chunqiao, and Yao Wenyuan for

their review. However, at this meeting nine months later, Wang and Zhang said they had not read them and indicated that they did not intend to ([176]: April 10, 1977, tr. in [82]: April 13, 1977: E19).

356

I.   *July 17, 1974*
II.   **MEETING OF THE POLITBURO OF THE CC CCP**
VI.   Mao Zedong (mention: [108]: 318,324; [273]: 637; [182]: January 14, 1977: 28; [270]: 389): criticizes Wang Hongwen, Zhang Chunqiao, Jiang Qing, and Yao Wenyuan and warns them not to become a small faction of four; tells Jiang not to pin labels on people and that it will be hard to mend her ways; declares Jiang only represents herself, not Mao.
IX.   This was the first time that Mao Zedong had raised the issue of a "Gang of Four" (mention: [108]: 318; [273]: 637).

Mao's statement that Jiang Qing did not represent him was first revealed in a wall poster at Beijing University in November 1976 (mention: [AFP]: November 15, 1977, tr. in [82]: November 15, 1977: E20).

357

I.   *October or November 1974*
II.   **MEETING OF THE POLITBURO OF THE CC CCP**
V.   Preparations for the Fourth National People's Congress
VI.   Zhu De (mention: [272]: February 15, 1977: 22): if Zhou Enlai is not premier, then I should be.

358

I.   *October 17, 1974*
II.   **MEETING OF THE POLITBURO OF THE CC CCP**
IV.   Mao Zedong was in Changsha and Zhou Enlai was hospitalized at the time of this meeting.
IX.   This meeting witnessed a clash between the Gang of Four and Deng Xiaoping, apparently in response to Mao Zedong's proposal on October 4, 1974, that Deng be named first vice-premier. The attack on Deng used as its pretext the "Fengqing" steamboat, an oceangoing vessel that was part of the effort to create a ship-building industry in China but was used by the Gang of Four as a symbol of the "worship of foreign things" and national betrayal ([273]: 637–38).

The next day, Wang Hongwen reported to Mao in Changsha on the clash. Mao in turn criticized Wang (mention: ibid.; [270]: 389).

359

I.   *November 1974*
II. **POLITBURO MEETING**
VI. Li Xiannian ([110]: May 1979: 86): conveys Mao Zedong's instruction "to push the national economy forward."

1975

360

I.   *January 8–10, 1975*
II.   **SECOND PLENUM OF THE TENTH CC CCP**
III. Beijing
IV.   Mao Zedong did not attend.
V.   Elevation of Deng Xiaoping; preparations for the January 13–17, 1975, First Session of the Fourth NPC (meeting 361).
VII. "Communique" (text: [182]: 4: January 24, 1975: 6): notes that this plenum:
      —Elected Deng Xiaoping vice-chairman of the CC CCP and a member of the Standing Committee of the Politburo of the CC CCP.
      —Decided to submit the following documents to the January 13–17, 1975, First Session of the Fourth NPC (meeting 361): "The Draft Revised Text of the Constitution of the PRC"; "The Report on the Revision of the Constitution"; "The Report on the Work of Government"; and the lists of nominees for membership in the Standing Committee of the NPC and for the State Council.
VIII. The plenum also approved Li Desheng's request to resign as party vice-chairman and member of the Standing Committee of the Politburo (the same posts Deng Xiaoping was appointed to) (mention: [108]: 319).
IX.   On January 5, 1975, just prior to this plenum, the Central Committee issued document no. 1, which announced the appointment of Deng Xiaoping as vice-chairman of the Military Affairs Commission and chief of staff of the PLA, and Zhang Chunqiao as head of the General Political Department of the PLA (mention: [273]: 639).

361

I.   *January 13–17, 1975*
II.   **FIRST SESSION OF THE FOURTH NPC**
III.   Beijing
IV.   2,864 delegates
V.   Approve the revised constitution, approve the government work report, elect and appoint government leaders
VI.   Zhou Enlai: "Report on the Work of the Government," January 13, 1975 (texts: [194]: January 21, 1975; [182]: 4: January 24, 1975: 21–25).

       Zhang Chunqiao: "Report on the Revision of the Constitution," January 13, 1975 (texts: [194]: January 20, 1975; [182]: 4: January 24, 1975: 18–20).

VII.   "Proclamation of the NPC," January 17, 1975 (text: [182]: 4: January 24, 1975: 11): provides name of appointees to the posts of premier, vice-premier, ministers, and ministers heading State Council commissions.

       "The Constitution of the People's Republic of China," January 17, 1975 (text: [182]: 4: January 24, 1975: 12–17).

       Other minor proclamations (texts in: ibid.).

IX.   Preparations for this congress began at least in October 1974 (mention: [194]: June 4, 1977 and [97]: no. 6, June 1977, tr. in [82]: June 7, 1977: E7).

362

I.   *February 25–March 8, 1975*
II.   **NATIONAL CONFERENCE OF PROVINCIAL PARTY SECRETARIES IN CHARGE OF INDUSTRY**
V.   Problems in rail transport
VI.   Deng Xiaoping: Speech (mention: [89]: 407; [270]: 392): on correcting problems with the railroads. Deng blamed these partly on supporting revolution to the neglect of production.
IX.   On the basis of Deng Xiaoping's speech and the discussion at this conference, the Central Committee decided to strengthen the railroad industry by putting the national railroads under the unified management of the Ministry of Railroads. Essential rules and regulations for the railroad system were restored and strengthened ([89]: 408).

363

I.   *March 1975*
II.   **MEETING OF FOREIGN AFFAIRS CADRES**
III. Beijing
IV.   Cadres at the consul level and above
VI.   Jiang Qing: Speech (text: [272]: June 1975: 122–25, tr. in [35]: Spring-Summer 1976: 49–61): discussion of revolutionary prospects in Asia and Africa; the spark of revolution in newly independent countries comes from unjust internal distribution, not foreign oppression; China supports revolutionary movements by giving, but not selling, arms; the decline of imperialism has weakened the United States and the Soviet Union and offers China a peaceful environment for economic and cultural development; revisionism is possible in Vietnam; the "*pi* Lin, *pi* Kong" campaign on the foreign affairs front; party leadership and political study is neglected in many of China's embassies.

364

I.   *March 1, 1975*
II.   **CONFERENCE OF DIRECTORS OF POLITICAL DEPARTMENTS IN MAJOR MILITARY UNITS**
V.   Danger of empiricism
VI.   Zhang Chunqiao (mention: [270]: 392): warns that the chief current danger is empiricism.

365

I.   *May 3, 1975*
II.   **MEETING OF THE POLITBURO OF THE CC CCP**
III. Beijing
IV.   Politburo members who were in Beijing at that time.
VI.   Mao Zedong (mention: [182]: January 14, 1977: 28; [273]: 646; [117: July 2, 1983, tr. in [82]: July 11, 1983: K3; [108]: 324; [110]: February 1979: 96 and April 1979: 111; [270]: 394): states the three do's and don'ts (practice Marxism-Leninism, not revisionism; unite, don't split; be open and above board, don't intrigue and conspire); warns Wang Hongwen,

Zhang Chunqiao, Jiang Qing, and Yao Wenyuan not to become a Gang of Four; criticizes them for their mistaken concept of empiricism and treatment of intellectuals.

IX.   Mao Zedong's criticism of the Gang of Four resulted in Deng Xiaoping's convening two Politburo meetings on May 27 and June 3, 1975, to criticize them further (mention: [270]: 394).

Jiang Qing later claimed that Mao Zedong had criticized "both sides" at this meeting ([110]: February 1979: 97).

366

I.   *May 27 and June 3, 1975*
II.   **MEETINGS OF THE POLITBURO OF THE CC CCP**
V.   Criticism of the Gang of Four
VI.   Deng Xiaoping, Ye Jianying, Li Xiannian, and others (mention: [273]: 646): criticized the Gang of Four on these counts: their reckoning of an eleventh two-line struggle; the "*pi* Lin, *pi* Kong" campaign; the issues of "walking in through the back door" and "oppose empiricism."
VIII.   Wang Hongwen made a self-criticism, but the other three denied they were a Gang of Four and refused to make a self-criticism.
IX.   These meetings resulted from Mao Zedong's criticism of the Gang of Four at a Politburo meeting on May 3, 1975.

One source mistakenly says these two meetings occurred in April and May ([110]: February 1979: 95).

367

I.   *June 24–July 15, 1975*
II.   **ENLARGED MEETING OF THE MILITARY AFFAIRS COMMISSION**
VI.   Deng Xiaoping: Speech, "The Task of Consolidating the Army," July 14, 1975 (text: [52]: 27–38): discusses the problems of bloating, laxity, conceit, extravagance, and inertia in the army; military equipment must be technologically upgraded and standardized; strategy, training, and political work in the army must be improved; demobilization and rotation of military cadres and officers should start with leading bodies; discusses the role of newly created post of adviser.

Ye Jianying: Speech, July 15, 1975 (mention: [89]: 409; [283]: 547–48; [273]: 642): consolidating the army requires solving the problems of reduction and reorganization of staff, making arrangements for excess cadres, overcoming the problem of weakness, laziness, and sloppiness in leading groups; resist bourgeois ideology, carry out party policies, and oppose factionalism.

VII.   "Guidelines" (mention: [9]: April 16, 1978, tr. in [82]: April 18, 1978: E2; [9]: April 25, 1978, in [82]: May 5, 1978: E23): stressed the need for education and training of troops, improvement in party and political work, preparedness for war, and resettlement of cadres.

VIII. Made preparations for convening an All-Army Political Work Conference ([9]: April 12, 1978, tr. in [82]: April 14, 1978: E8). This conference was not held due to interference from the Gang of Four.

Revised "Regulations on Internal Affairs" and "Regulations on Discipline," which were approved by Mao Zedong.

IX.   As a result of this meeting, the Military Affairs Commission demobilized several hundred thousand military cadres to do local work.

During this conference, Mao Zedong's criticism of the Gang of Four circulated among some participants ([176]: January 30, 1978, in [82]: January 31, 1978: E3).

Zhang Chunqiao declined a request to address this meeting ([115]: November 30, 1977 and [194]: December 1, 1977, tr. in [82]: January 31, 1978: E3).

368

I.   *July 20–August 4, 1975*
II.   **MEETING OF KEY ENTERPRISES OF NATIONAL DEFENSE INDUSTRIES**
VI.   Deng Xiaoping: Speech, "On Consolidating National Defense Industries," August 3, 1975 (text: [52]: 39–42).

369

I.   *July 30, 1975*
II.   **MEETING OF THE POLITBURO OF THE CC CCP**
VIII. Approved showing of the film "Haixia," which the Gang of Four opposed ([176]: March 15, 1977, in [82]: March 15, 1977: E2).

IX.   At this time, a directive of Mao Zedong was released, criticizing the Gang of Four for opposing the film "Pioneers."

370

I.   *Late 1975*
II.   **MEETINGS OF THE POLITBURO OF THE CC CCP**
VIII. Discussed the evaluation of the Cultural Revolution, criticized Deng

Xiaoping, stopped most of Deng's work [273]: 648–49).

371

I.   *September 15–October 19, 1975*
II.   **FIRST NATIONAL CONFERENCE ON LEARNING FROM DAZHAI IN AGRICULTURE**
III.   Xiyang County, Shanxi, and Beijing
IV.   Hua Guofeng, Ye Jianying, Deng Xiaoping, Zhang Chunqiao, Jiang Qing, Yao Wenyuan, Li Xiannian, Chen Xilian, Ji Dengkui, Wang Dongxing, Wu De, Wei Guoqing, Chen Yonggui, Wu Guixian, Su Zhen-hua, Saifudin, Tan Zhenlin, Ulanfu, Zhou Jianren, Li Suwen, Yao Lian-wei, Wang Zhen, Yu Qiuli, Gu Mu, Sun Jian, Xu Xiangqian, Nie Rong-zhen, Li Jingquan, and 3,700 delegates from around the country at all levels.
V.   "Learn from Dazhai" movement, agricultural mechanization
VI.   Chen Yonggui: Opening speech, September 15, 1975 (summary: [182]: September 19, 1975: 3–4): explains agenda for the conference; lauds the movement to learn from Dazhai, which has become the most widespread mass movement in the countryside; pace of agricultural production must increase.

Deng Xiaoping: Report, September 15, 1975 (mention: [182]: September 19, 1975: 3; excerpt: [2]: March 7, 1976, tr. in [82]: March 9, 1976: annex: 4; [97]: no. 11, November 1977, tr. in [82]: December 1, 1977: E13): military, party, local industries, culture, and education all need adjustment; Chairman Mao's revolutionary line has been primarily followed domestically for past twenty-five years, despite interference from opportunist and revisionist lines.

Jiang Qing: Speech, September 15, 1975 (mention: [182]: September 19, 1975: 4; [176]: December 24, 1976, in [82]: December 27, 1976: E19): accuses provincial first party secretaries of neglecting agriculture by not attending the conference [the Central Committee decided that first secretaries should not attend]; demands that her talk on the novel *Water Margin* be published and broadcast at the conference.

Guo Fenlian (party secretary of Dazhai production brigade): Speech (partial text: [176]: September 24, 1975, tr. in [82]: September 26, 1975: E1–9): detailed history of the Dazhai experience.

Wang Qinzi (Jinzi?) (deputy secretary of Xiyang Party Committee): Speech (partial text: [176]: September 27, 1975, tr. in [82]: October 1, 1975: E11–17): the success of Xiyang county in learning from Dazhai, becoming a Dazhai-type county, and achieving agricultural mechanization.

Hua Guofeng: Speech at a plenary session, "Mobilize the Whole Party, Make Greater Efforts to Develop Agriculture, and Strive to Build Dazhai-Type Counties Throughout the Country," October 15, 1975 (text: [176]: October 20, 1975, tr. in [82]: October 23, 1975: E1–11; partial English texts: [182]: October 31, 1975: 7–10,18; [176]: October 20, 1975, in [82]: October 22, 1975: E1–7): building Dazhai-type counties is a militant task of the whole party; county party committees are the key to building Dazhai-type counties; conducting education on the party's basic line is necessary; speed up agricultural mechanization; comprehensive planning and more effective leadership are necessary.

Chen Yonggui: Closing speech, October 19, 1975 (summary: [182]: October 31, 1975: 3; [176]: October 20, 1975, in [82]: October 22, 1975: E7–9): modernization of agriculture will guarantee the modernization of industry, national defense, and science and technology in its wake and will strengthen the material base in preparing against war and natural disasters; sets tasks of delegates after returning home from this conference.

IX. Mao Zedong ordered that Jiang Qing's speech on *Water Margin* not be published, distributed, or broadcast.

The *Renmin ribao* editorial on this conference is "Build Dazhai-Type Counties Throughout the Country" ([194]: October 21, 1975, tr. in [82]: October 22, 1975: E10–13).

Hua Guofeng's report was issued as Central Committee document no. 21 (1975) ([176]: December 24, 1976, in [82]: December 27, 1976: E19). Nevertheless, it is unusual that a meeting of this nature did not produce a document outlining policy direction nor give broad goals for the establishment of Dazhai-type counties. There is no indication that the delegates formally approved anything.

372

I. *September 23–October 21, 1975*
II. **FORUM ON RURAL WORK**
III. Beijing
V. Accounting units in the communes
VI. Deng Xiaoping: Speech, "Things Must Be Put in Order in All Fields," September 27 and October 4, 1975 (text: [52]: 47–50): party consolidation should focus on leading bodies at various levels; importance of selecting leading cadres, especially county party committees; give preference to middle-aged cadres; Mao Zedong Thought should be studied as an integral whole.
IX. On August 14, 1975, Chen Yonggui had advocated shifting the basic

accounting unit in communes from the team to the brigade level, as was done in Dazhai.

Reportedly, at this forum Zhao Ziyang and Tan Qilong strongly and persistently opposed Chen Yonggui's suggestion, to the point that the meeting adjourned without reaching agreement on this issue (mention: [270]: 397).

373

I.   *After early November 1975*
II.   **SEVERAL MEETINGS OF A PORTION OF THE POLITBURO MEMBERSHIP**
V.   Criticism of Deng Xiaoping
VIII. Stripped Deng of his work responsibilities other than in foreign affairs work ([270]: 398–99).
IX.   These meetings convened after Mao Yuanxin had convinced Mao Zedong that Deng Xiaoping was trying to reverse the verdict on the Cultural Revolution (ibid.).

374

I.   *Late November 1975*
II.   **MEETING OF THE POLITBURO OF THE CC CCP ("DA ZHAOHU" MEETING)**
III. Beijing
VI.   Hua Guofeng (mention: [273]: 649; [89]: 413): the problems emerging at Qinghua University are not isolated ones: they reflect the struggle between two classes, two roads, and two lines; it is a rightist wind to reverse correct verdicts; some people are unsatisfied with the Cultural Revolution.
IX.   Mao Zedong approved Hua Guofeng's speech ([270]: 399).

      The charge of a desire to reverse correct verdicts was most likely directed against Deng Xiaoping, who was later accused of favoring education and science policies discredited in the Cultural Revolution. The implicit criticism of Deng intensified over the following months until he was finally criticized by name in spring 1976.

1976_____

375

I.   *January 21 and 28, 1976*
II.   **MEETINGS OF THE POLITBURO OF THE CC CCP**
VIII. Mao Zedong proposed, and the Politburo agreed, that Hua Guofeng be appointed acting premier and be put in charge of the daily work of the Central Committee, and that Chen Xilian be put in charge of the daily work of the Military Affairs Commission.
IX.   These actions were made necessary by the death of Zhou Enlai and the political eclipse of Deng Xiaoping.
      Another source says that the appointment of Hua Guofeng occurred at a Politburo meeting on February 3, 1976 ([272]: January 15, 1977: 28).

376

I.   *Late January–early February 1976 (5 days)*
II.   **SECOND PLENUM OF THE TENTH CC CCP**
III. Beijing
VI.   Deng Xiaoping: Report on the work of the government (mention: [1]: March 17, 1976, in [82]: March 18, 1976: E1): includes mention of the five-year plan to begin that year.
      Yao Wenyuan and Zhang Chunqiao (mention: ibid.): criticism of Deng Xiaoping's report.
IX.   This plenum supposedly was scheduled to last eight days but ended after only five due to the disagreement brought on by Deng Xiaoping's report (ibid.; [1]: February 13, 1976, in [82]: February 17, 1976: E1–2).
      It was at this meeting that Hua Guofeng was chosen as acting premier as a compromise candidate (ibid.)
      The accounts of this plenum are based solely on rumors and may actually refer to the Politburo meetings on January 21 and 28 and February 3, 1976.

377

I.   *February 25–?, 1976*
II.   **CENTRAL MEETING OF PROVINCIAL, MUNICIPAL,
      AUTONOMOUS REGION, AND MILITARY REGION LEADERS**
VI.   Hua Guofeng: Speech representing the center, February 25, 1976 (men-

tion: [182]: December 24, 1976: 11; [108]: 330; [89]: 413; [273]: 650; [270]: 400): must criticize Deng Xiaoping and his revisionist line; Deng can be criticized by name.

Mao Yuanxin: a series of talks (mention: [273]: 650): reaffirms class struggle as the key link; veteran comrades who are dissatisfied with the Cultural Revolution are ideologically stuck in the stage of the bourgeois democratic revolution; capitalist roaders continue to exist in the party; the Cultural Revolution is 70 percent correct, the mistakes being "attack everything" and "all-around civil war."

IX.   Mao Zedong approved Hua Guofeng's speech.

On March 3, 1976, the Central Committee issued an instruction of Mao Zedong that criticized Deng Xiaoping by name ([89]: 413; [273]: 650).

This meeting suggests that the movement to criticize Deng Xiaoping met with a great deal of confusion, and perhaps opposition, around the country.

[89], [270], and [108] say that this meeting occurred on February 25 and mention only Hua Guofeng's talk. [273] says Mao Yuanxin gave a series of talks explaining Mao Zedong's instruction criticizing Deng Xiaoping by name; presumably, these talks were given to small group meetings and then Hua spoke at a plenary session.

378

I.   *March–June 1976*
II.   **THREE NATIONAL CONFERENCES CONVENED BY CENTRAL LEADING ORGANS**
V.   Unspecified issues
VI.   Wang Hongwen (mention: [182]: February 25, 1977: 17): a group of national betrayers exists in the foreign trade departments.

Zhang Chunqiao (mention: ibid.): the bourgeoisie and comprador bourgeoisie exist in the party and the Politburo; criticizes effort to create "a colonial economy" in China and importing of complete sets of equipment; accuses Hua Guofeng of using Mao Zedong's name to intimidate others.

Jiang Qing (mention: ibid.): China is shifting the international energy crisis onto its own people by exporting petroleum, which in turn has saved the first and second worlds.

Yao Wenyuan (mention: ibid.): the State Council is leasing China's natural resources to foreign countries and is engaged in national betrayal.

Hua Guofeng (mention: ibid.): imports of major items had Mao Zedong's approval.

379

I.   *March 13, 1976*
II.   **MEETING OF THE POLITBURO OF THE CC CCP**
IX.   At this meeting and another on June 25, 1976, the State Planning Commission gave a briefing on the plans to implement the industrial production plan. The Gang of Four criticized the importation of chemical fertilizers and complete sets of equipment for chemical fibers and the export of oil, even though Mao Zedong, the Politburo, and they themselves had approved the decisions. Yao Wenyuan criticized a proposal to establish several coal exporting bases, which were needed to facilitate the shipping of coal in exchange for foreign equipment and material needed by China ([110]: May 1979: 94–95).

380

I.   *April 1, 1976*
II.   **MEETING OF THE POLITBURO OF THE CC CCP**
VIII. Issued an instruction that characterized the "Nanjing incident" as a political event that [upheld] the party center with Mao as its leader but sought to reverse the general orientation of criticizing Deng Xiaoping [273]: 652).
IX.   In accordance with the sentiment of this meeting, on April 2, 1976, the Beijing Party Committee sent militia and police to interfere with and stop the people mourning for Zhou Enlai in Tiananmen Square. Before dawn on April 3 they removed the mementos that had been placed in Tiananmen Square (ibid.).

381

I.   *April 4, 1976*
II.   **MEETING OF THE POLITBURO OF THE CC CCP**
III.   Beijing
IV.   Not in attendance: Mao Zedong (ill), Ye Jianying, Zhu De, Xu Shiyou, and Li Xiannian (all not in Beijing).
V.   Demonstrations in Nanjing, Beijing, and elsewhere
VI.   Hua Guofeng (mention: [108]: 331; [273]: 652; [244]: November 30, 1984, tr. in [82]: December 19, 1984: K4): a group of people have come into the open to attack Mao Zedong and the Central Committee directly.
       Wu De (mention: [108]: 331; [244]: November 30, 1984, tr. in [82]:

December 19, 1984: K4): some central and Beijing municipal units have laid wreaths in Tiananmen Square; Deng Xiaoping has been making plans for demonstrations since 1974; current demonstrations are planned and counterrevolutionary.

Jiang Qing and others (mention: [89]: 415): advocate the arrest of demonstrators who make counterrevolutionary speeches and also the removal of wreaths.

VIII.   Decided to begin removing wreaths and poems from Tiananmen Square that evening, to deploy worker's militia and Public Security officers to surround the Monument to the Martyrs of the Revolution in the middle of Tiananmen, to prevent the masses from going to place flowers and meet with others, and to deploy a double row of garrison troops (ibid.; [108]: 331; [283]: 564).

IX.   Mao Zedong was ill and did not attend this meeting, but he approved a report given to him by Mao Yuanxin on the circumstances and the decisions of the meeting, including the counterrevolutionary nature of the demonstrations ([89]: 415; [108]: 331.

Additional quotes are in [270]: 401.

382

I.   *April 6, 1976*
II.   **MEETING OF THE POLITBURO OF THE CC CCP**
III.   Beijing
V.   Tiananmen Square demonstrations
VI.   Beijing Municipal Party Committee: Report on the Tiananmen Incident (mention: [89]: 416; [273]: 653).
VIII.   The meeting held that the Tiananmen demonstration was a counterrevolutionary riot; decided to keep thirty thousand garrison troops in the vicinity of Tiananmen and to call up nine battalions of reserves in Beijing; issued the Beijing Party Committee's report to the whole country to allow local areas to understand the situation and to make whatever plans were necessary ([89]: 416).
IX.   Mao Zedong approved the report given to him by Mao Yuanxin on these decisions.

383

I.   *April 7, 1976*
II.   **MEETING OF THE POLITBURO OF THE CC CCP**
III.   Beijing

V.   Tiananmen demonstrations
VIII.   Two decisions:
        —Resolution on the Appointment of Hua Guofeng as the First Vice-
        Chairman of the CC CCP and Premier of the State Council.
        —Resolution on the Dismissal of Deng Xiaoping from All Posts In and
        Out of the Party ([108]: 332; [89]: 417; [273]: 653).
IX.   These decisions were proposed by Mao Zedong and approved by the
        Politburo.
        Mao Zedong proposed that Deng Xiaoping retain his party member-
        ship and be given a light penalty to see if he would change his behavior
        ([273]: 653).
        These decisions were announced by *Renmin ribao* on April 8, 1976;
        that same day, the paper published the official assessment of the Tianan-
        men Incident and a speech by Wu De (ibid.).

384

I.   *April 30, 1976*
II.   **MEETING BETWEEN HUA GUOFENG AND MAO ZEDONG**
V.   National conditions following Qing Ming disturbances and ouster of
        Deng Xiaoping
VI.   Hua Guofeng (mention: [272]: March 15, 1977: 8): the general situation
        throughout the country is good, but the circumstances in several prov-
        inces are not very good.
        Mao Zedong (mention: ibid.): three written notes to Hua Guofeng:
        —Do not be in a hurry, there is no cause for alarm.
        —Act in accordance with past principles.
        —With you in charge, I am at ease.
IX.   Hua Guofeng showed only the first two notes to the Politburo (ibid.).

385

I.   *June 25, 1976*
II.   **MEETING OF THE POLITBURO OF THE CC CCP**
IX.   At this meeting and an earlier one on March 13, 1976, the State Planning
        Commission gave a briefing on the plans to implement the industrial
        production plan. The Gang of Four criticized the importation of chemical
        fertilizers and complete sets of equipment for chemical fibers and the
        export of oil, even though Mao Zedong, the Politburo, and they them-
        selves had approved the decisions. Yao Wenyuan criticized a proposal to
        establish several coal-exporting bases, which were needed to facilitate the

shipping of coal in exchange for foreign equipment and material needed by China ([110]: May 1979: 94–95).

386

I.   *July 1976*

II.   **NATIONAL CONFERENCE ON PLANNING WORK**

IX.   Little information is available on this conference other than that the Gang of Four launched an attack against Hua Guofeng and the State Council in an attempt to unsettle the succession arrangement established by Mao Zedong and the policies currently being implemented. The Ministry of Foreign Trade in particular was singled out for criticism ([194]: December 22, 1976, tr. in [82]: December 22, 1976: E2; [194]: July 16, 1977, tr. in [82]: July 18, 1977: E13; [182]: December 24, 1976: 11, January 7, 1977: 30, February 25, 1977: 18; [176]: April 21, 1977, tr. in [82]: April 26, 1977: E9; [9]: September 5, 1977, tr. in [82]: September 7, 1977: E13).

     This conference was convened by the CC CCP.

387

I.   *Summer (August?) 1976*

II.   **MEETING OF THE POLITBURO OF THE CC CCP**

IV.   Gang of Four did not attend.

V.   Tangshan earthquake

IX.   The Politburo held several meetings to hear reports on the relief efforts following the Tangshan earthquake on July 28, 1976. In contrast to the concern of most central leaders, the Gang of Four reportedly did not attend any of these meetings ([83]: November 15, 1976, tr. in [82]: November 22, 1976: E3).

388

I.   *September 1, 1976*

II.   **CONFERENCE ON ANTI-EARTHQUAKE AND RELIEF WORK**

III.   Beijing

IV.   Over 3,500 representatives from Tangshan, Tianjin, and Beijing. Central leaders: Hua Guofeng, Wang Hongwen, Ye Jianying, Zhang Chunqiao,

Jiang Qing, Yao Wenyuan, Li Xiannian, Chen Xilian, Ji Dengkui, Wang Dongxing, Wu De, Chen Yonggui, Wu Guixian, Su Zhenhua, Ni Zhifu, Guo Moruo, Ulanfu, Ngapo Ngawang-jigme, Zhou Jianren, Xu Deheng, Hu Juewen, Li Suwen, Wang Zhen, Gu Mu, Sun Jian, Shen Yanping, Jiang Hua.

V.   Earthquake relief efforts

VI.   Liu Zihou: Report (excerpts: [176]: September 2, 1976, tr. in [82]: September 3, 1976: E1–6): relief work in Tangshan.

Xu Xin: Report (excerpts: ibid.: E6–10): relief work in Tianjin.

Huang Zuochen: Report (excerpts: ibid.: E10–14): relief work in Beijing.

Hua Guofeng: Speech (summary: [176]: September 1, 1976, tr. in [82]: September 2, 1976: E2–5): central assistance to relief work and the rapid success of that work.

VIII. Approved message of salute to Mao Zedong ([176]: September 1, 1976, tr. in [82]: September 2, 1976: E5).

IX.   Wang Zhen presided over this conference (ibid.: E1).

389

I.   *September 29, 1976*

II.   **MEETING OF THE POLITBURO OF THE CC CCP**

VI.   Zhang Chunqiao (mention: [272]: January 15, 1977: 30): proposes that Jiang Qing be made party chairman.

IX.   At this meeting, Jiang Qing and others called on Hua Guofeng to resign.

390

I.   *Late September 1976*

II.   **MEETING OF THE POLITBURO OF THE CC CCP**

IX.   At this meeting, some veteran leaders criticized the Gang of Four for emphasizing the slogan "act according to the principles laid down" in their propaganda and ignoring the "three do's and don'ts" ([194]: December 17, 1976, in [182]: December 24, 1976: 9).

It was later discovered that "act according to the principles laid down" was a corruption of Mao Zedong's original written order to Hua Guofeng ("act according to past principles"), the difference resulting from the alteration of three characters in the original.

391

I.   *October 4, 1976*
II.   **MEETING OF THE POLITBURO OF THE CC CCP**
IV.   Gang of Four did not attend because they were not informed of meeting.
VIII.   Decided to arrest Gang of Four ([1]: February 8, 1977, in [82]: February 10, 1977: E21).
IX.   The arrests were carried out the evening of October 6, 1976 ([273]: 656).

392

I.   *October 5, 1976*
II.   **MEETING OF THE POLITBURO OF THE CC CCP**
IX.   Chen Xilian, Wu De, and Wang Dongxing allegedly forced Hua Guofeng to agree to nine demands in return for their support of the arrest of the Gang of Four ([20]: March 30, 1977, tr. in [82]: April 8, 1977: E2).

393

I.   *October 7, 1976*
II.   **MEETING OF THE POLITBURO OF THE CC CCP**
VI.   Hua Guofeng, Ye Jianying, and Wang Dongxing: Reports (mention: [172]: October 31, 1976, and November 1, 1976, tr. in [82]: November 3, 1976: E1-3): the arrest of the Gang of Four.
VIII.   Made the following decisions:
        —Approved arrest of the Gang of Four.
        —Elected Hua Guofeng chairman of the party and Military Affairs Commission.
        —Decided to build a memorial hall for Mao Zedong and to publish volume 5 of his *Selected Works* and prepare his *Collected Works* (ibid.: E3).

394

I.   *October 7-14, 1976*
II.   **CENTRAL MEETING**
III.   Beijing
IV.   Responsible leaders from central party, government, and military organs,

and from the provinces, municipalities, autonomous regions, and military regions.

VI.   Hua Guofeng (mention: [172]: November 1, 1976, tr. in [82]: November 3, 1976: E3; [270]: 404): must continue to criticize Deng Xiaoping and the right deviationist wind to reverse correct verdicts; problems in Liaoning and Shanghai.

Ye Jianying (mention: [270]: 404–405): arresting the Gang of Four is only an initial victory; must over the long term exert efforts to wipe out their ideological influence.

VIII.   Ratified decisions made by Politburo on October 7, 1976 (see meeting 393) ([272]: November 1976: 1).

IX.   The center convened a series of meetings with the responsible officials from the various units mentioned above. The object was to inform these key people about the Gang of Four incident, clarify issues that required immediate attention, and move things toward stability (mention: [270]: 404).

395

I.   *November 15–19, 1976*
II.   **PROPAGANDA WORK SEMINAR**
III.   Beijing
V.   Criticize Gang of Four
VIII.   Began to develop the propaganda line to be taken in criticism of the Gang of Four. Also, seized back leadership over propaganda work from the followers of the Gang of Four (mention: [270]: 405–406).
IX.   Reportedly, Hua Guofeng's own position at this conference kept the meeting focused on criticizing "rightism" rather than criticizing leftism. The meeting itself was convened by the party center (mention: ibid.).

396

I.   *December 10–27, 1976*
II.   **SECOND NATIONAL CONFERENCE ON LEARNING FROM DAZHAI IN AGRICULTURE**
III.   Beijing
IV.   More than five thousand representatives of party committees at all levels, army and public security forces, and farmers.
V.   Farm mechanization, agricultural development, criticism of Gang of Four
VI.   Li Xiannian: Opening speech, December 10, 1976 (mention: [176]: De-

cember 10, 1976, in [82]: December 13, 1976: E2).

Chen Xilian: Speech, December 10, 1976 (mention: ibid.).

Ji Dengkui: Speech, December 10, 1976 (mention: ibid.).

Chen Yonggui: Speech, December 10, 1976 (mention: ibid.).

Wu Guixian: Speech, December 10, 1976 (mention: ibid.).

Chen Yonggui: Report, "Thoroughly Criticize the 'Gang of Four' and Bring about a New Upsurge in the Movement to Build Dazhai-Type Counties Throughout the Country," December 20, 1976 (text: [176]: December 24, 1976, tr. in [82]: December 27, 1976: F16–30): describes attempt by Gang of Four to seize power, in particular their attempt to undermine the "Learn from Dazhai" movement; necessity of conducting education on the basic line of the party; sets targets for agricultural development.

Hua Guofeng: Speech, December 25, 1976 (mention: [176]: December 26, 1976, tr. in [82]: December 27, 1976: E30): reviews events of 1976 and discusses tasks for 1977.

Guo Fenglian: Speech (excerpts: [182]: February 4, 1977: 14–19): describes Jiang Qing's visits to Dazhai on eve of first Dazhai conference in September 1975 and again in September 1976 just before Mao Zedong died.

Speeches by delegates ([176]: December 16, 1976, in [82]: December 17, 1976: E1–4; [176]: December 21, 1976, in [82]: December 22, 1976: E15–17; [82]: supplement, January 21, 1977: 1–49; [182]: February 4, 1977: 5–10).

VIII. Made the following decisions:

—Reaffirmed the goal set forth at the first Dazhai conference of making one-third of all counties into Dazhai-type counties and basically achieving agricultural mechanization by 1980, and making production of grain, cotton, edible oil, and pork exceed the plan.

—Local areas must develop industrial enterprises that produce iron and steel, coal, chemical fertilizer, cement, and machinery to aid agricultural mechanization.

—Carry out the work of rectifying the party and work style in the villages and consolidate the leading groups.

—Strengthen brigade-run enterprises and raise the level (proportion?) of ownership of communes and brigades ([272]: January 15, 1977: 69).

1977 _____

397

I.   *January 21, 1977*
II.   **MEETING OF THE POLITBURO OF THE CC CCP**
V.   Investigation of Gang of Four
VI.   Ye Jianying: Report (mention: [1]: February 6, 1977, in [82]: February 7, 1977: E10): based on an inquiry by a commission headed by Ye, he reported that the Gang of Four, not Deng Xiaoping, was responsible for the most serious mistakes; recommended that Deng be reinstated as party vice-chairman and vice-premier.
VIII.   Politburo decided to ask Central Committee members for their opinions on what posts were to be given to Deng Xiaoping because it had been unable to agree after four days of discussion.
IX.   All information on this meeting comes from an unconfirmed report.

398

I.   *February ?-5-?, 1977*
II.   **FOUR DEFENSE CONFERENCES**
        (see IX below)
III.   Beijing
IV.   Eight hundred delegates
IX.   The four conferences were: a national conference on air defense; a conference convened by the Third Ministry of Machine Building (which produces weapons); a discussion meeting on planning; and a meeting on scientific research and production. The latter two were sponsored by the PLA's Science and Technology Commission for National Defense. These meetings were held simultaneously and are believed to have started a reevaluation of China's defense posture and military strategy ([176]: February 5, 1977, in [82]: February 7, 1977: E4; [177]: April 6, 1977: A11).

399

I.   *March 10–22, 1977*
II.   **CENTRAL WORK CONFERENCE**
III.   Beijing

V.   Political and economic conditions since the arrest of the Gang of Four; 1977 national economic plan

VI.   Hua Guofeng: Report, February 14, 1977 (mention: [283]: 578–79; [273]: 670–71; [108]: 360; [52]: 400; [194]: July 21, 1981, tr. in [82]: July 22, 1981: K5; [176]: August 22, 1977, in [82]: August 22, 1977: D32; [268]: August 1980, tr. in [82]: August 15, 1980: U1–17, passim): reaffirms the "two whatevers"; advocates the continuation of taking class struggle as the key link, the theory of continuous revolution, and supporting the achievements of the Cultural Revolution; refuses to reconsider verdicts on Deng Xiaoping and Tiananmen; describes "eight musts" for restoring order following Cultural Revolution.

Ye Jianying: Report (mention: [1]: May 29, 1977, in [82]: May 31, 1977: E1–2): the arrest of the Gang of Four.

Chen Yun (mention: [273]: 671): due to the needs of the Chinese revolution and the party, Deng Xiaoping should be allowed to return to work; must investigate the Gang of Four's scheme regarding Tiananmen.

Wang Zhen (mention: [273]: 671): the whole party, army, and nation want Deng Xiaoping to return to work at an early date; the Tiananmen Incident reflected the entire nation's opposition to the Gang of Four.

IX.   Hua Guofeng reportedly tried to prevent the circulation of Chen Yun's and Wang Zhen's calls for Deng Xiaoping's rehabilitation. Hua refused to let these speeches be printed in the meeting's bulletin ([270]: 407–8]. Although Hua Guofeng and others opposed Deng Xiaoping's return, the meeting reportedly agreed to let Deng resume his former posts (first vice-premier, party vice-chairman, and chief of General Staff), although the timing of his return would be decided by Hua ([1]: March 29, 1977, in [82]: March 30, 1977: E1).

According to a speech by Hu Jiwei, Zhang Pinghua led a drafting group that wrote on four theoretical issues to be included in Hua Guofeng's political work report at the Eleventh Party Congress: the criticism of productive forces, the theory of complete democracy, and the criticism of bourgeois rights are all correct, and distribution according to work is bourgeois. Although this central work conference objected strongly to these ideas associated with the Gang of Four, Zhang continued to hold that articles written by Zhang Chunqiao and Yao Wenyuan could not be criticized by name because Mao Zedong and the Central Committee had read and approved them. The conference decided that criticism of the Gang of Four must go beyond the four and criticize the entire "factional set-up": individuals in all locales and units could be criticized for being followers of the Gang of Four. Chen Yun, Wang Zhen, and Deng Yingchao were nominated to become Politburo members, but someone (Wang Dongxing, by implication) invoked Mao Zedong's criticism of Chen to block the nominations ([268]: August 1980, tr. in [82]: August 15, 1980: U1–17).

400

I. *March 24, 1977*
II. **MILITARY COMMISSION FORUM**
VI. Ye Jianying (mention: [270]): the military should move quickly to reverse the crimes of the Gang of Four in the military and to remove their poisonous influence there.

401

I. *April 20–May 13, 1977*
II. **NATIONAL CONFERENCE ON LEARNING FROM DAQING IN INDUSTRY**
III. Daqing (April 20–24) and Beijing (April 27–May 13)
IV. Seven thousand representatives.
VI. Li Xiannian: Opening speech, April 20, 1977 (text: [176]: April 22, 1977, tr. in [82]: April 25, 1977: E1–3).

Song Zhenming: Speech, April 20, 1977 (summary: ibid.: E3–5): describes Daqing's achievements over past seventeen years and its conflict with the Gang of Four.

Speeches by representatives of nine advanced units in Daqing, April 21–23 (mention: ibid.: E6).

Gu Mu: Speech, April 23, 1977 (mention: ibid.: E6).

Kang Shien: Speech, May 3, 1977 (summary: [176]: May 3, 1977, in [82]: May 4, 1977: E1–2): China is preparing a new leap forward that will exceed the 1958 leap in scale and impact; the petroleum industry has made great progress since the start of the Cultural Revolution.

Yu Qiuli: Report, "Let the Whole Party and the Entire Working Class Mobilize to Build Daqing-Type Enterprises Throughout the Country," May 4, 1977 (text: [176]: May 7, 1977, in [82]: May 9, 1977: E5–26): criticizes extensively the Gang of Four's interference in Daqing; reiterates Mao's policy on industrial management and support of Daqing; blames leadership at all levels for failure to enact Daqing's methods in all enterprises; economic and military capabilities must be strengthened; organizational consolidation and rectification of work style will be carried out once CC CCP makes the necessary arrangements; all enterprises must learn from the PLA and the Daqing experience.

Ye Jianying: Speech, May 9, 1977 (excerpts: [182]: May 20, 1977: 15–19): advocates learning from Dazhai, Daqing, and the PLA; elimination of classes on the way to communism will be a slow process; accelerate the building of industry in the interior in preparation for war; Mao's habit of convening national conferences and taking inspection tours was good and should be continued.

Hua Guofeng: Speech, May 9, 1977 (text: ibid.: 7–15): encourages the study and application of Mao Zedong Thought; promotes the Daqing experience; China must be prepared for war and any possible emergency; the pace of economic construction has fallen short of expectations.

Ji Dengkui: Closing Speech, May 13, 1977 (mention: ibid.: 4).

Other speeches: [82]: May 3, 1977: E8–14; May 4, 1977: E2–3; May 5, 1977: E1–2; May 7, 1977: E7–23.

IX.   Two *Renmin ribao* editorials were written to coincide with the opening and conclusion of this conference: "An Unprecedented Grand Meeting for Grasping the Key Link in Running the Country" ([194]: April 23, 1977, tr. in [82]: April 25, 1977: E10–14), and "The Chinese People Have High Aspirations" ([194]: May 14, 1977, tr. in [82]: May 16, 1977: E6–10).

A preparatory meeting was held by the State Council in December 1976 ([182]: December 24, 1976: 17; [176]: December 17, 1976, tr. in [82]: December 23, 1976: E1–2).

402

I.   *July 16–21, 1977*
II.   **THIRD PLENUM OF THE TENTH CC CCP**
III.   Beijing
VI.   Hua Guofeng: Speech (mention: [270]: 409; [182]: July 29, 1977: 3): continued to support the "two whatevers."

Ye Jianying: Speech (mention: [182]: July 29, 1977: 3).

Deng Xiaoping: Speech, July 21, 1977 (partial texts: [52]: 55–60; [110]: July 1978; summary: [273]: 672–73): Mao Zedong Thought must be understood in its entirety, especially regarding party building; sharply criticizes the Soviet Union; defends united front with all anti-Soviet nations; Sino-American relations will continue to improve; people-to-people ties with North Korea and Vietnam are strong, but relations between parties are like tofu: it breaks apart when pulled.

VII.   Communique, July 21, 1977 (text: [182]: July 29, 1977: 3–8; [176]: July 21, 1977: in [82]: July 22, 1977: E13–18): notes the following actions:

—Resolution on Confirming the Appointment of Comrade Hua Guofeng as Chairman of the CC CCP and Chairman of the Military Commission of the CC CCP;

—Resolution on Restoring Comrade Deng Xiaoping to His Posts;

—Resolution on the Anti-Party Clique of Wang Hongwen, Zhang Chunqiao, Jiang Qing, and Yao Wenyuan;

—Approved plans for convening the Eleventh Party Congress ahead of schedule.

IX.   A preparatory meeting was held in early July ([273]: 671–72).

Deng Xiaoping also gave a talk prior to the plenum to an ad hoc group that included Hua Guofeng. In his talk, Deng said the Cultural Revolution had shortcomings—chiefly, it loosened party discipline and let Lin Biao and the Gang of Four do their evil. The arrest of the Gang of Four cannot be credited to any individual but to the entire Central Committee. Although Hua was selected by Mao Zedong as his successor, it was due to Hua's performance in office that the older revolutionaries, including Deng, supported him and let him remain as leader ([110]: October 1977).

403

I.   *August 4–8, 1977*
II.   **SCIENCE AND EDUCATION WORK FORUM**
VI.   Deng Xiaoping (mention: [270]: 410): overall, science and education work during 1949–1966 pursued a ''red'' line, and most of the intellectuals concerned are laborers.
IX.   This meeting was convened by the party center (mention: ibid.).

404

I.   *August 12–18, 1977*
II.   **ELEVENTH NATIONAL CONGRESS OF THE CCP**
III.   Beijing
IV.   1,510 delegates representing more than 35 million party members.
V.   Political work report; elect new Central Committee; revise party constitution
VI.   Hua Guofeng: Political Work Report, August 12, 1977 (text: [176]: August 22, 1977, in [82]: August 22, 1977: D11–46, and September 1, 1977: Supplement: 11–46): praises Mao Zedong and his contribution to Marxism-Leninism; criticism of Gang of Four; supports the goals of the Cultural Revolution, especially continuous revolution and class struggle, but now is a time for stability; many more cultural revolutions will be needed in the future; renews support for Mao's ''three worlds'' theory of foreign affairs; the Soviet Union poses a greater threat because it is on the offensive, United States is on the defensive; now is the time for economic development and party building, consolidation, and rectification.

Ye Jianying: Report on the Revised Constitution, August 13, 1977 (text: [176]: August 23, 1977, in [82]: August 23, 1977: D1–15, and

September 1, 1977: Supplement: 49–63): Chairman Hua is a worthy successor who saved China; extensively praises Mao Zedong; China will remain a socialist country (and not become communist) so long as imperialism and the bourgeoisie continue to exist; Gang of Four is an excellent teacher by negative example; keep to and carry forward party work style and traditions.

Deng Xiaoping: Closing Speech, August 18, 1977 (text: [176]: August 24, 1977, in [82]: August 24, 1977: D1–2, and September 1, 1977: Supplement: 72–73): revive and carry forward party work style and traditions.

VII.   Communique, August 18, 1977 (text: [176]: August 20, 1977, in [82]: August 22, 1977: D2–10, and September 1, 1977: Supplement: 2–10).

Constitution of the Communist Party of China, August 18, 1977 (text: [176]: August 23, 1977, in [82]: August 23, 1977: D15–23, and September 1, 1977: Supplement: 63–71; [182]: September 2, 1977).

VIII.   Elected new Central Committee with 201 members and 132 alternate members (name list: [176]: August 20, 1977, in [82]: August 22, 1977: E1–3, and September 1, 1977: Supplement: 74–76).

IX.   This congress announced the official end to the Great Proletarian Cultural Revolution.

A preparatory meeting was held August 11. The congress met in plenary session August 12, 13, and 18.

405

I.   *August 19, 1977*
II.   **FIRST PLENUM OF THE ELEVENTH CC CCP**
II.   Beijing
V.   Election of new central leadership
VII.   Communique, August 19, 1977 ([176]: August 20, 1977, in [82]: August 22, 1977: E1, and September 1, 1977: Supplement: 74): reveals newly elected central leaders.

406

I.   *August ?–23–?, 1977*
II.   **MILITARY AFFAIRS COMMISSION FORUM**
V.   Education and training in the military
VI.   Deng Xiaoping: Speech, ''The Army Should Attach Strategic Importance to Education and Training,'' August 23, 1977 (partial text: [52]: 73–79): some worry that if the army is not consolidated it may not go into battle in

the event of enemy attack; leading bodies must be readjusted; peace-time education and training of cadres, officers, and troops are necessary to improve combat readiness and understanding of modern warfare.

407

I. *September 1977*
II. **MEETING OF THE POLITBURO OF THE CC CCP**
V. Restoration of presidency
VI. Su Zhenhua (mention: [177]: December 10, 1977: A2): Mao Zedong's opposition to Lin Biao as president does not mean he was opposed to the post itself.

Li Desheng (mention: ibid.): the question of restoring the presidency should be referred to the masses.
IX. According to a report based on intelligence sources in Taiwan (ibid.), a group of Deng Xiaoping's supporters advocated restoring the post of president at the Fifth National People's Congress. A Central Committee directive was reportedly issued to encourage debate on this issue.

The post of president was not restored until the Sixth National People's Congress in June 1983 (meeting 477).

408

I. *December 12–31, 1977*
II. **MEETING OF THE MILITARY AFFAIRS COMMISSION OF THE CC CCP**
VI. Deng Xiaoping: Speech, December 28, 1977 (text: [52]: 87–100): assesses the movement to criticize the Gang of Four and the related process of reorganizing leading bodies; it is possible to delay the outbreak of world war, but local wars may erupt at any time and China must be prepared to overcome superior forces with inferior equipment; the problem of training military cadres to do civilian work; one million soldiers are being demobilized every year; strict discipline must be enforced in the army, but without democracy there cannot be voluntary compliance with discipline; overcome factionalism.
VII. Nine documents ([52]: 403):

—Decision on Improving Education and Training in the Armed Forces;

—Decision on Running the Military Academies and Schools Well;

—Decision on Enhancing the Sense of Organization and Discipline of Our Army;

—Regulations of the Chinese People's Liberation Army on Guarding State Military Secrets;

—Decision on Speeding up the Modernization of Our Army's Weaponry and Equipment;

—Plan for Readjusting the Army Establishment and Organizational Structure;

—Draft Decision on the System of Military Service;

—Decision on Strengthening the Management of Factories, Horse Farms, Agricultural Production and Sideline Occupations in Our Army;

—Decision on Overhauling and Improving the Financial Work in Our Army.

VIII.   Set "Ten fighting tasks" for the army ([52]: 402–403; [273]: 685).

Affirmed the correctness of the Enlarged Meeting of the Military Affairs Commission that convened June 24–July 15, 1975 (meeting 367) ([270]: 413).

1978

409

I.   *January 28, 1978*
II.   **PROPAGANDA DEPARTMENT FORUM**
IV.   The deputy heads of twenty-six departments, ministries, and commissions of the Central Committee and the State Council.
V.   Effective deployment of the cadre force
VI.   Hu Yaobang (mention: [270]: 414): it is necessary quickly to allocate appropriate jobs to capable cadres, to make arrangements for old and weak cadres, and to complete the investigations of cadres under investigation.

410

I.   *February 18–23, 1978*
II.   **SECOND PLENUM OF THE ELEVENTH CC CCP**
III.   Beijing
V.   Preparations for Fifth National People's Congress and Fifth Chinese People's Political Consultative Congress.
VI.   Hua Guofeng: Speech (summary: [182]: March 3, 1978: 7–8; [176]: February 23, 1978, in [82]: February 23, 1978: E1–2): the country is

quickly on the mend following the arrest of the Gang of Four; local people's congresses have already been held; convocation of Fifth NPC is a major political event in the course of grasping class struggle as the key link.

VII.   Communique, February 23, 1978 (ibid.), reveals following actions:

—Discussed and approved three documents for submission to NPC and CPPCC: Government Work Report, (Draft) Outline for the Ten-Year Plan for the Development of the National Economy; Report on the Revision of the New Constitution.

—Approved all leadership appointments to be submitted to the NPC.

—Adopted new lyric for the national anthem.

411

I.   *February 26–March 5, 1978*

II.   **FIRST SESSION OF THE FIFTH NATIONAL PEOPLE'S CONGRESS**

III.   Beijing

IV.   3,497 delegates

VI.   Hua Guofeng: Report on the Work of the Government, February 26, 1978 (text: [62]: 1–118; [176]: March 6, 1978, in [182]: March 7, 1978: D1–38; [82]: March 10, 1978: 7–40).

Ye Jianying: Report on the Revision of the Constitution, March 1, 1978 (text: [62]: 173–220; [176]: March 7, 1978, in [82]: March 8, 1978: D28–42; [182]: March 17, 1978: 15–28).

VII.   Constitution, March 5, 1978 (text: [62]: 125–72; [176]: March 7, 1978, in [82]: March 7, 1978: D39–55; [182]: March 17, 1978: 5–14).

Proclamations (texts: [62]: 124, 221–32):

—Adopted constitution;

—Elected chairman, vice-chairmen, secretary-general, and other members of the NPC Standing Committee;

—Appointed Hua Guofeng premier;

—Appointed Jiang Hua president of the Supreme People's Court and Huang Huoqing chief procurator of the Supreme People's Procuratorate;

—Approved membership of the State Council;

—Appointed Guo Moruo president of the Chinese Academy of Sciences and Hu Qiaomu president of the Chinese Academy of Social Sciences;

—Adopted National Anthem.

VIII.   Adopted the Ten-Year Plan for the Development of the National Economy (ibid.: 119–23). The plan is outlined in Hua Guofeng's report.

IX.   Joint editorial by *Hongqi*, *Renmin ribao*, and *Jiefangjun bao* is available in [176]: March 5, 1978, in [82]: March 6, 1978: D17–21.

412

I.   *March 18–31, 1978*
II.   **NATIONAL SCIENCE CONFERENCE**
III. Beijing
VI.   Deng Xiaoping: Speech, March 18, 1978 (text: [52]: 101–16; [176]: March 21, 1978, in [82]: March 21, 1978: E4–15; [182]: March 24, 1978: 9–18): science is part of the productive forces; theoretical research must be allowed even though no practical applications are in sight at present; China must learn from the strong points of other countries; scientists should be excused from political work to concentrate on research; party committees must not interfere with scientific work.

   Fang Yi: Speech, March 18, 1978 (text: [176]: March 28, 1978, in [82]: March 29, 1978: E1–22; [182]: April 7, 1978: 6–14, 17): reviews development of science and technology since 1949 under Mao Zedong's guidance; discusses outline plan for the development of science and technology, including relevant policies and measures.

   Hua Guofeng: Speech, March 24, 1978 (text: [176]: March 25, 1978, in [82]: March 27, 1978: E1–8; [182]: March 31, 1978: 6–14): the four modernizations can only be achieved by relying on Mao Zedong Thought; must "raise the scientific and cultural level of the entire nation" (repeated nineteen times during speech); modernization of science and technology cannot be left to specialists; political and ideological work should be strengthened; China must continue to develop independently.

   Li Chang: Speech, March 30, 1978 (excerpts: [91]: April 2, 1978, tr. in [82]: April 13, 1978: E2–4): describes steps taken to reorganize and upgrade quality of research at the Chinese Academy of Science.

   Guo Moruo: Speech, March 31, 1978 (excerpts: [182]: April 7, 1978: 15–17; [176]: March 31, 1978, in ibid.: E1–2): on the importance to socialist development of scientific work.

IX.   Three days before this conference, China held a successful nuclear test ([182]: March 24, 1978: 3).

   A joint editorial of *Hongqi, Renmin ribao,* and *Jiefangjun bao* on this conference is available in [9]: March 17, 1978, tr. in [82]: March 20, 1978: E14–17.

   An article in *Hongqi* shortly after the conference was much closer to Hua Guofeng's position than Deng Xiaoping's. It advocated continued class struggle, and although it adopted Deng's suggestion of allowing scientists to devote five-sixths of their time to research, it used this to support strengthening political work, achieving better results in less time.

Although the article accepted Deng's definition of "redness" as being devoted to modernization, it also said that class background must be taken into account ([97]: April 1978, tr. in [82]: April 13, 1978: E5–11).

413

I.   *April 22–May 16, 1978*
II.   **NATIONAL EDUCATION WORK CONFERENCE**
III.   Beijing
V.   Countrywide development of education; rules and regulations for colleges, middle schools, and primary schools; clarify ideology, line, principles, and policies in education
VI.   Deng Xiaoping: Speech, April 22, 1978 (text: [52]: 119–26; [182]: May 5, 1978: 6–12): schools need not devote many hours to political and ideological education; primary and secondary schools must offer advanced science classes; importance of examinations; reward talent; education must keep pace with needs of the economy; raise political and social status of teachers.

   Liu Xiyao: Report, April 22, 1978 (mention: [176]: May 16, 1978, tr. in [82]: May 18, 1978: E1).

   Fang Yi: speeches at several group meetings (mention: ibid.: E3).

   Liu Xiyao: Closing speech, May 16, 1978 (mention: ibid.: E1).
VIII.   Several documents were discussed at this conference, but there is no indication whether further action was taken (ibid.: E3).
IX.   The *Renmin ribao* editorial on this conference is in [176]: May 16, 1978, tr. in [82]: May 18, 1978: E4–8.

   The conference emphasized professional standards in schools. For instance, all schools, even those that were not keypoint schools, were encouraged to establish separate tracks to train talented students ([176]: May 16, 1978, tr. in [82]: May 18, 1978: E1).

414

I.   *April 27–June 6, 1978*
II.   **ALL-ARMY POLITICAL WORK CONFERENCE**
III.   Beijing
IV.   Leading cadres in charge of political work at and above the army level and leading members of departments under the General Political Department.
VI.   Wei Guoqing: Report, May 2, 1978 (excerpts: [176]: June 7, 1978, tr. in [82]: June 9, 1978: E7–23): the need to train successors; must link criticism of Gang of Four with criticism of Lin Biao; review of damage done to army by Lin and Gang; company cadres must know families, class

origin, history, and ideology of everyone in company; improve militia work; strictly enforce discipline; establish a cadre evaluation system with promotions and demotions.

Hua Guofeng: Speech, May 29, 1978 (text: [176]: June 3, 1978, in [82]: June 5, 1978: E5–12; [182]: June 16, 1978: 6–12): contradiction between proletariat and bourgeoisie, between socialism and capitalism is still primary; political work is the lifeblood of our army; correct political line is more important than technical modernization in preparing for war with the Soviets; restore and carry forward tradition of political work.

Ye Jianying: Speech, May 29, 1978 (text: [182]: June 23, 1978: 6–13; [176]: June 4, 1978, in [82]: June 4, 1978: E12–21): political work is the lifeblood of our army in the present as it was in the past; strong defense of putting politics in command.

Deng Xiaoping: Speech, June 2, 1978 (text: [182]: June 23, 1978: 14–21, 29; [176]: June 5, 1978, in [82]: June 6, 1978: E1–10; [52]: 127–40): seeking truth from facts is essence of Mao Zedong Thought; must integrate basic principles of Marxism-Leninism-Mao Zedong Thought with reality to solve problems; restore and carry forward traditions of political work; army's role under current conditions; must combine criticism of Gang of Four with criticism of Lin Biao.

Geng Biao: Speech (mention: [176]: June 9, 1978, in [82]: June 9, 1978: E5): current international situation.

Wei Guoqing: Closing speech, June 6, 1978 (mention: ibid.: E6).

VIII.   Discussed and revised "Resolution on Strengthening Political Work," "Regulations for Political Work," and "Regulations for Cadres in Service" (ibid.).

IX.   During this conference, it was reported that the Military Affairs Commission had issued a decision on strengthening education and training in the army with an emphasis on actual combat ([9]: May 12, 1978, tr. in [82]: May 15, 1978: E9–10; [194]: May 14, 1978, in [82]: May 15, 1978: E10–13; [176]: May 14, 1978, in [82]: May 15, 1978: E13).

An article on "Lin Biao and the Gang of Four" appeared during this conference in *Renmin ribao* ([176]: May 18, 1978, in [82]: May 24, 1978: E2–11).

415

I.   *September or October 1978*
II.   **MEETING OF THE POLITBURO OF THE CC CCP**
VI.   Hua Guofeng (mention: [31]: November 23, 1978, in [82]: November 27, 1978: E11–12): Wu De is a good man who has made mistakes; he needs more help and less criticism.

Wang Dongxing (ibid.: E12): Wu De's action during the Tiananmen Incident is understandable because none dared openly to oppose Jiang Qing before her arrest.

Ye Jianying (ibid.): cannot blame Wu De alone for the suppression of Tiananmen demonstrations.

Deng Xiaoping (ibid.): does not hold personal grudge against Wu De, but public opinion demands his ouster.

Tan Zhenlin (ibid.): Wu De is a criminal.

IX. The source for this meeting is reportedly the minutes of a Politburo meeting contained in a report that circulated at Sichuan University.

Wu De was subsequently removed as first secretary and mayor of Beijing, but he remained on the Politburo. The decision to remove Wu was probably made at a Politburo meeting in early October, at which Zeng Shaoshan (head of Liaoning), Chen Xilian (commander of Beijing Military Region), and You Taizhong (commander of Chengdu Military Region) were also removed from their posts ([1]: October 14, 1978, in [82]: October 16, 1978: E1; [219]: October 12, 1978, tr. in [82]: October 12, 1978: E12).

A Politburo meeting around this time reportedly removed the labels of "renegade, hidden traitor, and scab" from Liu Shaoqi but still maintained that he mistakenly pursued a revisionist line ([268]: September 1, 1979, tr. in [82]: September 28, 1979: U2).

416

I. *October 1978*
II. **MEETING OF THE POLITBURO OF THE CC CCP**
IX. This meeting occurred prior to a national conference on resettling educated youth in the countryside. A briefing was given by the State Council's leading group on educated youth regarding helping youth settle in the countryside. The State Council held a similar, but separate, meeting around this time ([176]: December 14, 1978, tr. in [82]: December 15, 1978: E1).

417

I. *November 1978*
II. **MEETING OF THE STANDING COMMITTEE OF THE POLITBURO OF THE CC CCP**
VI. Deng Xiaoping (mention: [89]: 460): if every word of Mao Zedong Thought is correct, then Lin Biao's "theory of genius" was true.

IX.   This meeting occurred during the November 11–December 15, 1978, Central Work Conference (meeting 418).

418

I.   *November 11–December 15, 1978*
II.   **CENTRAL WORK CONFERENCE**
III.   Beijing
IV.   210 people from organs of the Central Committee, government, army, provinces, municipalities, autonomous regions, and mass organs; Deng Xiaoping was abroad for the early part of conference.
V.   Agricultural policy; economic plans for 1979 and 1980; Li Xiannian's speech at a State Council meeting on ideological guidelines.
VI.   Chen Yun: Speech, November 12, 1978 (text: [200]: 16–18): shifting the party's work to socialist modernization requires solving problems left over from history; must reverse the verdicts against Bo Yibo, Tao Zhu, Wang Heshou, Peng Dehuai, and others; must declare the Tiananmen Incident revolutionary; must expose Kang Sheng.

   Chen Yun (mention: [89]: 454; [64]: January 16, 1979, tr. in [82]: January 23, 1979: N2): gives his views on the "criterion of truth" debate, the "two whatevers," leaders' mistakes over last two years, restoration of party traditions, and agricultural policy.

   Tan Zhenlin and others ([273]: 687): proposes overturning Cultural Revolution verdicts on "February Adverse Current" and "Right Opportunist Wind to Reverse Correct Verdicts."

   Ye Jianying ([64]: January 16, 1979, tr. in [82]: January 23, 1979: N4): importance of fostering democracy and strengthening legal system.

   Hua Guofeng (ibid: N4; [176]: February 1, 1979, tr. in [82]: February 2, 1979: E17): the title "wise leader" should no longer be used; reviews work during past two years, questions leftover from history, "two whatevers," and criterion of truth.

   Deng Xiaoping: Speech, December 13, 1978 (text: [194]: July 1, 1983, tr. in [82]: July 5, 1983: K10–19; [200]: 19–33; [52]: 151–65): Lin Biao and the Gang of Four ruined party work style; wrong opinions and practices persist; a proper work style is marked by democratic centralism and adherence to rules of discipline; laws are needed for social and economic matters; mistakes of the past should be recognized, admitted, and redressed; decentralized management and responsibility systems are needed for the four modernizations.
VII.   Endorsed the proposal of the Politburo to shift the emphasis of the party's work from class struggle to socialist modernization ([273]: 687; [89]: 454).

Rejected "Resolution on Speeding Up the Pace of Agricultural Development (Draft for Discussion)," drafted by Ji Dengkui, because it poorly summed up past experience, did not correct the leftist methods of the past, and continued to uphold the "Learn from Dazhai" movement. However, a revised version was approved along with arrangements for the 1979 and 1980 economic plans ([273]: 688; [64]: January 16, 1979, tr. in [82]: January 23, 1979: N1).

Discussed whether or not the system of combining government affairs with commune management should be changed ([273]: 688).

IX.   Deng Xiaoping's speech served as the keynote speech to the following Third Plenum (meeting 422) ([200]: 19; [52]: 151).

Several sources give detailed, but unconfirmed, reports of the sharp debate at this work conference: [172]: December 22, 1978, tr. in [82]: December 22, 1978: E14–15; [64]: December 1978, tr. in [82]: December 29, 1978: N1–5; [117]: January 10, 1979, tr. in [82]: January 16, 1979: N1–5; [172]: January 15, 1979, tr. in [82]: January 18, 1979: E1–3; [64]: January 16, 1979, tr. in [82]: January 23, 1979: N1–6; [268]: January 16, 1979, tr. in [82]: January 30, 1979: N5–7).

A Central Committee document was reportedly issued during the work conference to limit the extent of demonstrations and criticism contained in wall posters, including the provision that Mao Zedong not be criticized by name ([1]: December 1, 1978, in [82]: December 1, 1978: E1).

Other prominent issues at the time of this work conference were the "Democracy Wall" demonstrations, normalization of diplomatic relations with the United States, and increasing tension with Vietnam.

419

I.   *December 12, 1978*
II.   **MEETING OF THE POLITBURO OF THE CC CCP**
VIII. Discussed and approved the documents resulting from a national conference on the resettling of educated youth in the countryside.

420

I.   *December 18–22, 1978*
II.   **THIRD PLENUM OF THE ELEVENTH CC CCP**
III.   Beijing
IV.   169 members and 112 alternate members of the Central Committee.
VI.   Hua Guofeng: Speeches (mentioned in communique, but no text or details are available).

Huang Huoqing: Speech (excerpts: [172]: July 12, 1979, tr. in [82]: July 27, 1979): shortcomings in the work of the procuratorate.

Ye Jianying: Speech (excerpt: [110]: May 1980: 75–78): China should take advantage of the current international and domestic stability to accomplish the four modernizations as soon as possible; Mao made many mistakes, but we cannot negate entirely Mao Zedong Thought; hopes this plenum does not turn into a retaliatory meeting, as did the Lushan Plenum.

Xu Shiyou: Speech (excerpt: ibid.: 78–80): recounts his warnings to Mao regarding Lin Biao's unreliability; Mao should be neither deified nor downgraded.

Tan Zhenlin: talk to a discussion group (excerpt: ibid.: 80–82): criticizes Wang Dongxing for trying to stifle debate on Mao.

Chen Yonggui: talk to a discussion group (excerpt: ibid.: 82–84): admits ignorance of Marxism and lack of competence for central positions; pledges continued allegiance to Mao and policies and verdicts of Cultural Revolution; is willing to be demoted by CC CCP.

VII. Communique, December 22, 1978 (text: [200]: 1–15; [176]: December 23, 1978, in [82]: December 26, 1978: E14–13; [182]: December 29, 1978: pp. 6–16): mentions the following actions taken:

—End of campaigns to criticize Lin Biao and Gang of Four;

—Shift of the party's work to socialist modernization;

—Numerous leadership changes;

—End of mass campaigns for class struggle or economic development;

—Discussed and approved arrangements for the 1979 and 1980 economic plans;

—Agreed to distribute nationally ''Decisions of the CC CCP on Some Questions Concerning the Acceleration of Agricultural Development (Draft)'' and ''Regulations on the Work in Rural People's Communes (Draft for Trial Use)'';

—Agreed to numerous policies aimed at reforming the existing agricultural system and increasing production;

—Reversed verdicts on the Tiananmen Incident and numerous veteran leaders;

—Postponed an evaluation of Mao Zedong and the Cultural Revolution, but made preliminary assessments;

—Established the Central Discipline Inspection Commission (CDIC).

IX. The documents on agricultural development and communes were not released, but their contents appear to be summarized in a *Renmin ribao* editorial ([194]: February 6, 1979, tr. in [82]: February 9, 1979: E17–19).

The plenum instructed the newly created CDIC to form a leading group to handle the cases of Lin Biao and the Gang of Four ([9]: September 27, 1981, tr. in [82]: September 29, 1980: L1).

421

I. *December 25, 1978*
II. **MEETING OF THE POLITBURO OF THE CC CCP**
VIII. Established posts of secretary-general and deputy secretary-general to be responsible for the daily work of the Central Committee. Hu Yaobang was named secretary-general and Hu Qiaomu and Yao Yilin deputy secretary-general. Wang Dongxing was dismissed from his post as head of the General Office. Decided to conduct an investigation of Kang Sheng and Xie Fuzhi (mention: [273]: 692).

1979

422

I. *1979*
II. **ENLARGED MEETING OF THE MILITARY AFFAIRS COMMISSION**
VI. Deng Xiaoping (mention: [269]: July 16, 1981, tr. in [82]: July 22, 1981: W1): proposes a plan of changing the organizational structure of the army.

Yang Dezhi (mention: ibid.): supports Deng Xiaoping's proposal.
IX. Although it is not clear what Deng Xiaoping's proposal contained, it reportedly met with great resistance from those who still believed in "the mountain-stronghold mentality." Yang Dezhi shortly afterward became chief of the General Staff as his reward for supporting Deng.

423

I. *January 18–April 3, 1979*
II. **PARTY CONFERENCE ON IDEOLOGICAL GUIDELINES FOR THEORETICAL WORK**
III. Beijing
IV. More than one hundred people from theoretical and propaganda units at

the center and in the Beijing region and liaison representatives from some provinces and municipalities (during the first stage of the conference), more from all provinces and municipalities in second stage.

V.   Guidelines for theoretical work in light of the changed emphasis in the party's work after the Third Plenum

VI.   Hu Yaobang: Speech, January 18, 1979 (text: [200]: 48–63): basic tasks of theoretical and propaganda work following the change in the party's work are to link theory with practice, research and solve new problems that will continually arise, and enrich and develop Marxism-Leninism-Mao Zedong Thought in practice.

Deng Xiaoping: Speech, "Uphold the Four Basic Principles," March 30, 1979 (text: [52]: 166–91; [200]: 80–108): China must adhere to the socialist road, the people's democratic dictatorship, the leadership of the party, and Marxism-Leninism-Mao Zedong Thought; bourgeoisie does not exist in the party and exploiting classes cannot emerge in a socialist society; theoretical work cannot be divorced from reality; society's shortcomings and mistakes are the fault of the party.

IX.   The first stage of this conference was convened by the Propaganda Department and the Chinese Academy of Social Sciences, the second stage was convened in the name of the Central Committee ([273]: 693).

Hu Sheng and Wu Lengxi reportedly made self-criticisms at this conference ([268]: June 1, 1979, tr. in [82]: June 12, 1979: U1).

424

I.   *February 16, 1979*
II.   **ENLARGED MEETING OF THE POLITBURO OF THE CC CCP**
III.   Beijing
IV.   High-level party, government, and army cadres
VI.   Deng Xiaoping: Speech (summary: [172]: March 3, 1979): discusses the conflict with Vietnam, its impact on the four modernizations, and China's military capability vis-à-vis the Soviet Union.
VIII. Decided to retaliate against Vietnam for repeated aggression along China's southern border.
IX.   Although the source for Deng Xiaoping's speech describes the meeting merely as a "central meeting" (*zhongyang huiyi*), Li Xiannian's speech to the April Central Work Conference (meeting 427) identifies it as an enlarged Politburo meeting ([200]: 111).

425

I.   *March 21, 1979*
II.   **MEETING OF THE POLITBURO OF THE CC CCP**
V.   1979 plan and economic readjustment

VI.   Chen Yun: Speech, "Readjust the National Economy, Insist upon Proportionate Development" (text: [200]: 74–79): the problems and social costs of attempting modernization under backward conditions; proportionate development is the fastest; the viability of foreign borrowing; two or three years of economic readjustment are necessary to overcome severe imbalances.

Deng Xiaoping (mention: [283]: 622): discusses economic readjustment, steel and grain production.

VIII.   Revised the 1979 plan and decided on a three-year period of economic readjustment ([283]: 624).

426

I.   *April 1979*

II.   **CCP SECRETARIAT WORK CONFERENCE**

VI.   Chen Yun: Speech (Summary: [109]: September 1979: 3–4): gives a generally downbeat military and economic assessment of the conflict with Vietnam; reveals that Deng Xiaoping called for the immediate withdrawal of troops in March 1979.

Chen Yun: Speech (summary: ibid.: 10–11; text: [110]: April 1980: 80–97): the masses are impatient for a better life; compares radical reform, moderate readjustment, and the status quo; if Lin Biao and the Gang of Four had solved the food and clothing problem in China, it would not have been so easy to defeat them; little progress has been made toward the four modernizations.

IX.   Chen Yun's speech on the economy formed the basis of Li Xiannian's speech to the April 5–28, 1979, Central Work Conference (meeting 427).

Although this meeting is described as a work conference of the Secretariat, that body was not officially reconstituted until the February 23–29, 1980, Fifth Plenum of the Eleventh CC CCP (meeting 432).

427

I.   *April 5–28, 1979*

II.   **CENTRAL WORK CONFERENCE**

III.   Beijing

IV.   Leaders of party, government, and army organs at central, provincial, municipal, and autonomous region levels.

V.   Economic readjustment

VI.   Li Xiannian: Speech (text: [200]: 109–47): gives overall assessment of economic accomplishments and mistakes since the arrest of the Gang of

Four; problems include imbalance, excessive capital construction, and use of foreign capital; proposes a three-year period of economic readjustment.

Deng Xiaoping ([82]: June 18, 1984, 1984: K2–3, tr. of *Nanfang ribao*, June 11, 1984): proposes the establishment of special economic zones in Guangdong.

VIII. Adopted the "eight-character" policy of readjustment, reform, consolidation, and improvement ([108]: 382–83; [283]: 624; [89]: 463).

Revised 1979 plan in light of new adjustment policy ([283]: 624).

Approved in principle five documents:

—Some Regulations to Expand the Administrative Authority of State-Run Industrial Enterprises;

—Regulations on the Percentage of Profits Allowed to Be Retained by State-Run Enterprises;

—Tentative Regulations on Raising the Depreciation Rate of the State-Run Industrial Enterprises' Fixed Assets and Improving the Methods of Spending the Depreciation Charge;

—Tentative Regulations on Levying Taxes on Fixed Assets of State-Run Industrial Enterprises;

—Tentative Regulations on Extending Full Credit to the Circulating Fund of the State-Run Industrial Enterprises ([176]: July 28, 1979; tr. in [82]: July 30, 1979: L5).

IX. Li Xiannian's talk was given on behalf of the party and State Council.

A joint *Renmin ribao*, *Hongqi*, and *Jiefangjun ribao* editorial on May 11, 1979, describes the two ideological lines that clashed at this Central Work Conference ([176]: May 11, 1979, in [82]: May 14, 1979: L3–14).

428

I. *June 18–July 1, 1979*

II. **SECOND SESSION OF THE FIFTH NATIONAL PEOPLE'S CONGRESS**

III. Beijing

IV. 3,312 deputies

V. Reports on government, economic, and financial work; adoption of new laws; leadership changes

VI. Ye Jianying: Opening speech, July 18, 1979 (mention: [108]: 384).

Hua Guofeng: Government Work Report, June 18, 1979 (excerpt: [200]: 157–60; text: [182]: July 6, 1979, 5–31; [176]: June 25, 1979, in [82]: July 2, 1979: Supplement: 1–32).

Yu Qiuli: Report on the Draft 1979 National Economic Plan, June 21, 1979 (text: [176]: June 28, 1979, in [82]: July 2, 1979: L13–28).

Zhang Jingfu: Report on the 1978 Final State Accounts and the 1979 Draft State Budget (text: [176]: June 29, 1979, in [82]: July 3, 1979: L6–19).

Peng Zhen: Explanation of Seven Draft Laws, June 26, 1979 (text: [176]: June 30, 1979, July 5, 1979: L9–19).

Jiang Hua: Written Report on the Work of the Supreme People's Court (summary: [182]: July 13, 1979: 35–36).

Huang Huoqing: Written Report on the Work of the Supreme People's Procuratorate (summary: ibid.).

Ye Jianying: Closing speech, July 1, 1979 (text: [176]: July 1, 1979, tr. in [82]: July 2, 1979: L3–7).

VII.   Communique of the State Statistical Bureau on the Fulfillment of China's 1978 National Economic Plan, June 27, 1979 ([182]: July 6, 1979: 37–41; [176]: June 27, 1979, in [82]: June 27, 1979: L11–19).

VIII. Numerous proclamations ([176]: July 1, 1979, tr. in July 2, 1979: L7–12).:

—Elected Peng Zhen, Xiao Jingguang, Zhu Yunshan, and Shi Liang vice-chairmen of the Standing Committee of the NPC;

—Endorsed Hua Guofeng's nomination of Chen Yun, Bo Yibo, and Yao Yilin as vice-premiers of the State Council (Chen Yun gave up his post of vice-chairman of the NPC Standing Committee), and Fang Yi as president of the Chinese Academy of Sciences.

—Approved all reports and approved the shift of the country's work to socialist construction and the "eight-character" policy of economic readjustment;

—Elected a Nationalities Committee with eighty-one members;

—Amended the constitution.

Approved seven draft laws:

—Organic Law of the Local People's Congresses and Local People's Governments of the PRC (text: [176]: July 11, 1979, tr. in [82]: July 27, 1979: Supplement: 1–12);

—Electoral Law of the PRC for the National People's Congress and Local Peoples' Congresses at All Levels (text: ibid.: 12–19);

—Organic Law of the People's Courts of the PRC (text: [176]: July 5, 1979, tr. in ibid.: 20–27);

—Organic Law of the People's Procuratorates of the PRC (text: ibid.: 27–33);

—Criminal Law of the PRC (text: [194]: July 7, 1979, tr. in ibid.: 33–62);

—Law on Criminal Procedure of the PRC (text: [176]: July 7, 1979, tr. in [82]: July 30, 1979: Supplement: 1–31);

—Law on Joint Ventures ([182]: July 8, 1979: 24–27; [176]: July 8, 1979, in, [82]: July 30, 1979: Supplement: 31–35).

IX.   The Organic Law for Local People's Congresses and Governments and the Electoral Law were revised by the November 26–December 10, 1982, Fifth Session of the NPC (meeting 473).

429

I.   *September 19, 1979*

II.   **MEETING OF THE POLITBURO OF THE CC CCP**

VI.   Wang Dongxing (mention: [129]: February 5, 1980: 11–13): self-criticism.

IX.   This report is translated from the Hong Kong journal *Chanwang*, January 16, 1980, which is the sole source of this information.

430

I.   *September 25–28, 1979*

II.   **FOURTH PLENUM OF THE ELEVENTH CC CCP**

III.   Beijing

IV.   189 members and 118 alternate members of the Central Committee, 16 observers from central organs and local party committees.

V.   Plans for the thirtieth anniversary of the founding of the PRC, especially Ye Jianying's speech for that occasion; agricultural reform

VI.   Hua Guofeng: Speech (mentioned in communique, but no details given).

VII.   Communique, September 28, 1979 (text: [182]: October 5, 1979: 32; [176]: September 28, 1979, in [82]: October 1, 1979: L1–2; [200]: 204–206): reveals the following actions:

    —Revised and approved "Decisions of the CC CCP on Some Questions in the Acceleration of Agricultural Development" ([200]: 177–203);

    —Approved Ye Jianying's speech on the thirtieth anniversary of the PRC, given September 29, 1979 (text: [200]: 207–48; [176]: September 29, 1979, in [82]: October 1, 1979: L8–34);

    —Added Wang Heshou, Liu Lanbo, Liu Lantao, An Ziwen, Li Chang, Yang Shangkun, Zhou Yang, Lu Dingyi, Hong Xuezhi, Peng Zhen, Jiang Nanxiang, and Bo Yibo to the Central Committee;

    —Added Zhao Ziyang and Peng Zhen to the Politburo.

IX.   The decisions on agricultural development were a revision of the draft disseminated by the Third Plenum.

1980

431

I.   *January ?–16–?, 1980*
II.   **10,000 CADRES CONFERENCE**
III.   Beijing
VI.   Deng Xiaoping: Speech, "The Present Situation and the Tasks Before Us" (text: [52]: 224–59; [200]: 306–43; [268]: March 1, 1980, tr. in [82]: March 11, 1980: Supplement: 1–27): outlines goals for the 1980s, international situation, and prerequisites for the four modernizations; strengthen party leadership and discipline; abolish the "four bigs."

432

I.   *February 23–29, 1980*
II.   **FIFTH PLENUM OF THE ELEVENTH CC CCP**
III.   Beijing
IV.   201 full and 118 alternate members of the CC CCP, 37 observers from various localities and departments.
V.   Resolution on holding the Twelfth Party Congress ahead of schedule; elect additional members to the Standing Committee of the Politburo; establish Secretariat; Guiding Principles for Inner-Party Political Life; revise draft constitution.
VI.   Ye Jianying: Speech, February 24, 1980 (text: [200]: 388–92): on the reestablishment of the Secretariat.

Chen Yun: Speech, February 24, 1980 (text: [28]: 241–44): discusses the reestablishment of the Secretariat and the resignations of Wang Dongxing, Ji Dengkui, Wu De, and Chen Xilian.

Deng Xiaoping: Speech, "Adhere to the Party Line and Improve Methods of Work," February 29, 1980 (text: [52]: 259–68): the Fifth Plenum has been devoted to establishing the organization line; three problem areas—plan succession, consolidate organs by weeding out unqualified party members, and overcome bureaucracy; need collective leadership and responsibility system at all levels; party committees should only be in charge of political matters; factory managers should be in charge of production.

Hua Guofeng, Li Xiannian, and Chen Yun: Speeches (mentioned in communique).

VII.   Communique, February 29, 1980 (text: [176]: February 29, 1980, tr. in
        [82]: February 29, 1980: L1–5; [182]: March 10, 1980: 7–10; [200]:
        436–43): reveals following actions:
            —Decided to hold the Twelfth Party Congress ahead of schedule;
            —Added Hu Yaobang and Zhao Ziyang to the Standing Committee of
        the Politburo;
            —Reestablished Secretariat with eleven secretaries;
            —Discussed revised draft of party constitution;
            —Adopted "Guiding Principles for Inner-Party Political Life" (text:
        [182]: April 7, 1980: 11–20; [176]: March 14, 1980, tr. in [82]: March
        17, 1980: L1–13; [200]: 414–35);
            —Rehabilitated Liu Shaoqi;
            —Removed Wang Dongxing, Ji Dengkui, Wu De, and Chen Xilian
        from party and state posts;
            —Proposed the deletion of the rights to "speak out freely, air views
        fully, hold great debates, and write big-character posters," as then stipu-
        lated in the constitution.
            Resolution on the Twelfth Party Congress, February 29, 1980 (text:
        [176]: March 1, 1980, tr. in [82]: March 3, 1980: L2–3).
            Resolution on the Establishment of the Secretariat, February 28, 1980
        (text: ibid.: L3).

IX.   The question of doing away with the life-long tenure system for cadres
        was raised at this plenum in connection with the revision of the party
        constitution.
            The party held a discussion meeting with around one hundred demo-
        cratic party and nonparty leaders on February 24–27 in connection with
        this plenum (mention: [176]: February 29, 1980, tr. in [82]: March 3,
        1980: L1–2).
            During this plenum, it was confirmed that Yang Dezhi had replaced
        Deng Xiaoping as chief of the General Staff, although it was not revealed
        when the change took place ([1]: February 25, 1980, in [82]: February 25,
        1980: L1).

433

I.   *?–March 12–?, 1980*
II.   **ENLARGED MEETING OF THE STANDING COMMITTEE OF
        THE MILITARY AFFAIRS COMMISSION OF THE CC CCP**
VI.   Deng Xiaoping: Speech, "Streamline the Army and Raise Its Combat
        Effectiveness," March 12, 1980 (text: [52]: 269–75): discusses reducing
        the "bloatedness in the army, reforming its organizational structure,
        improving training, and strengthening political and ideological work."

434

I.   *March 17, 1980*
II.   **MEETING OF THE STANDING COMMITTEE OF THE POLITBURO OF THE CC CCP**
VIII. Established finance and economic small group under Zhao Ziyang to replace the State Finance and Economic Commission. Other members include Yu Qiuli, Fang Yi, Wan Li, Yao Yilin, and Gu Mu (mention: [283]: 650).
      Established State Energy Commission, chaired by Yu Qiuli (ibid.).

435

I.   *Late March 1980*
II.   **STANDING COMMITTEE OF THE CC CCP**
VIII. Discussed the problem of promoting qualified cadres to proper posts (mention: [176]: March 24, 1980, tr. in [82]: March 27, 1980: L21).

436

I.   *April 1980*
II.   **MEETINGS OF THE SECRETARIAT OF THE CC CCP**
III. Tibet
VIII. With the approval of the CC CCP, issued a circular on ''summary of panel discussions on work in Xizang [Tibet]'' (mention: [176]: May 30, 1980, tr. in [82]: June 3, 1980: Q3).
IX.   Following these meetings, Hu Yaobang, Wan Li, and others went on an inspection tour of Tibet (mention: ibid.).

437

I.   *April 21, 1980*
II.   **MEETING OF THE SECRETARIAT OF THE CC CCP**
V.   Conditions in Beijing
VIII. Made four proposals (mention: [283]: 653–54):
      —Beijing should become a model for the whole country regarding public order and morality;
      —Improve Beijing's environment;

—Make Beijing the city with the most advanced science and technology and the highest level of education;

—The economy must continuously flourish and the people's lives must be stable and full of ease.

438

I.   *April 8–30, 1980*
II.   **ALL-ARMY POLITICAL WORK CONFERENCE**
III. Beijing
VI.   Hua Guofeng: Speech (summary: [176]: May 7, 1980, tr. in [82]: May 8, 1980: L4–6): even under the four modernizations, political work is the lifeline of economic and army work; adhere to and carry forward the army's tradition of political work; material rewards should be combined with moral encouragement; don't overemphasize production and development—spiritual development is also needed; foster a proletarian ideology and eliminate bourgeois ideology and exploiting classes.

Ye Jianying: Written remarks(?) (summary: ibid.: L1–2): party organs must select talented cadres and adhere to party discipline.

Xu Xiangqian: Speech (summary: ibid.: L2): political consciousness is the decisive feature in war; foster proletarian ideology, eliminate bourgeois ideology.

Nie Rongzhen: Speech (summary: ibid.): success at party building and education of party members creates a good army.

Geng Biao: Speech (summary: ibid.): discussion of the situation at home and abroad.

Wei Guoqing: Speech (summary: ibid.: L2–3; [176]: May 8, 1980, tr. in [82]: May 9, 1980: L1–4): conduct ideological and political education; restore and carry forward party traditions; select and train successors and readjust staff; strengthen party leadership over ideological and political work, promote proletarian ideology, and eliminate bourgeois ideology; train better troops, improve efficiency and performance.

IX.   Deng Xiaoping did not attend this conference, but the report cited above says Wei Guoqing relayed his instructions. Ye Jianying apparently also did not attend but was said to have "paid great attention to the conference" (ibid.).

A high-level CC CCP meeting preceded this conference at which Deng Xiaoping reportedly spoke. Wei Guoqing presumably based his speech on this earlier talk (mention: [Wen wie po]: May 15, 1980, tr. in [82]: May 15, 1980: U1).

439

I.   *Late May 1980*
II.   **TWO MEETINGS OF THE SECRETARIAT OF THE CC CCP**
V.   Education
IX.   These meetings preceded a National Forum on May 30, 1980. Little information is available on the results of the Secretariat meetings, other than the setting of a broad goal of "great developments in the cause of education." The National Forum discussed specific measures to realize this goal (mention: [176]: June 6, 1980, tr. in [82]: June 9, 1980: L2–4).

440

I.   *August 2–7, 1980*
II.   **NATIONAL LABOR AND EMPLOYMENT CONFERENCE**
III.   Beijing
IV.   Three hundred people from county level and above.
VI.   Wan Li: Speech (mention: [176]: August 12, 1980, tr. in [82]: August 13, 1980: L7): implementation of CC CCP policies and solution of problems in labor and employment must be done in accordance with local situations, not rigid uniformity.
VIII.   Issued Central Document no. 64 (1980) regarding the policy of having employment offices, independently organized labor, and independent occupations coexist under the unified plan and guidance of the state (mention: [200]: 981).
IX.   This conference was convened by the CC CCP.

441

I.   *August 18–23, 1980*
II.   **ENLARGED MEETING OF THE POLITBURO OF THE CC CCP**
III.   Beijing
VI.   Deng Xiaoping: Speech, "On the Reform of the System of Party and State Leadership," August 18, 1980, and approved by the Politburo on August 31, 1980 (text: [52]: 302–25; [200]: 510–25; [194]: July 2, 1983, tr. in [82]: July 6, 1983: K1–16; [272]: 15: 7: July 15, 1981: 106–39): increase production unit autonomy and power of local governments and economic units; promote younger people to top posts; bureaucratic problems result

from trying to control everything without administrative regulations or responsibility systems; separate functional responsibilities of party and government; abolish life-long tenure for cadres; all are equal before and responsible to the law; cadres should be selected and supervised by the masses; material well-being for individuals must not come at the expense of the state or the collective; oppose bourgeois ideology and feudal influences.

VIII.   Made following proposals to NPC:

—Zhao Ziyang to replace Hua Guofeng as premier;

—Deng Xiaoping, Li Xiannian, Chen Yun, Xu Xiangqian, Wang Zhen, and Wang Renzhong would not hold concurrent post of vice-premier;

—Approve Chen Yonggui's resignation as vice-premier.

IX.   A two-part article by Feng Wenbin in *Renmin ribao* gave a more detailed view of separating party and state functions and decentralizing authority (November 24 and 25, 1980, tr. in [82]: November 26, 1980: L23–30, and December 2, 1980: L9–15, respectively).

A speech by Liao Gailong discusses plans for a bicameral NPC and tricameral CCP, complete with checks and balances. Liao's speech, supposedly based on the results of this Politburo meeting and Deng's talk, appears to give the most thorough review of the reforms under discussion at this time (text: [110]: October 1981: 68–71 and November 1981: 81–110; excerpt: [190]: March 1, 1981, tr. in [82]: March 16, 1981: U1–16).

Following this meeting, many of those who attended suggested to the central authorities that Hua Guofeng be removed as chairman of the CC CCP and its Military Affairs Commission ([200]: 596).

442

I.   *August 30–September 10, 1980*
II.   **THIRD SESSION OF THE FIFTH NATIONAL PEOPLE'S CONGRESS**
III.   Beijing
IV.   More than 3,200 deputies
V.   Numerous reports and speeches; leadership changes; constitutional revision; adoption of laws
VI.   Ye Jianying: Opening speech, August 30, 1980 (text: [176]: August 30, 1980, tr. in [82]: September 2, 1980: L5–6).

Yao Yilin: Report on Arrangements for 1980 and 1981 Economic Plans, August 30, 1980 (text: [176]: September 11, 1980, tr. in [82]: September 23, 1980: Supplement: 1–16).

Wang Bingqian: Report on the Draft State Budget for 1980 and State Financial Estimates for 1981, August 30, 1980 (text: [176]: September 12, 1980, tr. in [82]: September 23, 1980: Supplement: 16–29).

Tan Zhenlin: Report on 1980 and 1981 Budgets, September 1, 1980 (excerpts: [176]: September 1, 1980, tr. in [82]: September 2, 1980: L32–33).

Peng Zhen: Report on the Work of the Standing Committee of the NPC, September 2, 1980 (text: [176]: September 13, 1980, tr. in [82]: September 23, 1980: Supplement: 29–40).

Jiang Hua: Report on the Work of the Supreme Court, September 2, 1980 (text: [176]: September 16, 1980, tr. in [82]: September 23, 1980: Supplement: 41–44).

Huang Huoqing: Report on the Work of the Supreme People's Procuratorate, September 2, 1980 (text: ibid.: 44–48).

Wu Xinyu: Report on Draft Nationality Law, September 2, 1980 (summary: [176]: September 3, 1980, tr. in [82]: September 4, 1980: L13–14).

Gu Ming: Report on the Joint Venture Tax Law, September 2, 1980 (summary: ibid.: L14–16).

Hua Guofeng: Speech, September 7, 1980 (text: [176]: September 14, 1980, tr. in [82]: September 23, 1980: Supplement: 49–68).

VII.   Income Tax Law of the PRC Concerning Joint Ventures with Chinese and Foreign Investment, September 10, 1980 (text: [176]: September 16, 1980, in [82]: September 16, 1980: L16–19).

Individual Income Tax Law of the PRC, September 10, 1980 (text: ibid.: L19–22).

Nationality Law of the PRC, September 10, 1980 (text: [176]: September 13, 1980, tr. in [82]: September 15, 1980: L26–28).

Marriage Law of the PRC, September 10, 1980 (text: [176]: September 15, 1980, tr. in [82]: September 19, 1980: L22–25).

VIII.   Numerous leadership changes (mention: [176]: September 10, 1980, tr. in [82]: September 10, 1980: L1).

Established a Constitution Revision Committee (mention: [176]: September 10, 1980, tr. in [82]: September 11, 1980: L5).

Revised Article 45 of the PRC Constitution by deleting the "four bigs" (ibid.)

443

I.   *August 31, 1980*
III.   **MEETING OF THE POLITBURO OF THE CC CCP**
VIII.   Endorsed Deng Xiaoping's speech to the enlarged Politburo meeting on

August 18, 1980 (meeting 441) (mention: [52]: 302; [200]: 510).

444

I.   *Mid-September 1980*
II.   **CONFERENCE CONVENED BY THE SECRETARIAT OF THE CC CCP**
III.   Beijing
IV.   First secretaries of all provinces, municipalities, and autonomous regions.
V.   Responsibility system in agriculture.
VII.   "On Several Questions Concerning Strengthening and Perfecting the Production Responsibility System in Agriculture," issued as Central Document no. 75 on September 27, 1980 (text: [200]: 541–49).
IX.   The document cited above was the minutes of the meeting called by the Secretariat at Zhongnanhai. It defined the fixing of agricultural output quotas for each household, pointing out that this "fixing under the leadership of the production team does not constitute a divorce from the socialist orbit."

     A report of this meeting is also in *Liaowang*, May 1981 (tr. in [82]: May 20, 1981: K10–11).

445

I.   *November 10–December 5, 1980*
II.   **SERIES OF ENLARGED MEETINGS OF THE POLITBURO OF THE CC CCP**
IV.   Liu Bocheng and Nie Rongzhen were too ill to attend; Chen Yonggui and Saifudin were not informed. In all, twenty-one members and one alternate member of the Politburo and seven members of the Secretariat attended.
V.   Hua Guofeng's fitness as party chairman.
VII.   "Communique of a Meeting of the Politburo of the CC CCP," December 5, 1980 (text: [200]: 596–600): reveals following actions:

     —Decided to propose to the upcoming Sixth Plenum that it approve Hua Guofeng's resignation as chairman of the CC CCP and its Military Affairs Commission, and the appointment of Hu Yaobang and Deng Xiaoping, respectively, to those posts; Hua will become vice-chairman and member of the Standing Committee of the Politburo;

     —Decided to circulate and solicit suggestion for the revision of the "Resolution on Some Questions in the History of Our Party Since the

Founding of the Country (Draft for Discussion)'';

—Prior to the Sixth Plenum, Hu Yaobang would unofficially take charge of the work of the Politburo and its Standing Committee and Deng Xiaoping the work of the Military Affairs Commission.

IX. The communique also reveals that Hua Guofeng twice offered to resign as chairman of the CC CCP and MAC (on November 10 and December 5) and that Deng Xiaoping turned down the nomination as party chairman but accepted the nomination as chairman of the Military Affairs Commission.

Hua was criticized for mistakes made in the four years since the arrest of the Gang of Four, especially the "two whatevers" policy and upholding Cultural Revolution slogans, although his mistakes were not described as an erroneous line. His contribution to the arrest of the Gang of Four was affirmed, but it was also concluded that he alone could not take sole responsibility for that event.

The Politburo was in session for nine days during this period: November 10, 11, 13, 14, 17, 18, 19, 29, and December 5, 1980.

446

I. *December 16–25, 1980*
II. **CENTRAL WORK CONFERENCE**
III. Beijing
V. Economic readjustment, political and ideological work, and socialist spiritual civilization
VI. Chen Yun: Speech, December 16, 1980 (text: [28]: 248–54; [200]: 601–607): decisions on foreign loans must consider China's ability to pay and the fact that capitalists are looking for profit; cannot stress economic laws alone, planned and proportionate methods are also needed; announces six-month price freeze; emphasize readjustment over reform; curtail development projects; centralize foreign economic relations and trade; emphasize agricultural over industrial crops; rely on personnel trained in 1950s and 1960s, not foreign experts or students sent abroad.

Zhao Ziyang: Speech, December 16, 1980 (text: [200]: 608–26): agricultural and industrial production are good, but deficits, excess currency, and inflation damage financial situation; announces $5 billion cut in administrative, capital construction, and military budgets, stronger central control over the economy, including price and foreign exchange controls, central approval for development projects, and the possible closing or merging of failing plants.

Deng Xiaoping: Speech, "Implement the Policy of Readjustment, Ensure Stability and Unity," December 25, 1980 (text: [52]: 335–55;

[200]: 627–48): this period of recentralization is an attempt to regain control over economic sabotage by leftist remnants and social disorders; reform must serve readjustment; fully outlines his program for socialist modernization, including the role of democratic centralism, the mass line, the need for successors and trained personnel, and the four basic principles.

Li Xiannian: Speech, December 25, 1980 (summary: [268]: February 1, 1980, tr. in [82]: February 2, 1980: U15; [283]: 676): accepts responsibility for economic errors since he was put in charge of the economic work for the State Council; need practical approach to planning and a balanced budget; consumption, not accumulation, should determine production; must guarantee a stable supply of grain but also develop various forms of management.

VIII. Decided to carry out further economic readjustment and create greater political stability ([273]: 713–15; [108]: 395; [283]: 674, 676–77; [137]: 101; [89]: 43).

Deng Xiaoping's speech was issued as a central document ([200]: 900).

The 1981 New Year's Day editorial in *Renmin ribao* summarized the conclusions of this Central Work Conference (tr. in [82]: January 2, 1981: L6–10), and its decisions are also reflected in [182]: March 23, 1981: 26–28.

A detailed, but unconfirmed, report of this work conference is in [64]: January 16, 1981 (tr. in [82]: January 22, 1981: U4–7).

1981

447

I.   *January 14–February 1, 1981*
II.   **ALL-ARMY POLITICAL WORK CONFERENCE**
III. Beijing
V.   Implementation of guidelines from December 16–25, 1980, Central Work Conference (meeting 446), strengthening political work, military modernization.
VI.   Wei Guoqing: Report (excerpts: [176]: February 3, 1981, tr. in [82]: February 4, 1981: L4–8): army must adhere to the four basic principles and study basic Marxist theories; readjustment of cadre ranks and leading bodies must emphasize political background; oppose bourgeois ideology; strengthen discipline and political work.

Hu Yaobang: Speech (summary: [176]: February 1, 1981, tr. in [82]: February 2, 1981: L3–4): reviews domestic situation and current policies; upholding party leadership is the key to the four basic principles; people's war is still China's best defense.

Geng Biao: Speech (mention: [176]: February 1, 1981, in [82]: February 3, 1981: L5).

Wei Guoqing: Summing-up speech (mention: ibid.: L6).

IX. Wei Guoqing's report conveyed Deng Xiaoping's instructions (mention: ibid.: L5).

448

I. *March 1981*
II. **MEETING OF THE POLITBURO OF THE CC CCP**
IX. Deng Xiaoping reportedly wanted Hua Guofeng to become party vice-chairman and member of the Standing Committee of the Politburo after resigning as chairman. Hua responded that he had the greatest role in overthrowing the Gang of Four and if he was not fit to be chairman, then he was also unfit for other leading posts (mention: [269]: July 6, 1981, tr. in [82]: July 9, 1981: W4).

449

I. *March 2, 1981*
II. **EIGHTY-EIGHTH MEETING OF THE SECRETARIAT OF THE CC CCP**
III. Beijing
V. Agricultural reform
VI. Zhao Ziyang: Speech (mention: *Liaowang*: May, 1981, tr. in [82]: May 20, 1981: K8): keep local conditions of soil, climate, and comparative advantage in mind when planning crop patterns; don't focus on grain production to the exclusion of all else.

Hu Yaobang (mention: ibid.): grain production must be grasped, not relaxed, but a diversified economy must also be developed.

Wan Li, Fang Yi, Song Renqiong, Yu Qiuli, and others (mention: ibid.: K9): on agricultural reform and a rural diversified economy.

IX. On March 30, 1981, the CC CCP and the State Council issued a three-thousand-character circular calling for the development of a diversified economy in rural areas (text: [200]: 740–58).

450

I.   *May or June 1981*
II.   **ENLARGED MEETING OF THE POLITBURO OF THE CC CCP**
IX.   This meeting read Chen Yun's May 8, 1981, report on promoting young and middle-aged cadres (text: [200]: 782–87). It likely convened around the time of the Sixth Plenum (meeting 452).

451

I.   *May 19, 1981*
II.   **ENLARGED MEETING OF THE POLITBURO OF THE CC CCP**
IV.   More than seventy people
VI.   Deng Xiaoping: Speech (text: [52]: 291–93; [200]: 459–61): discusses revision of the Resolution on Party History (passed at Sixth Plenum [meeting 452]), in particular the share of the blame to be given to Mao Zedong, the CC CCP, and individual leaders.

452

I.   *June 27–29, 1981*
II.   **SIXTH PLENUM OF THE ELEVENTH CC CCP**
III. Beijing
IV.   195 members and 114 alternate members of the CC CCP, 53 nonvoting participants
V.   Discussion and approval of the Historical Resolution, election and reelection of central party leadership
VI.   Li Xiannian: Speech (text: [110]: December 1981: 73): on the rationale of new party rankings.
      Hu Yaobang: Speech (text: ibid.: 74–77): most of the important contributions since the arrest of Gang of Four have been made by the veteran revolutionaries; the task of restoring order to the guiding ideology has been completed with the issuing of the Historical Resolution; leaders should devote themselves to the national economy.
      Chen Yun: Speech (text: ibid.: 78): gives his blessing to the actions of the plenum.
      Deng Xiaoping: Closing speech (text: ibid.: 78; [52]: 360): the Historical Resolution sets the parameters within which party members must confine themselves; all must obey this common organizational discipline even if they do not agree.

VII.   Communique, June 29, 1981 (text: [182]: July 6, 1981: 6–8; [176]: June 29, 1981, in [82]: June 29, 1981: K1–2; [200]: 847–49): reveals the following actions:

—Approval of "Resolution on Certain Questions in the History of Our Party Since the Founding of the PRC," June 27, 1981 (text: [182]: July 6, 1981: 10–39; [176]: June 30, 1981, in [82]: July 1, 1981: K1–38; [200]: 788–846);

—Numerous leadership changes, including Hua Guofeng's demotion to last of six party vice-chairmen and Hu Yaobang's promotion to party chairman.

IX.   This plenum had been postponed several times due to the ongoing debate over the fate of Hua Guofeng and revisions to the Historical Resolution.

The Historical Resolution was drafted by a small group headed by Hu Qiaomu under the supervision of Deng Xiaoping and Hu Yaobang. Deng's comments on various drafts are excerpted in ([52]: 276–96; [200]: 444–65).

A preparatory meeting was held June 15–25, 1981, during which Deng Xiaoping gave a speech (text: [52]: 293–96; [200]: 461–65); Hua Guofeng gave a self-criticism (mention: [Kyodo]: July 3, 1981, in [82]: July 6, 1981: K3); and a letter from Ye Jianying was read (text: [269]: July 31, 1981, tr. in [82]: August 3, 1981: W1). The dates for the meeting are given in ([108]: 400).

The CC CCP invited a number of nonparty leaders and industrialists to a June 22–25, 1981, discussion meeting to explain the Historical Resolution. Li Xiannian and Deng Liqun spoke, and Zhao Ziyang, Ulanhu, and Peng Chong also attended (mention: [176]: July 2, 1981, tr. in [82]: July 6, 1981: K1–3).

Chen Yun's May 8, 1981, article on promoting young and middle-aged cadres (text: [200]: 782–87) was read by those attending this plenum.

453

I.   *July 2, 1981*

II.   **DISCUSSION MEETING OF FIRST PARTY SECRETARIES OF PROVINCES, MUNICIPALITIES, AND AUTONOMOUS REGIONS**

VI.   Deng Xiaoping: Speech, "The Primary Task of Veteran Cadres Is to Select Young and Middle-aged Cadres for Promotion" ([52]: 361–66): the succession problem must be solved nationwide in three to five years.

Chen Yun: Speech (text: [28]: 267–73): discusses the need to promote young and middle-aged cadres and the organizational measures necessary to carry it out.

IX.   A letter from Nie Rongzhen to Deng Xiaoping, Hu Yaobang, and Chen Yun concerning the continued strength of factionalism (text: [200]: 850–52) was distributed at this conference.

454

I.   *July 17, 1981*
II.   **MEETING OF LEADERS OF CENTRAL PROPAGANDA DEPARTMENTS**
VI.   Deng Xiaoping: Speech, "Concerning Problems on the Ideological Front" (text: [52]: 367–78; [200]: 877–81): current problem is weak leadership and fear of criticizing wrong trends; antirightist movement of 1957 was necessary but its scope expanded too far; singles out the film script "Unrequited Love" and the newspapers *Jiefangjun bao* and *Wenyi bao* for criticism.
IX.   A national forum (meeting 455) was held soon afterward to discuss Deng's speech, which was also included in Central Document no. 30 (1981) (mention: [269]: October 1, 1981, tr. in [82]: October 28, 1981: W3).

455

I.   *August 3–8, 1981*
II.   **DISCUSSION MEETING ON PROBLEMS ON THE IDEOLOGICAL FRONT**
III. Beijing
IV.   More than three hundred people involved in propaganda, cultural, and education work at the provincial, municipal, and autonomous region level and in the military, from relevant CC CCP and State Council departments, and literary, art, theoretical, press, and publishing workers (mention: [176]: August 30, 1981, tr. in [82]: August 31, 1981: K3).
VI.   Xi Zhongxun: Speech (mention: ibid.: K2).
      Hu Yaobang: Speech, August 3, 1981 (text: [200]: 882–903; [110]: January 1984: 105–24): correcting mistakes in ideological work should not be directed against individuals or become an antirightist struggle; fear of criticizing erroneous ideas must be overcome; the party's policies toward intellectuals has not and will not change.
      Hu Qiaomu: Speech, "Some Problems on the Current Ideological Front," August 8, 1981 (text: [97]: December 1, 1981, tr. in [82]: December 15, 1981: K5–31; [200]: 904–51): weak leadership on the ideological front and the rise of bourgeois liberalism; Mao Zedong's opinion

on literature and art work; how literature and art should treat the Cultural Revolution and the seamy side of life.

IX.   Hu Yaobang's speech was issued with Deng Xiaoping's speech of July 17, 1981, as Central Document no. 30 (1981) (mention: [269]: October 1, 1981, tr. in [82]: October 28, 1981: W3).

456

I.   *November 1981*
II.   **ENLARGED MEETING OF THE POLITBURO OF THE CC CCP**
V.   The economy
IX.   The meeting discussed the current economic situation and guiding principles for future economic construction. The decisions reached at this meeting formed the basis for the policies approved by the November 30–December 13, 1981, Fourth Session of the Fifth NPC (meeting 457) (mention: [273]: 735–36), and presumably are reflected in Zhao Ziyang's report to that meeting.

457

I.   *November 30–December 13, 1981*
II.   **FOURTH SESSION OF THE FIFTH NATIONAL PEOPLE'S CONGRESS**
III.   Beijing
IV.   3,202 deputies
V.   Various reports and pending laws
VI.   Zhao Ziyang: Government Work Report, "The Present Economic Situation and the Principles for Future Economic Construction," November 30 and December 1, 1981 (text: [182]: December 21, 1981: 6–36; [176]: December 14, 1981, in [82]: December 16, 1981: K1–35; [200]: 994–1050).

Wang Bingqian: Report on the Final State Accounts for 1980 and the Implementation of the Financial Estimates for 1981, December 1, 1981 (text: [182]: January 11, 1982: 14–23; [176]: December 14, 1981, in [82]: December 18, 1981: K1–10).

Jiang Hua: Report on the Work of the Supreme People's Court, December 7, 1981 (text: [176]: December 15, 1981, in [82]: December 21, 1981: K1–5).

Huang Huoqing: Report on the Work of the Supreme People's Procuratorate, December 7, 1981 (text: [176]: December 14, 1981, in [82]: December 21, 1981: K5–9).

Yang Shangkun, Report on the Work of the Standing Committee of the NPC and explanation of three draft laws, December 7, 1981 (text: [176]: December 15, 1981, in [82]: December 18, 1981: K10–16).

Explanations of the three draft laws on foreign enterprise income tax, economic contracts, and civil procedure ([176]: December 8, 1981, tr. in [82]: December 9, 1981: K2–3, and December 10, 1981: K3).

VII.   Resolutions approving work reports, launching a nationwide tree planting campaign (texts: [176]: December 14 and 15, 1981, in [82]: December 17, 1981: K4–5), and postponing examination of revised draft of the state constitution (mention: [176]: December 13, 1981, in [82]: December 14, 1981: K1).

Foreign Enterprise Income Tax Law of the PRC, December 13, 1981 (text: [182]: December 28, 1981: 17–19; [176]: December 16, 1981, in [82]: December 17, 1981: K1–3).

VIII.   Adopted Foreign Enterprise Income Tax Law, law governing economic contracts, and approved in principle the draft civil procedure law (mention: [176]: December 13, 1981, in [82]: December 14, 1981: K1).

458

I.   *December ?–22–?,1981*
II.   **DISCUSSION MEETING CALLED BY CC CCP**
III.   Beijing
IV.   First party secretaries from all provinces, municipalities, and autonomous regions.
V.   Measures for economic development
VI.   Chen Yun: Speech, "Several Opinions on Economic Work," December 22, 1981 (text: [28]: 275–77; [200]: 1057–60): planned economy is primary, and market regulation secondary, for industry and agriculture; grain production must not be cut back for the sake of industrial or cash crops; China does not need more special economic zones, and the existing ones should sum up their experience; use of foreign exchange requires central approval.

459

I.   *December 15–26, 1981*
II.   **CENTRAL WORK CONFERENCE**
VI.   Hu Yaobang: Speech (mention: [172]: March 25, 1982, tr. in [82]: March 31, 1982: W4–5): on the likelihood of a comeback by the Gang of Four.
IX.   The only source for this meeting is the one cited above.

1982

460

I.   *January 5-12, 1982*
II.   **ALL-ARMY POLITICAL WORK CONFERENCE**
III. Beijing
IV.   Deputy directors of the General Political Department, leading cadres in charge of political work in large military units and corps-level units, and those attending a reading class for ranking cadres sponsored by the political academy (mention: [9]: January 12, 1982, tr. in [82]: January 13, 1982: K2).
VI.   Wei Guoqing: Speech, "The Basic Conditions of the Whole Army's Political Work in 1981 and the Main Tasks for 1982" (excerpts: [176]: January 13, 1982, tr. in [82]: January 15, 1982: K1–4): the need for political work will increase as the army becomes modernized and regularized.

    Geng Biao: Speech (mention: [176]: January 12, 1982, tr. in [82]: January 13, 1982: K1).

    Yang Shangkun: Speech (mention: ibid.).
IX.   Deng Xiaoping and Ye Jianying sent instructions to this conference. Those in attendance also read recent speeches by Hu Yaobang, Zhao Ziyang, and Chen Yun, and Chen's article "Tell the Truth; Do Not Save Face" (mention: ibid.).

461

I.   *January 11 and 13, 1982*
II.   **ENLARGED MEETING OF THE POLITBURO OF THE CC CCP**
V.   Deng Xiaoping, "Streamlining Organizations Constitutes a Revolution," January 13, 1982 (text: [52]: 374–79; [200]: 1105–10): announces the extent of staff reductions in CC CCP and State Council organs and says factionalism will inevitably occur during streamlining.
VII. "Urgent CC CCP Circular," January 11, 1982 [concerning cadre corruption] (text: [200]: 1092–93).

    "CC CCP Directive on Strengthening Political and Legal Work," January 13, 1982 (text: [200]: 1094–1104).
IX.   The two documents cited above are not identified as being passed by this Politburo meeting, but given the coincidence of their dates and the nature of their contents, it is quite likely that they were discussed and approved by the meeting.

462

I.   *January 14, 1982*
II.   **MEETING OF THE SECRETARIAT OF THE CC CCP**
VI.   Hu Yaobang, "On the Question of Foreign Economic Relations" (text: [200]: 1111–31): China must rely on its own strengths to modernize, but also utilize foreign investment, international markets, and foreign economic relations.

463

I.   *January 25, 1982*
II.   **AD HOC MEETING OF STATE PLANNING COMMISSION LEADERS**
IV.   Chen Yun, Yao Yilin, Song Ping, Chai Shufan, Li Renjun, Fang Weizhong, and Wang Yuqing.
VI.   Chen Yun: Speech, January 25, 1982 (text: [28]: 278–80; [200]: 1132–34): economic planning must remain prevalent in the countryside even after the institution of responsibility systems; living standards, especially food consumption, must be improved but not at the expense of accumulation needed for construction; projects must be approved and controlled by the center.

464

I.   *February 11–13, 1982*
II.   **DISCUSSION MEETING CALLED BY SECRETARIAT**
III.   Beijing
IV.   Sixty-eight people from the Secretariat, State Council, Military Affairs Commission, Central Discipline Inspection Commission (CDIC), relevant departments, Guangdong, and Fujian.
V.   Smuggling and speculation in Guangdong and Fujian
VI.   Hu Yaobang: Speech (mention: [273]: 726–27): current problems in the economic sphere (referring to corruption and other economic crimes) are much worse than during the "three-anti, five-anti" period.
        Zhao Ziyang, Hu Qiaomu, and others: Speeches (mention: [200]: 1171).
VII.   "Central Document Regarding the Minutes of a Discussion Meeting on Guangdong and Fujian," March 1, 1982 (text: [200]: 1169–83).

465

I.   *March (?) 1982*
II.   **MEETING OF THE STANDING COMMITTEE OF THE MILITARY AFFAIRS COMMISSION OF THE CC CCP**
VI.   Yang Shangkun: (mention: [172]: March 22, 1982, tr. in [82]: March 24, 1982: W4): it is necessary to streamline military organs, reduce the number of soldiers, and retire cadres.
IX.   All information on this meeting comes from the one source cited above.

466

I.   *April 3, 1982*
II.   **MEETING OF THE CC CCP**
VI.   Deng Xiaoping (mention: [273]: 729): organizational revolution, combating economic crime, building a spiritual civilization, and party consolidation are necessary for the four modernizations.

467

I.   *April 10, 1982*
II.   **MEETING OF THE POLITBURO OF THE CC CCP**
V.   Discuss "Decision of the CC CCP and State Council on Combating Economic Crime"
VI.   Deng Xiaoping: Speech, "Combat Economic Crime" (text: [52]: 380–82; [200]: 1256–80): current struggle against economic crimes is more serious than the "three-anti, five-anti" campaign because the magnitude of crimes is greater; CDIC has determined that smuggling of gold and silver out through Hong Kong is harming China's foreign exchange reserves; each province must harshly punish several cases.
VII.   "Resolution of the CC CCP and State Council Regarding Combating Serious Criminal Behavior in the Economic Sphere," April 13, 1982 (text: [200]: 1241–55).

468

I.   *?–July 4–?, 1982*
II.   **FORUM OF THE MILITARY AFFAIRS COMMISSION OF THE CC CCP**
IV.   More than sixty senior army, navy, and air force leaders.

VI.   Yang Shangkun: Speech (mention: [52]: 386; [200]: 1299): on structural
        reform in the military.
            Deng Xiaoping: Speech, July 14, 1982 (text: [52]: 386–90; [200]:
        1299–1303): the present structure, method of leadership, and organiza-
        tion are too complicated and must be streamlined; the problem of appoint-
        ing young and qualified cadres has not been solved.
VII.   ''Regulations Concerning the Military Service of Army Officers
        (Draft)'' (mention: [52]: 389; [200]: 1302).

469

I.   *July 30, 1982*
II.   **ENLARGED MEETING OF THE POLITBURO OF THE CC CCP**
VI.   Deng Xiaoping: Speech, ''Advisory Commissions Will Be a Transitional
        Measure for the Abolition of Life Tenure in Leading Posts'' (text: [52]:
        391–93): the Central Advisory Commission (CAC) is an interim measure
        until a more appropriate retirement system can be devised; the succession
        problem must be solved in the next ten to fifteen years and the CAC
        dissolved.

470

I.   *August 6, 1982*
II.   **SEVENTH PLENUM OF THE ELEVENTH CC CCP**
III.   Beijing
IV.   185 full and 112 alternate members of the CC CCP, and 21 observers.
VI.   Hu Yaobang: Closing speech (text: [200]: 1311–14): reviews accomplish-
        ments of past several years.
VII.   Communique, August 6, 1982 (text: ibid.: 1304–1305; [176]: August 6,
        1982, in [82]: August 6, 1982: K1): reveals the following actions:
            —Twelfth Party Congress will convene on September 1, 1982;
            —Approved work report and draft constitution to be presented to the
        congress;
            —Sent letters of congratulation to Liu Bocheng and Cai Chang upon
        their retirement (texts: [200]: 1306–10).
IX.   This plenum was preceded by a six-day preparatory meeting (mentioned
        in the communique), at which Hua Guofeng reportedly objected to the
        slogan ''practice is the sole criterion of truth,'' arguing that communism
        has not yet been realized or tested, yet it will inevitably triumph (mention:
        [268]: November 1, 1983, tr. in [82]: November 9, 1983: W2).

471

I.   *September 1–11, 1982*

II.   **TWELFTH NATIONAL CONGRESS OF THE CC CCP**

III.   Beijing

IV.   1,600 official delegates and 149 alternate delegates (representing over 39 million party members), and other non-CC CCP observers.

V.   Hu Yaobang's political work report; new constitution; new CC, CDIC, and CAC

VI.   Deng Xiaoping: Opening speech, September 1, 1982 (text: [52]: 297–99): this is the most important Party Congress since the Seventh in 1945; the line of the Eighth Party Congress was correct but the party was unprepared to carry it out; China should learn from other countries, but not copy from them; China's foreign policy is based upon independence and the open door; sets tasks for the rest of the century.

Hu Yaobang: Political Work Report, September 1, 1982 (text: [182]: September 13, 1982: 11–40; [176]: September 7, 1982, in [82]: September 8, 1982: K1–30): sections deal with development since the end of the Cultural Revolution; the economy; spiritual and material civilization; socialist democracy; foreign policy; and party work style.

Ye Jianying: Speech, September 6, 1982 (text: [176]: September 6, 1982, in [82]: September 7, 1982: K17): now is the time for younger cadres to be promoted and to work in close cooperation with the old.

Chen Yun: Speech, September 6, 1982 (text: ibid.: K18–19): the succession of young people to leading posts will allow for the close scrutiny of party ranks; political integrity is to be given priority over professional competence.

Du Runsheng: Speech at a discussion meeting (summary: [194]: September 16, 1982, tr. in [82]: September 21, 1982): reviews recent reforms in rural policy.

Li Xiannian: Closing speech, September 11, 1982 (text: [176]: September 11, 1982, in [82]: September 13, 1982: K12–14).

VII.   Constitution, September 6, 1982 (text: [182]: September 20, 1982: 8–21; [176]: September 8, 1982: K1–19).

VIII.   Elected a CC CCP with 210 full and 138 alternate members (name list of full members: [176]: September 10, 1982, in [82]: September 10, 1982: K1–2; alternate members in [176]: September 11, 1982, in [82]: September 13, 1982: K8–9).

Elected CDIC with 132 members (name list in ibid.: K9), and approved its work report (text: ibid.: K9–12).

Elected CAC with 172 members (name list in [176]: September 10, 1982, in [82]: September 10, 1982: K2).

IX.   Position of party chairman was abolished and replaced by post of general secretary.

   This Party Congress was preceded by a preparatory meeting on August 30–31, 1982 (mention: [108]: 411–12).

   An analysis of the behind-the-scenes maneuvering at this congress is in [268]: October 1, 1982, tr. in [82]: October 15, 1982: W1–6.

472

I.   *September 12–13, 1982*
II.   **FIRST PLENUM OF THE TWELFTH CC CCP**
III. Beijing
IV.   210 full and 138 alternate members of the CC CCP, 149 members of the CAC, and Huang Kecheng.
V.   Election of new central leadership
VI.   Hu Yaobang: Speech, September 13, 1982 (text: [194]: October 22, 1982, tr. in [82]: October 22, 1982: K1–4): planning of party consolidation will be the central task of the Secretariat in the coming year; a draft document on consolidation will be on the agenda of the next party plenum; if all goes well, education, labor, wage, and price reforms will begin in 1984.
VII. Communique, September 12, 1982 (text: [176]: September 12, 1982, in [82]: September 13, 1982: K1–2): includes name lists of new central leading organs (see also [182]: September 20, 1982: 6).
IX.   Plenary sessions of the CDIC and CAC were also held on September 13, 1982; name lists of the leadership of those commissions are in ibid. Excerpts from Deng Xiaoping's speech to the CAC are in [Zhongguo xinwen she]: October 22, 1982, tr. in [82]: October 27, 1982: K5–6; and [30]: October 29, 1982, in [82]: October 29, 1982: K15–16.

473

I.   *November 26–December 10, 1982*
II.   **FIFTH SESSION OF THE FIFTH NATIONAL PEOPLE'S CONGRESS**
III. Beijing
IV.   3,040 deputies
VI.   Zhao Ziyang: Report on the Sixth Five-Year Plan for National Economic and Social Development, November 30, 1982 (text: [182]: December 20, 1982: 10–35; [176]: December 13, 1982, in [82]: December 14, 1982: K1–34).

   Wang Bingqian: Report on the Implementation of the State Budget for 1982 and the Draft State Budget for 1983, December 1, 1982 (text: [176]:

December 14, 1982, in [82]: December 14, 1982: K36–48).

Peng Zhen: Report on Revision of the Constitution, December 5, 1982 (text: [82]: December 20, 1982: 9–23; [176]: December 5, 1982, in [82]: December 7, 1982: K33–48).

Xi Zhongxun: Explanation of draft laws (text: [194]: December 16, 1982, tr. in [82]: December 21, 1982: K1–8).

Yang Shangkun: Written report on the work of the Standing Committee of the NPC, December 6, 1982 (text: [176]: December 16, 1982, tr. in [82]: December 17, 1982: K1–6).

Jiang Hua: Written report on the work of the Supreme People's Court, December 6, 1982 (text: [194]: December 17, 1982, tr. in [82]: December 21, 1982: K8–13).

Huang Huoqing: Written report on the work of the Supreme People's Procuratorate, December 6, 1982 (text: ibid., tr. in [82]: December 23, 1982: K21–26).

Ye Jianying: Closing speech, December 10, 1982 (text: [182]: December 27, 1982: 10–29; [176]: December 10, 1982, in [82]: December 10, 1982: K2–3).

VII. Constitution of the PRC, adopted December 4, 1982 (text: [182]: December 27, 1982: 10–29; [176]: December 4, 1982, in [82]: December 7, 1982: K1–28).

National Economic and Social Development Plan for 1983 (excerpts: [194]: December 20, 1982, tr. in [82]: December 23, 1982: K10–21).

Sixth Five-Year Plan for National and Social Development (1981–1985) (excerpts: [194]: December 13, 1982, tr. in [82]: December 20, 1982: K5–42).

Revised Organic Law of the Local People's Congresses and Local People's Governments, adopted December 10, 1982 (text: [176]: December 15, 1982, tr. in [82]: December 20, 1982: K43–54).

Revised Electoral Law of the NPC and Local People's Congresses, adopted December 10, 1982 (text: [176]: December 15, 1982, in [82]: December 17, 1982: K14–21).

Organic Law of the NPC, adopted December 10, 1982 (text: [194]: December 15, 1982, in [82]: December 17, 1982: K6–13).

Organic Law of the PRC State Council, adopted December 10, 1982 (text: [176]: December 14, 1982, tr. in [82]: December 15, 1982: K1–2).

474

I. *December 31, 1982*
II. **ENLARGED MEETING OF THE POLITBURO OF THE CC CCP**
VI. Chen Yun: Speech, December 31, 1982 (excerpt: [28]: 247): discusses the importance of raising different points of view in inner-party meetings.

1983 _____

475

I.   *January 7–22, 1983*
II.   **NATIONAL CONFERENCE ON IDEOLOGICAL AND POLITICAL WORK**
III. Beijing
IV.   Over 900 people from various departments
V.   Ideological and political work among staff and workers in light of the Twelfth Party Congress and the Fifth Session of the Fifth NPC; guidelines for implementing reforms announced at those meetings
VI.   Deng Liqun: Opening speech, January 7, 1983 (mention: [176]: January 7, 1983, tr. in [82]: January 10, 1983: K1).

Lin Jianqing: Speech, January 7, 1983 (mention: ibid.: K1–2): ideological and political work must serve economic work by safeguarding the socialist nature of enterprises; leftism is still prominent among ideological and political workers; main task is to oppose commercializing everything.

Yuan Baohua: Speech, January 7, 1983 (mention: ibid.: K2): on strengthening ideological and political work.

Hu Yaobang: Speech, "On Questions Regarding the Four Modernizations and Reforms," January 20, 1983 (excerpts: [176]: January 20, 1983, tr. in [82]: January 21, 1983: K1): stresses that organizational, economic, and other reforms are necessary for the modernization program; whether reforms are conducive to the development of the nation and the prosperity of the people is the criterion for judging right from wrong reforms.

Deng Liqun: Speech (mention: [176]: January 22, 1983, tr. in [82]: January 25, 1983: K2): party organizations in enterprises must spend more time on ideological and political work and less on administrative details.

Feng Jian: Speech (excerpts: [176]: January 13, 1983, tr. in [82]: January 21, 1983: K2–3): ideological and political work at Shoudu Iron and Steel Company.

Chen Liemin: Speech (mention: ibid.: K4): ideological and political work at Daqing.

VIII. This conference prepared documents to be submitted to the CC CCP on strengthening ideological and political work among staff and workers (mention: [176]: January 22, 1983, tr. in [82]: January 25, 1983: K1).

The Chinese Society for the Study of Ideological and Political Work among Workers and Staff Members was created on January 18, 1983, with Deng Liqun listed first among its leaders (mention: [176]: January 18, 1983, tr. in [82]: January 21, 1983: K2).

IX.   *Renmin ribao* carried an editorial on this conference on January 23, 1983 (tr. in [82]: January 25, 1983: K2–5).

476

I.   *March 10, 1983*
II.   **FORTY-FIFTH MEETING OF THE SECRETARIAT OF THE CC CCP**
V.   Rural and higher education
IX.   The meeting focused on the need rapidly to develop education and train qualified personnel and intellectuals to assist China's modernization. Following a similar State Council executive meeting on April 16, 1983, the CC CCP and State Council issued a "Circular on Certain Questions Concerning the Strengthening and Reform of Rural School Education" on May 6, 1983.

All information comes from a June 1983 article in *Liaowang* (summary: [176]: June 15, 1983, tr. in [82]: June 16, 1983: K13–14).

477

I.   *June 6–21, 1983*
II.   **FIRST SESSION OF THE SIXTH NATIONAL PEOPLE'S CONGRESS**
III.   Beijing
IV.   2,877 deputies
VI.   Peng Zhen: Opening speech, June 6, 1983 (summary: [176]: June 6, 1983, in [82]: June 7, 1983: K7).

Zhao Ziyang: Report on the Work of the Government, June 6, 1983 (text: [182]: July 4, 1983: Supplement; [176]: June 23, 1983, in [82]: June 23, 1983: K1–26).

Yao Yilin: Report on the 1983 Plan for National Economic and Social Development, June 7, 1983 (text: [176]: June 24, 1983, in [82]: June 24, 1983: K1–11).

Wang Bingqian: Report on the Final State Accounts for 1982, June 7, 1983 (text: ibid.: K11–17).

Jiang Hua: Report on the Work of the Supreme People's Court, June 7, 1983 (text: [176]: June 25, 1983, tr. in [82]: June 27, 1983: K1–9).

Yang Shangkun: Report on the Work of the Standing Committee of the NPC, June 7, 1983 (text: ibid.: K9–14).

Huang Huoqing: Report on the Work of the Supreme People's Procuratorate, June 7, 1983 (text: [176]: June 25, 1983, tr. in [82]: June 28, 1983: K1–7).

Li Xiannian: Speech, June 21, 1983 (text: [176]: June 21, 1983, in [82]: June 22, 1983: K3–5).

Peng Zhen: Closing speech, June 21, 1983 (text: ibid.: K5–11).

VIII. Numerous leadership changes, in particular Li Xiannian's appointment to the newly restored post of president, creation of a State Central Military Commission, and a Ministry of State Security ([182]: June 27, 1983: 4–12; [176]: June 20, 1983, in [82]: June 21, 1983: K1–5).

IX. Liao Chengzhi was to have become vice-president, but he died during this NPC ([182]: June 27, 1983: 5).

478

I.   *October 11–12, 1983*
II. **SECOND PLENUM OF THE TWELFTH CC CCP**
III. Beijing
IV. 201 full and 136 alternate members of the CC CCP; 150 members of the CAC, 124 members of the CDIC, and 11 leading members of central and local party committees as observers.
V.   Party rectification, spiritual pollution, additions to CC CCP and CAC
VI. Deng Xiaoping: Speech, October 12, 1983 (text: [110]: April 1984: 100–11): discusses the goals and targets of party rectification; spiritual pollution is creating distrust of socialism and the party; political line since the Third Plenum has been correct, but implementation has been slack.

Chen Yun: Speech, October 12, 1983 (text: [28]: 293–96): excerpt: [194]: December 20, 1983, tr. in [82]: December 29, 1983: K17): weeding out the "three kinds of people" and building up the third echelon of leaders are the two halves of party rectification; the party has changed greatly since coming to power; we must fully see the problems that have emerged simultaneously with the opening to the outside world.

VII. Communique, October 12, 1983 (text: [9]: October 12, 1983, tr. in [82]: October 13, 1983: K17): reveals following actions:

—Adopted "Decision of the CC CCP on Party Consolidation" (text: [182]: October 17, 1983: supplement; [176]: October 12, 1983, in [82]: October 13, 1983: K2–16).

—Elected a twenty-seven-member Central Commission for Guiding Party Rectification (CCGPR), with Hu Yaobang chairman and Bo Yibo permanent vice-chairman (mention: ibid.: K18).

—Decided to hold a meeting in coming months on strengthening ideological work.

—Elected new members to CC CCP and CAC.

IX.   A forum on party rectification was held immediately after this plenum to explain the campaign to more than 270 non-CCP leaders. Both Peng Zhen and Hu Yaobang spoke at this forum (excerpts: [176]: October 23, 1983, tr. in [82]: October 24, 1983: K2–6; [176]: October 27, 1983, tr. in [82]: October 31, 1983: K3–4).

Renmin ribao carried an editorial on party rectification on October 14, 1983 (tr. in [82]: October 14, 1983: K1–4).

479

I.   *November 1983*
II.   **ENLARGED MEETING OF THE POLITBURO OF THE CC CCP**
V.   Spiritual pollution
VI.   Hu Yaobang and Zhao Ziyang: Speeches (mention: [268]: February 1, 1984, tr. in [82]: February 7, 1984: W6): eliminating spiritual pollution should be limited to literature and art fields; some ultraleftists are using the spiritual pollution campaign to negate the line of the Third Plenum; open-door policies will continue.
IX.   Around this same time, the Secretariat issued its "Report on the Investigation of the Enlargement of the Scope of the Work of the Elimination of Spiritual Pollution" (mention: ibid.).

All information comes from the one source cited above.

480

I.   *December 1983*
II.   **NATIONAL RURAL WORK CONFERENCE**
III.   Beijing
IV.   More than four hundred people in charge of rural and financial work in the provinces, municipalities, and autonomous regions, and from relevant central departments.
V.   Analyze rural work since the issuance of Central Document no. 1 of 1983; formulate guidelines for 1984; make proposals to CC CCP to meet needs of rural work.
VI.   Wan Li: Speech (excerpts: [176]: December 28, 1983, tr. in [82]: January 3, 1984: K12–13): increased agricultural production resulting from the household responsibility system requires making the superstructure and

the relations of production fit the changing situation; if the problem is not solved, what has already been achieved may be lost.

Du Runsheng: Speech, "Several Problems in Making Progress in the Rural Areas" (mention: ibid.: K14): discusses questions regarding the household responsibility system in agriculture, including its effects on large-scale efficiency and whether long-term use of farmland would constitute de facto ownership.

Yao Yilin and Tian Jiyun: Speeches (mention: ibid.: K13).

IX.   It was suggested at this conference that contracts should be expanded beyond the current one- to three-year period (ibid.: K12).

1984

481

I.   *February 24, 1984*
II.   **CENTRAL FORUM**
III.   Beijing
V.   Special economic zones (SEZs) and the further opening of coastal cities to the outside.
VI.   Deng Xiaoping (mention: [82]: June 18, 1984: K4, tr. of *Nanfang ribao*, June 11, 1984): some policies of the SEZs can be implemented in other coastal cities.
IX.   This forum took place following an inspection tour of the SEZs by Deng, Wang Zhen, and Yang Shangkun.

The discussion at this forum was described as "heated," suggesting serious objection to the policy of opening areas of China to the West (mention: ibid.).

482

I.   *March 26–April 6, 1984*
II.   **FORUM CONVENED BY SECRETARIAT AND STATE COUNCIL**
III.   Beijing
IV.   More than ninety people
V.   Open-door policy
VI.   Liang Xiang: Speech (mention: [82]: June 18, 1984: K5, tr. of *Nanfang ribao*, June 11, 1984): on the development of Shenzhen.

Yuan Geng: Speech (mention: ibid.): on the development of Shekou.

Gu Mu (mention: ibid: K6): study classes should be held in Shenzhen and Shanghai to share their experiences.

Hu Yaobang and Zhao Ziyang (mention: ibid.): Shanghai should be more aggressive in using its superior level of development.

Zhao Ziyang: Speech, April 6, 1984 (mention: ibid.: K6–7): China has not yet gained enough experience in its open-door policy; opening of coastal cities will rely on central policies, not central financial support.

VIII.   Fourteen coastal cities opened to foreign trade and investment, with special privileges similar to SEZs ([176]: April 6, 1984, in [82]: April 9, 1984; [82]: June 18, 1984: K4–7, tr. of *Nanfang ribao*, June 11, 1984).

IX.   The decision of this forum was approved by the Politburo on April 30, 1984 (meeting 483).

483

I.   *April 30, 1984*
II.   **ENLARGED MEETING OF THE POLITBURO OF THE CC CCP**
III.   Beijing
IV.   Politburo members, leaders from the Secretariat, State Council, CAC, and other organs.
V.   Open-door policy
VIII.   Fourteen coastal cities given some of the special privileges and policies available in SEZs.
IX.   This meeting confirmed a decision made by the March 26–April 6, 1984, forum on the opening of these fourteen cities (meeting 482).

484

I.   *May 15–31, 1984*
II.   **SECOND SESSION OF THE SIXTH NATIONAL PEOPLE'S CONGRESS**
III.   Beijing
IV.   2,625 deputies
VI.   Zhao Ziyang: Report on the Work of the Government, May 15, 1984 (text: [182]: June 11, 1984: supplement; [176]: May 31, 1984, in [82]: June 1, 1984: K1–20).

Wang Bingqian: Report on the Final State Accounts for 1983 and the Draft State Budget for 1984, May 16, 1984 (text: [176]: June 1, 1984, in [82]: June 4, 1984: K1–10).

Song Ping: Report on the Draft 1984 Plan for National Economic and

Social Development, May 16, 1984 (text: [176]: June 1, 1984, in [82]: June 5, 1984: K1–14).

Ngapoi Ngawang Jigme, Explanation of "Law on Regional Autonomy for Minority Nationalities," May 22, 1984 (text: [194]: June 4, 1984, in [82]: June 13, 1984: K11–18).

Yang Dezhi: Explanation of Military Service Law, May 22, 1984 (text: [176]: June 4, 1984, in [82]: June 6, 1984: K14–21).

Chen Pixian: Report on the Work of the Standing Committee of the NPC, May 26, 1984 (text: [176]: June 5, 1984, in [82]: June 11, 1984: K1–9).

Zheng Tianxiang: Report on the Work of the Supreme People's Court, May 26, 1984 (text: [176]: June 6, 1984, in [82]: June 15, 1984: K1–8).

Yang Yichen: Report on the Work of the Supreme People's Procurator-ate, May 26, 1984 (text: [176]: June 6, 1984, in [82]: June 19, 1984: K3–9).

Peng Zhen: Closing Speech, May 31, 1984 (mention: [176]: May 31, 1984, in [82]: June 1, 1984: K26).

VII. Military Service Law, adopted May 31, 1984 (text: [176]: June 4, 1984, tr. in [82]: June 6, 1984: K1–10).

Law on Regional Autonomy for Minority Nationalities, adopted May 31, 1984 (text: [176]: June 4, 1984, in [82]: June 14, 1984: K3–13).

VIII. Hainan Island given the status of an administrative region (mention: [176]: May 31, 1984, in [82]: June 14, 1984: K3–13).

485

I. *July (?) 1984*
II. **MEETING OF THE STANDING COMMITTEE OF THE POLITBURO OF THE CC CCP**
VIII. Adopted proposal by the Secretariat to add Peng Zhen and Wan Li to the Standing Committee of the Politburo (mention: [268]: August 1, 1984, tr. in [82]: August 3, 1984: W1).
IX. If this decision was in fact made, it was never implemented.

486

I. *October 20, 1984*
II. **THIRD PLENUM OF THE TWELFTH CC CCP**
III. Beijing
IV. 321 full and alternate members of the CC CCP; 297 observers from the CAC, CDIC, and local and central departments; Ye Jianying did not attend due to illness.

VI.   Chen Yun: Written report, October 20, 1984 (text: [28]: 297–300): dis-
        cusses agreement with Great Britain to return Hong Kong to Chinese
        sovereignty; reform of the economic structure; material and spiritual
        civilizations.

VII.   Communique, October 20, 1984 (text: [176]: October 20, 1984, in [82]:
        October 22, 1984: K1).

        "Decision of the Third Plenary Session of the Twelfth Central Com-
        mittee of the Communist Party of China on the Convocation of a National
        Conference of Party Delegates" (text: ibid.: K20–21).

        "Decision of the CC CCP on Reform of the Economic Structure"
        (text: ibid.: K1–19; [182]: October 29, 1984: supplement).

IX.   This plenum was preceded by a six-day preparatory meeting (mentioned
        in communique).

487

I.   *November 1, 1984*
II.   **MEETING OF THE MILITARY AFFAIRS COMMISSION OF THE
        CC CCP**
VI.   Deng Xiaoping: Speech (excerpts: [9] and [176]: November 1, 1984, in
        [82]: November 2, 1984: K11–13): all branches of the PLA should give
        up some of their personnel, technology, and equipment to aid national
        economic development; higher levels must promote younger people to
        leading bodies; older personnel must retire, and surplus personnel must
        be reduced.
IX.   On December 22, 1984, forty senior officers from the General Staff
        Department retired (mention: [176]: December 29, 1984, in [82]: De-
        cember 31, 1984: K2).

488

I.   *November 15, 1984*
II.   **MEETING OF THE SECRETARIAT OF THE CC CCP**
IV.   Those who normally attend Secretariat meetings and members of the
        Central Commission for Guiding Party Rectification (mention: [176]:
        November 26, 1984, tr. in [82]: November 27, 1984: K1).
V.   Party rectification
VIII.   Approved in principle a document of the CCGPR on "The Basic Situation
        of First-Stage Party Rectification and Opinions about the Plan for Sec-
        ond-Stage Party Rectification" (excerpts: ibid.: K1–5).

489

I.   *December 1984*
II.   **MEETINGS OF THE POLITBURO AND SECRETARIAT OF THE CC CCP**
V.   Policy toward literature and art
VI.   Hu Yaobang (mention: [268]: February 1, 1985, tr. in [82]: February 7, 1985: W1): criticizing rightism in literature and art while combating "leftism" in the economic sphere is neither logical nor practical; writers and critics should have more freedom; criticizes spiritual pollution campaign.

Zhao Ziyang (mention: [268]: ibid.): emphasis on economic development and structural reform should continue; criticism of spiritual pollution should cease.

VIII.   The Secretariat decided to end discussion of spiritual pollution and give writers greater freedom to choose themes. This discussion was conveyed to a preparatory meeting for the Fourth Congress of the Writer's Association in late December 1984 (ibid.: W1-2).
IX.   All information on these meetings (which are not differentiated) comes from the one source cited above.

490

I.   *December 14-21-?, 1984*
II.   **NATIONAL RURAL WORK CONFERENCE**
III.   Beijing
V.   Building a market-oriented rural economy
VI.   Hu Qili and Xi Zhongxun: Speeches, December 14, 1984 (mention: [176]: December 30, 1984, tr. in [82]: January 2, 1985: K23).

Wan Li: Speech (mention: ibid.: K25): rural cadres must find new methods, study domestic and foreign experiences, and abandon policies and work styles of the past; increased grain production is causing problems.

Du Runsheng: Speech (mention: ibid.): relationship between workers and peasants, urban and rural areas, and production and consumption in the course of rural reform.

Zhao Ziyang: Speech, December 21, 1984 (mention: [176]: December 30, 1984, in [82]: December 31, 1984: K18 and January 2, 1985: K23): peasants should base production on market demands; the government should use economic measures to administer rural work; state commerce should participate in market regulation to protect producers and consumers.

1985 _____

491

I.   *February 8, 1985*
II.   **MEETING OF THE SECRETARIAT OF THE CC CCP**
V.   Journalism
VI. Hu Yaobang: Speech, "On the Party's Journalism Work," (text: [194]: April 14, 1985, tr. in [82]: April 15, 1985: K1–15): the party's journalism must reflect the line and policies of the party and government and provide guidance, not simply represent the views of the editor; the interests of the party and government are identical with the interests of the people, so it is unnatural to express different opinions on basic issues; defends curtailment of campaign against spiritual pollution.

492

I.   *March 27–April 10, 1985*
II.   **THIRD SESSION OF THE SIXTH NATIONAL PEOPLE'S CONGRESS**
III. Beijing
IV. 2,628 deputies
V.   Hear various reports; approve Sino-British agreement on Hong Kong; authorize State Council to make provisional regulations on domestic and foreign economic reforms.
VI. Zhao Ziyang: Report on the Work of the Government, March 27, 1985 (text: [9]: March 27, 1985, tr. in [82]: March 29, 1985: K1–17; [182]: April 22, 1985: supplement).

    Wang Bingqian: Report on Execution of the State Budget for 1984 and on the Draft State Budget for 1985, March 28, 1985 (text: [176]: April 12, 1985, in [82]: April 15, 1985: K20–29).

    Song Ping: Report on the Draft 1985 Plan for National Economic and Social Development, March 28, 1985 (text: [176]: April 12, 1985, in [82]: April 12, 1985: K1–12).

    Chen Pixian: Report on the Work of the NPC Standing Committee, April 3, 1985 (text: [176]: April 14, 1985, in [82]: April 23, 1985: K1–11).

    Wu Xueqian: An Explanation of the Sino-British Joint Declaration of the Question of Hong Kong, April 3, 1985 (text: [218]: April 4, 1985, tr. in [82]: April 4, 1985: W1–3).

    Zheng Tianxiang: Report on Work of the Supreme People's Court,

April 3, 1985 (text: [176]: April 15, 1985, in [82]: April 25, 1985: K2–9).

Yang Yichen: Report on the Work of the Supreme People's Procurator-ate, April 3, 1985 (text: [176]: April 15, 1985, in [82]: April 26, 1985: K1–6).

VIII. Approved Sino-British agreement on Hong Kong (mention: [182]: April 15, 1985: 6).

Approved inheritance law (mention: [176]: April 9, 1985, tr. in [82]: April 16, 1985: K13–15).

IX. Chen Muhua and Wang Bingqian made self-criticisms at a Presidium meeting over excessive bank lending and the budget deficit in 1984 (text: [176]: April 4, 1985, in [82]: April 5, 1985: K1–2).

493

I. *May 3, 1985*
II. **MEETING OF THE SECRETARIAT OF THE CC CCP**
V. Education reform
VI. Hu Yaobang (mention: *Liaowang*: June 10, 1985, tr. in [82]: June 21, 1985: K12–13): implementation of seven-year mandatory education system will be easier in economically developed areas but difficult in old liberated and minority areas and border regions.

Zhao Ziyang (mention: ibid.: K13): different requirements for education reform should be proposed for areas where economic development is slow.

Bo Yibo (mention: ibid.): must understand that economic and cultural development in China is uneven.

VIII. Discussed the eighth draft of the document on education reform (mention: ibid.: K12).
IX. The document on education reform was ultimately approved by the Politburo on May 27, 1985 (meeting 496), following the May 15–20, 1985, National Education Conference.

494

I. *May 13, 1985*
II. **MEETING OF THE SECRETARIAT OF THE CC CCP**
V. Education reform
VIII. Discussed ninth draft of the document on education reform.
IX. This meeting was followed by the National Conference on Education.

All information on this meeting comes from the journal *Liaowang*, June 10, 1985 (tr. in [82]: June 26, 1985).

495

I.   *May 23–June 6, 1985*
II.   **ENLARGED MEETING OF THE MILITARY AFFAIRS COMMISSION OF THE CC CCP**
IV.   Senior military officers
V.   Troop reductions
VI.   Hu Yaobang: Speech, June 4, 1985 (mention: [176]: June 11, 1985, tr. in [82]: June 12, 1985: K1): national defense must be subordinate to national economic development; not only are reductions coming in the military, but veteran officers and cadres will be replaced by young ones.

Deng Xiaoping: Speech, June 4, 1985 (mention: ibid.: K1–2; [30]: June 14, 1985, in [82]: June 14, 1985: K1): troops will be reduced by one million.

Yang Shangkun: Speech, June 4, 1985 (mention: [176]: June 11, 1985, tr. in [82]: June 12, 1985: K2): on army's acceptance of reductions.

Yang Dezhi (mention: ibid.: K2): report on structural reform, reduction in strength, reorganization, and expediting military modernization and regularization.

Yu Qiuli, Zhang Aiping, and Hong Xuezhi: Speeches (mention: ibid.): on structural reform, reduction in strength, and reorganization.
VIII.   Reduced the number of military regions from eleven to seven and selected leading bodies of new military regions (ibid.: K3; name list: [Wen wei po]: June 14, 1985, tr. in [82]: June 14, 1985: W1; [218]: June 16, 1985, tr. in [82]: June 17, 1985: W1–2).
IX.   *Jiefangjun bao* carried an editorial on this conference on June 13, 1985 (tr. in [82]: June 18, 1985: K15–17).

After this meeting, local work conferences were held on resettling retired military cadres (mention: [176]: June 24, 1985, tr. in [82]: June 25, 1985: K7).

A further report on this conference is in [7]: July 10, 1985 (tr. in [82]: July 26, 1985: K2–4).

496

I.   *May 27, 1985*
II.   **MEETING OF THE POLITBURO OF THE CC CCP**
V.   Education reform
VIII.   Gave approval to eleventh and final draft of "Decision of the CC CCP on Reform of the Education System," published the following day (mention: *Liaowang*: June 10, 1985, tr. in [82]: June 26, 1985: K12); the text of the

"Decision" is in [176]: May 28, 1985 (tr. in [82]: May 30, 1985: K1–11).

497

I.   *September 16, 1985*
II.   **FOURTH PLENUM OF THE TWELFTH CC CCP**
III.   Beijing
IV.   188 full and 129 alternate members of the CC CCP; 130 CAC members, 121 CDIC members, and 40 others as observers (Ye Jianying absent due to illness).
V.   Numerous resignations from central leadership; discussion of Seventh Five-Year Plan
VII.   Communique, September 16, 1985 (text: [176]: September 16, 1985, in [82]: September 16, 1985: K7): reveals the following actions:
         —Decided to convene CCP conference on September 18, 1985;
         —Approved in principle the proposed Seventh Five-Year Plan for submission to the CCP conference;
         —Approved requests to resign of numerous members and alternate members of CC, CAC, and CDIC (texts: ibid.: K5–6, and September 17, 1985: K4–6);
         —Sent congratulatory letters to Ye Jianying and Huang Kecheng (texts: ibid.: K2–4).
IX.   This plenum was preceded by four days of preparatory meetings (mentioned in communique).

498

I.   *September 18–23, 1985*
II.   **NATIONAL CONFERENCE OF THE CC CCP**
III.   Beijing
IV.   992 delegates
V.   Seventh Five-Year Plan; election of additional members to central party organs
VI.   Hu Yaobang: Opening speech, September 18, 1985 (text: [176]: September 18, 1985, in [82]: September 18, 1985: K1–5): discusses the return of democratic centralism in the party's central leading organs in recent years; a resolution is now being drafted on the succession issue; readjustment of younger leaders is nearly complete.
         Zhao Ziyang: Speech, September 18, 1985 (summary: [182]: October

7, 1985: supplement: I-V; [176]: September 25, 1985, in [82]: September 26, 1985: K24–30): explanation of Seventh Five-Year Plan.

Deng Xiaoping: Speech, September 23, 1985 (text: [182]: September 30, 1985: 15–18; [176]: September 23, 1985, in [82]: September 23, 1985: K8–13): predominance of the public sector and common prosperity are the fundamental principles in the reform of the economic structure; some party members have lost confidence in Marxist and communist ideals, thereby weakening discipline.

Chen Yun: Speech, September 23, 1985 (text: [28]: 303–307; [82]: September 30, 1985: 18–20; [176]: September 23, 1985, in [82]: September 23, 1985: K13–16): grain production has dropped due to rural reforms; market regulation remains subordinate to planning in China's economy; some party members have lost their socialist and communist ideals; democratic centralism must be adhered to.

Li Xiannian: Closing speech, September 23, 1985 (text: [176]: September 23, 1985, in [82]: September 24, 1985: K1–3): summary of conference proceedings and tasks for the future.

VII. Proposal of the CC CCP for the Seventh Five-Year Plan for Economic and Social Development, adopted September 23, 1985 (text: [182]: October 7, 1985: supplement: VI-XXIV; [176]: September 25, 1985, in [82]: September 26, 1985: K1–24).

VIII. Elected new members to central party organs (name lists: [176]: September 22, 1985, tr. in [82]: September 23, 1985: K2–3, and September 25, 1985: K1).

499

I.   *September 24, 1985*
II.   **FIFTH PLENUM OF THE TWELFTH CC CCP**
III. Beijing
IV.   202 full and 128 alternate members of the CC CCP; 172 CAC members and 127 CDIC members as observers.
V.   Election of new central leadership
VII. Communique, September 24, 1985 (text: [176]: September 24, 1985, in [82]: September 24, 1985: K6–7): reveals following actions:

—Elected Tian Jiyun, Qiao Shi, Li Peng, Wu Xueqian, Hu Qili, and Yao Yilin to Politburo;

—Approved resignations of Xi Zhongxun, Gu Mu, and Yao Yilin from Secretariat, elected Qiao Shi, Tian Jiyun, Li Peng, Hao Jianxiu, and Wang Zhaoguo to that body;

—Approved election of new leaders and members of CAC and CDIC.

500

I.   *September 25, 1985*
II.   **MEETING OF THE SECRETARIAT OF THE CC CCP**
III.   Beijing
VIII. Two decisions (mention: [134]: November 16, 1985, tr. in [82]: November 26, 1985: W2-3):
       —Division of labor on Secretariat: Hu Qili becomes permanent secretary; Tian Jiyun and Li Peng will concentrate on their State Council work; Hao Jianxiu will be responsible for mass organizations; Wang Zhaoguo will continue as head of the General Office and become director of the Policy Research Center;
       —Agreed on work style norms.
IX.   All information comes from the one source cited above.

501

I.   *November (?), 1985*
II.   **MEETING OF THE SECRETARIAT OF THE CC CCP**
V.   Fiftieth anniversary of December 9th movement
VIII. Set principles for handling emergencies. A special organ was created, with Li Peng in charge and other members from the Central Propaganda Department, Education Commission, and Ministry of Public Security (mention: [268]: December 1, 1985, tr. in [82]: December 13, 1985: W2).
IX.   These steps were taken in anticipation of anti-Japanese demonstrations on college campuses.
       All information on this meeting comes from the one source cited above.

502

I.   *December 5-21, 1985*
II.   **CENTRAL RURAL WORK CONFERENCE**
III.   Beijing
IV.   240 officials in charge of agriculture work from central and local departments and rural issue experts.
VI.   Wan Li: Speech, "Analyze Experience, Persist in Making Reforms," given December 6, 1985 (text: [176]: December 31, 1985, tr. in [82]: January 6, 1986: K1-7): defense of the reform movement despite the

decline in grain production in 1985; problems are inevitable due to lack of experience and contradiction between old and new systems during transition; peasants would lose enthusiasm for production if reforms are reversed.

Tian Jiyun: Report, "Develop the Results Achieved in the Reform, Promote the Commodity Economy," December 12, 1985 (text: [176]: January 15, 1986, tr. in [82]: January 16, 1986: K1–10): explains declines in cotton and grain production and measures to encourage more grain output; development of a diversified economy cannot be neglected for the sake of grain; agricultural prices will not change in 1986.

Zhao Ziyang: Speech, December 18, 1985 (mention: [176]: December 30, 1985, in [82]: December 30, 1985: K4): no new rural reforms will be introduced in 1986 in order to consolidate and perfect the reforms already in place.

Du Runsheng: Speech (mention: [176]: December 30, 1985, tr. in [82]: January 3, 1986: K16): explains prospects for rural reform, policy of letting some people get rich first, objective of common prosperity, and commodity economy and cooperative system.

VIII. Agreed on general tasks for rural work in 1986 (mention: ibid.).

1986

503

I. *January 6 and 9, 1986*
II. **CENTRAL CADRES CONFERENCE**
III. Beijing
IV. Eight thousand leading cadres from central party, government, and army organs and Beijing municipality.
V. Party work style
VI. Tian Jiyun: Speech, "Issues Concerning the Current Economic Situation and Reforms of the Economic Structure," January 6, 1986 (text: [176]: January 11, 1986, tr. in [82]: January 13, 1986: K5–22): the economy has shown signs of instability since end of 1984, mostly because China lacks experience in microeconomic invigoration and macroeconomic control; incomes have risen faster than prices; income gaps have been criticized by the masses; the planned economy will remain predominant, with guidance favored over mandatory planning.

Hu Yaobang: Speech, "Central Organs Must Set an Example for the Whole Country," January 9, 1986 (text: [176]: January 10, 1986, tr. in ibid.: K1–5): central organs must pay attention to the problems of efficiency, study, discipline, and party spirit.

Wang Zhaoguo: Speech, "Issues Regarding the Improvement of Party Style in Central Organs," January 9, 1986 (text: [176]: January 12, 1986, tr. in [82]: January 14, 1986: K1–9): central organs should take the lead in overcoming bureaucratism, liberalism, individualism, departmentalism, favoritism in personnel matters, and lax party discipline; Secretariat is drafting regulations to overcome these unhealthy tendencies.

Yang Shangkun: Speech, "The Army Should March in the Vanguard of Rectifying Party Style," January 9, 1986 (text: ibid.: K9–13): discussion of unhealthy tendencies in the army.

Zhao Ziyang: Speech, January 9, 1986 (summary: [176]: January 10, 1986, tr. in ibid.: K14–15): the leading party, government, and army organs in Beijing are the key to improving the work style of the whole party and the social mood of the country.

Hu Qili: Speech (mention: ibid.: K15): the Secretariat has set up a leading group to rectify work style in central organs, headed by Qiao Shi with Wang Zhaoguo and Jiang Xiaochu as deputy heads.

504

I.   *January 11–20, 1986*
II.   **NATIONAL CONFERENCE ON PLANNING AND ECONOMIC WORK**
III. Beijing
IV.   CC CCP and State Council leaders, including Zhao Ziyang, Tian Jiyun, Yao Yilin, Chen Muhua, Zhang Jingfu, and Song Ping.
VI.   Lu Dong: Speech, January 11, 1986 (summary: [176]: January 11, 1986, tr. in [82]: January 15, 1986: K6–7): tasks for 1986 and the period of the Seventh Five-Year Plan.

Yuan Baohua: Speech, January 11, 1986 (summary: ibid.: K8–9): on the simultaneous development of spiritual and material civilizations, ideological-political work in enterprises, and improving party work style.

Zhao Ziyang: Speech, January 13, 1986 (summary: [176]: January 17, 1986, tr. in [82]: January 22, 1986: K1–3): economic results were better than expected in 1985, the first year of overall reform; investments and the money supply must be controlled; no new price reforms will be taken in 1986; horizontal ties between regions and departments will be encouraged in production and circulation.

505

I.   *January 17, 1986*
II. **MEETING OF THE STANDING COMMITTEE OF THE POLITBURO OF THE CC CCP**
V.   Cadre behavior
VI. Deng Xiaoping: Speech (mention: [176]: January 29, 1986, tr. in [82]: January 29, 1986: D2; [218]: February 12, 1986, tr. in [82]: February 12, 1986: W1; [268]: March 1, 1986, tr. in [82]: March 14, 1986: W1–6): criticizes the behavior of a writer, Zhou Erfu, who reportedly visited the Yosukuni Shrine of Japanese war dead, watched pornographic movies in his hotel room, and visited the red light district while on a trip to Japan.
IX. Zhou Erfu was subsequently fired from his post of vice-president of the Chinese People's Association for Friendship with Foreign Countries and expelled from the party (mention: [176]: March 3, 1986, in [82]: March 3, 1986: K1).

506

I.   *March 25–April 11, 1986*
II. **FOURTH SESSION OF THE SIXTH NATIONAL PEOPLE'S CONGRESS**
III. Beijing
VI. Zhao Ziyang: Report on the Seventh Five-Year Plan for National Economic and Social Development, March 25, 1986 (text: [182]: April 21, 1986: supplement; [12]: March 25, 1986, tr. in [82]: March 28, 1986: K1–28).

Wang Bingqian: Report on the Implementation of the State Budget for 1985 and on the Draft State Budget for 1986, March 26, 1986 (text: [176]: April 15, 1986, in [82]: April 22, 1986: K3–16).

Song Ping: Report on the Draft 1986 Plan for National Economic and Social Development, March 26, 1986 (text: [176]: April 15, 1986, in [82]: April 21, 1986: K9–19).

Li Peng: Explanation of Compulsory Education Law, April 2, 1986 (text: [176]: April 17, 1986, tr. in [82]: April 24, 1986: K10–17).

Chen Pixian: Report on the Work of the Standing Committee of the NPC, April 2, 1986 (text: [176]: April 18, 1986, tr. in [82]: April 25, 1986: K1–14).

Wang Hanbin: Explanation of the General Principles of the Civil Code, April 2, 1986 (text: [176]: April 16, 1986, tr. in [82]: April 23, 1986: K4–11).

Zheng Tuobin: Explanation of the Draft Law Governing Wholly Owned Foreign Enterprises, April 2, 1986 (summary: [176]: April 2, 1986, in [82]: April 6, 1979: K14–15).

Zheng Tianxiang: Report on the Work of the Supreme People's Court, April 8, 1986 (text: [176]: April 19, 1986, tr. in [82]: April 28, 1986: K4–16).

Yang Yichen: Report on the Work of the Supreme People's Procuratorate, April 8, 1986 (text: [176]: April 19, 1986, tr. in [82]: April 29, 1986: K11–19).

VII.   Seventh Five-Year Plan for National Economic and Social Development, approved April 12, 1986 (excerpts: [182]: April 28, 1986: supplement; [176]: April 14, 1986, in [82]: April 18, 1986: K1–37).

General Principles of the Civil Code.

Compulsory Education Law, approved April 12, 1986 (text: [176]: April 17, 1986, tr. in [82]: April 22, 1986: K17–19).

Law Governing Wholly Owned Foreign Enterprises, adopted April 12, 1986 (text: [182]: May 5, 1986: 16–17; [176]: April 12, 1986, in [82]: April 14, 1986: K13–16).

VIII. Leadership changes: Qiao Shi named vice-premier, Song Jian named state counsellor, and Chu Tunan named vice-chairman of the Standing Committee of the NPC.

507

I.   *June 28, 1986*

II.   **MEETING OF THE STANDING COMMITTEE OF THE POLITBURO OF THE CC CCP**

VI.   Deng Xiaoping: Speech (mention: [268]: October 1, 1986, tr. in [82]: October 9, 1986: K10–11): criticizes interference of CDIC in party rectification and criminal investigation work.

Chen Yun (mention: ibid.): defends activism of the CDIC.

IX.   The text of Deng's speech was reportedly carried in the August or September edition of the Chinese journal *Organization and Personnel* (mention: ibid.).

The *Zheng ming* article is the sole source of information on this meeting.

508

I.   *September 29, 1986*
II.   **SIXTH PLENUM OF THE TWELFTH CC CCP**
III. Beijing
IV.   199 full and 126 alternate members of the CC CCP; 161 CAC members, 122 CDIC members, and 25 leading comrades as observers.
VI.   Deng Xiaoping: Speech (text: [51]: 142–43): criticizes trend of bourgeois liberalization.
      Hu Yaobang: Speech (mention: [82]: September 30, 1986: K1).
VII. Communique, September 28, 1986 ([176]: September 28, 1986, tr. in [82]: September 29, 1986: K1): reveals the following actions:
      —Adopted CC CCP Resolution on the Guiding Principles for Socialist Spiritual Construction (text: [182]: October 6, 1986: supplement; [176]: September 28, 1986, tr. in September 29, 1986: K2–12);
      —Agreed to hold the Thirteenth Party Congress in October 1987 (text of resolution: ibid.: K13);
      —Promoted Yin Changmin to full membership in the CC CCP.
IX.   This plenum was preceded by a five-day preparatory meeting, during which Yao Yilin gave a report on the current economic situation (mentioned in communique). Earlier preparations were made during the summer at Beidaihe (mention: [Wen wei po]: August 8, 1986, tr. in [82]: August 11, 1986: W1–2).

509

I.   *?–November 8–?, 1986*
II.   **CENTRAL RURAL WORK CONFERENCE**
V.   Current situation in rural economy; rural work for 1987
VI.   Tian Jiyun: Speech, "Persist in Reform and Promote the Sustained and Steady Development of the Rural Economy," November 8, 1986 (text: [176]: November 25, 1986, tr. in [82]: November 28, 1986: K3–13): reviews current situation in rural work; outlines production targets and improvements in rural work planned for 1987.
      Wan Li: Speech, "How to Understand and Approach the Building of Socialist Spiritual Civilization in Rural Areas," November 8, 1986 (text: [176]: November 26, 1986, tr. in [82]: December 1, 1986: K1–7): explains relationship of material and spiritual civilizations.

510

I.   *Late November 1986*
II.   **MEETING OF THE SECRETARIAT OF THE CC CCP**
V.   Redistribution of power within the Secretariat
VIII.   Tentatively decided that Zhao Ziyang would replace Hu Yaobang as general secretary at the Thirteenth Party Congress; decided that Deng Xiaoping's retirement would no longer be discussed (mention: [268]: February 1, 1987, tr. in [82]: January 29, 1987: K2).
IX.   Hu Yaobang reportedly angered Deng Xiaoping, Wang Zhen, and others by encouraging Deng's retirement so that he could replace Deng as chairman of the MAC and CAC, causing Deng to lose confidence in Hu and contributing to Hu's ouster in January 1987 (mention: ibid.).

        The meeting discussed the question of who would replace Zhao as premier but apparently did not reach an agreement (mention: ibid.: K8).

        All information on this meeting comes from the one source cited above.

511

I.   *December 11–25, 1986*
II.   **ENLARGED MEETING OF THE MILITARY AFFAIRS COMMISSION OF THE CC CCP**
III.   Beijing
IV.   Commanders of army corps
VI.   Yu Qiuli: Speech, December 11, 1986 (summary: [176]: December 27, 1986, tr. in [82]: December 29, 1986: K13–16): intensification of political work in the army is an unchanging policy.

        Yang Dezhi: Speech (mention: [176]: December 26, 1986, tr. in ibid.: K17): on military work.

        Zhang Aiping: Speech (mention: ibid.): on defense building.

        Hong Xuezhi: Speech (mention: ibid.): on logistics work.

        Yang Shangkun: Closing speech, December 25, 1986 (summary: ibid.: K17–18): main task of the army is to shift its attention from preparedness for war to national construction in time of peace.
IX.   This was the largest MAC meeting since 1978 (mention: [176]: December 25, 1986, tr. in December 29, 1986: K1–2).

Bibliography

[1]   Agence France Presse.
[1A]   Ahn, Byung-joon. "Ideology, Policy, and Power in Chinese Politics and the Evolution of the Cultural Revolution, 1959–65." Ph.D. dissertation, Columbia University, 1971.
[2]   *Asahi shimbun* (Asahi News). Tokyo: Asahi Shimbunsha.
[3]   *Atlas*, April 1967, pp. 12–17.
[4]   *Ba er wu zhanbao* (August 25 Combat News). Canton, February 14, 1967. Translated in *JPRS*, no. 41450 (June 19, 1967).
[5]   *Ba yi san hongweibing* (August 13 Red Guards). Investigation Team of the Tianjin University "August 13" Red Guards Liaison Station for Criticizing Liu, Deng, and Tao Dispatched to Baoding, April 17, 1967.
[6]   *Ba ba zhanbao* (August 8 Battle News). Joint Committee of the Central United Front and Nationalities Committee System to Thoroughly Smash the Counterrevolutionary Revisionist Line, April 21, 1967.
[7]   *Banyuetan*.
[8]   Baum, Richard, and Frederick C. Teiwes. *Ssu-Ch'ing: The Socialist Education Movement of 1962–1966*. Berkeley: Center for Chinese Studies, University of California, 1968.
[9]   Beijing Domestic Service.
[10]   *Beijing gongshe* (Beijing Commune). Beijing: August 8 Fighting Squad, Beijing Commune of Central College of Finance and Currency.
[11]   *Beijing ribao* (Beijing Daily). Paper of the Organs of the Beijing Revolutionary Committee, June 10, 1967.
[12]   Beijing Television Service.
[13]   Bennett, Gordon. "Activists and Professionals: China's Revolution in Bureaucracy, 1949–65: A Case Study of the Finance-Trade System." Ph.D. dissertation, University of Wisconsin, 1973.
[14]   Bowie, Robert R., and John K. Fairbank. *Communist China 1955–1959: Policy Documents and Analysis*. Cambridge: Harvard University Press, 1962.
[15]   Bridgham, Philip. "Mao's 'Cultural Revolution': Origin and Development." *The China Quarterly* 29 (January–March 1967): 1–35.
[16]   *The Broadsheet*. London: China Policy Study Group, December 1969, vol. 6, no. 12.
[17]   *CAS Bulletin*.
[18]   *Caimao hongqi* (Red Flag of Finance and Trade). Revolutionary Rebel Liaison Committee of National Finance and Trade Organizations, February 15, 1967.
[19]   *The Case of P'eng Teh-huai*. Hong Kong: Union Research Institute, 1968.

[20] *Central Daily News.*

[21] *Chairman Mao on the Revolution in Education.* Beijing: People's Publishing House, 1967. Translated in *CB* 888 (August 22, 1969): 1–20.

[22] Chang, Parris Hsu-cheng. "Patterns and Processes of Policy-making in Communist China, 1955–1962: Three Case Studies." Ph.D. dissertation, Columbia University, 1969.

[23] Charles, David. "The Dismissal of Marshal P'eng Teh-huai." *The China Quarterly* 8 (October-December 1961): 63–76.

[24] *Chedi cuihui Liu Deng fangeming xiuzhengzhuyi luxian* (Totally Smash the Counter-revolutionary Revisionist Line of Liu and Deng). Beijing: The Capital's Liaison Committee to Totally Smash the Counterrevolutionary Revisionist Line of Liu and Deng, April 12, 1967.

[25] Chen, Jerome. *Mao.* London: Oxford University Press, 1965.

[26] Chen, Jerome. *Mao Papers: Anthology and Bibliography.* London: Oxford University Press, 1970.

[27] Chen Yun. *Chen Yun wenxuan (1949–1956)* (Selected Writings of Chen Yun [1949–1956]). Beijing: Renmin chubanshe, 1984.

[28] Chen Yun. *Chen Yun wenxuan (1956–1985)* (Selected Writings of Chen Yun [1956–1984]). Beijing: Renmin chubanshe, 1986.

[29] *Chi wei jun* (Red Guard Army), April 14, 1967.

[30] *China Daily.*

[31] *China News Analysis.* Hong Kong.

[32] *The China Quarterly* 34 (April-June 1968).

[33] *Chinese Communist Affairs: Facts and Features.* Taipei: Institute of Political Research, January 22, 1969.

[34] *Chinese Communist Party Documents on the Great Proletarian Cultural Revolution.* Hong Kong: Union Research Institute, 1968.

[35] *Chinese Law and Government.* Armonk, N.Y.: M. E. Sharpe.

[36] *Chinese Sociology and Anthropology* 2, 1–2 (Fall-Winter 1969–70): 40.

[37] *Chuan dan* (Hand-out Sheet). Canton, December 1967.

[38] *Collected Works of Liu Shaoqi 1958–1967.* Hong Kong: Union Research Institute, 1968.

[39] *Collection of Documents Concerning the Great Proletarian Cultural Revolution.* Vol. 1. Beijing: Propagandists of Mao Zedong Thought, Beijing College of Chemical Engineering, May 1967. Translated in *CB* 852 (May 6, 1968): 1–121; with addition of ten documents from other Red Guard publications, pp. 122–36.

[40] "Communique of Eleventh Plenary Session of the Eighth Central Committee of the Communist Party of China." Beijing: Foreign Languages Press, 1966. English text also available in *SCMP* 3762 (August 17, 1966); *Documents of the Chinese Communist Party Central Committee September 1956-April 1969*, vol. 1 (see [61]); *Beijing Review* 34 (August 19, 1968): 4–8. Chinese text available in *Renmin ribao* (People's Daily), August 14, 1966; *Hongqi* (Red Flag) 182 (August 21, 1966): 2–7.

[41] "A Condensation of P'eng Teh-huai's Talks at the Lushan Conference in 1959." *Chinese Communist Affairs: Facts and Features* (Taipei) 2, 9 (February 19, 1969): 27–29.

[42] *Cui jiu zhanbao* (Crushing the Old Combat News). Editorial Board of *Crushing the Old Combat News*, the Combat Regiment for Completely Crushing the Old Beijing Municipal Committee, May 25, 1967.

[43] *Current Background.* Hong Kong: U.S. Hong Kong Consulate General.

[44] *Dadao gongjiao zhanxian shang di hei bazhu sanfan fenzi da pantu Bo Yibo)* (Overthrow the Black Chieftain of the Industry and Communications Front—

Three-Anti Traitor Bo Yibo). *East Is Red*, February 15, 1967.

[45] *Dadao Li Jingquan zhuankan* (Special Issue on Down with Li Jingquan), July 27, 1967, p. 3.

[46] *Dadao da yinmoujia, da yexinjia, da junfa Peng Dehuai* (Down with the Big Conspirator, Big Ambitionist, Big Warlord Peng Dehuai). Beijing: Capital's Red Guard Congress, Qinghua University Jinggangshan Corps, November 1967. Reprinted in *Zuguo* (China Monthly) (see [232]) 50 (May 1, 1968): 31–32. Translated in *CB* 851 (April 26, 1968), and *Chinese Communist Affairs: Facts and Features* (see [33]) 2, 9 (February 19, 1969): 27–29.

[47] *Dadao Deng Xiaoping* (Down with Deng Xiaoping). Beijing: Beijing Institute of Physical Education for Workers, Farmers, and Soldiers Regiment of Maoist Soldiers, Propaganda Section, March 1967.

[48] *Da pipan tongxun* (Big Criticism Bulletin). Correspondence Team in Canton for East Is Red Regiment of Tongji University of Shanghai, October 5, 1967.

[49] *Dazibao xuanbian, di san ji* (Selection of Big-Character Posters, Vol. 11). Beijing: Beijing College of Aviation, April 1967.

[50] Deng Xiaoping. *Build Socialism with Chinese Characteristics*. Beijing: Foreign Languages Press, 1985.

[51] Deng Xiaoping. *Jianshe you Zhongguo tese di shehuizhuyi (zengding ben)* (Build Socialism with Chinese Characteristics [revised edition]). Beijing: Renmin chubanshe, 1987.

[52] Deng Xiaoping. *Selected Works of Deng Xiaoping (1975–1982)*. Beijing: Foreign Languages Press, 1984.

[53] *Deng Xiaoping fandang fan shehuizhuyi fan Mao Zedong sixiang di yanlun zhai bian* (Excerpts From Deng Xiaoping's Anti-party, Anti-socialist, Anti-Mao Zedong Thought Speeches). Beijing: First Division of the People's University Three-Red Grab Liu and Deng Group of the Capital's Red Guard Congress, April 1967.

[54] *Deng Xiaoping zai tongyi zhanxian, minzu, zongjiao gongzuo fangmian di fangeming xiuzhengzhuyi yanlun huibian* (Collection of Deng Xiaoping's Counterrevolutionary Revisionist Speeches on the United Front, Nationalities, and Religion). East Is Red Commune of the CC CCP United Front Department; Materials Office of the Joint Committee of the Central United Front and Nationalities Committee System to Thoroughly Smash the Counterrevolutionary Revisionist Line, July 1967, pp. 12–13.

[55] *Deng Xiaoping zi bai shu* (Deng Xiaoping's Confession. *Looking Forward*. Reprinted from a Handout "Reprinted" by the Tiger-taming Combat Squad of the Guangdong Youths Sent Up to the Mountains and Down to the Villages. Reprinted in *Studies in Chinese Communism* (see [272]) 3, 11 (November 10, 1969): 90–94, 200. Translated in *Chinese Law and Government* 3, 4 (Winter 1970–71): 278–291.

[56] *Dianying zhanbao* (Movies Combat News). Canton: *Movies Combat News* Editorial Board, Revolutionary Rebels Committee on Criticizing Reactionary Movies, August 8, 1967.

[57] *Dianying zhanbao* (Movies Combat News), July 10, 1967.

[58] *Dianying geming* (Revolution in Films). Jointly Managed by Revolution in Films Liaison Station and the Revolutionary Rebel General Headquarters of the "August 1" Film Studio, May 18, 1967.

[59] Dittmer, Lowell. *Liu Shao-ch'i and the Chinese Cultural Revolution: The Politics of Mass Criticism*. Berkeley: University of California Press, 1974.

[60] Dmitriyev, F. *Whither China? Comments on the Economic Policy of Mao Tse-tung*. Moscow, 86 pp. Pp. 76–79 cited in Klaus Mehnert, "Mao and Maoism: Some Soviet Views." *Current Scene* 8, 15:16.

[61] *Documents of the Chinese Communist Party Central Committee, September 1956–*

April 1969. Vol. 1. Hong Kong: Union Research Institute, 1971.

[62] *Documents of the First Session of the Fifth National People's Congress.* Beijing: Foreign Languages Press, 1978.

[63] *Documents of the National Conference of the Communist Party of China (March 1955).* Beijing: Foreign Languages Press, 1955, p. 64.

[64] *Dongxiang.*

[65] *Dongfang hong* (East Is Red). Beijing: Beijing College of Mining, Red Guard Congress of the Capital's Universities and Colleges.

[66] *Dongfang hong* (East Is Red). Beijing: Revolutionary Liaison Station of the Red Guard General Headquarters for the Capital's Universities and Colleges.

[67] *Dongfang hong zhanbao* (East Is Red Battle News), June 15, 1967.

[68] *Dou pi gai* (Struggle-Criticism-Transformation). Beijing: Third Red Guard Head-quarters, People's University, Metropolitan Red Guards Congress. Translated in *SCMM-S* 19 (March 4, 1968): 10–13.

[69] *Dou Tao zhanbao* (Struggle Against Tao Combat News). Beijing: Preparatory Office for Criticizing Tao Chu, Capital's Red Guard Congress, April 18, 1967.

[70] *The Draft Program for Agricultural Development in the PRC, 1956–1967.* Beijing: Foreign Languages Press, 1956.

[71] Editorial Departments of *People's Daily, Red Flag,* and *Liberation Army News.* "Carry the Great Revolution on the Journalistic Front Through to the End." *Beijing Review* 37 (September 13, 1968): 18–27.

[72] *Eighth National Congress of the Chinese Communist Party.* Vol. 1. Beijing: Foreign Languages Press, 1956.

[73] *Eighth Plenary Session of the Eighth Central Committee of the Communist Party of China.* Beijing: Foreign Languages Press, 1959.

[74] "Events Surrounding the Ch'ang-kuan-lou Counterrevolutionary Incident." *East Is Red* (see [217]), April 20, 1967. Translated in *SCMP-S* 187 (June 15, 1967): 23–36.

[75] *Extracts from China Mainland Magazines.* Hong Kong: U.S. Hong Kong Consulate General. (Later entitled *Selections from China Mainland Magazines*.) (See [205].)

[76] Fan, K. *Mao Tse-tung and Lin Piao: Post-Revolutionary Writings.* New York: Doubleday, 1972.

[77] *Fan xiu zhanbao* (Antirevisionism Combat News). Canton: *Anti-Revisionism Combat News* Editorial Board, July 8, 1967. Translated in *SCMP* 3933 (May 5, 1967): 10.

[78] *Fan geming xiuzhengzhuyi fenzi Bo Yibo shi da zuizhuang* (The Ten Great Crimes of the Counterrevolutionary Revisionist Bo Yibo). *Jinggangshan* (see [124]), January 1, 1967. Translated in *SCMP-S* 162 (February 14, 1967): 11–15.

[79] *Fangzhi zhanbao* (Textile Battle Bulletin). Shanghai, April 24, 1967.

[80] *Feiqing yanjiu* (Communist Studies). Taipei.

[81] *Fen qi Mao Zedong sixiang di qian jun bang chedi za lan Liu Shaoqi di xiuzheng-zhuyi jiaoyu luxian* (Wield the Mighty Crudgel of Mao Zedong Thought to Thoroughly Smash Liu Shaoqi's Revisionist Educational Line). Tianjin: Advanced Guards Revolutionary Rebel Department of the Chemical Industry Office of Tianjin Engineering College.

[82] *Foreign Broadcast Information Service.* Washington, D.C.: National Technical Information Service.

[83] Fujian Front PLA Radio.

[84] *Guodeng jiaoyu lingyu liang tiao luxian douzheng dashi ji* (Chronology of the Two-line Struggle in the Realm of Higher Education). Beijing: Editorial Team of *Pedagogical Criticism*, Cultural Revolution Committee of Beijing University, April 20, 1967. Translated in *SCMM-S* 18 (February 26, 1968): 1–31.

[85] Gittings, John. *The Role of the Chinese Army*. New York: Oxford University Press, 1967.

[86] Goldman, Merle. "Party Policies Toward the Intellectuals: The Unique Blooming and Contending of 1961–1962." In *Party Leadership and Revolutionary Power in China*, ed. John Lewis. London: Cambridge University Press, 1970. Also appeared in *The China Quarterly* 37 (January–March 1969): 54–83.

[87] *Gongren ribao*.

[88] Grow, Roy. "The Politics of Industrial Development in China and the Soviet Uniion: Organizational Strategy as a Linkage Between National and World Politics." Ph.D. dissertation, University of Michigan, 1973.

[89] *Guanyu jianguo yilai dang di luogan lishi wenti di jueyi zhushi ben* (Annotated Edition of the Resolution on Some Questions in the History of the Party since the Founding of the Country). Beijing: Renmin chubanshe, 1983.

[90] *Guanyu jianguo yilai dang di luogan lishi wenti di jueyi zhushi ben* (Report on the Problem of Luo Ruiqing's Mistakes). Red Guard publication. Reprinted in *Chinese Communist Yearbook* (see [271]), vol. 2, sec. 7, 1970. Translated in *Chinese Law and Government* 4, 3–4 (Fall-Winter 1971–72): 287–314.

[91] *Guangming ribao* (Brightness Daily). Shanghai.

[92] *Guangming ribao* (Brightness Daily), July 21, 1967. Translated in *CB* 836 (September 25, 1967): 34.

[93] Hinton, Harold. *Communist China in World Politics*. Boston: Houghton Mifflin, 1966.

[94] *He qi du ye!* (How Vicious They Are!) Beijing: Liaison Station for Criticizing Liu, Deng, and Tao, "Red Flag Commune" of Beijing Railways Institute, Red Guard Congress, April 1967. Translated in *SCMP-S* 208 (October 26, 1967): 1–30.

[95] *Hongqi* (Red Flag). Beijing: "Red Flag" Combat Team of Beijing Aeronautical Institute, April 4, 197. Translated in *SCMP-S* 180 (May 1, 1967): 1–6.

[96] *Hongqi zhanbao* (Red Flag Combat News). Beijing, December 1, 1966. Translated in *SCMP-S* 162 (February 14, 1967): 16–21.

[97] *Hongqi zazhi* (Red Flag Magazine).

[98] *Hong fan jun* (Red Rebel Army). Beijing: Red Rebel Army of Beijing Institute of Commerce, The Capital's Red Guard Congress, May 20, 1967.

[99] *Hong Bei ying* (Red Beijing Motion Picture Studio). Beijing: Editorial Board of Red Beijing Motion Picture Studio Revolutionary Committee, 1967. Reprinted in *Qingdao ribao* (Qingdao Daily), March 1, 1968.

[100] *Hongse zhanbao* (Red Combat News). Beijing: Red Rebel Squad of the February Seventh Railroad Factory, February 11, 1967.

[101] *Hongse xuanchuan bing* (Red Propaganda Soldier). Beijing: Revolutionary Rebel Committee of the Capital's Publishing System.

[102] *Hongse gongjiao* (Red Industry and Communication). Liaison Committee for Attacking Bo Yibo, Criticizing Yu Qiuli, and Criticizing Gu Mu, July 1, 1967.

[103] *Hongse baodong* (Red Riot). Canton: "Red Rebels" of Central-South Forestry Institute, Red Guard Headquarters of Canton, February 27, 1967.

[104] *Hongse pipanzhe* (The Red Critic) (Beijing) 5 (May 24, 1967).

[105] *Hongse zaofanzhe* (The Red Rebels) (Shanghai) 4 (May 13, 1967).

[106] *Hongse zaofan bao* (Red Rebel News), August 5, 1967. Same document, under different title and publisher, translated in *CB* 834 (August 17, 1967).

[107] *Hongweibing xiaocezi* (Red Guard Pamphlet), 1967. Reprinted in *Zuguo* (China Monthly) (see [232]) 50 (May 1, 1968).

[108] Hu Hua. *Zhongguo shehui zhuyi geming he jianshe jiangyi* (Teaching Materials on China's Socialist Revolution and Construction). Beijing: Zhongguo ren da chubanshe, 1985.

[109]   *Inside China Mainland.*

[110]   *Issues & Studies.* Taipei: Institute of International Relations.

[111]   *Jian xun* (News in Brief) (Canton) 1 (December 1967)

[112]   Jiang Baiying. *Deng Zihui chuan* (Biography of Deng Zihui). Shanghai: Renmin chubanshe, 1986.

[113]   *Jiang Qing tongzhi lun wenyi* (Comrade Jiang Qing on Literature and Art), May 1968.

[114]   *Jiaoyu geming* (Educational Revolution). Beijing: Educational Revolution Liaison Committee of Beijing Municipality.

[115]   *Jiefang jun bao* (Liberation Army News). Beijing: Liberation Army News Press.

[116]   *Jin jun bao* (Charge). Red Guard Corps of the Mao Zedong Thought Philosophy and Social Science Department.

[117]   *Jing bao.*

[118]   *Jingji pipan* (Economic Criticism). Beijing: Capital Liaison Station for Thoroughly Criticizing the Counterrevolutionary Revisionist Economic Line of Liu and Deng, May 20, 1967, p. 4.

[119]   *Jingji yanjiu* (Economic Research) 10 (October 17, 1958): 37.

[120]   *Jingxin dongpo di wenyi zhanxian da bodou—wenyi zhanxian liang tiao luxian douzheng dashi ji, 1949–1966* (The Big Startling Struggle in the Literary Front— A Chronology of the Two-Line Struggle on the Literary Front, 1949–1966). Beijing: Red Guards Congress of the Capital's Universities and Colleges, June 7, 1967.

[121]   *Jinggangshan.* Beijing: Beijing Normal University Revolutionary Committee and the Red Guard Congress of the University's Jinggangshan Commune, August 1, 1967. Republished in *Zuguo* (China Monthly) (see [232]) (November 1969): 42– 46.

[122]   *Jinggangshan.* Jinggangshan Revolutionary Rebel Group of the Central Musical Troupe, May 24, 1967.

[123]   *Jinggangshan.* Beijing: Editorial Board of Jinggangshan, Jinggangshan Commune of Beijing Normal School, Red Guard Congress of Universities and Colleges in Beijing.

[124]   *Jinggangshan.* Beijing: Editorial Board of Jinggangshan News, Qinghua University.

[125]   *Jinggangshan.* (See [124]), March 27, 1967. Translated in *SCMP-S* 195 (July 31, 1967): 20–28.

[126]   *Jinggangshan.* (See [124]). Reprinted in *Qingdao ribao* (Qingdao Daily), November 23–29, 1967.

[127]   *Jing song* (Strong Pines). Canton: Shanghai Liaison Station for Headquarters of Wuhan Regional Revolutionary Rebels of Mao Zedong Thought Red Guards, February 7, 1967.

[128]   *Jiu Peng Luo zhanbao* (Grab Peng and Luo Combat News). The Fighting Squad of Guangdong Especially for Grabbing Peng and Luo, 1968, p. 2. Reprinted in *Qingdao ribao* (Qingdao Daily), June 18, 1968.

[129]   *Joint Publication Research Service.* Washington, D.C.: National Technical Information Service.

[130]   *Kang da* (Anti-Japanese University). Beijing: Editorial Department, Kang Da Commune of Central Nationalities' Institute Red Guard Congress, June 15, 1967. Translated in *SCMP-S* 201 (September 15, 1967): 13–25.

[131]   Kau, Michael Y. M., ed. *The Lin Biao Affair.* White Plains, N.Y.: International Arts and Sciences Press, 1975.

[132]   *Keji zhanbao* (Scientific Technology Combat News). Editorial Board of Scientific Technology Combat News, Revolutionary Rebel Faction of the Na-

tional Scientific Committee System.

[133] *Gongzuo tongxun* (Bulletin of Activities). General Political Department of the Chinese PLA, April 5, 1961. Translated in *The Politics of the Chinese Red Army*, ed. J. Chester Cheng. Stanford: Hoover Institution Press, 1965.

[134] Kuang Chiao Ching.

[135] Lardy, Nicholas, and Kenneth Lieberthal, eds. *Chen Yun's Strategy for China's Development*. Armonk, N.Y.: M.E. Sharpe, 1983.

[136] Li Rui. *Huai nian shipian*. Beijing: Renmin chubanshe.

[137] Liao Gailong. *Quanmian jianshe shehui zhuyi di daolu* (The Path of the Overall Establishment of Socialism).

[138] Lampton, David. "The Politics of Public Health in China: 1949–1969." Ph.D. dissertation, Stanford University, 1973.

[139] *Lianhe bao* (United News) (Taipei), January 22, 1967.

[140] *Liang Chen anjian zhuankan* (Special Issue on the Case of the Two Chens). Reprinted in *Ming bao Monthly* (see [173]), May 1, 1968.

[141] *Liao lian zhanbao* (Liaoning Alliance Battle News) (Great Alliance Committee of the Liaoning Revolutionary Rebel Faction), July 21, 1967.

[142] Lieberthal, Kenneth. "Mao Versus Liu? Policy Towards Industry and Commerce: 1946–49." *The China Quarterly* 47 (July-September 1971): 494–520.

[143] Lieberthal, Kenneth, and Michel Oksenberg. *Bureaucratic Politics and Chinese Energy Development*. Washington, D.C.: GPO, 1986.

[144] Liu Shaoqi. *Collected Works of Liu Shaoqi, 1945–1957*. Hong Kong: Union Research Institute, 1969.

[145] Liu Shaoqi. *Report on the Draft Constitution of the People's Republic of China*. Beijing: Foreign Languages Press, 1954.

[146] Liu Shaoqi. *Liu Shaoqi xuanji (shang)* (Selected Works of Liu Shaoqi [vol. 1]). Beijing: Renmin chubanshe, 1985.

[147] Liu Shaoqi. *Liu Shaoqi xuanji (xia)* (Selected Works of Liu Shaoqi [vol. 2]). Beijing: Renmin chubanshe, 1981.

[148] *Liu Shaoqi fan Mao Zedong sixiang yi bai li* (A Hundred Examples of Liu Shaoqi Opposing Mao Zedong Thought). *Jinggangshan* (see [124]), February 1 and 8, 1967. Translated in *SCMP-S* 173 (April 4, 1967): 1–20.

[149] *Liu Shaoqi fandui Mao zhuxi jiaoyu geming luxian wu shi li* (Fifty Instances of Liu Shaoqi's Opposition to Chairman Mao's Educational Line). *Jiaoyu geming* (Educational Revolution) (see [114]), April 16, 1967. Translated in *SCMP-S* 196 (August 3, 1967): 23–33.

[150] *Liu Shaoqi di fandong yanlun* (Liu Shaoqi's Reactionary Speeches). Beijing: Liaison Station for Criticizing Liu, Deng, and Tao, Red Flag Commune of Beijing Railways Institute Red Guard Congress, April 1967. Translated in *SCMM-S* 25 (May 13, 1968): 1–37.

[151] *Liu Shaoqi zai linshi gong, hetong gong zhidu zhong di hei cailiao (xiaocezi)* (Black Materials of Liu Shaoqi Concerning the Systems of Temporary Workers and Contract Workers [Pamphlet]). Red Rebel Squad of the Labor Department and Red Staff and Worker Revolutionary Rebel Squad of the Labor Department, January 1, 1967. Reprinted by Canton Red Combat Regiment for Criticizing Liu, January 1968.

[152] *Liu Shaoqi zui xing lu* (Record of Liu Shaoqi's Criminal Activities). Combat Regiment of Organs of Xiangtan Administrative Bureau, September 1967. Translated in *SCMM-S* 26 (June 27, 1968): 16–22.

[153] *Liu Shaoqi dui kang Mao Zedong sixiang san bai li* (Three Hundred Examples of Liu Shaoqi's Opposition to Mao Zedong Thought). Beijing: Social Struggle-Criticism-Transformation Liaison Station, Red Flag Commune of the Beijing

Railways Institute, Red Guard Congress, April 11, 1967.

[154] *Liu Deng fan geming xiuzhengzhuyi jituan Lu Dingyi, Zhou Yang zhi liu zai zhong xiao xue jiaocai bianshen gongzuo zhong fan dang fan shehuizhuyi fan Mao Zedong yanlun zhailu* (Excerpts of the Anti-Party, Anti-Socialist, Anti-Mao Zedong Thought Speeches of the Likes of Lu Dingyi and Zhou Yang of the Counterrevolutionary Revisionist Clique of Liu and Deng and Respect to Editing and Reviewing Middle and Primary School Teaching Materials). Revolutionary Rebel Liaison Squad of People's Educational Press, December 7, 1967.

[155] *Long Live Leninism!* Beijing: Foreign Languages Press, 1960.

[156] Lu Ting-i. *Let 100 Flowers Bloom, 100 Schools of Thought Contend!* Beijing: Foreign Languages Press, 1958.

[157] *Lu Dingyi fandui Mao Zedong sixiang tuixing xiuzhengzhuyi jiaoyu luxian yanlun zhaibian* (Excerpts from Lu Dingyi's Speeches Opposing Mao Zedong Thought but Promoting the Revisionist Educational Line). Beijing: Capital Liaison Committee for Criticizing the Reactionary Academic "Authority" of the Bourgeois Class, May 1967.

[158] MacFarquhar, Roderick. *The Origins of the Cultural Revolution.* Vol. 1. New York: Columbia University Press, 1974.

[159] *Mainichi shimbun* (Mainichi News). Tokyo and Osaka: Mainichi Shimbunsha.

[160] *Mainichi shimbun,* January 28–29, 1967.

[161] *Manjiang hong.* East Is Red Commune of the Central College of Industrial and Fine Arts, Red Guard Congress, May 31, 1967.

[162] Mao Zedong. *On the Correct Handling of Contradictions Among the People.* Beijing: Foreign Languages Press, 1957.

[163] Mao Zedong. *Selected Works of Mao Tse-tung.* Vol. 5. Beijing: Foreign Languages Press, 1977.

[164] Mao Zedong. *Socialist Upsurge in China's Countryside.* Beijing: Foreign Languages Press, 1957.

[165] Mao Zedong. *Zai Zhongguo gongchandang quan guo xuanchuan gongzuo huiyi shang di jianghua* (Talk at the CCP National Conference on Propaganda Work). Beijing: People's Publishing House, 1964. Translated in *Selected Readings from the Works of Mao Tse-tung* (see [203]), pp. 480–98.

[166] *Mao Zedong sixiang wan sui* (Long Live Mao Zedong Thought). 1967.

[167] *Mao Zedong sixiang wan sui* (Long Live Mao Zedong Thought). 1969.

[168] *Mao Zedong zhuzuo xuandu (jia zhong ben)* (Selected Readings from the Works of Mao Zedong [Edition A]). June 1964.

[169] *Mao Zedong zhuyi zhandou bao (wenhua fenglei)* (Maoism Combat News [Winds and Thunder in Culture]). (Joint Committee of Revolutionary Rebel Factions for Crushing the Ministry of Culture), February 23, 1967.

[170] *Mao zhuxi dui Peng, Huang, Zhang, Zhou fan dang jituan di pipan* (Chairman Mao's Criticism of the Anti-Party Clique of Peng, Huang, Zhang, and Zhou). Translated in "In Camera Statements of Mao Tse-tung," *Chinese Law and Government* 1, 4 (Winter 1968–69).

[171] *Mao zhuxi wenxuan* (Selected Essays of Chairman Mao). Translated in *JPRS,* nos. 49826 (February 12, 1970—Part 1) and 50794 (June 23, 1970—Part 2).

[172] *Ming bao.*

[173] *Ming pao Monthly.* Hong Kong.

[174] *Miscellany of Mao Tse-tung Thought.* 2 vols. *JPRS,* nos. 612691–92 (February 20, 1974).

[175] Myers, James T. "The Fall of Chairman Mao." *Current Scene* 6, 10 (June 15, 1968): 1–17.

[176] New China News Agency.

[177]   *The New York Times.*
[178]   *Nihon keizai shimbun* (Japan Economic News). Tokyo, April 6, 1967.
[179]   *Nongye jixie jishu* (Agricultural Machinery Technique) 5 (August 8, 1967). Translated in *SCMM* 610 (January 15, 1968): 18.
[180]   Oliver, Adam (pseud.). "Rectification of Mainland Chinese Intellectual, 1964–65." *Asian Survey* (October 1965): 475–90.
[181]   *Pai hsing.* Hong Kong.
[182]   *Peking Review* (Beginning in 1979, *Beijing Review*). Beijing.
[183]   *Peng Dehuai cailiao huiji* (A Collection of Materials Concerning Peng Dehuai). Beijing: Jinggangshan Regiment of Qinghua University. Translated in *CB* 851 (April 26, 1968): 1–31.
[184]   *Peng Zhen fan geming xiuzhengzhuyi yanlun zhaibian* (Excerpts From Peng Zhen's Counterrevolutionary Revisionist Speeches). Beijing: New People's University Commune Mao Zedong Thought Red Guards of the Chinese People's University, May 1967.
[185]   *Peng Dehuai zishu* (Autobiography of Peng Dehuai). N.p., 1981.
[186]   *People's China.* Beijing, November 1, 1955, pp. 3–16. Text also in Bowie and Fairbank, *Communist China 1955–1959* (see [14]) pp. 94–105.
[187]   *People's China.* Beijing.
[188]   Perkin, Linda. "The Chinese Communist Party: The Lushan Meeting and Plenum, July–August 1959." M.A. essay, Columbia University, 1971.
[189]   *Pi Tao zhanbao di 12 hao* (Combat News for Criticizing Tao No. 12). Beijing: The Capital's Committee on Criticizing Tao Zhu, the New Representative of the Liu-Deng Line.
[190]   *Qishi niandai* (The Seventies). Hong Kong.
[191]   *Quan wu di* (Entirely Matchless). Beijing: *Entirely Matchless* Editorial Board of the Capital Medical Revolution Committee and Yanan Commune Health Bulletin.
[192]   *Quan wu di* (Entirely Matchless). *Entirely Matchless* Editorial Board of the Public Health System, March 10, 1967.
[193]   *Quotations from Chairman Mao Zedong.* Beijing: Foreign Languages Press, 1966.
[194]   *Renmin ribao* (People's Daily). Beijing.
[195]   *Renmin shouce* (People's Handbook). Beijing.
[196]   *Ren da san hong* (Three Reds of People's University). Beijing: Three Reds of the Chinese People's University, Red Guard Congress of the Capital, May 11, 1967.
[197]   Rice, Edward E. *Mao's Way.* Berkeley: University of California Press, 1974.
[198]   Robinson, Thomas. "The Wuhan Incident: Local Strife and Provincial Rebellion During the Cultural Revolution." *The China Quarterly* 47 (July–September 1971): 413–38.
[199]   *Sankei jiji* (Industrial and Economic Review). Tokyo.
[200]   *San zhong quanhui yilai zhongyao wenxian xuanbian* (Selected Important Documents since the Third Plenum). Changchun: Renmin chubanshe, 1983. Reprinted as *Zhonggong shouyao jianghua ji wenjian xuanbian* (Selected Important Speeches and Documents since the Third Plenum of the Eleventh Central Committee of the Chinese Communist Party). Taipei: Zhonggong yanjiu zazhi chubanshe, 1983.
[201]   Schram, Stuart R., ed. *Chairman Mao Talks to the People.* New York: Pantheon, 1974.
[202]   *Second Session of the Eighth National Congress of the Chinese Communist Party.* Beijing: Foreign Languages Press, 1958.
[203]   *Selected Readings from the Works of Mao Tse-tung.* Beijing: Foreign Languages Press, 1971.

[204] *Selected Works of Mao Tse-tung.* Vol. 4. Beijing: Foreign Languages Press, 1961.
[205] *Selections from China Mainland Magazines.* Hong Kong: U.S. Hong Kong Consulate General (see [75]).
[206] *Selections from China Mainland Magazines-Supplement.* Hong Kong: U.S. Consulate General.
[207] *Sheng zhi hong qi* (Red Flag Organs Directly Under the Province). *Red Flag Organs Directly Under the Province* Editorial Department of the Provincial Organs' Revolutionary Liaison Station, January 1968.
[208] *Shi qi nian lai jiaoyu zhanxian shang liang tiao luxian dou zheng dashi ji* (Chronology of the Two-Line Struggle on the Educational Front in the Past Seventeen Years). *Jiaoyu geming* (Educational Revolution) (see [114]). Translated in Peter J. Seybolt, *Revolutionary Education in China: Documents and Commentary.* White Plains, N.Y.: International Arts and Sciences Press, 1973.
[209] *Shoudu hongweibing* (Capital's Red Guards). Beijing: General Headquarters of Red Guards and Revolutionary Rebels of the Capital's Universities and Colleges.
[210] *Shoudu hongweibing* (Capital's Red Guards). Reprinted in *Qingdao ribao* (Qingdao Daily), February 21, 1967.
[211] *Sikai Wang Guangmei di huapi (xiaocezi)* (Tear off Wang Guangmei's Painted Mask [pamphlet]). Beijing: ''Red Flag Events'' Editorial Board of Beijing Engineering College for Chemical Textiles, Red Guard Congress, May 1967.
[212] Simmonds, J. D. ''P'eng Teh-huai: A Chronological Reexamination.'' *The China Quarterly* 37 (January-March 1969): 120–38.
[213] *Sixth Plenary Session of the Eighth Central Committee of the Communist Party of China.* Beijing: Foreign Languages Press, 1958.
[214] Solomon, Richard. *Mao's Revolution and the Chinese Political Culture.* Berkeley: University of California Press, 1971.
[215] Stavis, Benedict. ''Political Dimensions of the Technical Transformation of Agriculture in China.'' Ph.D. dissertation, Columbia University, 1972.
[216] *Survey of China Mainland Press.* Hong Kong: U.S. Hong Kong Consulate General.
[217] *Survey of China Mainland Press-Supplement.* Hong Kong: U.S. Hong Kong Consulate General.
[218] *Ta kung pao.* Hong Kong.
[219] Tanjug (Yugoslav Press Agency).
[220] *Tantan Zhongguo gongchandang di zhengdang zhengfeng* (Discussions on the Rectification of the Chinese Communist Party). Fujian: Renmin chubanshe, 1984.
[221] *Tao Zhu jiu shi zhongnan diqu di Heluxiaofu (xiaocezi)* (Tao Zhu Is No Other Than the Khrushchev of the Central-South [pamphlet]). Canton Liaison Station of the Wuhan Region Revolutionary Rebel Headquarters of Mao Zedong Thought Red Guards, January 14, 1967.
[222] *Tao Zhu fan dang fan shehuizhuyi fan Mao Zedong sixiang di yanlun zhailu (Tao Zhu zuixing huibian, di yi ji)*(Excerpts from Tao Zhu's Anti-Party, Anti-Socialism, Anti-Mao Zedong Thought Speeches [A Compilation of Tao Zhu's Criminal Activities], vol. 1). Beijing: Preparatory Office for Criticizing Tao Zhu, the Capital's Red Guard Congress, March 1967.
[223] Teiwes, Frederick. ''Establishment and Consolidation of the New Regime.'' In *Cambridge History of China*, vol. 14. Cambridge: Cambridge University Press, 1987.
[224] Teiwes, Frederick. ''Rectification Campaigns and Purges in Communist China, 1950–1961.'' Ph.D. dissertation, Columbia University, 1971.

[225] *Tiyu zhanxian* (Physical Education Front).

[226] *Tiyu zhanxian* (Physical Education Front). Beijing: Beijing Worker-Peasant-Soldier Physical Education College and the Mao Zedong Thought Corps of the Capital's Red Guard Congress, April 21, 1967. Translated in *JPRS*, no. 41446 (June 19, 1967): 52–59.

[227] *Tiyu zhanbao* (Physical Education Combat News).

[228] *Tiyu zhanbao* (Physical Education Combat News). April 26, 1967.

[229] *Tiyu zhanbao* (Physical Education Combat News). May 6, 1967.

[230] *Tokyo shimbun* (Tokyo News). Tokyo, May 30, 1967.

[231] *Zou shehuizhuyi daolu hai shi zou zibenzhuyi daolu?* (Shall We Take the Socialist Road or the Capitalist Road?). *Hongqi* (Red Flag) 13 (August 17, 1967): 4–13.

[232] *Zuguo* (China Monthly). Hong Kong: Union Research Institute.

[233] *Union Research Service* (Hong Kong) 1, 19 (November 18, 1955). Cited in Vogel, *Canton Under Communism* (see [235]), p. 164, n. 196.

[234] *Union Research Service* (see [233]) 49, 13 (November 14, 1967).

[235] Vogel, Ezra. *Canton Under Communism*. Cambridge: Harvard University Press, 1969.

[236] Walder, Andrew G. *Chang Ch'un-ch'iao and Shanghai's January Revolution*. Ann Arbor: Center for Chinese Studies, University of Michigan, 1978.

[237] *Wan shan hong bian* (Ten Thousand Mountains Red All Over). Beijing: Workers, Peasants, and Soldiers Literature and Art Commune of Beijing, April 1967. Translated in *SCMM-S* 33 (February 20, 1969): 1–26.

[238] *Wan shan hong bian* (Ten Thousand Mountains Red All Over, No. 1). Ten Thousand Mountains Red All Over Rebel Propaganda Team, Art and Drama Institute for Chinese Children, April 1967.

[239] *Wei dong* (Tianjin East [play on words—can also mean "Protect the East"]). Tianjin: *Wei dong* Editorial Office of the Nankai University Red Guards of the Red Guard Congress.

[240] *Wenhui bao* (Literary News). Shanghai.

[241] *Wenyi geming* (Revolution in Literature and Art), July 13, 1967.

[242] *Wenhui bao.*

[243] *Wenyi bao* (Literary Gazette) 8–9 (September 30, 1964): 15–20.

[244] *Wenzhai bao.*

[245] *Wuchanzhe zhi sheng* (Voice of the Proletariat). Wuzhou, Guangxi: Political Propaganda Department of Wuzhou Proletarian Red Guard Alliance Headquarters, no. 10, January 1968. Reprinted in *Zhao cong* (A Sketch of the Course of the Cultural Revolution Movement), part 55. *Zuguo* (China Monthly) (see [232]) 101 (August 1, 1972): 23–26.

[246] *Wuchan jieji wenhua da geming dashi ji* (The Great Proletarian Cultural Revolution—A Record of Major Events. September 1965–December 1966). Beijing: "Chuan-min-chieh-ping" and "Chung-hsiao-han" Combat Teams of the 28th Regiment of the Jinggangshan Corps of Tsinghua University. Translated in *JPRS*, no. 42349 (August 25, 1967): 1–167.

[247] *Wuhan gang er si* (Wuhan Steel Second Headquarters). Canton: Revolutionary Rebel Headquarters for Mao Zedong Thought Red Guard in Wuhan Region, September 8, 1967.

[248] *Wu Lengxi tan bai shu* (Wu Lengxi's Confession). Red New China (Rebel Faction of New China News Agency). Reprinted in *Qingdao ribao* (Qingdao Daily), July 9, 1968. Translated in *SCMM* 662 (June 28, 1969): 1–8.

[249] Xiao Yang. *Huiyi Zhang Wentian* (Remember Zhang Wentian). Hunan: Hunan chubanshe, 1985.

[250] *Xin Beida* (New Beijing University). Beijing: Editorial Board of New Beijing

University, Cultural Revolution Committee of Beijing University.

[251] *Xin Beida* (New Beijing University), February 25, 1967. Translated in *SCMP-S* 180 (May 1, 1967): 11–16.

[252] *Xin gang yuan* (New Steel Institute). Beijing: Editorial Board of New Steel Institute, Revolutionary Rebel Commune of Beijing Institute of Iron and Steel.

[253] *Xinhua ban yue kan* (New China Semimonthly). Beijing: New China Monthly Press.

[254] *Xinhua ribao* (New China Daily). Nanjing.

[255] *Xinhua yue bao* (New China Monthly). Beijing: New China Monthly Press.

[256] *Xin nong da* (New Agricultural University). East Is Red Branch of Beijing Agricultural University, Red Guard Congress, April 1, 1967.

[257] *Xin ren wei* (New People's Health) (June 1967). Translated in *SCMM-S* 22 (April 8, 1968): 1–16.

[258] *Qingdao ribao* (Qingdao Daily). Hong Kong.

[259] *Xuexi ziliao* (Study Materials). Translated in *SCMM-S* 30 (October 6, 1969): 9–14.

[260] *Xuexi ziliao* (Academic Research) 3 (May 5, 1966).

[261] Yao Wenyuan. "Ping Zhou Yang fan geming liang mian pai" (Criticize Zhou Yang, Two-faced Counterrevolutionary Element). *Hongqi* (Red Flag) 1 (January 1, 1967): 14–36. Translated in *JPRS*, no. 39853 (February 9, 1967): 1–52.

[262] *Yomiuri shimbun* (Yomiuri News). Tokyo.

[263] *Zhanbao* (Combat News).

[264] *Zhanbao* (Combat News), January 18, 1967. Translated in *SCMP-S* 165 (March 10, 1967): 19.

[265] *Zhan dou bao* (Battle News), February 23, 1967, p. 4. *Zhang Wentian xuanji* (Selected Works of Zhang Wentian). Beijing: Renmin chubanshe, 1985.

[266] Zhao Han, ed. *Tantan Zhongguo gongchandang di zhengfeng yundong* (Talks about the Chinese Communist Party's Rectification Campaigns). Beijing: China Youth Publishing Company, 1957.

[267] *Zhengfa hongqi* (Red Flag [of the College of ?] Politics and Law), October 17, 1967.

[268] *Zheng ming*. Hong Kong.

[269] *Zheng ming ribao*. Hong Kong.

[270] *Zhonggong dang shi dashi nianbiao* (Major Events in the Party's History). Beijing: Renmin chubanshe, 1987.

[271] *Zhonggong nianbao* (Chinese Communist Yearbook). Taipei: Chinese Communist Research Periodical Press.

[272] *Zhonggong yanjiu* (Studies in Chinese Communism). Taipei: Chinese Communist Research Periodical Press.

[273] *Zhongguo gongchandang liushi nian, xia* (Sixty Years of Chinese Communist Party History, Vol. 2).

[274] *Zhongguo jiaoyu nianjian, 1949–1981* (A Chronology of Education in China, 1949–1981). Shanghai: Zhongguo dabaike quanshu chubanshe, 1984.

[275] *Zhongguo qingnian* (China Youth).

[276] *Zhongguo qingnian bao* (Chinese Youth), August 29, 1965, p. 1.

[277] *Zhongguo renmin zhengzhi xieshang huiyi di er ju quanguo weiyuanhui huiyi wenjian* (Documents of the First Session of the Second CPPCC National Committee). 3 vols. Beijing: Renmin chubanshe, 1955–1957.

[278] *Zhongguo renmin zhengzhi xieshang huiyi di yi ju quanti huiyi jianghua baogao fayan* (Collected Speeches, Reports, and Pronouncements of the First Session of the CPPCC). Shanghai: New China Bookstore, 1949.

[279] *Zhonghua Renmin Gongheguo di yi ju quanguo renmin daibiao dahui huiyi wenjian*

(Documents of the First NPC of the PRC). 4 vols. Beijing: Renmin chubanshe, 1955.

[280] *Zhonghua Renmin Gongheguo di yi ju quanguo renmin daibiao dahui di san zi huiyi hui kan* (Collected Materials of the Third Session of the First NPC of the PRC). Beijing: Renmin chubanshe, 1956.

[281] *Zhonghua Renmin Gongheguo di yi ju quanguo renmin daibiao dahui di si zi huiyi hui kan* (Collected Materials of the Fourth Session of the First NPC of the PRC). Beijing: Renmin chubanshe, 1957.

[282] *Zhonghua Renmin Gongheguo di san ju quanguo renmin daibiao dahui di yi zi huiyi zhuyao wenjian* (Major Documents of the First Session of the Third NPC of the PRC). Beijing: Renmin chubanshe, 1965.

[283] *Zhonghua Renmin Gonheguo jingji dashiji (1949–1980)* (Economic Chronology of the People's Republic of China [1949–1980]). Beijing: Zhongguo shehui kexue chubanshe, 1984.

[284] *Zhonghua Renmin Gongheguo kai guo wenxian* (Founding Documents of the People's Republic of China). Hong Kong: New Democratic Publishing Company, 1949.

[285] *Zhonghua yue bao* (China Monthly). Shanghai.

[286] Zhou Enlai. *Zhou Enlai xuanji* (Selected Writings of Zhou Enlai). Beijing: Renmin chubanshe, 1986.

[287] *Zhu ying dongfang hong* (Pearl River Films East Is Red). Canton: Pearl River Films East Is Red of Pearl River Film Studio, Red Guard Headquarters of Organs of Joint Committee of Red Rebels, September 13, 1967. Translated in *SCMP*, no. 4036 (October 6, 1967): 1–6.

[288] *Ziliao zhuanji* (Special Collection of Materials). Canton: Political Department of the Canton Workers' Congress. Translated in *SCMP-S* 246 (March 12, 1969): 1–18.

[289] MacFarquhar, Roderick, Timothy Cheek, and Eugene Wu, eds. *A Mao for All Seasons*. Cambridge: Harvard University Press, est. 1989.

Index to Meeting Summaries

About the Authors

A graduate of Dartmouth College, KENNETH G. LIEBERTHAL received his M.A., East Asian Institute Certificate, and Ph.D. in political science from Columbia University. He has taught at Swarthmore College and the University of Michigan. He is currently professor of political science and director of the Center for Chinese Studies at the University of Michigan. He serves as a consultant to the Department of State, The Rand Corporation, the China Advisory Group of the Government Research Corporation, and The China Group. Professor Lieberthal has traveled to China more than fifteen times and has had opportunities to talk with many of the participants in the meetings described in the current volume. He has written extensively on elite politics and policy process in China, and his books include *Bureaucratic Politics and Chinese Energy Development* (with Michel Oksenberg, 1986), *Revolution and Tradition in Tientsin, 1949–52* (1980), and *A Research Guide to Central Party and Government Meetings in China, 1949–1975* (1976).

BRUCE J. DICKSON received a B.A. in political science and English literature and an M.A. in Asian Studies from the University of Michigan. He is currently a doctoral pre-candidate in political science, the University of Michigan. He has taught and done research at the University of Michigan, the Brookings Institution, the Center for Strategic and International Studies, and the U.S. Department of Commerce. He has co-edited *Economic Relations in the Asian-Pacific Region* (with Harry Harding, 1987), *The Emerging Pacific Community: A Regional Perspective* (with Robert L. Downen, 1984), and edited *The Emerging Pacific Community Concept: An American Perspective*.